GERMAN
FIGHTER ACES

of

WORLD WAR ONE

GERMAN FIGHTER ACES

of

WORLD WAR ONE

Terry C. Treadwell & Alan C. Wood

TEMPUS

First published 2003

Tempus Publishing Ltd
The Mill, Brimscombe Port
Stroud, Gloucestershire GL5 2QG
www.tempus-publishing.com

British Library Cataloguing in Publication Data.
A catalogue record for this book is available from the British Library.

ISBN 0 7524 2808 X

Typesetting and origination by Tempus Publishing.
Printed and bound in Great Britain.

CONTENTS

Introduction   7
Glossary   9

PART I
GERMAN AIRMEN OF WORLD WAR ONE

1   Introduction, Prussia and Greater Germany   19
2   The German Army Air Services   23
3   German Airmen of World War One   33
4   Holders of the Orden Pour le Mérite   53
5   Biographies of German Airmen   57
6   Victory Totals of German Airmen   177

PART 2
GERMAN AIRCRAFT MANUFACTURERS AND THEIR AIRCRAFT

German Aircraft Manufacturers of World War One   185
Allgemeine Electrizitäts GmbH   192
Albatros Werke GmbH   199
Automobil und Aviatik AG   208
Deutsche Flugzeug-Werke GmbH   214
Fokker Flugzeug-Werke GmbH   219
Flugzeugbau Friedrichshafen GmbH   230
Gothaer Waggonfabrik AG   240
Halberstädter Flugzeug-Werke GmbH   249
Hannoversche Waggonfabrik AG   254
Hansa-Brandenburgische Flugzeug-Werke GmbH   258
Junkers Flugzeug-Werke AG   264
Luftfahrzeug GmbH   268
Luftverkehrs GmbH   277
Pfalz Flugzeug-Werke GmbH   282
Rumpler Flugzeug-Werke GmbH   290
Sablatnig Flugzeugbau GmbH   296
Siemens-Schuckert Werke GmbH   299
Zeppelin Werke Staaken GmbH   308

Index   317

INTRODUCTION

Worlld War One – 1914 to 1919 – was a global conflict with fifty-seven nations involved. The main fighting Powers were: the Allies or the Triple Entente (Britain with its Empire and Commonwealth, France and Russia); and the Central Powers (Germany and Austria-Hungary).

As World War One progressed, other nations joined one or other of the main Power blocks: Italy and Belgium (which had been invaded by the Germans) officially joined the Allies in 1916 and 1915 respectively; Turkey joined the Central Powers in 1914. In 1917 America aligned itself with the Allies.

With aviation in its infancy only eight nations had an air arm to their fighting Services: Britain and its Allies – America, Italy, Belgium, France, and Russia – and the Central Powers comprising Germany and Austria-Hungary.

The first section of this book deals with German airmen, whilst the second part deals with the aircraft manufacturers who supplied the German Army Air Service. It would be impracticable in this book to include biographies of all those German airmen who scored over five aerial victories – they are legion. Such a biographical listing would require several volumes or one massive tome. Similarly, to list all the German aircraft of World War One would require another massive tome; thus only the most important aircraft are dealt with.

Ehrenbecher Silver Victory Cup – awarded by German aviation firms
for one victory. Later eight to nine victories were required
and the cup was made of iron not silver.

GLOSSARY

AFP	Armee Flugpark	Supply depot
AG	Aktiengesellschaft	Corporation
Bogohl	Bombengeschwader der Obersten Heeresleitung	Bombing squadron
	Ballonzug	Balloon Section
Dipl.Ing	Diplomingenieur	College-trained engineer
	Dreidecker	Triplane
	Eindecker	Monoplane
FA	Flieger Abteilung	Flying unit
FA(A)	Flieger Abteilung Artillerie	Flying unit artillery
FEA	Flieger Ersatz Abteilung	Pilot training unit
FFA	Feldflieger Abteilung	Field aviation unit
	Flugzeugmeisterei	Air Ministry
Fr.	Freiherr von	Baron of

	Geschwader	Squadron
GmbH	Gesellschaft mit beschränkter Haftung	Limited company
Idflieg	Inspektion der Fliegertruppen	Inspectorate of Aviation Troops
Jasta	Jagdstaffel	Fighting squadron
JaSch	Jastaschule	Fighter pilot school
JG	Jagdgeschwader	Jasta group (permanent)
Jgr	Jagdgruppe	Jasta group (temporary)
	Jäger	Fighter pilot/fighter plane
	Kanone Ace	German pilot with ten or more aerial victories
Kagohl	Kampfgeschwader der Obsten	Combat squadrons
Kasta	Kampfstaffel	Fighting unit or section
Kek	Kampfeinsitzer Kommando	Fighter group
	Kampfeinsitzer	Single-seat fighter
Kest	Kampfeinsitzer Staffel	Home defence squadron
KG	Kampfgeschwader	Bombing squadron
Kofl	Kommandeur der Flieger	Commanding Officer – army aviation
Kogenluft	Kommandierender General Luftstreitkrafte	GOC German Aviation
MFJ	Marine Feld Jasta	Marine fighting squadron
	Reihenbildzug	Photographic unit
RFA	Riesenflugzeug Abteilung	Giant aircraft unit
	Ritter von	Knight of (title awarded by Royal Decree)
SFA	Seefrontstaffel	Marine unit
SflS	Seeflug Station	Naval air base
SST	Schutzstaffel	Ground support unit (escort) Protection Flight
Schusta	Schlachstaffel	Ground support unit (fighting) Battle Flight

Ranks

Army

Feldmarschall	Field Marshal
General Oberst	no equivalent
General Kavallerie	General
General Leutnant	Lieutenant General
Generalmajor	no equivalent
Oberst	Colonel
Oberstleutnant	Lieutenant-Colonel
Major	Major
Rittmeister	Cavalry Captain
Hauptmann	Army Captain
Oberleutnant	Lieutenant
Leutnant	Second Lieutenant
Fähnrich	Officer Cadet
Offizierstellvertreter	Warrant Officer or Acting Officer
Vizefeldwebel/Wachtmeister	Sergeant Major
Feldwebel	Sergeant
Unteroffizier	Corporal
Gefreiter	Lance Corporal
Flieger	Private

Navy

Kapitänleutnant	Naval Captain
Korvettenkapitän	Lieutenant Commander
Leutnant zur See	Naval Lieutenant
Oberflugmeister	Naval Aviation Senior NCO
Vizeflugmeister	Naval Aviation Junior NCO
Flugmeister	Naval Aviation Airman

'Der Reserve' denotes *of the reserve*.
'Zur See' after the rank denoted a regular officer in the navy and not a reserve.

CLASSIFICATION OF GERMAN AIRCRAFT

A	Unarmed monoplanes
B	Unarmed biplanes: observation and training
C	Armed biplanes: reconnaissance and bombing
CL	Light C plane
CLS	Schlachtflieger: C plane for ground attack
D	Single-seat armed biplane fighter
DJ	Single-seat ground attack
Dr	Single-seat armed triplanes
J	Two-seater ground attack infantry support aircraft.
E	Single-seat armed monoplanes
F	First Fokker Dr.Is
G	Grossflugzeug: twin-engined biplane bombers
R	Riesenflugzeug: multi-engined armed biplane long-range bombers
S	Schlachtflugzeug: ground attack aircraft

The aircraft serial number on the sides of the fuselage or fin(s) showed the maker, type, serial no. and year of production: e.g, Udet's Fokker D.VII Nr.4253/18.

The Germans' Austro-Hungarian allies used a slightly different system:

A	Monoplane
B	Older biplane of up to 150hp
C	Biplane two-seater 150hp to 250hp
D	Single-seater fighter
F	Single-engined biplane 350hp upwards
G	Twin-engined bomber
R	Giant bomber

There was also a manufacturer's number code. Each manufacturer was allocated an identifying letter and number abbreviation.

AWARDS TO THE GERMAN ARMY AIR SERVICE IN WORLD WAR ONE

Each of the twenty-six kingdoms, duchys, principalities, states and cities that comprised Greater Germany had their own range of orders, decorations and medals. However, not all gave aviation awards; the list below is of the ones who did and of the awards that they gave.

Germany's allies – Turkey and Austria-Hungary – also awarded orders, decorations and medals to personnel of the German Army Air Service.

Kingdom of Prussia

Order of the Red Eagle, 3rd Class with Crown and Swords
Orden Pour le Mérite
Royal Hohenzollern House Order, Knight's Cross with Swords (Officers)
Royal Hohenzollern House Order, Knight's Cross
Crown Order, 4th Class
Crown Order, 4th Class with Swords
Royal Hohenzollern House Order, Member's Cross with Swords (NCOs)
Royal Hohenzollern House Order, Member's Cross
Golden Military Merit Cross
Merit Cross 3rd Class with Swords
Iron Cross 2nd Class
Iron Cross 1st Class
Member's Cross, Order of the Griffin
Pilot's Badge

Bavaria

Military Max-Joseph Order, Knight's Cross
Military Merit Order, 3rd Class with Crown and Swords
Military Merit Order, 4th Class with Crown and Swords
Military Merit Order, 4th Class with Swords
Golden Military Merit Cross
Military Merit Cross, 2nd Class with Crown and Swords
Military Merit Cross, 2nd Class with Swords
Mecklenburg Military Cross of Merit with Swords
Gold Bravery Medal
Silver Bravery Medal
Pilot's Badge

Saxony

Military St Henry Order, Knight's Cross
Military St Henry Order, Commander 2nd Class
Military St Henry Order, 4th Class
Albert Order, Knight 1st Class with Crown and Swords
Albert Order, Knight 1st Class with Swords
Albert Order, Knight 2nd Class with Swords
Saxon Merit Order, Knight 1st Class with Swords
Saxon Merit Order, Knight 2nd Class with Swords
Gold St Henry Medal
Silver St Henry Medal
Honour Cross with Swords

Württemberg

Military Merit Order, Knight's Cross
Friedrich Order, Knight's Cross with Swords
Friedrich Order, Knight's Cross 2nd Class with Swords
Württemberg Military Merit Order, Knight's Cross
Gold Military Merit Medal
Silver Military Merit Medal
Merit Cross with Swords
Wilhelm Cross with Swords

Brunswick

War Merit Cross 2nd Class

Anhalt

Ducal House Order of Albert the Bear, Knight 1st Class with Swords
Ducal House Order of Albert the Bear, Knight 2nd Class with Swords
Friedrich Cross 1st Class
Friedrich Cross 2nd Class

Baden

Order of the Zähringer Lion, Knight's Cross 2nd Class
Military Karl-Friedrich Merit Order, Knight's Cross

Hesse

Order of Philip
Hesse Decoration for Bravery

Oldenburg

Order of the Royal House of Oldenburg
Friedrich August Cross 1st Class

THURINGIAN STATES

Grand Duchy of Saxe-Weimar

Order of the White Falcon, Knight's Cross 1st Class
Order of the White Falcon, Knight's Cross 2nd Class with Swords
General Honour Decoration in Gold
General Honour Decoration in Gold with Swords

General Honour Decoration in Silver
General Honour Decoration in Silver with Swords

Duchy of Saxe-Altenburg

Ducal Ernestine House Order, Commander's Cross with Swords
Ducal Saxe-Ernestine House Order, Knight's Cross with Swords
Ducal Saxe-Ernestine House Order, Knight's Cross 2nd Class with Swords
Ducal Saxe-Ernestine House Order, Commander 2nd Class with Swords
Ducal Saxe-Ernestine House Order, Merit Cross
Ducal Saxe-Ernestine House Order, Gold Merit Medal
Ducal Saxe-Ernestine House Order, Gold Merit Medal with Swords
Ducal Saxe-Ernestine House Order, Silver Merit Medal
Ducal Saxe-Ernestine House Order, Silver Merit Medal with Swords

Duchy of Saxe-Coburg

Gold Duke Ernst Medal
Silver Duke Ernst Medal
Silver Duke Ernst Medal with Swords
Silver Duke Ernst Medal with Oak Leaf
Silver Duke Ernst Medal with Oak Leaf and Swords
Duke Ernst Medal 1st Class with Swords
Saxe-Altenburg Bravery Medal

Duchy of Saxe-Gotha

Duke Carl Eduard Military Service Medal
Duke Carl Eduard War Cross
Duke Carl Eduard Medal 2nd Class with Swords

Duchy of Saxe-Meiningen

Saxe-Meiningen Cross for Merit in War (Officers)
Saxe-Meiningen Medal for Merit in War (NCOs)

Principality of Reuss

Reuss Honour Cross
Reuss Honour Cross 3rd Class with Swords
Gold Merit Medal
Gold Merit Medal with Crown
Silver Merit Medal
Reuss War Merit Cross

Principality of Schwarzburg

Schwarzburg Honour Cross 1st Class with Swords
Schwarzburg Honour Cross 2nd Class with Swords
Schwarzburg Honour Cross 3rd Class with Swords
Silver Honour Medal for Merit in War

City State of Bremen

Bremen Hanseatic Cross

City State of Hamburg

Hamburg Hanseatic Cross

Principality of Lippe

Order of the House of Lippe, Schaumberg Cross

City State of Lübeck

Lübeck Hanseatic War Service Cross

Greater Germany

Wound Badge in Gold (Army & Navy)
Wound Badge in Silver (Army & Navy)
Wound Badge in Black (Army & Navy)
Army Pilot's Badge
Land Based Pilot's Badge (Navy)
Observer's Badge (Army)
Observer's Badge (Navy)

Turkish Ottoman Empire

Turkish War Medal (Star of Gallipoli)
Imtiaz Medal, Gold
Imtiaz Medal, Silver
Liakat Medal, Gold
Liakat Medal, Silver

Part One

GERMAN AIRMEN OF WORLD WAR ONE

I
PRUSSIA &
GREATER GERMANY

The German Empire (*das Deutsche Reich*) followed the Franco-Prussian War of 1870-1871, with the German states continuing their process of unification to counterbalance the power of Russia, France and Austria-Hungary. The then King of Prussia became the first 'Kaiser' (*emperor*) with the new Germany being given a Federal Constitution.

The new German Empire was a confederation of twenty-six states: the kingdoms of Prussia, Bavaria, Saxony and Württemberg; the grand duchies of Baden, Hesse, Mecklenberg-Schwerin, Mecklenberg-Strelitz, Saxe-Weimar and Oldenburg; the duchies of Anhalt, Brunswick, Saxe-Alteberg, Saxe-Coburg-Gotha and Saxe-Meiningen; the principalities of Lippe, Ruess-Greiz, Reuss-Schleiz, Schaumburg Lippe, Schwarzburg-Rudolstadt, Schwarzburg-Sonderhausen and Waldeck; the territory of Alsace-Lorraine; and the cities of Bremen, Lübeck and Hamburg. By 1910 the population of Germany was 65 million with Prussia having over 40 million.

The first Kaiser, Wilhelm I, ruled Germany from 1871 to 1888, being followed by Friedrich III during 1888, and finally by Wilhelm II from 1888 until 1918. They were all members of the aristocratic Prussian Hohenzollern dynasty which was descended from Frederick the Great.

Within the Federal Constitution some armies were under the control of the Prussian Army, but some – the Royal Armies of Saxony and Württemberg – retained their own

Orden Pour le Mérite – Prussian Order for bravery and outstanding service. Eighty-one were awarded to German air servicemen during World War One.

war ministries, headquarters staff and establishments. The Royal Bavarian Army remained autonomous under the command of its king, with its own headquarters staff and headquarters establishment. The various military forces of the smaller states and provinces became integrated with the Prussian Army. At the outbreak of World War One, however, the military forces of the Imperial German Empire were under unified command, with only Bavaria maintaining a separate establishment.

Each of the kingdoms and states had their own range of orders, decorations and medals that they awarded to their subjects and others to whom they saw fit to reward.

The Orden Pour le Mérite, Prussia's most famous award, was originally awarded for individual gallantry on the battlefield. It was not Germany's highest military award, but it was Prussia's. Because Germany was fragmented at that time with various principalities, states and duchies, there were no overall awards for gallantry; each of the states had their own. For example, Bavaria's highest military honour, the Military Max-Joseph Order, was only awarded to Bavarians, yet the Prussian Order Pour le Mérite had been awarded to nine aviators from Bavaria. How the awards were given and to whom they were given was decided by the individual state. The introduction of the Orden Pour le Mérite to aviators was given not for just one act of bravery, but for the highest military conduct over a period of time and it was only given to officers. Eighty-one Orden Pour le Mérites were awarded to aviation personnel during World War One. The award was discontinued after the defeat of Germany in 1918.

It is considered by some, that the colloquial name for the Orden Pour le Mérite – 'Blue Max' which was introduced during World War One – was named thus after

Prussian Military
Merit Cross in Gold
– awarded to NCOs
for bravery. It was
regarded as the
equivalent of the
Orden Pour le
Mérite for officers.

the death of the first military aviation recipient of the order, Max Immelmann, but
there is nothing to substantiate this. However, in the operational history of
Jagdgeschwader Nr.2, an entry for 18 September 1918 reads:

> September 18 was once again a special day for Lt Büchner who succeeded for the
> second time in downing three enemies in one day, thereby gaining his 30th, 31st and
> 32nd victories. And still the 'Blue Max' did not come! High time the whimsical god
> of war was gracious to him!

The famous Iron Cross was instituted by Friedrich Wilhelm III, King of Prussia, in
1813 as an award for gallantry in combat.

The 1st and 2nd Classes of the Iron Cross were reinstated for the Franco–German War of 1870 to 1871 and continued to be awarded until the end of World War One. There were 219,300 awards made of the Iron Cross 1st Class and 5.5 million of the Iron Cross 2nd Class from 1813 to 1918.

The Imperial German Aviation Service was regarded until 1916 as part of ground communications troops, although a separate command had been established in March 1915 but had not been unified. Naval and military aviation remained separate.

2
THE GERMAN ARMY
AIR SERVICES

Germany's military interest in aviation began in 1884 with the use of reconnaissance balloons by the Prussian Army. During the next seven years, both free-flown and moored balloons came into use and by 1896 the original balloon concept had developed into kite balloons, designed by a Major von Parseval and Hauptmann von Sigsfeld.

On 2 July 1900 the rigid airship, Graf Zeppelin LZ.1, flew over Lake Constance on a fifteen-minute successful air test. However, it was scrapped the following year because of a cash-flow problem. Another Graf Zeppelin design, the LZ.2, took to the air and had just two test flights before it was damaged beyond repair in a violent storm in January 1906.

Graf Zeppelin carried on producing airships, making flights in his LZ.3 and LZ.4. The LZ.4 made a record-breaking twenty-hour flight on 4 August 1908, but was destroyed during a storm at Stuttgart (Echterdingen airport). This disaster ruined Zeppelin, but the German people rallied round and raised an amazing 6 million marks to enable him to continue his work.

However, the non-rigid airship Parseval Luftschiff 1 was accepted by the German military for service.

The German Army Air Service began to take shape with the appointment in May 1907 of Hauptmann Wolfram de la Roi of the Prussian War Ministry to head an

Aviation Test Project, with a technical section under the control of Major Hesse. This established the basis of the German Army Air Service. The results were so encouraging that Generalleutnant Freiherr von Lyncker was put in charge of the Inspectorate of Transport Troops, under which umbrella the German Army Air Service grew.

Hauptmann de la Roi believed that the future lay with heavier-than-air aeroplanes and reported to the War Ministry that this was the way ahead for German military aviation. The War Ministry saw differently: they had ordered fifteen rigid airships to be in military service by 1910.

During the following years both civil and military pilots were licensed by the German Aviation Association and the Inspectorate of Military Transport (military only). The first pilots' certificates were issued to August Euler and Hans Grade on 1 February 1910. Euler – an engineer – went on to become an aircraft designer; Hans Grade, to produce aircraft. In Germany there was a certain social attitude towards flying aircraft in the early years. Prior to 1914 gentlemen of means employed chauffeurs to drive their cars and the piloting of an aircraft was regarded in the same manner.

During the spring of 1910 the first flying schools were set up. By December 1910, ten officers had completed their flying training and had been awarded their certificates.

The German War Department – encouraged by the results of military pilot training – allocated the sum of 110,000 marks to the purchase of military aircraft. Hermann Dorner and Hans Grade were among the first to be allocated money to produce aeroplanes. Seven aircraft were bought: one Aviatik Farman, one Albatros Farman, one Etrich Taube, one Farman, one Albatros Sommner and two Frey aeroplanes.

The future German Army Air Service was slowly coming into being and when World War One broke out on 4 August 1914, Germany had approximately 228 aircraft on strength plus a small reserve. Twleve airships were on strength: LZ.4, LZ.5, LZ.6, LZ.7, LZ.8, LZ.9, S12, M4, P4, the DELAG *Hansa*, *Viktoria Louise* and *Sachsen*. Around twenty-five kite and free balloons were also in service. Aircrew strength stood at 600 officer pilots and 220 NCO pilots. Five hundred officers had qualified as observers – a total of 1,320 flying personnel.

This complement was allocated to forty-three Flieger Abteilungen (*flying units*) of which thirty-three were Feldflieger Abteilungen (*field aviation units*). Ten Festung Abteilungen (*fortress units*) were designated to defend strategic towns.

German army aircraft were placed under the control of the military whilst their large fleet of airships was placed under the control of the navy. At this time German thinking was that aircraft and airships were to be used for reconnaissance: aircraft for short-range missions, such as artillery spotting and photo reconnaissance, and airships for long-range reconnaissance duties. The tactical use of aircraft as fighters and bombers came later. By the end of 1914 five airships had been lost during daylight operations but only three new airships came into service; this attrition caused airships to be relegated to night use only. Z5 came down in Russia, Z6, Z7 and Z8 were lost to small arms fire and Z9 was destroyed in a hangar raid by Lieutenant R.L.G. Marix, RNAS, flying a Sopwith Tabloid Scout.

This confused situation reigned until 8 October 1916, when General Ernst von Hoeppner was appointed officer commanding the Imperial German Air Service and

Generaleutnant der Kavallerie Ernst von
Hoeppner, Commanding General of the
German Air Service. He was awarded
the Orden Pour le Mérite for his abilities
and service to the German air arm.

immediately began to reorganise its command structure. The final classification was: fighter units of eighteen aircraft each; ground attack units of six to twelve aircraft; bomber units with about twenty-four aircraft each; reconnaissance units; artillery units; and single-seater aircraft for home defence.

The Imperial German Naval Air Service, however, remained independent, operating flying boats from some thirty-two bases on German and occupied coasts; they also operated land-based aircraft for coastal defence.

The first pilots were drawn from the ranks of non-commissioned officers, while the commissioned officers – usually cavalrymen some with the rank Freiherr (*baron*) – acted as observers and sat in the rear cockpit. This sometimes caused great problems: in the early years most of the 'cavalrymen' insisted on being properly dressed and that included the wearing of a sword. As the aircraft were made of wood and fabric, this caused holes to be torn in the fuselage and the practice of carrying a sword was very soon dropped.

The first long-range bomber units – Kampfgeschwader (KG) – were formed in October 1914 and came under army command. The first such unit was a clandestine one codenamed Brieftauben Abteilung Ostende (BAO: *Ostend Carrier Pigeon Flight*), under the command of Major Wilhelm Siegert.

The German High Command soon realised that their relatively slow reconnaissance and observation aircraft needed protection from faster enemy fighters, so that they could carry out their essential missions unmolested. Early German fighters – such as the Aviatik C1 – were two-seaters with the pilot and observer firing machine guns sidewards and rearwards from their cockpits. The aircrew were unable to fire forward through the propeller arc as no firing interrupter gear had yet been perfected. Some aircraft had machine guns mounted on the upper wing to fire over the propeller arc but this was not very successful.

It was not long before a reliable firing interrupter mechanism was developed. The mechanism was said to have been invented by Anthony Fokker after seeing the French pilot Roland Garros's design on his Morane Parasol, after it had been shot down. (It is now accepted that it was probably the brainchild of Heinrich Luebbe, a member of Fokker's design team.) On 23 May 1915 his Fokker Eindecker – equipped with a machine gun firing through the propeller – came into front line service with FA.62 at Douai. German Army Air Service fighter aircraft now came into their own: single-seaters with machine guns firing forward through the propeller arc.

This development attracted the attention of Hauptmann Oswald Boelcke and Oberleutnant Max Immelmann – both already famous in Germany as pilots. Boelcke and Immelmann immediately went into combat with the new Eindeckers of FA.62. Boelcke shot down a Morane Parasol on 4 July and Immelmann a BE2c on 1 August 1915. Both earned Prussia's most prestigious decoration – the Orden Pour le Mérite – on 12 January 1916.

Anthony Fokker with Leutnant Wintgens in studio poses. (*Sanke Card Nr.400*)

Leutnant Max Immelmann in the cockpit of a Fokker E.I.

Hauptmann Oswald Boelcke seated in an Albatros D.I – purportedly taken just before his ultimate sortie.

With the arrival of the Eindeckers and their forward firing guns, the German Army Air Service attained air superiority over the Allied Air services – until the Allies produced their own aircraft with forward firing machine guns.

The aerial experience of war began to show that the German Army Air Service needed some central command structure. The War Ministry approved a unified aviation command in 1915 and appointed Major Hermann von der Leith-Thomsen as Chief of Field Aviation with a brief to reorganise the Service. By the summer of 1915 the German Army Air Service had been expanded to eighty Abteilungen. The BAO bomber unit was enlarged to six squadrons of six aircraft each, and another separate unit – Brieftauben Abteilung Metz (BAM) – was formed at Metz. The latter bombardment squadron's codename was translated as 'Carrier Pigeon Detachment Ostend/Metz'.

Recognising the need for specific fighter pilot training, Kampfeinsitzer Abteilung Nr.1 was formed at Mannheim on 1 August 1915. All of the trainees were already qualified two-seater aircraft pilots. When trained, these fighter pilots would fly and protect the vital two-seaters engaged in artillery spotting and reconnaissance missions.

Major Leith-Thomsen rapidly improved the Air Service and in autumn 1916 was appointed Chief of the General Staff to the Commanding General of the Air Service, Generalleutnant Ernst von Hoeppner.

Shrewdly, the German War Ministry realised the propaganda value of casting their pilots and observers as national heroes, by awarding honours and decorations for the number of enemy aircraft shot down. Intially, four victories were needed to receive 'ace' status; the Germans did not use this term, preferring Kanone (*cannon*). Six kills were rewarded with the award of the Knight's Cross of the Royal Hohenzollern House Order and eight with the award of the Orden Pour le Mérite. Famous airmen

A Sanke card photograph of Direktor
Anthony Fokker in civilian flying clothing.

began to emerge: Boelcke, Immelmann and Wintgens won the 'Blue Max' for their
exploits and were immortalised on the famous Sanke Postcards. These postcards
carried the portraits of the aerial pilots in various heroic poses and were avidly
bought and collected by an admiring German public.

The measure of any fighter pilot at the time was determined by the number of
aircraft he shot down. As their scores steadily mounted so did their fame, to such an
extent that magazines carried stories of these 'Teutonic Knights of the Air'. Stories
of chivalrous acts toward their defeated enemy abounded and almost all of them were
in the minds of the writers. In truth every trick or ruse in the book was used to gain
the upper hand over their adversaries and little or no quarter was given or expected.
If a lone aircraft was jumped by a patrol, or the enemy aircraft had run out of ammunition, or the crew member or members had been wounded, all were fair game.
Unlike the infantryman who fired at an individual, the pilot of an aircraft fired at,
for all intents and purposes, an inanimate object. This was the truth of aerial warfare,
and the realisation that there was a person in the other aircraft only came home when
they examined the burnt out, crumpled wreckage of their victim. As one German
pilot said, after examining the wreckage of one of his victims and seeing the mangled,
burnt bodies still inside, 'Better them than me.'

During the winter of 1916 the tempo of aerial conflict increased and the number
of victories required for high honours increased. To gain the Orden Pour le Mérite,
sixteen kills were needed; this later rose to twenty and finally thirty by the end of the
war. Strangely, some pilots with high scores – including Leutnant Paul Billik with
thirty-one kills and Josef Mai with thirty kills – were never awarded the Blue Max.

Thirty-five other pilots scored between fourteen and twenty-six victories but were not decorated with the Orden Pour le Mérite.

Nineteen known pilots were actually awarded the Order but never received it for various reasons – including death. The decoration could only be awarded to a living officer. Non-commissioned ranks received the Golden Military Merit Cross of which eighty awards were given.

During the Battle of the Somme the Allies regained air superiority so, in August 1916, the German Army Air Service Command formed permanent fighter squadrons equipped with the new D-type aircraft coming into service. These squadrons – Jagdstaffeln (*hunting squadrons*) – soon became known as Jastas. Their primary function was to hunt, attack and destroy enemy fighters (and other aircraft and balloons) so that German artillery spotting and reconnaissance aircraft could carry out their duties unhindered. This fixed fighter role was to prove successful.

The new Albatros D.I and D.II scouts were in service and could outfly most of the aircraft of the Allied Air Services, which was handicapped by the lack of an aircraft which could out perform the formidable Albatros. The British Pup and the French Nieuport were the best the Allies could put in the air. By the end of 1916 the German Army Air Service had twenty-four fully staffed operational Jastas and these began to take an even higher toll of Allied aircraft. Many fighter pilots began to rise

Offizierstellvertreter Edmund Nathanael (fifteen victories) was one of the early pilots, and flew with FFA.42 in 1916. He was killed in action on 11 May 1917 by Capt. C.K. Cochrane-Partick of 19 Squadron RFC.

A Sanke card photograph of Leutnant Rudolf Wendelmuth (fourteen victories) who was killed in an aerial collision on 30 November 1916.

Unser erfolgreicher Kampfflieger
Leutnant Jul. Schmidt

A Sanke card photograph of Leutnant Julius Schmidt, who served with KG4 and Jasta 3. He had fifteen confirmed victories, and one unconfirmed. He died on 2 July 1944.

to prominence, including Hartmut Baldamus, Erwin Böhme, Frtiz Otto Bernert, Albert Dossenbach, Wilhelm Frankl, Heinrich Gontermann, Max Müller, Hans Müller and Werner Voss. Fate, however, took a hand and the famous Hauptmann Oswald Boelcke died in combat with DH2s of 24 Squadron RFC on 28 October 1916 – his aircraft colliding with one of his former flying pupils Erwin Böhme. Boelcke's death brought the most famous of all German aces – Manfred Freiherr von Richthofen – to the fore. By the end of 1916 he had fifteen confirmed victories to his credit.

In January 1917 Richthofen took command of Jasta 11 and, under his inspired leadership, it became the second highest scoring Jasta in the German Army Air Service. During April 1917, known to the Allies as 'Bloody April', Richthofen's Jasta 11 shot down eighty-nine enemy aircraft with their Albatros D.IIIs. Richthofen had his Albatros painted red after his fourteenth victory and gained the nickname 'The Red Baron'.

To counteract their numerical inferiority, Jastas were combined into fighter squadrons: Jagdgeschwader (JG). Jastas 4, 6, 10, and 11 were combined as Jagd-geschwader Nr.1 under the command of Manfred von Richthofen. Being highly mobile JG.1 soon became known as the 'Flying Circus' from its ability to move quickly from battlefront to battlefront. JG.1 was the first of the permanent groups with Manfred von Richthofen as its leader. It wasn't until 1917 that JGs 2, 3 and 4 appeared, the latter in October 1918.

These Jagdgeschwaders were known collectively as 'circuses', because like JG.1, they moved all over the front line as and when they were needed. Because of the

Leutnant Hartmut Baldamus. He had earned eighteen victories, but was killed in an aerial collision in 1917. (*Sanke Card Nr.390*)

A Sanke card photograph of Leutnant Julius Schmidt, who served with KG4 and Jasta 3. He died on 2 July 1944.

colourfully painted aircraft these Jagdgeschwaders adopted, allied units often claimed they had been in conflict with 'Richthofen's Flying Circus'. It was a myth that only Richthofen's aircraft was painted red; a number of other German pilots had their aircraft painted the same colour but not whilst serving in the same JG as Richthofen.

Around thirty Jastas had been formed by the end of 1916 and only one, Jasta 25, operated outside of France. Operating on the Macedonian front, Jasta 25, under the command of Hauptmann Friedrich-Karl Burckhardt, supported the Bulgarians and Austrians against the Allies based in Salonika.

More and more German fighter pilots rose to national (and international) fame: Karl Allmenröder, Lothar von Richthofen, Karl Emil Schäfer, Adolf Ritter von Tutschek and Kurt Wolff. The German Army Air Service, though outnumbered, had air superiority over the Allies in the early years with the RFC taking heavy casualties, but as time moved on and the Americans entered the war the tide turned.

3

GERMAN AIRMEN
OF WORLD WAR ONE

During the spring of 1917 the Germans found that their Jastas were outnumbered in aerial combat by Allied squadrons. The German's problem was that their individual Jasta units were numerically smaller that their opponents' larger squadrons. An individual Jasta was no match for a larger Allied squadron in spite of the German pilots' superb flying skills and zest for combat.

In an attempt to counter this inferiority, commanders of the German Army Air Service decided to group their Jastas into larger fighting units. The following message was sent:

Supreme Headquarters, 26 June 1917

By order of the Chief of the General Staff of the Field Army, dated 23 June 1917 (Ic Nr.5834 op.), Jagdgeschwader 1 is formed from Jagdstaffeln Nrs. 4, 6, 10, 11. The Geschwader is a closed unit. It is appointed for the purpose of fighting and securing aerial superiority in crucial combat sectors.
Chief of the General Staff
[signed] Thomsen

RICHTHOFEN JAGDGESCHWADER NR.1

Accordingly, at the end of June 1917, the following Jastas were combined into one unit – Jagdgeschwader Nr.1 (a permanent fighting group of Jastas) more commonly known as JG.1: Jasta 4 (Royal Prussian) commanded by Oberleutnant Kurt-Bertram von Döring; Jasta 6 (Royal Prussian) commanded by Leutnant Eduard Dostler; Jasta 10 (Royal Prussian) commanded by Oberleutnant Ernst Freiherr von Althaus; and Jasta 11 (Royal Prussian) commanded by Leutnant Kurt Wolff. This was the Army's first Geschwader, the Army Air Service up to this point had been made up of Staffeln.

Chosen to command JG.1 was the already legendary Rittmeister Manfred Freiherr von Richthofen. The Red Baron, as he was known to the Allies, had fifty-six confirmed victories to his credit by 25 June 1917 and had been awarded Prussia's high decoration the Orden Pour le Mérite and a host of other decorations and medals.

The Red Baron led JG.1 until his death in action on 21 April 1918 – he was just twenty-six years old. The next commander of JG.1 was Hauptmann Wilhelm Reinhard on 22 April 1918, but he died in an air crash, and the much decorated Oberleutnant Hermann Göring assumed command on 8 July 1918.

The thinking behind the creation of JG.1 was that it could achieve temporary air superiority over a given area, by having a larger amount of aircraft in combat and, importantly, being highly mobile. The squadrons switched from battlefront to battle-front as required or directed, and JG.1 quickly became the élite aerial fighting unit of the German Army Air Service.

The fighter aircraft flown by JG.1 were mainly Albatros D.Vs, Fokker Dr.Is, Fokker D.VIIs, Pfalz D.IIIs and a few Fokker D.VIIIs. Contrary to popular belief JG.1 was not composed entirely of Germany's foremost fighter aces – or Kanone as they were known in Germany. At its inception JG.1 had but one Kanone: Oberleutnant Hans Klein with sixteen victories.

Peculiar to the German Army Air Service was that the shooting down of an observation balloon counted as a victory. One Kanone, Leutnant Heinrich Gontermann, shot down eighteen balloons out of his victory total of thirty-nine.

JG.1 became a proving ground under the leadership of Richthofen and many aces emerged. Those pilots who did not fit in with Richthofen's aggressive ideas of attacking and destroying the enemy, were dismissed to other units. Symbolic of the spirit of JG.1 was the incredible Leutnant Walther Karjus who flew with one arm, his left; the right arm had been amputated. Some of Germany's most famous (and one later infamous Oberleutnant Hermann Göring) fighter pilots fought with JG.1: Oberleutnant Ernst Udet, Leutnant Karl Wüsthoff, Leutnant Kurt Wolff, Leutnant Hans Kirchstein and Leutnant Erich Löwenhardt.

Uniquely, Leutnant Lothar von Richthofen (brother of Manfred) and his cousin Leutnant Wolfram von Richthofen flew with Rittmeister Manfred von Richthofen, their relative and commanding officer. Manfred von Richthofen's policy of selection of the best pilots survived his death, and resulted in JG.1 having 892 confirmed victories to its credit by the war's end on 11 November 1918.

During JG.1's operational career fifty-eight of its pilots were killed; forty-seven wounded; eleven taken prisoner; five killed in accidents; and four injured in accidents.

Commanders of JG.1

Rittmeister Manfred Freiherr von Richthofen	25 June 1817 – 21 April 1918
Oberleutnant Kurt-Bertram von Döring	7 July – 25 July 1917 (acting CO)
Hauptmann Wilhelm Reinhard	22 April 1918 – 3 July 1918
Oberleutnant Erich Löwenhardt	June-July 1918 (acting CO)
Oberleutnant Hermann Göring	8 July 1918 – Armistice

JASTA 4 (ROYAL PRUSSIAN)

Formed from pilots from Kek Vaux (a group of fighting aircraft), Armee Flugpark Nr.2 and Fokker Kommando Süd 23 (*Fokker flying detachment south*), on 25 August 1916, flying Fokker Scout and Halberstadt D.II aircraft.

First commander was Oberleutnant Rudolf Berthold then Oberleutnant Hans Joachim Buddecke on 28 August 1916. Command then passed to Oberleutnant Ernst Freiherr von Althaus from 14 December until January 1917, when Leutnant Wilhelm Frankl assumed command. By then, the Jasta had been equipped with the formidable Albatros D.II single-seat fighter with a top speed of 109mph. The twin Spandau machine-gunned D.II outclassed Allied aircraft and wreaked havoc on British BE2c reconnaissance planes.

Leutnant Frankl had scored twenty victories and earned the award of the Orden Pour le Mérite before he was killed in action on 8 April 1917. When the Nazis came to power in Germany, Leutnant Frankl, who was Jewish, had his name deleted from

Oberleutnant Ernst Freiherr von Althaus (Orden Pour le Mérite) died on 29 November 1946.

the honour roll of World War One airmen; this was rectified after World War Two and Luftwaffe JG.74 now bears his name.

On 8 April 1917 Kurt-Bertram von Döring assumed command of Jasta 4. He held the Iron Cross 1st Class and was awarded the Knight's Cross of the Royal Hohenzolllern House Order on 14 December 1917. When the Red Baron was away from the front due to wounds, von Döring took temporary command of JG.1. Whilst with Jasta 4, von Döring scored nine victories and two more with Jasta 1. He survived World War One and joined the Luftwaffe in 1934. He became a group commander of the Richthofen Geschwader and rose to the rank of Leutnantgeneral.

During von Döring's temporary absence as Geschwaderführer of JG.1, Oberleutnant Oskar Freiherr von Boenigk took command of Jasta 4 and scored seven victories with the unit. His total war tally was twenty-six and his impressive array of decorations included the Orden Pour le Mérite. He survived the war and served in the Nazi Luftwaffe, rising to the rank of Generalmajor.

In February 1918 the twenty-one-year-old Leutnant Kurt Wüsthoff became commander of Jasta 4. He scored all his twenty-seven victories with the Jasta and was awarded the Orden Pour le Mérite in addition to other decorations. He survived the war but died in an aircrash in July 1926.

By early 1918, Jasta 4 was flying Albatros Scouts, Pfalz Scouts and Fokker Dr.I Dreideckers. Their Albatros and Pfalz Scouts carried black and white fuselage identification bands and their triplanes red and turquoise striped wings and fuselage markings.

During 1918 – the last year of the war – Jasta 4 saw plenty of aerial combat on German Army Fronts 2, 6, 7 and 17. Some famous airmen commanders emerged during this last year of war: Leutnant Hans Georg von Osten, Leutnant Johann Janzen and Oberleutnant Ernst Udet.

Jasta 4 was credited with 189 victories with the loss of eleven pilots, nine wounded and two taken as POWs. The Jasta was dissolved on 16 November 1918.

Staffelführer of Jasta 4

Oberleutnant Rudolf Berthold	25 August – 28 August 1916
Oberleutnant Hans Joachim Buddecke	28 August – 14 December 1916
Oberleutnant Ernst Freiherr von Althaus	14 December 1916 – 1 January 1917
Leutnant Wilhelm Frankl	1 January 1917 – 8 April 1917
Oberleutnant Kurt-Bertram von Döring	8 April 1917 – 22 February 1918
Oberleutnant Oskar von Boenigk	7 July – 25 July 1917 (acting CO)
Leutnant Kurt Wüsthoff	22 February – 16 November 1918

The personnel of Jasta 4 with their total war victories, where known, are as follows:

Oberleutnant Ernst Freiherr von Althaus	10
Leutnant Fritz Gerhard Anders	7
Oberleutnant von Alvensleben	0
Leutnant Raven Freiherr von Barnekow	11
Leutnant Frtiz Otto Bernert	27

Oberleutnant Rudolf Berthold	44
Oberleutnant Oskar Freiherr von Boenigk	26
Leutnant der Reserve Bouillon	0
Oberleutnant Hans Joachim Buddecke	13
Vizefeldwebel Clausnitzer	0
Oberleutnant Kurt-Bertram von Döring	11
Leutnant H. Drekmann	11
Leutnant der Reserve Fischer	0
Leutnant Wilhelm Frankl	20
Leutnant der Reserve Geppert	0
Leutnant Gluszewski	0
Leutnant der Reserve Graul	0
Leutnant Gisbert-Wilhelm Groos	7
Leutnant von Hartmann	0
Leutnant Held	0
Leutnant der Reserve Hertz	0
Leutnant der Reserve Hildebrandt	0
Leutnant der Reserve Hirschfeld	0
Leutnant Walter Höhndorf	12
Leutnant Hüber	0
Vizefeldwebel Alfred Hübner	0
Leutnant Johann Janzen	13
Leutnant Jessen	0
Leutnant der Reserve Joschkowitz	0
Leutnant Hans Klein	22
Leutnant der Reserve E. Koepsch	9
Leutnant der Reserve Kraut	0
Leutnant der Reserve Krüger	0
Leutnant Krüger	0
Leutnant Alfred Lenz	6
Vizefeldwebel Marquardt	0
Leutnant H. Maushake	6
Leutnant Friedrich Theodor Noltenius	21
Leutnant Hans Georg von Osten	5
Vizefeldwebel Patermann	0
Leutnant Victor von Pressentin	15
Leutnant von Puttkammer	0
Flieger Rhode	0
Leutnant Rouselle	0
Sergeant Otto Schmutzler	0
Leutnant E. Siempelkamp	5
Leutnant Skauradzun	0
Oberleutnant Ernst Udet	62
Leutnant Joseph Veltjens	35
Leutnant der Reserve Wilde	0

Fokker E.V (D.VIII) of Jasta 6, late 1918. The unit's markings of black and white striping are visible on the tail and wheel discs.

Leutnant Hans Ritter von Adam (twenty-one victories) was killed in action on 15 November 1917 when he was shot down by Lieutenant K.B. Montgomery, 45 Squadron RFC. (*Sanke Card Nr.557*)

Leutnant von Winterfield	0
Vizefeldwebel Wüstoff	0
Leutnant Kurt Wüsthoff	27
Leutnant Zwiters	0

JASTA 6 (ROYAL PRUSSIAN)

Jasta 6 was created on 25 August 1916 from Fokkerstaffel Sivry and equipped with Fokker E.IV Eindeckers (obsolete by then). The Jasta went to 2. Armee on the western front in the area of the Somme, where it re-equipped with Albatros D.I Scouts and one Fokker D.V.

The first commander was Leutnant Josef Wulf in September, followed by Leutnant Fritz Otto Bernert who took over command on 1 May 1917. Bernert did not stay for long and Leutnant Eduard Dostler assumed command in the first week of June 1917.

Dostler had eight victories to his credit and had been decorated with the Knight's Cross with Swords of the Royal Hohenzollern House Order when he joined Jasta 4 on 10 June. By 21 August 1917 he had scored a total of twenty-six downed Allied aircraft. Shortly before his death at the hands of pilots O'Callaghan and Sharples flying an RE8 of 7 Squadron RFC, he was awarded the Orden Pour le Mérite and, posthumously, was made a Ritter (*knight*) and awarded the Bavarian Military Max-Joseph Order.

Jasta 6 moved base to Courtrai in early June and took on charge Albatros D.IIIs and D.Vs, and Fokker Dr.Is. Some of the later Fokker Dr.Is had red-and-white-painted engine cowlings; many of the Albatros had black and white stripes on their elevators. Most pilots had personal insignia on their fuselages: Leutnant Franz Hemer had blond wavy hair and his aircraft had a white or yellow wavy line along its fuselage – an allusion to his blond hair.

Jasta 6 was incorporated into JG.1 in July 1917 and stayed with it until the end of the war on 11 November 1918.

When von Dostler was killed in combat in August, Leutnant Hans Ritter von Adam assumed command but three months later on 15 November, he too was killed flying Albatros D.V Nr.5222/17 – after recording twenty-one victories in aerial combat. His victorious opponent was Lieutenant L.K. Montgomery flying a Camel.

The successor to von Adam as Jasta commander was Oberleutnant Wilhelm Reinhard who took over on 26 November 1917. Reinhard had six victories to his credit when he joined Jasta 6 and scored another six before he took command of JG.1 on 22 April 1918 after Manfred von Richthofen was killed on 21 April 1918.

Several other pilots assumed command of Jasta 6. They were: Leutnant Johann Janzen (thirteen victories), Leutnant Hans Kirschstein (twenty-seven victories), Leutnant Paul Wenzel (twelve victories) and lastly, on 1 September 1918, Leutnant Ulrich Neckel (thirty victories).

As part of 'the Flying Circus' JG.1, Jasta 6 had to move from battlefront to battlefront to stem the Allied mounting pressure on the ground, but JG.1 still had the tactical advantage of aerial combat over or within their lines. Their enemy had to come to them.

In May 1918 Jasta 6 acquired Fokker D.VIIs then Fokker E.Vs, and continued to score against the Allies but to no avail. By mid-September JG.1 was moved from opposing British sector aircraft to the quieter American sector.

11 November 1918 saw the end of fighting on the Western Front. Jasta 6 was de-activated on 16 November 1918 at Darmstadt. Jasta 6 recorded 196 victories at a cost of ten pilots killed in action; two further pilots killed and four injured in accidents. Nine were wounded and three taken as prisoners of war.

Staffelführer of Jasta 6

Leutnant Josef Wulf	September 1916–1 May 1917
Leutnant Fritz Otto Bernert	1 May 1917 – June 1917
Oberleutnant Eduard Ritter von Dostler	June 1917 – 21 August 1917
Leutnant Hans Ritter von Adam	21 August 1917 – 15 November 1917
Oberleutnant Wilhelm Reinhard	26 November 1917 – 21 April 1918
Leutnant Johann Janzen	21 April 1918 – 9 June 1918
Leutnant Hans Kirchstein	9 June 1918 – 16 July 1918
Leutnant Paul Wenzel	16 July 1918 – 1 September 1918
Leutnant Ulrich Neckel	1 September 1918 – Armistice

Nominal roll of pilots of Jasta 6 with their believed total war victories:

Leutnant Hans Ritter von Adam	21
Vizefeldwebel Bachmann	0
Leutnant L. Beckmann	8
Leutnant Fritz Otto Bernert	27
Vizefeldwebel Beschow	0
Flieger Blümener	0
Leutnant der Reserve Bretschneider-Bodemer	0
Leutnant O. von Breiten-Landberg	5
Leutnant Czermak	0
Leutnant Karl Deilmann	6
Oberleutnant Eduard Ritter von Dostler	26
Vizefeldwebel Ey	0
Leutnant der Reserve Galetschky	0
Leutnant Franz Hemer	18
Vizefeldwebel Häusler	0
Vizefeldwebel Hemer	0
Vizefeldwebel Holler	0
Leutnant Johann Janzen	13
Leutnant Jantzen	0
Leutnant Hans Kirchstein	27
Leutnant der Reserve Koch	0

Vizefeldwebel F. Krebs	13
Vizefeldwebel Heinrich Küllmer	0
Leutnant der Reserve Küppers	0
Hauptmann Lischke	0
Leutnant Fritz Loerzer	11
Leutnant Friedrich Mallinckrodt	6
Leutnant Markgraf	0
Leutnant der Reserve Matzdorf	0
Leutnant Nauk	0
Leutnant Ulrich Neckel	30
Vizefeldwebel Niess	0
Leutnant der Reserve Nöldecke	0
Leutnant Friedrich Theodor Noltenius	21
Leutnant der Reserve Pollandt	0
Leutnant der Reserve Raffay	0
Leutnant der Reserve Reiher	0
Unteroffizier Reimers	0
Hauptmann Wilhelm Reinhard	20
Leutnant der Reserve Rieth	0
Leutnant der Reserve Rödiger	0
Leutnant der Reserve Rolfe	0
Leutnant Schliewen	0
Leutnant Julius Schmidt	15
Feldwebel Leutnant Schubert	0
Leutnant Skowronski	0
Leutnant Stock	0
Vizefeldwebel Stumpf	0
Leutnant Tüxen	0
Leutnant von der Wense	0
Leutnant Paul Wenzel	10
Leutnant Richard Wenzel	12
Leutnant Wever	0
Leutnant der Reserve Zschunke	0

JASTA 10 (ROYAL PRUSSIAN)

Jasta 10 was formed on 28 September 1916 at Pfalempin, near Douai, from Kek 3 and equipped with four Fokker E.IVs, two Fokker D.IIs, one Halberstadt D.II and two Albatros D.IIs. Jasta 10's activation was on 6 October 1916 and its first attachment was to 5. Armee. It was initially known as Jasta Linck after its first Staffelführer Oberleutnant Ludwig Karl Wilhelm Linck who had been posted from FA.18. However, on 22 October 1916 Linck was killed in action and his command was taken over by Oberleutnant Karl Rummelsbacher who remained as such until June 1917.

In February 1917, Jasta 10 was sent to support 4. Armee near Courtrai, where they spent the next ten months in support actions until they were assigned to JG.1.

Some of the pilots lasted only a short time. Flieger Rudolf Ihde had his first sortie with Jasta 10, flying alongside Manfred von Richthofen, but was shot down and killed in his first dogfight with Allied fighters. Leutnant der Reserve Fritz Friedrichs, who had been badly wounded whilst serving on the ground as an infantryman and discharged as medically unfit, became a pilot and fought with great distinction alongside Richthofen. He claimed twenty-one victories by the end of the war.

Karl Rummelsbacher was replaced – albeit briefly – by Leutnant Albert Dossenbach from June 1917 to 3 July 1917, then in turn by Oberleutnant Ernst Freiherr von Althaus, who like Richthofen had come from a calvary unit where he had been awarded the Knight's Cross of the Military St Henry Order for Bravery. Von Althaus had failing eyesight and had to give up his Jasta 10 command to Leutnant Werner Voss. Voss was killed in action on 23 September 1917 and Jasta 10 had another commander, Leutnant Hans Klein, until he was badly wounded in action against British fighters on 19 February 1918.

It was not until April 1918 that Jasta 10 acquired a new commander: Oberleutnant Erich Löwenhardt. He lasted until June 1918 when he was wounded in a dogfight. Leutnant Alois Heldmann assumed command until Löwenhardt returned to duty. On 10 August 1918, during an aerial battle with SE5as of 56 Squadron, Royal Air Force, Löwenhardt's aircraft collided with that of Leutnant Alfred Wenz of Jasta 11 causing both pilots to abandon their crashing aircraft and take to their parachutes. Löwenhardt's parachute failed to open and he fell to his death.

The last commander of Jasta 10, Leutnant Arthur Laumann, was posted from Jasta 66 as a stopgap and stayed until the end of hostilities on 11 November 1918.

During its two-year existence a variety of aircraft were used: Fokker D.VIIs, Fokker D.VIIIs, Fokker Dr.Is, Albatros D.Vs; and Pfalz D.IIIs. The Fokker Dreideckers were distinctive with their engine cowlings painted black and white.

In its short action span Jasta 10 acquitted itself well, with 157 recorded victories but lost twenty-two pilots, four taken as prisoners of war, ten badly wounded and one killed in an accident.

Staffelführer of Jasta 10

Oberleutnant Ludwig Karl Wilhelm Linck	6 October 1916 – 22 October 1916
Oberleutnant Karl Rummelsbacher	22 October 1916 – 8 June 1917
Leutnant Albert Dossenbach	10 June 1917 – 3 July 1917
Oberleutnant Ernst Freiherr von Althaus	3 July 1917 – 31 July 1917
Leutnant Werner Voss	31 July 1917 – 23 September 1917
Leutnant Hans Klein	23 September 1917 – February 1918
Oberleutnant Erich Löwenhardt	April – June 1918
Leutnant Alois Heldmann	June 1918 – 6 July 1918
Oberleutnant Erich Löwenhardt	6 July 1918 – 10 August 1918
Leutnant Arthur Laumann	10 August – 11 November 1918

Pilots of Jasta 10 with their believed total war victories:

Leutnant Adomeit	0
Oberleutnant Ernst Freiherr von Althaus	10
Offizierstellvertreter Paul Aue	10
Leutnant der Reserve Baehren	0
Vizefeldwebel Barth	1
Gefreiter Beerendon	1
Leutnant der Reserve Bellen	1
Leutnant Bender	1
Unteroffizier Biewers	0
Leutnant Bohlein	1
Unteroffizier Breitel	0
Gefreiter Brettel	2
Vizefeldwebel Burggaller	0
Vizefeldwebel Delang	2
Leutnant Demandt	0
Unteroffizier Derflinger	1
Leutnant Albert Dossenbach	15
Leutnant der Reserve Feige	0
Leutnant der Reserve Fritz Friedrichs	21
Leutnant Gilles	0
Leutnant der Reserve Justus Grassmann	10
Unteroffizier Hardel	0
Vizefeldwebel Hecht	0
Leutnant Alois Heldmann	15
Unteroffizier Hennig	0
Leutnant Ernest Hess	17
Leutnant der Reserve Kirst	0
Unteroffizier Klamt	0
Leutnant Hans Klein	22
Leutnant der Reserve W. Kohlbach	5
Leutnant Kortüm	0
Leutnant der Reserve Krayer	0
Leutnant der Reserve Kühn	3
Leutnant der Reserve Arthur Laumann	28
Leutnant der Reserve Lehmann	0
Gefreiter Lemke	0
Oberleutnant Ludwig Karl Wilhelm Linck	0
Oberleutnant Erich Löwenhardt	54
Leutnant der Reserve Malesky	0
Leutnant Friedrich Mallinckrodt	6
Leutnant Meise	0
Gefreiter Möller	1
Flieger Nitsche	0

Leutnant der Reserve Ohirau	1
Unteroffizier Oppel	1
Leutnant Otto	1
Leutnant der Reserve Rademacher	0
Flieger Riensberg	0
Leutnant Römer	0
Leutnant der Reserve Rüdenberg	0
Leutnant der Reserve Schibilsky	0
Vizefeldwebel F. Schumacher	5
Leutnant Stoy	0
Unteroffizier Strecker	0
Offizierstellvertreter Viereck	0
Leutnant Werner Voss	48
Vizefeldwebel Wawzin	1
Oberleutnant Weigand	3
Leutnant der Reserve Hans Weiss	16
Unteroffizier Werkmeister	0

Not all the above named pilots served with Jasta 10 throughout the war. A number of the pilots were transferred from other Jastas albeit for only a short time: for example, Vizefeldwebel Ernst Bürggaler lasted only two months before being returned to the air depot.

JASTA 11 (ROYAL PRUSSIAN)

On the morning of 14 January 1917, the German Army Air Service squadron Jasta 11 was destined to became a household name. This was the day that Leutnant Manfred Freiherr von Richthofen was given his first command and became its commanding officer.

The squadron at the time was based at La Brayelle, outside Douai on 6. Armee Front, and the appointment of Richthofen as its commanding officer was to place Jasta 11, and its subsequent involvement with the Richthofen Geschwader, into the annals of aviation history.

Two days previously, one day after receiving word of his first command, Manfred von Richthofen received a telegram from Army Headquarters. It read: 'His Majesty the Kaiser has awarded The Orden Pour le Mérite to Leutnant von Richthofen.' There was some speculation about the reason for the delay in Richthofen receiving Prussia's highest award, because up to this point his number of victories numbered sixteen. Some theorists put it down to the fact that he had not shot down any obser- vation balloons. It is hard to believe that such an award would literally hang on the demise of a balloon. In Richthofen's final total of eighty victories not one balloon was claimed.

Richthofen brought his personal Albatros D.III with him to Jasta 11, painted in the usual olive green and brown on the wings and natural wood finish on the fuselage. For whatever reason, he decided to have the aircraft painted partly red. Such was the confidence of the man in his own ability, he realised that from the moment he engaged and destroyed an enemy aircraft, he would soon become a target for every Allied fighter pilot.

As Jasta 11's successes soared, some of the pilots expressed concern about their leader. It wasn't his leadership that they were concerned about – *that* was beyond question – but the fact that Manfred, already known to the Allies, had a price put on his head. Lothar von Richthofen had recently joined his brother in Jasta 11, and implored his brother to allow all the other aircraft in the Staffel to be painted red to draw some of the attention away from Manfred. Richthofen agreed in principle and allowed the Staffel's aircraft to be painted a soft red with individual markings.

On 23 January 1917 the newly emblazoned pack took to the air for the first time and headed over the trenches near Lens. As they approached, a squadron of eight British fighters appeared. Without hesitation Richthofen dived to action. In less than fifteen minutes the skirmish was over and three British aircraft had been destroyed; the Jasta had been 'blooded' and the price had just gone up on the head of the now acclaimed Red Baron.

As the Jasta went from strength to strength, a number of pilots fell by the wayside. They were not up to the standard expected by Manfred von Richthofen and were replaced. Among the early replacements were: Leutnant Karl Allmenröder, who was later awarded the Orden Pour le Mérite; Vizefeldwebel Sebastian Festner; and Leutnant Kurt Wolff. Such was the reputation of Jasta 11 that Leutnant Karl Emil Schäfer, of KG.2, sent Manfred von Richthofen a telegram saying, 'Can you use me?' Richthofen, already aware of Schäfer's aggressive and skilful reputation, replied, 'You have already been requested.'

Slowly, Richthofen put together an élite squadron of fighter pilots of the highest standard and among these was Leutnant Walther Karjus who, despite only having one hand, was able to hold his own with the best of them. The Jasta's reputation went before it, and whenever the Allied fighters saw the red-painted aircraft, accompanied by other softer-red-painted aircraft, they knew they were in for a hard fight. Between 23 January and 22 April 1917, Jasta 11 shot down 100 enemy aircraft. However, 22 April was marred by the report that Schäfer was missing. The following day he turned up – he had crash-landed his aircraft close to a Bavarian section of the German army. At first he didn't understand their dialect, and thought he had landed close to enemy lines, but soon realised that the soldiers were indeed part of the German army.

Jasta 11 continued to score heavily against the Allies but at a cost. One after another the experienced pilots were shot down and killed but Richthofen seemed to lead a charmed life. In 6 July 1917 Richthofen's luck ran out. He clashed with a flight of FE2ds from 20 Squadron, RFC, and was forced to land suffering from a head injury. However, his luck held, he had landed close to a German Army Field Hospital.

Richthofen's place as Jagdgeschwader commander was taken by Oberleutnant Kurt-Bertram von Döring. It was only a short command – Richthofen returned on 25 July. New aircraft were required and in October new Fokker Dreideckers arrived, they were later a success.

The Jagdgeschwader continued to lose top pilots. Kurt Wolff, then Alfred Hübner, followed by Oberleutnant von Dostler and Werner Voss, and most devastating of all, the wounding of the Red Baron's brother, Lothar von Richthofen.

On Sunday 21 April 1918 the greatest loss of all occurred: Manfred von Richthofen died in combat. He was involved in a dogfight with Allied fighters over Vaux-sur-Somme. It is not clear who actually fired the fatal bullet, but one thing was certain, the Red Baron crashed and was found dead in the wreckage of his aircraft.

This spelled the beginning of the end for Jasta 11 and for JG.1. With their leader gone the spell was broken and Richthofen's place was taken by Oberleutnant Hermann Göring, whose charismatic leadership was to lead him into infamy in the Third Reich.

On Armistice Day, 11 November 1918, in a last act of defiance, Hermann Göring, who had been ordered to take JG.1 aircraft to Strasbourg and hand them over to the French, instructed his pilots to have accidents whilst landing, thus rendering the aircraft useless. Later at a meeting in a monastery wine cellar, fifty-three officers and 473 men listened to their last commander Hermann Göring tell them that they had acquitted themselves gloriously and had accounted for 644 British, French and American aircraft. The sum total of Allied casualties included the loss of fifty-six Allied officers and enlisted pilots, six ground crew killed, and fifty-two officers and seven enlisted men wounded. A splendid record by any standards.

The Richthofen Jagdgeschwader had left its mark in the annals of aviation history.

Staffelführer of Jasta 11

Oberleutnant Rudolf Emil Lang	11 October 1916 – 14 January 1917
Oberleutnant Manfred von Richthofen	14 January 1917 – 26 June 1917
Leutnant Karl Allmenröder	26 June 1917 – 27 June 1917
Leutnant Kurt Wolff	27 June 1917 – 2 July 1917
Leutnant Gisbert-Wilhelm Groos	2 July – 11 September 1917 (acting CO)
Oberleutnant Kurt Wolff	11 September 1917 – 15 September 1917
Leutnant Lothar von Richthofen	15 September 1917 – March 1918
Leutnant Hans Weiss	March – September 1918
Leutnant Eberhardt Mohnicke	March – September 1918
Leutnant Wolfram von Richthofen	March – September 1918
Oberleutnant Erich-Rüdiger von Wedel	8 September 1918 – Armistice

Pilots of Jasta 11 and their victories with the Jasta:

Leutnant Karl Allmenröder	30
Vizefeldwebel Baierlein	1
Leutnant der Reserve Bahr	0
Leutnant Raven Freiherr von Barnekow	0
Leutnant Bockelmann	2
Leutnant H. von Boddien	0
Leutnant der Reserve Walter Bordfeld	0

Leutnant Otto Brauneck	3
Leutnant O. von Breiten-Landenberg	5
Leutnant von Conta	0
Unteroffizier Eiserbeck	0
Leutnant Max Festler	0
Vizefeldwebel Sebastian Festner	12
Vizefeldwebel Willi Gabriel	11
Leutnant Alfred Gerstenberg	0
Leutnant Gisbert-Wilhelm Groos	7
Oberleutnant Hermann Göring	22
Leutnant S. Gussmann	5
Leutnant der Reserve Hans Hintsch	3
Leutnant Graf von Hohenau	0
Feldwebel Jagla	0
Leutnant der Reserve Erich Just	6
Leutnant Walther Karjus	0
Leutnant Keseling	0
Leutnant der Reserve von Köckeritz	3
Leutnant Egon Koepsch	9
Leutnant Krefft	0
Vizefeldwebel Josef Lautenschlager	0
Leutnant von Linsingen	0
Leutnant E. Lübbert	0
Leutnant Otto Maashoff	3
Unteroffizier Martens	0
Leutnant der Reserve Karl Meyer	2
Leutnant Mentz	0
Leutnant Eberhardt Mohnicke	9
Leutnant der Reserve Franz Müller	2
Leutnant A. Niederhoff	7
Leutnant Friedrich Theodor Noltenius	21
Leutnant Hans Georg von Osten	5
Leutnant Plüschow	1
Leutnant von Raczek	0
Leutnant der Reserve Günther Pastor	0
Oberleutnant Wilhelm Reinhard	20
Oberleutnant Manfred von Richthofen	80
Leutnant Lothar von Richthofen	40
Leutnant Wolfram von Richthofen	8
Leutnant Karl Emil Schäfer	30
Oberleutnant Scheffer	0
Vizefeldwebel Edgar Scholtz	6
Leutnant K. von Schönebeck	3
Leutnant von Schweinitz	0
Leutnant der Reserve Schulte-Frohlinde	4

Vizefeldwebel Willi Gabriel (eleven victories) (extreme left) with Jasta 11 pilots.

Leutnant Georg Simon	0
Leutnant Stapenhorst	4
Leutnant W. Steinhäuser	4
Vizefeldwebel Alfred Niemz	4
Leutnant Ernst Udet	3
Oberleutnant Erich-Rüdiger von Wedel	13
Leutnant der Reserve Hans Weiss	16
Leutnant Richard Wenzel	1
Oberleutnant Kurt Wolff	33
Leutnant Hans Joachim Wolff	9
Oberleutnant Zander	1

By the summer of 1917 the RFC – aided by Sopwith Triplanes of the RNAS – had regained control of the air. New aircraft, such as the Bristol F.2b, the Sopwith Camel, and the SE5, were coming into front line service and restored the balance. The French Air Service squadrons of Spad V.II and Spad X.IIIs came into service and scored many successes.

The Allies' objective was to overwhelm the German Army Air Service in the air by numerical superiority but the Allied pilots were, to a certain extent, not as skilled airmen as the Germans at this time. The RFC were soon to change this and gain the edge. Tactical bombing by DH4 and then DH9 day bombers was increased. Fighting back, the German Army Air Service took delivery of the Albatros D.V and Pfalz

Leutnant Otto Brauneck of Jasta 25 (ten victories) was killed in action on 26 July 1917 when he was shot down by Captain N.N.W. Webb of 70 Squadron RFC over Zonnebeke. (*Sanke Card Nr.508*)

D.VIII but these fighters made little impact, in spite of the then superior flying skills of the German pilots.

The Fokker Dr.I Dreidecker came into service in the autumn of 1917 but had to be withdrawn with wing root problems. It re-entered service later and Kurt Wolff was killed in action flying the new triplane on 15 September. The high-scoring Werner Voss, also flying a Fokker Dr.I, fell in action against SE5s of the élite 56 Squadron RFC. Another ace, Heinrich Gontermann, destroyer of eighteen balloons, was killed when his triplane's top wing folded in flight.

German airmen continued to die in aerial combat: Karl Emil Schäfer, Eduard von Dostler and Erwin Böhme fell and the Red Baron himself was wounded and hospitalised. New airmen appeared in the sky: Fritz Rumey and Otto Könnecke of Jasta 5 took up the challenge and many Allied aircraft fell beneath their guns. Walter von Bülow-Bothkamp died on 6 January and Max Ritter von Müller on 9 January under the guns of the RFC. The brave Müller jumped to his death from his blazing aircraft: a quick death rather than the agony of dying in the flames of his fighter.

January 1918 also saw the Fokker Dreidecker come into its own when Richthofen discovered the agility of the machine in a dogfight. Again he had his aircraft painted in red. Some Jastas were equipped with the triplanes, others partly equipped. The triplanes of Richthofen's 'Flying Circus' scored the most victories during March and April 1918.

The Red Baron met his end on 21 April 1918 when he was shot down in action by Australian ground forces on the Somme.

With the United States of America entering in the war in April 1917, the German government realised that they would have to increase their air arm to compete with America's industrial might. Forty new Jastas were thus created as well as two new Jagdgeschwaders. Hauptmann Adolf von Tutschek commanded JG.2 and Oberleutnant Bruno Loerzer JG.3.

Aircrew reinforcements became available from the now defunct Russian front: these pilots and observers were battle hardened from flying in Russia and provided a valuable reserve of support. Other pilots began to show their worth. Oberleutnant Ernst Udet – who ended the war with sixty-two victories and was the highest surviving ace – was posted to Jasta 11. Oberleutnant Hermann Göring – later to become Reichsmarschall of Nazi Germany – was appointed to command Richthofen's JG.1 but only scored one more kill to bring his total to twenty-two victories.

During April 1918 JG.1 began to receive one of Germany's best fighters of World War One: the Fokker D.VII. This machine went on to become the outstanding German fighter of the war.

By the end of May most of the German Army Air Service was battling against the French and United States Air Services on the Aisne front. The RFC had established air superiority over the British section of the front and was flying sorties without opposition over and behind German lines. The Allies' war of attrition began to take its toll and the German Army Air Service began to run out of experienced aircrew. The last of the airmen took to the sky in the summer of 1918 flying their Fokker D.VIIs into combat.

A Halberstadt CL.II two-seater battle aircraft crewed by Pilot Hubener and Gunner Schaesberg.

The German Army Air Service was fighting on other fronts – Palestine, Italy and the Dardanelles – where Hauptmann Hans Joachim Buddecke gained the third Orden Pour le Mérite of the war on 14 April 1916. During 1917 to 1918, Emil Meinecke and Theo Croneiss of Ottoman FA.6 were in action against the Royal Naval Air Service and Greek forces. In Italy the German Army Air Service had been assisting their allies, the Austro-Hungarians, with Jastas 1, 31 and 39. With the big German offensives in France in progress during 1918, these Jastas were withdrawn and the Austro-Hungarians fought on unaided.

The Imperial German Naval Air Service with their own seaplane fighters and land-based aircraft, duelled with their British counterparts over the North Sea. Oberleutnant zur See Friedrich Christiansen won his Orden Pour le Mérite on 11 December 1917. His exploits included an air to surface battle against a British submarine: the C.25 in the estuary of the River Thames. Two other naval fliers – Oberleutnant zur See Gotthard Sachsenberg and Oberleutnant zur See Theodor Osterkamp – scored many kills and both were awarded the Orden Pour le Mérite.

The German Naval Airship Division flying Zeppelins made many raids over England. Kapitänleutnant Horst Treusch Freiherr von Buttlar-Brandenfels won his Orden Pour le Mérite for flying nineteen missions against England, and Fregattenkapitän Peter Strasser won the supreme award in 1917, but lost his life in Zeppelin LZ.70 when leading a mass Zeppelin attack against England.

The last three months of the war saw the German Army Air Service still hard at battle. On 8 August 1918 the RAF suffered its highest casualty total of World War One. Its pilots went down to aces Otto Könnecke, Erich Löwenhardt, Lothar von Richthofen, Ernst Udet and Arthur Laumann.

The ground war, however, was going badly for the Germans, but their air service was – though hard pressed and outnumbered three to one – still an effective fighting force. During August 1918 they inflicted the most aerial casualties sustained by the Allies since April 1917.

At 11:00 on 11 November 1918 World War One effectively ended and Germany capitulated. The German Army Air Services were bruised, battered, bloodied but unbowed. They had fought a good fight, largely with honour, but had succumbed to the overwhelming material power and resources of the Allies. Some but not many of the German airmen survived World War One. Some were to die between the wars by murder, revolution and accident, and some to serve again in World War Two for their Fatherland: Nazi Germany.

4
HOLDERS OF THE ORDEN POUR LE MÉRITE

The following airmen were awarded the Orden Pour le Mérite:

Leutnant Karl Allmenröder
Oberleutnant Ernst Freiherr von Althaus
Leutnant Paul Bäumer
Leutnant Oliver Freiherr von Beaulieu-Marconnay
Oberleutnant Fritz Otto Bernert
Oberleutnant Hans Berr
Hauptmann Rudolf Berthold
Leutnant Walter Blume
Hauptmann Oswald Boelcke
Oberleutnant Oskar Freiherr von Boenigk
Leutnant Erwin Böhme
Rittmeister Karl Bolle
Leutnant Heinrich Bongartz
Kapitänleutnant Horst Treusch Freiherr von Buttlar-Brandenfels
Hauptmann Ernst von Brandenburg
Leutnant Julius Buckler

Leutnant Franz Buchner
Hauptmann Hans Joachim Buddecke
Leutnant Walter von Bülow-Bothkamp
Oberleutnant zur See Friedrich Christiansen
Leutnant Carl Degelow
Leutnant Albert Dossenbach
Oberleutnant Eduard Ritter von Dostler
Leutnant Wilhelm Frankl
Hauptmann Hermann Fricke
Oberleutnant Hermann Wilhelm Göring
Leutnant Heinrich Gontermann
Oberleutnant Robert Ritter von Greim
Oberleutnant Jurgen von Grone
Leutnant der Reserve Wilhelm Griebsch
Leutnant Walter Höhndorf
General de Kavallerie Ernst von Hoeppner
Oberleutnant Erich Homburg
Oberleutnant Hans-Georg Horn
Oberleutnant Max Immelmann
Leutnant der Reserve Josef Carl Peter Jacobs
Hauptmann Alfred Keller
Leutnant Hans Kirchstein
Leutnant Otto Kissenberth
Leutnant Hans Klein
Hauptmann Rudolf Kleine
Leutnant Otto Könnecke
Hauptmann Hermann Köhl
Oberleutnant Heinrich Claudius Kroll
Leutnant Arthur Laumann
Leutnant Gustav Leffers
Oberst Hermann von der Leith-Thomsen
Hauptmann Leo Leonhardy
Hauptmann Bruno Loerzer
Oberleutnant Erich Löwenhardt
Oberleutnant Carl Menckhoff
Leutnant Max Ritter von Müller
Oberleutnant Albert Müller-Kahle
Leutnant Max Ritter von Mulzer
Leutnant Ulrich Neckel
Leutnant Landwehr Friedrich Nielebock
Oberleutnant zur See Theodor Osterkamp
Leutnant Otto Parschau
Hauptmann Paul Freiherr von Pechmann
Leutnant Fritz Pütter
Oberleutnant Lothar Freiherr von Richthofen

Leutnant Walter Höhndorf (Orden Pour le Mérite, with twelve victories) died in an aerial accident on 5 September 1917 while testing an AEG D.I. (*Sanke Card Nr.389*)

A Sanke card photograph of Hauptmann Alfred Keller (Orden Pour le Mérite). He served with Kagohl 27 and Kagohl 40, and commanded Bogohl 1 Night Bombers.

Rittmeister Manfred Freiherr von Richthofen
Leutnant der Reserve Peter Rieper
Oberleutnant Friedrich Ritter von Röth
Leutnant Fritz Rumey
Oberleutnant zur See Gotthard Sachsenberg
Leutnant Karl Emil Schäfer
Hauptmann Eduard Ritter von Schleich
Leutnant Wilhelm Paul Schreiber
Fregattenkapitan Peter Strasser
Leutnant Karl Thom
Leutnant Emil Thuy
Hauptmann Adolf Ritter von Tutschek
Oberleutnant Ernst Udet
Leutnant Joseph Veltjens
Leutnant Werner Voss
Hauptmann Franz Walz
Leutnant Rudolf Windisch
Leutnant Kurt Wintgens
Oberleutnant Kurt Wolff
Leutnant Kurt Wüsthoff

The following airmen were awarded/nominated/recommended for the Orden Pour le Mérite but were never actually decorated with the honour. Leutnant Gustav Doerr was awarded the Golden Military Merit Cross when an NCO, and then the Orden Pour le Mérite in 1919 when a Leutnant. Others died before they could receive it or due to Germany's surrender in 1918.

Name	Date awarded	History
Oberleutnant Harald Auffahrt	3 September 1918	29 victories
Leutnant Hermann Becker	5 November 1918	23 victories
Oberleutnant Hans Bethge	18 March 1917	20 victories Killed in action 18 March 1917
Leutnant Paul Billik	10 August 1918	31 victories
Leutnant Gustav Doerr	17 January 1919	35 victories
Leutnant Hans von Freden	10 November 1918	20 victories
Leutnant der Reserve Fritz Friedrichs	20 July 1918	21 victories Killed in action 15 July 1918
Leutnant Otto Fruhner	20 September 1918	27 victories
Leutnant Georg von Hantelmann	30 October 1918	25 victories
Leutnant Josef Mai	3 September 1918	30 victories
Leutnant Georg Meyer	5 November 1918	24 victories
Leutnant Max Nather	29 October 1918	26 victories
Leutnant Friedrich Theodor Noltenius	8 January 1918	21 victories
Leutnant Karl Odebrett	October 1918	21 victories (16 confirmed)
Leutnant Werner Preuss	29 October 1918	22 victories
Hauptmann Wilhelm Reinhard	*died before award was approved*	20 victories Killed in action 3 July 1918
Oberleutnant Franz Schleiff	3 April 1918	12 victories
Oberleutnant Otto Schmidt	27 October 1918	20 victories
Leutnant der Reserve Hans Weiss	22 April 1918	16 victories

5
BIOGRAPHIES OF GERMAN AIRMEN

RITTMEISTER MANFRED FREIHERR VON RICHTHOFEN

The legendary Red Baron was born at Breslau on May 2 1892, into the aristo-cratic Prussian family of Albrecht Freiherr von Richthofen, a Major in the 1st Regiment of Cuirassiers, and the Baroness von Richthofen.

Blue-eyed, blond-haired and of medium height, he was destined to leave his mark on aviation history during his relatively short life. At the age of eleven he entered the military school at Wahlstatt followed by admission to the Royal Prussian Military Academy. Easter 1911 saw him join a famous regiment of lancers: Uhlan Regiment Nr.1 'Kaiser Alexander III'. In the autumn of 1912 he was commissioned as a Leutnant in the 1st Uhlans. On the outbreak of World War One he went with his Uhlans into Russian Poland but within two weeks the regiment was transferred to the Meuse in France, where his regiment was allocated to the Crown Prince's German 5th Army.

Trench warfare ended Richthofen's cavalry unit. He was attached to 6th Army Corps and awarded the Iron Cross 2nd Class for his active service with the Uhlans. He transferred to the Air Service in May 1915. After four weeks training as an observer at Flieger Ersatz Abteilung 7 (FEA.7) Cologne and FEA.6 Grossenhain, he was posted to Flieger Abteilung 69 (FA.69) on the Eastern Front as an observer in

Rittmeister Manfred Freiherr von Richthofen (Orden Pour le Mérite, with eighty victories). He was the greatest of the German aces and the highest scoring fighter pilot of World War One.

an Albatros B.II. His pilot Leutnant Zeumer was dying from tuberculosis and had a death wish to die in action. The section to which they had been posted was being formed on the Eastern Front as part of Brieftauben Abteilung Ostende at Ostend. This innocuous title of 'Mail Carrier Pigeon Unit' was the cover name for a long-range bomber unit training to bomb England.

On 1 September 1915 Richthofen got his first taste of aerial combat. Flying as an observer in an AEG with Leutnant Zeumer, he spotted a Royal Flying Corps Farman flying nearby and ordered Zeumer to close to combat. Armed with a Mauser rifle, Richthofen opened fire on the Farman but missed with his four shots. The observer in the Farman replied and scored several hits on Richthofen's AEG. A week later Richthofen flying as an observer in an Albatros piloted by Leutnant Osteroth sighted a solitary Farman flying over French lines. Ordering his pilot to the attack Richthofen opened fire with his machine gun and poured 100 rounds at the enemy aircraft. The stricken Farman plunged to earth and crashed nose first behind French lines. However, the victory was unconfirmed and Richthofen was not credited with his first aircraft downed.

On 1 October 1915 Richthofen was posted to Metz to join another bomber unit. En route by train he met the already legendary Oswald Boelcke whom he engaged in conversation. Fired by Boelcke's example Richthofen decided to become a pilot and asked Leutnant Zeumer to teach him to fly. His first attempt to fly ended in disaster when he crashed on landing. He persisted in training and on Christmas Day 1915 qualified as a pilot. Posted to Russia, it was not until March 1916 that he returned to the Western Front but was ordered to fly a two-seater Albatros – not a single-seat fighter. He adapted the two-seater Albatros by fitting a machine gun on the upper wing which he could fire from the pilot's seat.

On 26 April 1916, he brought his machine gun into action against a French Nieuport over French lines. The Nieuport – riddled with bullets – crashed behind French Lines at Douamont. Again his victory was unconfirmed. Richthofen had not yet opened his score – officially.

Richthofen joined Oswald Boelcke's Jasta 2 on 1 September 1916 flying new Albatros D.IIIs. On 17 September Boelcke led his eight-strong Jasta into action and sighted eight BE2cs of 12 Squadron RFC and six FE2bs of 11 Squadron bombing Marcoing railway station. Richthofen – flying Albatros D.III Nr.491/16 – chose an FE2b as his target; he opened fire but missed. The enemy aircraft returned T.A. Lewis'

Manfred von Richthofen visiting his pilots, accompanied by his father (centre). Left to right are: Leutnant Brauneck, Rittmeister Manfred von Richthofen, Albrecht von Richthofen, Leutnant Böhme and Leutnant Kreft.

machine-gun fire. Avoiding the gunfire Richthofen banked out of range then came back under and behind the FE2b. Closing to point blank range – and unseen by the enemy aircraft's crew – he opened a burst of fire on the FE2b's engine and cockpit which wounded both the pilot, 2nd Lieutenant L.B.F. Morris, and his observer, Lieutenant T. Rees. The doomed FE2b plunged downwards with the dying pilot Morris managing to land the crippled aircraft behind German lines. Richthofen followed it down and landed nearby where he found the pilot mortally wounded and the observer dead. Richthofen had scored his first officially confirmed victory and, to mark the event, had a silver cup made by a Berlin silversmith to commemorate the victory.

By the end of October 1916 Richthofen had six confirmed victories to his credit. On 28 October Boelcke was killed in an aerial collision with fellow pilot Erwin Boheme and Jasta 2 was renamed Jasta Boelcke (Royal Prussian) with Oberleutnant Stephen Kirmaier in command.

Richthofen's victory score continued to increase; by 20 November 1916 he had ten confirmed kills. Two days later he shot down the Royal Flying Corps's leading ace – Major Lanoe Hawker, VC, DSO, flying a DH2 of 24 Squadron – in a dogfight. When Richthofen learned who his opponent had been, he flew over British lines and dropped a message to inform 24 Squadron of Major Hawker's death. Jasta Boelcke pilots arranged a military funeral for Major Hawker but Richthofen did not attend. It was not the done thing.

Richthofen was promoted to flight commander with Jasta Boelcke and subsequently had his Albatros aircraft painted red. This was to let his aerial opponents know with whom they fought and led to his most famous title: 'The Red Baron'.★ When he scored his sixteenth victory on 4 January 1917 the Kaiser awarded him – by special citation – the Orden Pour le Mérite. He was but twenty-four years old and now Germany's national hero.

With the decoration came promotion to Rittmeister (*cavalry captain*) and command of Jasta 11. On 11 April 1917 Richthofen had taken his score to forty confirmed kills; by the end of April it had risen to fifty-two confirmed. On 30 April he crossed swords with the Canadian ace Billy Bishop (who ended the war with seventy-two kills) over Drocourt. Try as he might Richthofen could not best Bishop, who outflew him and riddled his Albatros with bullets. Richthofen broke off the duel and retreated eastward towards safer territory.

On 26 June the German High Command grouped Jastas into Jagdgeschwaders and Richthofen took command of JG.1, which comprised Jastas 4, 6, 10 and 11. With its highly mobile and brightly painted aircraft, JG.1 soon earned the nickname of 'The Flying Circus'.

Richthofen continued to increase his score. On 6 July when flying his red Albatros with Jasta 11, he attacked six FE2ds of 20 Squadron RFC and, in the ensuing

---

★ As mentioned previously, Richthofen was not the only German pilot who painted his aircraft red; there are a number of reports of an all-red German aircraft being involved in skirmishes with the RFC and RNAS, and all in different places at the same time.

5 unserer erfolgreichsten Kampfflieger.

Vizefeldwebel Festner Leutnant Schäfer
Leutnant Frhr. von Richthofen
Rittmeister Frhr. von Richthofen   Leutnant Wolff

Jasta 11 pilots in 1917. Between these five, they were credited with 195 combat victories in total for World War One. Left to right are: Vizefeldwebel Sebastian Festener (twelve victories); Leutnant Karl Emil Schäfer (thirty victories); Rittmeister Manfred Freiherr von Richthofen (eighty victories); Leutnant Lothar Freiherr von Richthofen (forty victories); and Oberleutnant Kurt Wolff (thirty-three victories).

The Red Baron with his brother Lothar alongside a Fokker D.I. Both are wearing their Orden Pour le Mérite.

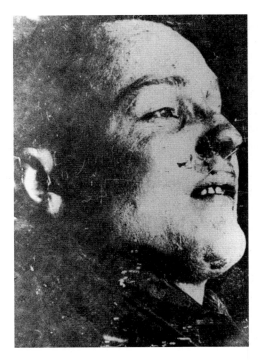

A poor quality picture of the bruised and battered face of the dead Red Baron.

His body was taken from his aircraft by the British and buried with full military honours at Bertangles. The Australian Army Guard of Honour fired three volleys of shots over his coffin before interment. Wreaths were laid by officers of the Royal Air Force.

dogfight, the observer of one of the FEs wounded the Red Baron in the head causing him to break off combat and make a heavy landing near Wericq. After being hospitalised, Richthofen returned to duty but was plagued with headaches and dizziness.

Nevertheless he managed to fly and score victory after victory, and by 30 November 1917 he had shot down sixty-three enemy aircraft. In the Red Baron's last year – 1918 – he shot down eleven aircraft during March making his total seventy-four. On 2 April he was awarded the last of his twenty-six decorations – the Order of the Red Eagle with Crowns and Swords – by the Kaiser. By 20 April he achieved what was to be his final score: eighty confirmed victories.

On Sunday, 21 April 1918 the Red Baron took off from his base at Cappy, France, with Jasta 11, on what was to be his final flight. Jasta 11 engaged the aerial enemy over Le Hamel and a huge dogfight ensued, with the Red Baron in the thick of it. Richthofen swung onto the tail of a 209 Squadron Camel flown by a young pilot Lieutenant Wilfred May and gave chase. Captain A. Roy Brown, DSC, flying above saw May's perilous position and dived to the rescue. Coming up on Richthofen's aircraft from behind, Brown opened fire and scored a long burst on the red triplane. Apparently unharmed Richthofen continued to chase and machine gun May's Camel. As Richthofen flew low over Morlancourt Ridge he came under a hail of fire from Australian ground gunners. Machine gun fire raked the red triplane and the gunners saw the Red Baron's head snap backwards in his cockpit. His aircraft sideslipped then glided into the ground nose first. The Red Baron was dead – killed in action.

The following message was dropped by a British aircraft and was addressed to the German Flying Corps:

To,
The German Flying Corps
Rittmeister Baron Manfred von Richthofen was killed in aerial combat on April 21, 1917.
He was buried with full military honours.
From British Royal Flying Corps

Baron Manfred von Richthofen was buried with Military Honours at Bertangles with his coffin draped with the Imperial German flag. Pilots of the German Army Air Service flew over his grave and dropped wreaths unhindered. His remains were returned to Berlin in 1925 and reburied at the Invaliden.

LEUTNANT KARL ALLMENRÖDER

Karl Allmenröder was born in the small town of Wald, near Solingen, on 23 May 1896, the son of a Lutheran pastor. His strict upbringing and education were instrumental in his decision to become a doctor, but his studies were interrupted by the outbreak of war. He enlisted in the German army joining Ostfriesisches Feldartillerie-Regiment Nr.62 in Oldenburg and, after training, was posted to 1. Posenches Feldartillerie-Regiment Nr.20, but within months he returned to

Leutnant Allmenröder

Leutnant Karl Allmenröder (Orden Pour le Mérite, with thirty victories) was killed in action on 27 June 1917.

Feldartillerie-Regiment Nr.62. He saw active service in Poland and was awarded the Iron Cross 2nd Class at the beginning of March 1915. On 30 March he was granted a commission. At the beginning of August his leadership resulted in him being awarded the Friedrich August Cross 1st Class.

By this time his brother Willi had enlisted in the German army and together they applied, and were accepted, for the German Army Air Service on 29 March 1916. They reported to FEA.5 at Hanover for pilot training at the Halberstadt Jastaschule, they were both posted to Flieger Abteilung Artillerie 227 (FA(A).227) and in November 1916 to the newly created Jasta 11 (Royal Prussian). Jasta 11 was led by a Bavarian officer from Flieger Abteilung 6b (FA.6b), Oberleutnant Rudolf Lang, who was the commanding officer when Jasta 11 was set up in October 1916. Lang had been joined by Leutnant Konstantin Kreft, Feldwebel Hans Howe and Leutnant der Reserve Hans Hintsch. Three more pilots joined: Leutnants Kurt Wolff, Georg Simon and Vizefeldwebel Sebastian Festner. With the total of pilots now at eight, Lang was ready for operations, but under his command not one confirmed 'kill' was made by any pilot. In January 1917, Lang was replaced as commander of Jasta 11 by the legendary Manfred von Richthofen, who was destined to make Jasta 11 the second highest scoring Jasta in the German Army Air Service.

Within weeks Manfred von Richthofen had shown the rest of his squadron the way forward by shooting down two Allied aircraft on 23 and 24 February 1917. Karl Allmenröder scored his first victory on 16 February 1917 when he shot down a BE2c of 16 Squadron RFC. On 21 February, the Jasta's pool of pilots was enriched with the arrival of Leutnant Karl Emil Schäfer, and then on 6 March 1917 the Jasta welcomed another pilot, Leutnant Lothar von Richthofen, Manfred's younger brother.

By the end of March Allmenröder had raised his tally to four and had been awarded the Iron Cross 1st Class. April started well with a victory over a BE2c of 13 Squadron RFC, over Lens. Between 25 and 27 March he shot down three aircraft on consecutive days, bringing his tally to eight. This success was marred by the news that his brother Willi, who had two victories, had been severely wounded in combat and invalided out of the German Army Air Service.

The Battle of Arras opened on 9 April, and the RFC and RNAS suffered horrendous casualties, losing a number of experienced pilots to the German Army Air Service. Losses were not confined to the Allies: Vizefeldwebel Festner was shot down and killed on 25 April, just two days after receiving the distinguished Member's Cross with Swords of the Royal Hohenzollern House Order.

Schäfer had been scoring so rapidly that decorations that were awarded to him became submerged in paperwork. He was assigned to take command of Jasta 28 – the command that had been given to Oberleutnant Lang – who had proved equally ineffective there as he had been with Jasta 11. One day after taking command, Schäfer was awarded the Knight's Cross with Swords of the Royal Hohenzollern House Order and the prestigious Orden Pour le Mérite.

At the beginning of May, Manfred von Richthofen went on leave and passed command of Jasta 11 to Lothar. Leutnant Wolff was given command of Jasta 29 after its commander Leutnant Ludwig Dornheim had been killed; this then left Karl Allmenröder as second in command in Jasta 11.

Thirteen victories in May brought Karl Allmenröder's tally to twenty-one. The month of June saw his relentless pursuit of the enemy bring his tally to twenty-five. On 13 May, Lothar von Richthofen was shot down by groundfire whilst returning from a sortie so command of Jasta 11 passed to Karl Allmenröder who ran the Jasta until the middle of June, when Manfred von Richthofen returned from leave.

On 6 June Allmenröder was awarded the Knight's Cross of the Royal Hohenzollern House Order and the following day the Orden Pour le Mérite. With the top aces of Jasta 11 either being shot down or given commands of their own, Karl Allmenröder suddenly found himself second only to Manfred von Richthofen.

Although June was to start dramatically well for Karl Allmenröder, it was to end tragically. On 18, 24, 25 and 26 June, four more British aircraft were to fall under his guns, bringing his tally to twenty-nine. At 09:45 on 27 June 1917 his patrol was attacked by British fighters over Zillebeke. After a fierce battle, Allmenröder flew toward his own lines at a very low altitude but his aircraft was hit by sustained groundfire and crashed – killing him instantly. A very graphic report on his demise said to have been witnessed by a German soldier in the trenches and published in the newspaper *Wuppertaler General Anzeiger*, a provincial newspaper in the small town of Wuppertal, close to the home of Karl Allmenröder at Wald. It read:

On 27th June 1917, from 8 to 10 o'clock, the infantryman Max Feuerstein of the 4th Company of the Bavarian 6th Reserve Infantry Regiment lay in a grenade shelter next to an alarm post. Nearby was an earth-covered concrete bunker in which his comrades slept and cleaned their weapons. Cloudy skies covered Flanders, heavy clouds rolled over the land from the sea.

Then, in a flock, the first English fliers arrived at the front. They go back and forth across the lines at low altitude like a swarm of hornets. Their keen eyes missed no movement. Then, rapidly, and violently out of the clouds, it broke loose like a storm: blood-red single-seater fighters, well known by every soldier in Flanders, shot lightning-like below the English hornets. The first blue-white-red cockade pulled out toward its own lines, burning in a cloud of black smoke. Fleeing, the enemy sought its own territory. A red arrow shot out after it. Far behind the enemy lines the pursuer pressed on.

Then the red arrow came back from the other side. Artillery and machine gun fire directed at it created a roar. It exploded and crashed around the plane. Gripping fear came over the field grays in the cratered field as the red machine veered and then spun. One wing broke off. A plume of smoke trailed behind. A tongue of fire shot out of the aircraft explosive like. It shuddered, fell, crashed out of control into the depths. The splintered machine with its doomed occupant fell into the mud near the bunker. Barely two hundred metres in front of the first English positions the red Albatros had bored itself into the ground enveloped in fire and smoke.

Leutnant Karl Allmenröder was posthumously awarded the Oldenburg Friedrich August Cross 1st and 2nd Class and the Bavarian Military Merit Order 4th Class on 20 July 1917. He was twenty-one years old.

Oberleutnant Ernst Freiherr von Althaus

The son of the Adjutant to the Duke of Saxe-Coburg-Gotha, Ernst Althaus was born on 19 March, 1890, at Coburg, Bavaria. At the age of sixteen he joined the Saxon 1 Husaren-Regiment König Albert Nr.18 as an Ensign, being promoted to Leutnant in 1911.

Three years later war broke out and the 1 Husaren-Regiment König Albert Nr.18 were immediately into action. On 27 January 1915, von Althaus was awarded the Saxon Knight's Cross to the Order of St Heinrich for his bravery through a number of clashes with the enemy and the Iron Cross 2nd Class. But his sights were set on joining the German Army Air Service; on 4 April 1915 he was transferred to the Fliegertruppe and posted to FEA.6 for pilot training at Grossenhain. During training he was promoted to Oberleutnant. On completion of training he was posted first to FFA.23, flying one of the few Fokker Eindeckers, then to Kek Sivry and then Kek Vaux.

Ernst Freiherr von Althaus recorded his first victory on 3 December 1915, when he shot down a BE2c of 13 Squadron whilst flying West of Roye. His next victory was a French Voisin belonging to Escadrille VB.101 on 2 February 1916, followed by another BE2c on 26 February. On 19 March he raised his tally to four when he shot down a Caudron G.IV, followed by a Farman on 30 April, over St Mihiel. At the end of April 1916 having increased his tally to five, he was wounded in the leg during a dogfight. Von Althaus was taken to hospital for treatment and it was there that he met a nurse who was later to be his wife. He returned to his unit after convalescence to be told that he had been awarded the Iron Cross 1st Class and the Knight's Cross with Swords of the Royal Hohenzollern House Order. This was followed in July 1916 by the coveted award the Orden Pour le Mérite. Von Althaus continued to fly with his unit until 4 March 1917, when he was again wounded in combat. During the time he was in hospital, Kek Vaux became Jasta 4 and von Althaus's tally totalled nine.

After a period of recuperation he was posted to Jasta 14 as acting leader, but shortly afterwards was assigned to Jasta 10, replacing Leutnant Albert Dossenbach who had taken over command after Manfred von Richthofen had been injured. Whilst with Jasta 10 he flew Albatros D.V Nr.D1119/17 with his nickname 'HA' (Hussar Althaus) painted in morse code – five dots and one dash ($\cdot\ \cdot\ \cdot\ \cdot\ \cdot\ -$) – on the side.

Von Althaus lasted just three weeks as leader of Jasta 10, when it is believed that he was removed on the insistence of Manfred von Richthofen. Various reasons have been given: that he was burnt out as a fighter pilot; that he was a loner who preferred to fight alone rather than in 'Richthofen-type' tight formations or his lack of leadership ability. Whatever the reasons, Manfred von Richthofen's power, even from a hospital bed, was quite considerable.

Leutnant Frankl, Oberleutnant Althaus and Leutnant Lenz with a shot-down BE2c on 1 July 1916.

Von Althaus's last confirmed victory was on 24 July 1917, when he shot down Sopwith Camel No.B3825 of 70 Squadron RFC. One month later he relinquished command of Jasta 10 to Werner Voss, when his eyesight started to fail. He was given command of Jastaschule 11 for a time but his eyesight continued to worsen. He later returned to army duties where he commanded an infantry company in the Verdun area. He was captured by the US Army on 15 October 1918 and was imprisoned in a POW camp until the end of September 1919.

At the end of the war he entered the legal profession and became a barrister, but went blind in 1937. Despite his blindness he continued to study law and during World War Two was appointed the Director of the County Court of Berlin. In 1945 he worked for a short time with the Allies as an interpreter, but died after a short illness on 29 November 1946. His list of decorations was extremely impressive and, in addition to the Orden Pour le Mérite and the Knight's Cross with Swords of the Royal Hohenzollern House Order, he had the Saxe-Ernestine House Order Knight 2nd Class with Swords, the Brunswick War Merit Cross 2nd Class and the Hesse Honour Decoration for Bravery.

Vizefeldwebel Johann Baur

Born in Mulhdorf on 24 April 1897 Baur was a two-seater pilot serving with Bavarian FA.295 and flying Hannover CLIII aircraft. His usual observer was Leutnant Georg Ritter von Hengl (b.1897 – d.1952).

Baur and Hengl opened their victory tally on 17 July 1918 when they clashed with a seven-strong French Spad patrol over the Fôret de Courton. Within two minutes, two Spads went down in flames and another two were forced down. Baur and Hengl had their two Spads confirmed as shot down but not the two forced down. Baur was awarded the Iron Cross 1st Class and the Bavarian Silver Bravery Medal for the action.

During the third Battle of the Aisne they were shot down over British lines and captured by British troops but made their escape with the assistance of German soldiers of a Württemburg regiment.

On 20 August 1918 Baur and Hengl had an unconfirmed victory over a French Breguet XIV. On 22 October they had two confirmed victories over French aircraft and on 29 October they shot down four Spads of which two were unconfirmed. Their unofficial total at the Armistice was six confirmed and three unconfirmed victories. Hengl was awarded the Iron Cross 1st Class and the Knight's Cross of the Max-Joseph Military Order, becoming Ritter von Hengl.

Baur joined the Nazi Luftwaffe when it was formed and flew Ju52 and FW200 Condor transport aircraft. He became Adolf Hitler's personal pilot and rose to the rank of Generaloberst in the Waffen SS. He was captured by the Russians in 1945 and sent to Siberia for ten years – probably because he was in the Waffen SS. During his captivity he contracted gangrene in his leg which had to have a primitive amputation without anaesthetic. Nevertheless Johann Baur survived the operation and died in 1993.

Hengl survived World War One and during World War Two enlisted in Alpine Jäger troops where he rose to the rank of General. He was awarded the Knight's Cross of the Iron Cross. General Hengl died on 19 March 1952.

Leutnant Oliver Freiherr von Beaulieu-Marconnay wearing his Iron Cross 1st Class, which was won when he was with 4 Prussian Dragoon Regiment at the age of just seventeen years.

LEUTNANT OLIVER FREIHERR VON BEAULIEU-MARCONNAY

The son of an aristocratic Prussian army officer, Oliver Beaulieu-Marconnay was born in Berlin on 14 September 1898. During his early childhood he was brought up in Hochschule (*college*) in the typical military fashion of the day, so it was no surprise when at seventeen he joined up as a cadet one year after the beginning of World War One. He enlisted in his father's old regiment, the 4 Prussian Dragoon Regiment, and was soon in combat. By July of 1916, after battles in the Rokitno Swamps, he had been awarded the Iron Cross 1st Class and been promoted to the rank of Leutnant.

The young Leutnant Beaulieu-Marconnay had been observing the rise of the German Army Air Service and saw that it offered him the chance of achieving his ambition: one-to-one combat. He applied to be transferred out of the army and into the air service. Early in the spring of 1917 he was accepted and sent to flying training school, graduating in November. On 1 December 1918, he was posted first to Jasta 18 (Royal Prussian), then a few months later to Jasta 15 (Royal Prussian) under the command of Leutnant Joseph Veltjens.

Under the tutelage of Veltjens he progressed rapidly and on 28 May 1918, 'Bauli' as he became known, scored his first victory: an AR.2 over Soissons. This was quickly followed on 6 June by two victories: a DH4 from 27 Squadron RFC; and an SE5a from 32 Squadron. By the end of June he had raised his tally to eight, shooting down three Sopwith Camels, an SE5a and a DH4. On 9 August he increased his tally to ten in a space of fifteen minutes when he shot down a Sopwith Camel and a Spad 2. Then on 2 September he was given command of Jasta 19 (Royal Prussian) – he was just nineteen years old. By the end of September he had raised his tally to twenty-one. A remarkable achievement considering the responsibilities of command and his age.

Beaulieu-Marconnay continued to fly combat sorties and in the first two weeks of October had raised his tally to twenty-five. Then on 10 October 1918, whilst flying his favourite aircraft, a Fokker D.VII with his personal insignia – '4D' (the 4th Dragoons) – painted on the side of the blue fuselage, fate caught up with him. During a combat sortie, in which his Jasta was attacked by Allied aircraft, his aircraft was caught in the crossfire from a Fokker D.VII of Jasta 74 and he was mortally wounded. He managed to land his aircraft and was rushed to hospital. When the Kaiser was told of his injuries and that he would not recover, he awarded him the Orden Pour le Mérite. As he lay dying he was informed that he had been awarded the decoration – the youngest recipient of the prestigious order in World War One at the age of 20 years and one of the very few to be awarded the decoration without having the Royal Hohenzollern House Order. He succumbed to his injuries and died on 26 October 1918.

OBERLEUTNANT FRITZ OTTO BERNERT

The son of the Burgermeister of Ratibor, Upper Silesia, Fritz Otto Bernert was born on 6 March 1893. After leaving school he joined Infanterie-Regiment Nr.173 as a cadet, being commissioned as a Leutnant just after the outbreak of World War One. His infantry regiment was one of those who were soon in the thick of action. Bernert was wounded in November and was awarded the Iron Cross 2nd Class for his part in the action in which he had received his wound. By the end of 1914 Bernert had been wounded twice more; none of the wounds proved to be serious. In December 1914, during particularly heavy close-quarter hand-to-hand fighting, he received a bayonet wound in his left arm which severed the main nerve. He was deemed to be unfit for further military duties, but he applied to join the German Army Air Service as an observer.

How Bernert passed the medical examination for the Air Service is a mystery, but he did and in February 1915 was sent for training. After graduating he was posted to FFA.27 and for six months carried out reconnaissance and scouting missions. In July of 1915, Bernert was posted to FFA.71. By this time he was looking toward flying aircraft himself and applied for pilot training. In November his application was accepted and he was posted to Jastaschule for training. Again he was able to conceal the fact that he only had one arm that was fully operational and the other arm which had very limited mobility. In addition to this he was only one of three Jasta pilots in the German Army Air Service who were known to wear glasses. On graduating at the end of March 1916, Bernert was assigned to Kek Vaux where on 17 April he opened his tally by shooting down a Nieuport fighter.

During the summer months of 1916, there appeared to be a lull in the action in Bernert's sector and in late August he was posted to Jasta 4. On 6 September he scored his second victory when he shot down a Caudron whilst on patrol over

Oberleutnant Fritz Otto Bernert (Orden Pour le Mérite, with twenty-eight victories) was one of the few German pilots who wore spectacles. He died of influenza on 18 October 1918.

Dompierre. Another victory, a Nieuport fighter over Allenes on 11 September, raised his tally to three. By the end of November Bernert had raised his score to seven, the last three all on 9 November: two DH2s and an FE8.

In February of 1917, Bernert was posted to Jasta 2 and awarded the Iron Cross 1st Class, the Knight 2nd Class with Swords of the Saxon Albert Order and Knight's Cross with Swords of the Royal Hohenzollern House Order. To celebrate, Bernert opened his score with his new Jasta by shooting down a Sopwith Camel whilst on patrol over Ecourt-Mory, this brought his tally to eight. A BE2d at the end of March seemed to set the scene for April, when on consecutive days starting on the 1st, Bernert scored four victories. He continued to score almost daily, then on 23 April he was awarded Prussia's highest accolade, the Orden Pour le Mérite. As if to celebrate this honour, on the following day 24 April, he claimed five victories: three BE2es (all from 9 Squadron RFC), a DH4 and a Sopwith 1½ Strutter. On 1 May, Bernert was appointed Staffelführer of Jasta 6 with his tally standing at twenty-four. Bernert added three more victories to his score by the end of May before taking command of Jasta 2 Boelcke on 9 June 1917.

He continued to fly but with no more successes and on 18 August was wounded again. On his release from hospital in November, he was deemed to be unfit for flying duties and was assigned to the office of the Idflieg (Inspector of the Flying Service) with a promotion to Oberleutnant. In early September 1918, Fritz Otto Bernert contracted influenza and died in hospital in his home town on 18 October.

Oberleutnants Althaus and Berr (wearing the Orden Pour le Mérite decoration round their necks) pictured with pilots of Jasta 5 in 1916 (second and third, respectively, from left in the front row).

OBERLEUTNANT HANS BERR

Hans Berr was born on 20 May 1890 in Brunswick, Bavaria, and was the son of the President of the Brunswick High Postal Administration. He wanted to be a soldier from his earliest years and as soon as he was of age he enrolled in the army as a cadet. By the time he was eighteen years of age he had been commissioned as an Infantry Leutnant in the Magdeburgisches Jäger-Battailon Nr.4. When World War One broke out in 1914, Berr was serving with the Leicht Infanterie (Reserve) Regiment Nr.7 and was soon in action on the Western Front. He was wounded in action on 6 September 1914, which resulted in his being awarded the Iron Cross 2nd Class. He continued to serve in the Infantry and was promoted to Oberleutnant on 27 January 1915, but like so many other young German aristocrats, he wanted to leave infantry ground combat and take to the air to do battle in a more exciting and personal way.

He applied to join the German Army Air Service on 3 March 1915 and trained as an observer at Grossenhain. On graduation he was posted to FFA.60 flying reconnaissance and artillery spotting missions on the Western Front. After several months flying reconnaissance missions, Berr applied for pilot training and was accepted. He was posted to Jastaschule at Metz where he trained to fly single-seat fighters. Upon graduation he was posted to Kampfeinsitzer Kommando, flying Fokker Eindeckers. This Staffel later became Jasta 5.

On 8 March 1916 he opened his tally of kills when he shot down a Nieuport of Escadrille MS 3 over the Verdun sector of the front. A week later he downed a Caudron also over Verdun. With but two victories to his credit he was appointed to command Jasta 5 (Royal Prussian) on 21 August 1916, based at Bechamp near Verdun in 5. Armee area. With the appointment came the awards of the Bavarian

Military Merit Order 4th Class with Swords and the Brunswick War Merit Cross. Jasta 5 had been the Avillers Fokker Staffel and was originally equipped with Fokker Eindeckers, then re-equipped with Albatros D.II Scouts and Halberstadt D.Is.

On the morning of 7 October 1916, he shot down a Caudron over Combles then a BE2b of 34 Squadron also over Combles. These two victories brought his total to four confirmed but between 20 October and 26 October 1916, he added three more aircraft: two FE2bs, a Morane Parasol, and a balloon shot down. His total now stood at eight and recognition followed in the form of decorations from Imperial Germany and its various states in the form of the Hanseatic Cross from Hamburg, the Ruess War Merit Cross and Honour Cross 3rd Class with Swords. By the time he had scored his tenth and final victory on 3 November 1916, he had been awarded: the Iron Cross 1st Class; the Knight's Cross with Swords of the Royal Hohenzollern House Order; the Bavarian Military Merit Order 4th Class with Swords; the Brunswick War Merit Cross; the Ruess War Merit Cross and Honour Cross 3rd Class with Swords; and the Hamburg Hanseatic Cross.

On 4 December 1916 Hans Berr was awarded the Orden Pour le Mérite. This was before the German High Command had altered the required victory total to qualify for the Blue Max to sixteen aircraft shot down and confirmed. Hans Berr continued to fly in combat but did not add to his total victories.

Taking off with his Jasta 5 on Good Friday 6 April 1917, his Jasta engaged in aerial combat with 57 Squadron, Royal Flying Corps. In the heat of battle Vizefeldwebel Paul Hoppe – a fellow Jasta 5 pilot – had just moved in behind a Vickers Gunbus when Berr came swooping in from the right-hand side and crashed into Hoppe. Eyewitnesses said there was a big dust cloud and the tangled remains of both aircraft plunged toward the ground, killing both pilots instantly.

LEUTNANT WALTER BLUME

Walter Blume was born on 10 January 1896, in Hirschberg, a village at the foot of the Silesian mountains. After graduating from school in 1911, he took an apprenticeship as a tool maker in a machine factory. At the outbreak of the war, he enlisted in the Silesian Jäger-Battailon Nr.5 and was posted to East Prussia. The battalion had only been at the front a matter of months, when during heavy fighting near the town of Lyck, Blume was severely wounded. Whilst in hospital Blume considered his position and decided to apply for transfer on his release to the newly formed German Army Air Service.

On 30 June, with his application being approved, Blume reported to the Flying Reserve Unit at Grossenhaim and was then posted to the Jastaschule at Leipzig-Mockau. On graduating and receiving his pilot's badge, Blume was assigned to the Research and Exercise Field West Unit near St Quentin on the Western Front. After two months he was assigned to Army Aeroplane Park 'A' at Strasbourg to await a posting to another unit. On 18 June 1916, Blume was assigned to FFA.65 as a reconnaissance pilot, then one month later to FA(A).280. Although being a reconnaissance pilot was not what Blume wanted, he quickly distinguished himself and was awarded an Iron Cross 2nd Class on 24 July and promoted to Vizefeldwebel on 23 August

Leutnant Walter Blume (Orden Pour le Mérite, with twenty-eight victories) survived World War One. He died on 27 May 1964.

1916. Further flights during the rest of the year culminated in him being given a commission to Leutnant der Reserve on 31 January 1917.

At the beginning of March 1917, Blume was selected by Bruno Loerzer and Hermann Göring to be one of the pilots to form the nucleus of Jasta 26. One month later, after conversion and tactical training, the squadron was ready and was assigned to the St Quentin area. Within days of arriving, the Jasta was in action in some of the heaviest aerial fighting. On 10 May, Blume opened his tally when he shot down a DH4 from 55 Squadron RFC whilst on patrol over Gouzencourt. He continued to score steadily and by the end of November had raised his score to six and had been awarded the Iron Cross 1st Class. On 29 November during a patrol, his flight encountered Bristol fighters from 48 Squadron RFC and during the skirmish Blume was wounded in the chest. Managing to keep control of his aircraft, which had suffered considerable damage, and fighting waves of unconsciousness, Blume managed to guide his crippled aircraft back to his base. He was critically wounded, but the skill of the surgeons and three months' hospitalisation aided his recovery.

On 5 March 1918, Blume returned to the front in command of Jasta 9 and was assigned to the Champagne Front. Within days Blume was back in action. On 21 April he shot down a Spad whilst on patrol over Chiry-Ourscamp, taking his total of 'kills' to seven. The following three months accounted for ten more Allied aircraft, bringing his tally to seventeen. The shooting down of a Spad over Bazoches on 6 August, heralded the award of the Knight's Cross with Swords of the Royal Hohenzollern House Order. By the end of September, Blume had raised his score to twenty-six, this was followed on 2 October by his twenty-eighth victory and the Jasta's 100th. On landing back at his base, Blume was ceremoniously awarded the Orden Pour le Mérite. Blume scored his final victory on 28 October, a Sopwith Camel from 209 Squadron over Remaucourt, then came the Armistice and the end of the war.

Blume returned home to complete his engineering studies, earning a degree. He became a designer with the Arado and Albatros aviation companies and was responsible for contributing to many of the designs of aircraft used in World War Two. Walter Blume died on 27 May 1964.

HAUPTMANN OSWALD BOELCKE

One of six children, Oswald Boelcke was born in Giebichenstein, near Halle, in Saxony on 19 May 1891. His father was a schoolteacher who ensured that all his children were educated to their full extent and gave them enquiring minds. In Oswald Boelcke's case, this was to manifest itself in later years when he wrote his famous report on air fighting and tactics. After leaving school, Boelcke decided on a military career, much against the wishes of his family. In March 1911 he joined the Prussian Cadet Corps and was posted to Nr.3 Telegrapher Battailon at Koblenz. After completing his initial training, he was posted to War School at Metz to complete his officer training.

After graduating, Boelcke applied for transfer to the German Army Air Service for training as a pilot and was accepted. He was posted to Jastaschule in Halberstadt – completing his flying training in October 1914. Boelcke was assigned to Trier in the

A studio pose of Hauptmann Oswald Boelcke wearing his Orden Pour le Mérite, which was awarded on 12 January 1916. He was one of the first two pilots to be so decorated. Unfortunately, Boelcke died in an aerial collision with Erwin Böhme in October 1916.

first instance and two weeks later was posted to his first combat unit: FA.13, near Montmédy, where his older brother Wilhelm was stationed as an observer. The two brothers became a team, flying reconnaissance missions over the Argonne region. In October 1914, Oswald Boelcke was awarded the Iron Cross 2nd Class for his work flying reconnaissance missions.

Boelcke continued flying reconnaissance missions into the first quarter of 1915 and received the Iron Cross 1st Class on 4 February. In May Boelcke was transferred to FA.62 which had recently been equipped with LVG C.Is. On 4 July 1915, together with his observer Leutnant Heinz von Wühlisch, Boelcke was on patrol over Valenciennes when he encountered a Morane Parasol. After a short skirmish the Morane Parasol was shot down and Boelcke had opened his score. His enthusiasm for engaging enemy aircraft whenever possible prompted the squadron commander to transfer him to single-seater fighters. Single-seat Fokker Eindeckers had recently been assigned to the squadron for scouting and protection of reconnaissance aircraft. Early in July, Boelcke saved the life of a fourteen-year-old French boy, for which he was awarded a Life Saving Medal.

On 19 August, Boelcke, flying a Fokker Eindecker from Douai, notched up his second victory when he shot down a Bristol biplane over the front lines. It was at Douai that he came into contact with Max Immelmann where they both learned from each other. By the end of the year, Boelcke had raised his score to six and had been awarded the Knight's Cross with Swords of the Royal Hohenzollern House Order.

In the first two weeks of January 1916, Boelcke shot down three more Allied aircraft bringing his total to nine and the Orden Pour le Mérite. Boelcke was the first fighter pilot to receive the award.

Boelcke's funeral at Cambrai Cathedral, France, on 31 October 1916.

Every month, communiques to the German High Command mentioned the name of Boelcke as he steadily increased his tally. By the end of June 1916 his score had reached nineteen and he was a household name in Imperial Germany.

When Max Immelmann died in June, the German High Command sent Boelcke on an inspection/public relations tour of Vienna, Budapest, Belgrade and Turkey. The long journeys gave him the chance to formulate a theory of air fighting and he wrote a thesis, 'The Theory of Air Fighting Tactics', which he submitted to the German High Command. This thesis was to become the 'bible' of air combat among German fighter pilots. No such thesis had ever been written before in the new science of military aviation.

At the end of July Boelcke was recalled from his tour and given command of Jasta 2 and promotion to Hauptmann. He decided to choose his Jasta 2 pilots: among those chosen were, Manfred von Richthofen, Max Müller and Erwin Böhme. The latter was to play a significant part in Boelcke's demise later that year. On 2 September, Boelcke scored his twentieth victory when he shot down a DH2 from 37 Squadron RFC. By the end of the month he had shot down nine more, bringing his tally to twenty-nine.

Jasta 2 was creating a reputation for itself amongst the Allies, as being one of the most feared in the German Army Air Service. October was just as good for Boelcke in terms of victories and by 26 October he had shot down a further eleven, bringing his total to forty.

On 28 October on patrol with Richthofen and Böhme, Boelcke came in contact with seven enemy aircraft and dived to attack. Boelcke and Böhme flying in tandem chased a British fighter as they closed in. Richthofen, chasing another British fighter, cut across in front of them. Erwin Böhme rolled his Albatros out of the way as Boelcke did – but the two aircraft collided. Böhme managed to control his aircraft, but Boelcke's Albatros D.II was badly damaged and spun in towards the ground. Boelcke's stricken Albatros crashed behind a German gun emplacement where the crew pulled him from the wreckage. Oswald Boelcke had died instantly in his cockpit in the mid-air collision. He never wore a seatbelt or helmet.

OBERLEUTNANT OSKAR FREIHERR VON BOENIGK

The son of an army officer, Oskar Boenigk was born near Bunzlau, Silesia, on 25 August 1893. On leaving school, he followed the family tradition and became an army cadet. He was commissioned into the Grenadier-Regiment König Friedrich III (2 Schlesisches) Nr.11 on 22 March 1912. By the time World War One broke out, Boenigk was a platoon leader with his regiment and was soon in action. In October 1914, during the battle of Longwy, he was badly wounded in the chest and spent many months in hospital. He was awarded the Iron Cross 2nd Class on his return to his unit in the early spring of 1915, and was soon in action once more on the French Front where he was wounded again. He returned after recuperating and fought at Loretto Heights and Arras. Boenigk soon began to weary of the cold and the mud, and looked toward the newly formed German Army Air Service. He applied for transfer to the Air Service and was accepted. He was then posted to the observer school FEA.7 in December 1915 and after training, was posted to Kasta 19 of KG.4 in March 1916.

Boenigk spent the next four months on reconnaissance and scouting missions, then was posted to Kasta 32. At the beginning of January 1917 he applied to Jastaschule for training as a pilot and on graduating was posted to Jasta 4 on 24 June 1917. Boenigk opened his tally on 20 July when he shot down a Sopwith Camel over Tembrielen. One week later he shot down another Sopwith Camel from 70 Squadron RFC over Moorslede. By the end of September he had taken his score to five and was rewarded with the Iron Cross 1st Class and the command of Jasta 21 on 21 October 1917. By the end of the year he had raised his tally to six.

Oskar Boenigk had taken command of Jasta 21 when its commander Oberleutnant Eduard Schleich went on leave. The temporary change of command happened at a time when there was a purge on 'foreigners' within the German Army Air Service. By 'foreigners' it meant Bavarians, Saxons, Prussians, etc. Schleich, a Bavarian, was in command of a Prussian formation and it was decided by the various hierarchies that each formation would be commanded by their own people. It was decided that Boenigk, a Prussian, would take command of the Prussian formation of Jasta 21. Schleich was given command of the Royal Bavarian Jasta 32. All the infighting between the various states and principalities paled into insignificance in 1918 when it became increasingly obvious that a unified front was all that was left. As if to endorse this, in March 1918, Jasta 21 became part of the Royal Saxon Army.

The pressure of command and easing of hostilities meant that matters were very quiet in the first six months of 1918 for Oskar Boenigk. But at the beginning of June this all changed. The first week of June, Boenigk claimed six more victories: two Spads, one Breguet XIV and three balloons, bringing his total to twelve. By the end of August he had increased it to nineteen and had been awarded the Knight's Cross with Swords of the Royal Hohenzollern House Order. He was also given command of JG.11 on 31 August and promoted to Oberleutnant. The Geschwader was moved to the St Mihiel Front in September to oppose the American forces gathering there. By the end of the month Boenigk had raised his personal tally to twenty-six. At the beginning of October he received the Saxon Albert Order 2nd Class with Swords, the Sax-Ernestine House Order, Knight 2nd Class with Swords, and the Prussian Order of St John, Knight of Honour. It was the latter award that enabled him to use the title Freiherr. On 25 October, Oberleutnant Oskar Freiherr von Boenigk was awarded Prussia's high accolade, the Orden Pour le Mérite. By the end of the war he had raised his score to twenty-six.

His days of action were not over and he served in the post-war revolution with some distinction.

During World War Two Boenigk served in the Luftwaffe as commander of various airfields, then as area commander attaining the rank of Generalmajor. He was captured by the Russians in May 1945 and died in a prison camp the following year.

LEUTNANT ERWIN BÖHME

Erwin Böhme was born in Holzminden, on the Weser, on 29 July 1879. After finishing school, he went to Dortmund and studied engineering at technical college. On qualifying, Böhme worked in Germany and Switzerland before going to East

Leutnant Erwin Böhme (twenty-four victories) was in an aerial collision with Oswald Boelcke which resulted in Boelcke's death. Böhme was killed in action on 29 November 1917. (*Sanke Card Nr.302*)

Africa. It was in East Africa that he learned to fly, a skill he put to use some years later. Böhme had just returned to Germany when the war broke out and he immediately volunteered to join a Jäger regiment. In the spring of 1915 he volunteered for flying duties with the newly formed German Army Air Service and, due to his experience as a pilot, was accepted and retained as an instructor. This was not what Böhme wanted but, as a staunch defender of the Fatherland, he realised that his role was just as important.

In June 1916, Böhme applied for a posting to a front line unit and, because there was a sudden desperate need for experienced pilots on the front, he was posted at the end of July to Jasta 10, a unit within Kagohl 2 commanded by Hauptmann Wilhelm Boelcke, brother of Oswald Boelcke. Böhme opened his tally on 2 August by shooting down a Nieuport XII whilst on patrol over Radzyse. Later that month he was introduced to Oswald Boelcke who was forming a new fighter unit Jasta 2. The two of them hit it off right away and quickly became friends. Boelcke asked for Böhme to be assigned to his Jasta and by the beginning of September Jasta 2 was ready for action. On 17 September Böhme scored his second victory, a Sopwith 1½ Strutter from 70 Squadron RFC, over Hervilly and was awarded the Iron Cross 2nd Class.

On 28 October tragedy struck for Böhme. With his tally now standing at five, he was on patrol with Oswald Boelcke when their two aircraft collided in mid-air. Böhme managed to keep control of his aircraft, but Boelcke's aircraft plunged to the ground killing him instantly. Böhme was devastated, but dedicated himself to continuing the fight against the enemy. By the end of the year he had raised his tally to eight. On 7 January 1917, he opened the new year by shooting down a DH2 from 32 Squadron RFC over Beugny. Two more victories on 4 February – another DH2 from 32 Squadron RFC and a BE2c from 15 Squadron RFC – brought his score to eleven.

On 11 February he was wounded in a fight with a Sopwith 1½ Strutter but although he managed to land his aircraft, he was hospitalised for a month. Whilst in hospital he was awarded the Iron Cross 1st Class, this was followed on 12 March by the award of the Knight's Cross with Swords of the Royal Hohenzollern House Order.

On his release from hospital at the end of March, Böhme was given the post of instructor as part of his recuperation. Then on 2 July he was posted to Jasta 29 as commander, but only managed to claim one more victory before being posted back to Jasta 2 as its commander. He was wounded again on 10 August 1917 when his aircraft was shot up by a Sopwith Camel whilst he was attacking a two-seater bomber. The wound was to his hand and kept him behind the desk at Jasta 2 for a month. Two more 'kills' in September and six in October brought his tally to twenty-one. On 6 November he shot down a Sopwith Camel from 65 Squadron RFC, followed by a Nieuport Scout from 1 Belgian Escadrille. Then on 24 November he was awarded the Orden Pour le Mérite, but he enjoyed fame for only a few days. On 29 November, whilst on patrol over Zonnebecke, his flight was attacked by a patrol from 10 Squadron RFC. During the action Böhme shot down a Sopwith Camel, but failed to see an AWFK.8 behind him. Seconds later he was dead with his aircraft crashing into British lines. Two days later he was buried by the British with full military honours at Keerselaarhook. His remains were reinterred at Hinter den Linden after the war.

RITTMEISTER KARL BOLLE

Karl Bolle was born in Berlin on 20 June 1893, the son of an academic. After finishing school in Berlin, Bolle went to Oxford University in 1912 to read economics. Just before the outbreak of World War One, Bolle returned to Germany and joined Kurassier-Regiment von Sedlitz (Magdeburgisches) Nr.7 with the rank of Leutnant and was sent to France to fight on the Western Front. At the beginning of 1915, the regiment was moved to the Eastern Front and fought in Poland and Kurland. At the end of 1915, after receiving the Iron Cross 2nd Class, Bolle applied for transfer to the newly formed German Army Air Service. His application was accepted and in February 1916 he was posted to Johannisthal for his initial flying training. On completion he was posted to Flieger Ersatz Abteilung 5 in Hannover for final training.

On completion of his training in July 1915, he was awarded his pilot's badge and posted to Kagohl 4 as a reconnaissance pilot. After spending several months carrying out scouting and reconnaissance missions, Bolle was posted to Kampstaffel 23 at the end of 1915. Throughout 1916, Bolle and his observer carried out many dangerous reconnaissance flights and on one of them, in October of 1916, Bolle was badly wounded during an attack by five French fighters. Despite his wounds, Bolle managed to bring his aircraft down and carry his badly wounded observer to safety. On his return to duty two months later, he found that the application he had made some months earlier to transfer to single-seater fighters had been accepted, and he was posted to Jastaschule at the beginning of 1917.

On graduating in July 1917, he was posted to Jasta 28 as Adjutant because he was still recovering from his wounds. Under the tutelage of Offizier-Stellvertreter Max Müller, Karl Bolle opened his tally on 8 August 1917 by shooting down a DH4 from 57 Squadron RFC over Kachten. His second, a Martinsyde G100 bomber from 27 Squadron RFC, was shot down over Seclin on 21 August. It wasn't until 18 December that he scored his next victory, a Sopwith Camel from 65 Squadron RFC. On January 29 1918, Bolle scored his fourth victory when he shot down another Sopwith Camel from 65 Squadron. The following day he raised his tally to five by shooting down a DH4 from 5 Squadron RNAS.

In September 1917, Karl Bolle was awarded the Württemberg Friedrich Order and the Knight 2nd Class with Swords.

In January 1918, Max Müller was killed after his aircraft had been set on fire during a fight with an RE8. His place as commanding officer of Jasta 2 was taken by Leutnant Otto Höhne, a former member of Jasta 2 who had been hospitalised after being shot down and badly wounded a year earlier. It soon became obvious that Höhne was not up to the job and, so despite his relative inexperience, Bolle was given command of Jasta 2 on 20 February 1918 and promoted to Oberleutnant. Bolle immediately set about making it one of the best, but it was to be two months before he himself got back into the air and started scoring again. On 3 April he shot down a DH9 bomber over Frezenberg and on 25 April a Sopwith Camel, raising his tally to seven.

The next three months of the war in the air were frantic. The Allies started making their big push and the skies were filled with aircraft. By the end of July, Karl Bolle had shot down a further twenty-one Allied aircraft bringing his score to twenty-eight. He was awarded the Max-Joseph Order, the Mecklenburg Military Cross of Merit with Swords, and the Knight's Cross with Swords of the Royal Hohenzollern House Order. Then on 28 August 1918 he received the Orden Pour le Mérite.

Bolle continued to fight on and by the end of the war had raised his score to thirty-six. On leaving the army, Bolle became an instructor, then in the early 1920s was appointed Director of the German Transportation Flying School, in charge of all pilot training. When World War Two started, Bolle became special advisor to the Luftwaffe, a post he held throughout the war. Karl Bolle died in Berlin on 9 October 1955.

LEUTNANT HEINRICH BONGARTZ

The son of a schoolteacher, Heinrich Bongartz was born in Gelsenkirchen, Westphalia, on 31 January 1892. Throughout his childhood it was obvious that he would follow the family tradition and become a schoolteacher. After leaving school, Bongartz went to college and trained as a teacher. In August 1914 at the outbreak of war, he volunteered for the army and joined Infanterie-Regiment Nr.16, then later the Reserve-Infanterie-Regiment Nr.13 with the rank of Sturmoffizier. The regiment was stationed on the Western Front near Verdun and throughout 1915 Bongartz saw some of the heaviest fighting of the war. In March 1916 his bravery and leadership qualities earned him a commission to Leutnant and the award of the Iron Cross 2nd Class. But the fighting in the cold climate had taken its toll of him, and he applied for transfer to the German Army Air Service. He was accepted and posted for training as a pilot to FA.5 in the autumn of 1916. On completion of training in October, he was posted to Kagohl 5 as a reconnaissance and scouting pilot. At the beginning of January 1917, he was posted to Jasta 27 (which later became Schusta 8) where he stayed until the beginning of April 1917 when he was posted to Jasta 36.

Within days of arriving at Jasta 36, Bongartz had opened his tally when he shot down a Spad VII from Spa 31 over Viry. By the end of the month he had increased his score to four. He continued to score steadily until 13 July 1917 when whilst on patrol alone he attacked an English bomber flight. During the fight, Bongartz was hit several times and was wounded in the upper and lower arm. As the aircraft, which was also badly damaged, spiralled down out of control, Bongartz managed to regain control at the last minute but crashed on making an emergency landing. The wounds put him out of commission for two months, but on 26 September he celebrated his return to duty by shooting down a Sopwith Triplane over Houthulst Forest.

At the end of September, Bongartz became the Commanding Officer of Jasta 36. In the following two months Bongartz scored another fourteen victories, bringing his total to twenty-five and earning the award of the Knight's Cross with Swords of the Royal Hohenzollern House Order. Bongartz finished the year by shooting down another two Allied fighters and raising his tally to twenty-seven. Then on 23 December 1917, he was awarded the Orden Pour le Mérite.

The New Year started quietly for Bongartz, with only one victory on 29 January 1918: a Sopwith Camel over Poelcapelle. Two more victories in February and three in March took his score to thirty-three, but on 29 March he was again wounded in action.

The following month on 25 April he was slightly wounded, but on 29 April was seriously wounded. Whilst on patrol over Kemmel Hill, he clashed with fighters from 74 Squadron RFC and, during the dogfight, he was wounded in the head. The bullet passed right through his left temple, his eye and his nose. His aircraft crashed near Kemmel Hill and he was taken unconscious to hospital. The following is the record of the incident from the German War Diary for Jasta 36:

The Jasta took off for afternoon patrol and shortly after take-off Ltn. Bongartz returned to Halluin airfield with a defective motor and landed safely, he took the reserve aircraft, Fokker Dr.I 575/17 and started to the front wanting to catch up with the rest of the unit. At the front near Kemmel he was attacked by three Sopwith fighters, one flying cover for the two that attacked, one from the front and one from behind. It was a burst from behind that hit Bongartz's Triplane. One round penetrated his left temple, and destroyed his left eye. Semi-conscious in his spinning aircraft the wounded pilot somehow righted his machine and crash landed at 1300 hours near Ploegsteert Forest and overturned, pinning him beneath it in the cockpit, wounded but alive.

The wounds were so serious that he lost his left eye and finished his wartime career. He later took over as Director of the Aeroplane Inspectorate at Aldershof, where he stayed until the end of the war and helped to deactivate the German Army Air Service.

Leutnant Heinrich Bongartz (Orden Pour le
Mérite, with thirty victories) died on
23 January 1946.

During the post-war revolution Bongartz fought against the Spartacists, a group of German left-wingers who formed the nucleus of the German Communist Party. But again he was wounded, this time in the leg and seriously. It finally finished his military career and he was invalided out. Bongartz could not stay away from aviation and became the Director of Deutschen Luftreederei (German Air Trade), a department that was concerned with using airships for trade and transport. In January 1921 he was involved in a crash and again was seriously injured but recovered later in the year. Heinrich Bongartz died of a heart attack on 23 January 1946.

HAUPTMANN ERNST BRANDENBURG

One of the oldest pilots in World War One, Ernst Brandenburg was born on 4 June 1883 in Westphalia. On leaving school, Brandenburg joined the army as a cadet and after graduating, joined the 6 Westpreussisches Infantrie-Regiment Nr.149 based in Schneidemühl.

In 1911 he was assigned to the Research Institute for the Aviation System to study the merits of military aviation. He progressed steadily in the army and at the outbreak of war in 1914, was an Oberleutnant and Regiments Adjutant. The regiment was soon in action on the Western Front and the sight of reconnaissance aircraft spotting for the infantry rekindled Brandenburg's interest in aviation. After a year on the front, in which he was awarded the Iron Cross 2nd Class, he was seriously wounded and

Hauptmann Ernst Brandenburg (Orden Pour le Mérite) was one of the oldest pilots of World War One. He died in Berlin in 1952.

declared unfit for the trenches. He applied for transfer to the German Army Air Service on 1 November 1915 and was accepted.

After graduating as an observer in the spring of 1916, Brandenburg was assigned to Kasta S.2, a reconnaissance unit attached to the infantry. He carried out numerous missions for which he was awarded the Iron Cross 1st Class and the Knight's Cross with Swords of the Royal Hohenzollern House Order. On 10 January 1917, he was asked by General Hoeppner to put together a bomber squadron for the express purpose of carrying out raids against the British, the main target being London. These raids were to be the first of their kind and posed numerous problems, the main ones being the reliability of the aircraft and the weather. Brandenburg formed Kagohl 3, also known as the Englandgeschwader, and began intensive training with both air and ground crews. He discovered that the fuel carried by the Gotha bombers was insufficient to complete the round trip, so auxiliary tanks were fitted. The Gotha's attack altitude of 14,000ft afforded it a large degree of protection – and once it had unloaded its bombs it could climb higher. To protect the three-man crews from the elements, each member of the crew was given extra thick clothing and the bombers were equipped with two small cylinders of compressed oxygen. A rubber pipe was attached and the crew members sucked on the pipe just like they would on an oriental pipe. Many pilots said that they would have preferred a swig of cognac.

Although Kagohl 3 was attached to 4. Armee, it operated independently and received its orders from Oberste Heeresleitung (OHL: *colonel command*). At the beginning of June 1917, Brandenburg decided that they were ready and planned the first raid. The unpredictable British weather intervened, not once but twice.

However, on 13 June, although the weather was inclement, Brandenburg decided to delay no longer. At 10:00 on 13 June 1917, eighteen Gotha bombers took off from Ghent and headed across the English Channel. As they crossed the English coast alarm bells started ringing in England and at 13:00 the aircraft appeared over London. They immediately encountered anti-aircraft fire from the defences around London, but it was ineffective. The guns had been badly positioned and the crews poorly trained. The bombers started unloading their bombs on predetermined targets; they destroyed docks, railway stations and warehouses. Of the thirty British fighters that scrambled to intercept them, not one was effective. A number of Gothas were hit but two hours after bombing London the entire squadron landed in Ghent.

The following day, 14 June, Brandenburg was summoned to Supreme Headquarters and, in front of the Kaiser and all the High Officers, described the raid in detail. He was promoted to Hauptmann and the Kaiser personally awarded Brandenburg the Orden Pour le Mérite and invited him to stay the weekend. Early on the following Tuesday Brandenburg's Albatros aircraft, with his pilot Oberleutnant Freiherr von Trotha at the controls, took off. As the aircraft lifted from the runway the engine spluttered and the Albatros plunged into the ground. Brandenburg was pulled from the wreckage seriously injured with a shattered leg, which was later amputated.

After recuperating he resumed the leadership of the squadron, which was redesignated Bombengeschwader 3, and planned other raids. Brandenburg organised numerous bombing raids, including a thirty-eight Gotha bomber night-time raid on England on 19/20 May 1918. Of the thirty-eight aircraft that took off, twenty-eight actually made it to England where forty-nine people were killed and 177 injured in the attack. Six of the bombers were shot down and a number were badly damaged. The High Command decided that these raids by the Englandgeschwader were too high a price to pay for the results they were achieving so the strategic bombing of England was abandoned.

At the end of the war Brandenburg's squadron was disbanded and he returned to Germany. In 1924 he became the Director of the Civil Aviation, a department within the transport ministry, under whose umbrella the Luftwaffe was born. Former senior army officers were enrolled in commercial pilot schools and over 27 million marks were channelled to the Reichswehr through the ministry for military aviation. With the rise of the Nazis, Brandenburg was pushed aside in favour of Ernst Udet and faded into obscurity. He died in 1952 in Berlin.

Leutnant Julius Buckler

Julius Buckler was born in Mainz on 28 March 1894. He was a bright schoolboy who had aspirations of being an architect. At fifteen years old he went to work for a short time with Anthony Fokker, the Dutch aircraft builder and designer, in his design office, but circumstances at home were instrumental in Buckler joining the army. In 1913 he joined Infanterie-Leib-Regiment Nr.117 as the war clouds were gathering. Within days of the outbreak of war, Buckler and his regiment were in action on the Western Front. Within weeks he received the Iron Cross 2nd Class. In August he was badly wounded and, after being released from hospital in October

Leutnant Julius Buckler (Orden Pour le Mérite, with thirty-six confirmed victories) died in Berlin on 23 May 1960.

1914, was deemed to be unfit for army service. Buckler, despite having been involved in some of the heaviest fighting and suffering some terrible injuries, still wanted to be part of the war.

In November 1914, he volunteered for flying duties and was accepted for training as an observer. He joined FEA.6 two weeks later and passed his flight exams after only four weeks' instruction. Such was the natural aptitude and ability of Buckler that he remained at FEA.6 as an instructor. After spending just over six months at FEA.6, he was posted to FA(A).209 as an observer. Buckler spent nearly a year with FA(A).209, in which he was awarded the Iron Cross 1st Class. In the spring of 1916 he requested pilot training. He was accepted and on completion of his training in November, Buckler was posted to Jasta 17 with the rank of Vizefeldwebel and was immediately in action over Verdun. On 17 December he opened his victory score by shooting down a twin-engined Caudron over Bras.

Two more Caudrons on 14 and 15 February brought his score to three, and by the end of April he had raised his tally to six. Buckler continued to score steadily until 17 July 1917, when the Jasta ran into a patrol of Sopwith Camels and Pups over Keyem. After shooting down one Sopwith Pup, Buckler was badly wounded in a fight with another, but he managed to break away and return to his airfield. On 12 August, with his score standing at thirteen, he was again wounded in a dogfight with a Sopwith Camel and again managed to break away and return to his airfield. On 12 November after his twenty-fifth victory, he was promoted to Leutnant and awarded the Golden Military Merit Cross the same day. He marked this by shooting down an RE8 from 21 Squadron RFC on 15 November, followed by two balloons and an RE8 on 18 November. Buckler crashed on 30 November after being attacked by Allied fighters – surviving an horrendous plummet to the ground from 800 metres. Considering the impact, his injuries were extremely light: two broken arms and numerous bruises. His score at this time stood at thirty and whilst in hospital, he was awarded the Orden Pour le Mérite on 4 December 1917.

Buckler returned to Jasta 17 at the beginning of April 1918 and was soon back in action. On 16 April he shot down a Breguet XIV over Vaux and on the 21st another Breguet XIV over Mareuil. He was wounded again on 6 May, this time in the ankle. It was a wound that was to put him in hospital for nearly eight weeks and was to win him the award of a Golden Wound Badge – it being his fifth wound. He returned to Jasta 17 at the beginning of July and to a period of inactivity. On 22 September 1918, he was made Staffelführer, a post he held until the end of the war. His tally at the end of hostilities stood at thirty-six.

During World War Two, Julius Buckler served with training squadrons of the Luftwaffe. He died in Berlin on 23 May 1960, one of the few pilots to serve through two world wars.

Hauptmann Hans Joachim Buddecke

The son of a wealthy businessman, Hans Joachim Buddecke was born in Berlin on 22 August 1890. After leaving school in 1904 at the age of fourteen, he joined the army as a cadet and was commissioned as a Leutnant in 1910 at the age of twenty. After three years he resigned his commission and went to work for his uncle in America as an engineer in his uncle's car plant. One year later, Buddecke had earned enough to buy a French Nieuport aeroplane and set about learning to fly. He soon became competent and could see that there was going to be a future in aviation. With the help of his uncle he decided to set up his own factory and to build aircraft to his own design. But World War One erupted in Europe and Buddecke made his way back to Germany aboard a Greek freighter.

In June of 1915, Buddecke joined the German Army Air Service and given the rank of Leutnant because of his previous army experience. After a brief period at Jastaschule, he was posted to FFA.23 as a scout and reconnaissance pilot flying Fokkers. Here he became close friends with Rudolf Berthold and it was when flying with him on patrol that he claimed his first victory. The patrol was flying over St Quentin when they sighted a patrol of British aircraft from 8 Squadron RFC. As the two patrols closed on each other, Berthold came under attack from a BE2c. Quickly Buddecke closed on the British aircraft and shot it down: it was to be the first of many. Buddecke scored a second BE2c on 23 October and a third BE2c on 11 November, bringing his tally to three by the end of the year and earning him the Iron Cross 2nd Class.

At the end of December Buddecke was posted to Gallipoli with Ottoman FA.6, flying Halberstadt D.IIs, D.Vs, and Fokker E.IIIs as a scout and reconnaissance pilot. FA.6 was based at Smyrna and was heavily involved in the evacuation from Gallipoli. On 6 January Buddecke scored his fourth victory: a Maurice Farman from 2 Squadron RNAS over Cape Narors. By the end of the month, he had raised his total to seven and had been awarded the Silver Liaket Medal and the Iron Cross 1st Class.

At the end of April 1916, he was awarded the coveted Orden Pour le Mérite, the Golden Liaket Medal, the Saxon Military St Henry Order 4th Class, and the Knight's Cross with Swords of the Royal Hohenzollern House Order. The Turks had nicknamed him El Schahin, or 'The Shooting Hawk' and the 'Hunting Hawk'. The Ottoman Empire also awarded Buddecke the Imtiaz Medal with Clasp and Sabres in both Gold and Silver, in addition to a uniquely designed Turkish Pilot's Badge.

On his return, Buddecke was posted back to France at the beginning of August and was appointed Staffelführer of Jasta 4 on 28 August 1916. He increased his tally during September to ten, but was then posted back to Turkey in the middle of December to join Ottoman FA.5. The rest of 1916 for Buddecke was extremely quiet and his flying consisted mainly of scouting and reconnaissance missions.

Action picked up in March 1917. On the 30th, whilst on patrol over Smyrna, he came across a patrol of British reconnaissance aircraft. After a short skirmish, Buddecke shot down a Farman F27 and a Nieuport XII from 2 Squadron RNAS, raising his score to twelve. The action quietened down again and for the rest of the year he flew reconnaissance and scouting missions.

At the beginning of 1918, he received a message from his friend Rudolf Berthold, who was now commander of Jasta 18, asking him to join him as his deputy. Buddecke, tired of the inactivity in Turkey, immediately accepted the offer and arranged for a posting to Jasta 18. He returned to France at the beginning of February, firstly going to Jasta 30 for two days, then to Jasta 18. On 19 February 1918, over Neuve Chapelle, he shot down a Sopwith Camel from 80 Squadron RFC.

However, the long periods of inactivity in Turkey were taking effect and on 10 March 1918, whilst on patrol with Berthold, his luck ran out. The patrol was over Harnes when it clashed with a patrol of Sopwith Camels from 3 Squadron RNAS. Berthold was attacked and Buddecke went to his aid, but was caught by another Sopwith Camel. His lack of combat experience during the long periods of inactivity caught up with him and he was shot down and killed. He was buried in Berlin with full military honours on 22 March 1918.

Leutnant Walter von Bülow-Bothkamp

Walter von Bülow-Bothkamp was born on 24 April 1894 at Borby, near Eckernforde, Holstein. Von Bülow was a very bright pupil and went on to study law at Heidelberg University. At the onset of war, he joined the famous Saxon Husaren-Regiment Nr.17 (the 'Death's Head' Hussars) whose commander was the legendary Feldmarschall August von Mackensen. The Hussars were soon in action and early in 1915 saw heavy fighting in the Alsace region. Walter von Bülow stood out from the rest of the men and after a series of skirmishes, in which he distinguished himself, was given a field commission to Leutnant and was awarded the Iron Cross 2nd Class.

Even at this early stage of the war, von Bülow could see that the days of the Hussars were numbered. The days of the cavalry wearing elaborate uniforms and charging with lance and sword were gone; mechanisation was the key to war. In the spring of 1915, von Bülow applied for transfer to the newly formed German Army Air Service and was accepted. He was posted to Valenciennes for pilot training in June and on graduating was assigned to FA.22, flying reconnaissance missions in twin-engined AEG G.II biplanes. On 10 October 1915, von Bülow opened his tally when he shot down a Voisin whilst flying on a reconnaissance mission over Metz. The next day he scored another victory: a Maurice Farman whilst patrolling the Champagne region. For these victories he was awarded the Iron Cross 1st Class.

In January 1916 Leutnant Walter von Bülow was posted to FA.300 in Palestine. It was a welcome relief as far as the weather was concerned, but there was comparatively little aerial action. It wasn't until 8 August that von Bülow scored his next victory: an EA over El Arish, Suez. Then on 17 September he scored two Sopwith Babys, the first one from the seaplane carrier *Ben-my-Chree*, again over El Arish. Von Bülow was posted back to the Western Front to join Jasta 18 in December of 1916 after numerous requests.

Von Bülow took his tally to six on 23 January 1917 when he shot down a Sopwith 1½ Strutter from 45 Squadron RFC and an FE8 from 41 Squadron over Gheluvelt in his Albatros D.V. By the end of April, he had increased his score to twelve and had been awarded the Knight's Cross with Swords of the Royal Hohenzollern House Order, and the Saxon Military St Henry Order. This was followed on 10 May by his promotion to commander of Jasta 36. Von Bülow continued to score regularly and, by the beginning of October 1917, had raised his tally to twenty-one. On 8 October he had the honour of receiving the Orden Pour le Mérite. Von Bülow continued to increase his score and, when on 13 December he was made commander of Jasta 2 Boelcke, it had reached twenty-eight.

Leutnant Walter von Bülow-Bothkamp (Orden Pour le Mérite, with twenty-eight victories) was killed in action on 6 January 1918.

However, his appointment as commander of the prestigious Jasta Boelcke was not to last long. Whilst on patrol in his Albatros D.V over Ypres, east of Passchendaele, his patrol was jumped by British fighters from 23 and 70 Squadrons RFC. After a brief fight, Leutnant Walter von Bülow-Bothkamp's aircraft was seen to spin out of control and crash into the front line trenches. His body was recovered and buried with full military honours. He was aged twenty-two.

LEUTNANT CARL DEGELOW

Carl Degelow was born on 5 January 1891 in Munsterdorf, Germany. The wander-lust he had in his childhood years resulted in his move to America when he was twenty-one, working at various jobs throughout the United States from Chicago to El Paso, Texas. Degelow returned to Germany after hearing that there was going to be war in Europe and arrived back in Germany just before the start of World War One.

At the onset of war Degelow joined the Nassauischen Infantrie-Regiment Nr.88 and after training was sent to the Western Front. His regiment was in action almost immediately and Degelow showed his leadership qualities within weeks of being there. Within three months he had been promoted from Gefreiter to Unteroffizier and had been awarded the Iron Cross 2nd Class. At the beginning of 1915, the regiment was posted to the Russian Front. Once again Degelow showed his leader-ship qualities by leading a succession of offensives against the Russians, for which he was promoted to Vizefeldwebel and awarded the Iron Cross 1st Class. It was on one of theses offensives against the Russians that Degelow was badly wounded in the arm. On 31 July, whilst in hospital, he was awarded a commission to Leutnant, but his thoughts were looking toward getting away from the Russian Front, so he decided to apply for a transfer to the German Army Air Service.

On release from hospital, Leutnant Degelow returned to the Russian Front. In April 1916, his transfer came through and he was posted to Jastaschule in Germany. After graduating at the beginning of 1917, he was posted to FA(A).216 on the Somme as a reconnaissance pilot. Together with his observer Leutnant Kurten, they flew artillery support and reconnaissance missions in their Albatros C.V. It was whilst on a artillery support flight south west of Braye on 22 May 1917 that they were attacked by a Caudron G.IV. During the ensuing fight they managed to get the better of it and shot it down, but it was unconfirmed. Three days later, whilst on a reconnaissance mission over Bailly-Braye, they were attacked by another Caudron G.IV; again they shot it down, but this time it was confirmed and Degelow opened his score.

Degelow applied for transfer to single-seater fighters. After a short time at the Armee Flugpark, he was posted to Jasta 36 for training, but within days he had been returned to his unit after accidentally shooting an airmen whilst carrying out gunnery practice on the ground. The incident had occurred when Degelow, who was involved in mock combat above the airfield, suddenly and inexplicably left his 'opponent' and dived toward a target area set aside for strafing practice. Special permission was required to carry out strafing practice on this target area and Degelow

Leutnant Carl Degelow (fourth from left) with Bristol F.2b No.E2260 of 48 Squadron, RFC, that he shot down on 20 September 1918.

Leutnant Carl Degelow (Orden Pour le Mérite, with thirty victories) standing by his Fokker D.VII which bore his personal insignia – a leaping stag.

did not have it. On the ground observing the aerial combat was Leutnant Kreuzer, who the moment he saw Degelow set up his strafing run, hit the ground. How he wasn't killed is still a mystery as bullets exploded the dirt all around him. One of the rounds, however, hit him in the foot. Kreuzer was immediately hospitalised: the result of 'friendly fire'.

On 17 August 1917, Degelow was posted to Jasta 7 where he notched up another two victories, but again they were unconfirmed. He managed a victory on 25 January 1918 with a BF2b of 20 Squadron; another on 21 April, a Sopwith Camel from 54 Squadron; and on 16 May, an RE8, raising his tally to four. Degelow was posted to Jasta 40 on 16 May 1918, taking command on 11 July. As if to celebrate his appointment to commander, Degelow shot down six more aircraft in July bringing his score to thirteen.

He was awarded the Knight's Cross with Swords of the Royal Hohenzollern House Order on 9 August and celebrated the award by shooting down another six Allied aircraft during September. By the end of October he had shot down another ten Allied aircraft, raising his total to twenty-nine. He brought the total to thirty on 4 November 1918 when he shot down a DH9 near the Dutch border. Then five days later he was awarded the Orden Pour le Mérite, the last airman ever to receive this prestigious award.

After the war Degelow created the Hamburg Zeitfreiwilligen Korps and fought against the communists in the post-war revolution. At the beginning of World War Two, he joined the Luftwaffe, becoming a Major. After surviving the war, Degelow went into business and died in Hamburg on 9 November 1970.

LEUTNANT GUSTAV DOERR

Very little is known of Gustav Doerr prior to his joining the air service, but he was wounded twice during the first year of the war. Whilst convalescing from the second wound he saw a notice asking for volunteers for the Fliegertruppe. Doerr applied and was accepted. In July 1915, he was sent to the Jastaschule at Döberitz for his initial training and then on to FEA.3 at Gotha. On 2 February 1916 Gustav Doerr graduated and was posted to Armee Flugpark B on the Western Front for assignment and was posted to FA(A).68 at Habsheim. One of the pilots at FA(A).68 was Vizefeldwebel Ernst Udet, later to become one of the top aces of the German Army Air Service and holder of the Orden Pour le Mérite.

On arriving at FA(A).68 he was assigned his observer Oberleutnant Serger, just in time to be involved in the start of the Somme offensive by the British. Doerr and his observer were re-assigned to FA.6, later to become FA(A).257. On arriving at FA.6 on 22 December 1916, he discovered that he had been promoted to Offizier-Stellverterer. On 17 April 1917 Gustav Doerr received the Iron Cross 1st Class, having received the Iron Cross 2nd Class as an infantryman.

During the following months Doerr and his observer carried out a number of reconnaissance flights, but on 10 June Doerr was returning to his base when his aircraft developed aileron and elevator problems, possibly the result of anti-aircraft fire, and crashed into the ground from a height of 4,000ft. Doerr survived the crash, suffering serious injuries to his face (his jaw was broken in six places amongst other injuries), but his observer on this particular fight, Leutnant Hans Bohn, was killed. After three months in hospital, Doerr was assigned to FEA.1 at Altenburg as a test pilot.

After six months of testing aircraft, Gustav Doerr became restless for the excitement of battle and applied to become a fighter pilot. He was assigned to Jasta 45 and was in action at once. Flying on his first mission over Verdun with other members of the Jasta, Doerr scored his first victory. They were jumped by Allied fighters as they approached Verdun and were outnumbered four to one. After a fierce fight Doerr shot down a Sopwith Camel, before discretion became the better part of valour and the Jasta pilots flew rapidly out of the area.

On 28 May 1918 having just scored his third victory, he was attacked and his aircraft set on fire. Fortunately he was at a low altitude and he managed to set the flaming aircraft down and escape with just minor burns. In the next three months Doerr scored at an amazing rate, shooting down twenty aircraft within this period. In September he was promoted to Leutnant and awarded the Golden Military Merit Cross. Such was his standing with his fellow pilots that on 25 October 1918 the Kommandeur der Flieger der 7. Armee, Hauptmann Hugo Sperrle, recommended Leutnant Gustav Doerr for the prestigious award of the Orden Pour le Mérite.

Gustav Doerr continued to score steadily and by the time the Armistice drew a halt to the hostilities, his tally had reached thirty-five. The Orden Pour le Mérite was never awarded. Like many of the German pilots who flew and fought in the war and achieved very high scores, they were forgotten for one reason or another.

Leutnant Gustav Doerr (thirty-five confirmed victories) did not receive his Orden Pour le Mérite as World War One ended before he could do so. He died on 11 December 1928.

LEUTNANT ALBERT DOSSENBACH

The son of a local innkeeper, Albert Dossenbach was born in St Blasien in the southern part of the Black Forest. A very intelligent young man, he had no intentions of following in his father's footsteps but decided to enter the world of medicine and attended medical school. He was starting his hospital internship when war was declared. Dossenbach enlisted in the army and joined the Grossherzoglich Mecklenburgisches Füsilier-Regiment Nr.90. Because of his background and training, he was promoted to Gefreiter within weeks. Four weeks after joining the army, Dossenbach was awarded the Iron Cross 2nd Class for carrying his wounded commanding officer away from the front line to safety. Within four months, after being involved in a number of missions, Dossenbach was been awarded the Iron Cross 1st Class, the Military Merit Cross 2nd Class of the Grand Duchy of Mecklenburg-Schwerin, and promotion to Unteroffizier.

The new year started brightly for Albert Dossenbach when he was commissioned to Leutnant on 27 January 1915. By the end of the year his thoughts had turned to the air service and he applied for transfer to the German Army Air Service. In spring 1916, Dossenbach was posted to Jastaschule at FEA.3 at Gotha for initial training and then on to FEA.4 for further training, graduating in June 1916. Posted to FA.22, he joined up with his new observer, Oberleutnant Hans Schilling, flying an Albatros C.II. They were in the thick of action immediately and, only three months after graduating, Dossenbach and his observer were credited with shooting down eight Allied aircraft on 27 September. The last of the eight victims managed to inflict

Leutnant Albert Dossenbach (Orden Pour le Mérite, with fifteen victories) was killed in action on 3 July 1917.

considerable damage to Dossenbach's aircraft before crashing himself, causing Dossenbach to crash land. Both he and his observer were slightly burned in the ensuing fire, but were soon in action again. Dossenbach was awarded the Knight's Cross 2nd Class with Swords of the Order of the Zähringer Lion. One month later on 21 October 1917, he was awarded the Knight's Cross of the Royal Hohenzollern House Order. Both he and his observer marked the awards by shooting down an FE2b of 25 Squadron over Tourmignies. During the fight his observer was badly wounded, which took the edge off the celebrations.

On 11 November 1916, Leutnant Albert Dossenbach was awarded the Orden Pour le Mérite, the first two-seater pilot ever to receive the prestigious award. A further award was made on 9 December when he was given the Knight's Cross of the Military Karl-Friedrich Merit Order. Unfortunately, this honour was overshadowed by the death of his friend and former observer Hans Schilling, who was killed whilst on a bombing mission with another pilot. Dossenbach applied to go to Jasta Boelcke, the former Jasta 2 that had been renamed after the late Oswald Boelcke, for single-seater training. After graduating he took command of Jasta 36 on 22 February 1917 and set the standard by scoring the unit's first victory: a French Caudron from Escadrille Spa.12 on 5 April. By the end of the month Dossenbach had raised his personal tally to fourteen.

A bomb attack on his airfield on 2 May left Dossenbach badly wounded from bomb shrapnel and put him in hospital for two months. On release from hospital he was given command of Jasta 10 and took up the post on 21 June 1917. He opened his score with the Jasta on 27 June by shooting down an observation balloon over Ypres, raising his tally to fifteen. Then on 3 July 1917, whilst on patrol over Frenzenberg, his patrol was jumped by British fighters from 57 Squadron RFC. Heavily outnumbered, Dossenbach was attacked by four fighters and during the ensuing mêlée his aircraft caught fire. It is not certain whether he jumped or fell from his blazing aircraft, but his remains were returned to the Germans who buried him with full military honours at Frieberg.

OBERLEUTNANT EDUARD RITTER VON DOSTLER

Eduard Dostler was born on 3 February 1892 in Pottenstein, Bavaria. After leaving school he joined the 2nd Pioneer Battalion of the Bavarian Army as a cadet and, after graduating on 28 October 1912, was commissioned a Leutnant and assigned to the 4th Pioneer Battalion. In 1913, during a military exercise which involved crossing the heavily flooded Danube River, Dostler saved the life of a fellow officer. For this extreme act of bravery, he was awarded the Bavarian Life Saving Medal.

At the outbreak of war in August 1914, Dostler's engineering unit was sent to the front into the thick of the fighting and he was awarded the Iron Cross 2nd Class in November. In March 1915, he was awarded the Iron Cross 1st Class and the Bavarian Military Merit Order 4th Class with Swords. He continued to fight with his battalion until November when he heard that his brother, a pilot, had been killed in action. Dostler then decided that he would apply to be transferred to the German Army Air Service and in February 1916 was posted to Schleissheim for flight training.

Oberleutnant Eduard Ritter von Dostler
(Orden Pour le Mérite, with twenty-six
victories) was killed in action on 21 August
1917.

Graduating on 15 June he was posted to Kasta 36, flying Roland C.Is. With his observer Leutnant Boes, Dostler carried out reconnaissance missions throughout 1916. On 17 December 1916, he opened his tally when he shot down a Nieuport Scout whilst carrying out reconnaissance over Verdun.

Ten days later both Dostler and his observer were posted to Jasta 13; they increased their tally by shooting down a Caudron over Nixeville on 22 January. Early in February they were posted again, this time to Jasta 34. They stayed with Jasta 34 until the beginning of June, by which time their tally had risen to eight. On 10 June, Dostler was given command of Jasta 6. By the end of the following month his score had risen to twenty-one and he was awarded the Knight's Cross with Swords of the Royal Hohenzollern House Order. This was followed by the prestigious award of the Orden Pour le Mérite. Interestingly, when on 6 August Dostler was informed that he was to be awarded the Orden Pour le Mérite, Manfred von Richthofen, who was on sick leave, visited Jasta 6 and at a party given for Dostler, decorated Dostler with his own Orden Pour le Mérite for the purposes of a photograph.

Dostler's tally continued to mount and by 18 August had reached twenty-six. On 21 August whilst on patrol over the east Roulers area his luck ran out. Spotting what he thought was an unarmed photo-reconnaissance RE8, Dostler led his patrol into attack. The observer in the RE8, however, had spotted the patrol and concentrated his fire on the lead Albatros. Dostler's aircraft took the first burst of fire and erupted into flames. Dostler's aircraft plunged to the ground, killing its pilot. The remainder of the patrol came under attack and were driven off by Spad fighters of 19 Squadron RFC who came to the aid of the RE8.

Dostler's death was a bitter blow to his Jasta as he was a well-liked and respected officer. He was posthumously awarded the Bavarian Military Max-Joseph Order, making him a knight. The award was backdated to 18 August.

VIZEFELDWEBEL GOTTFRIED EHMANN

Among the list of pilots who became household names and who were awarded decorations and medals from the various principalities were a small number of non-pilot aviators who also left their mark. Among these was Vizefeldwebel Gottfried Ehmann who was the most successful aerial gunner in the German Army Air Service during World War One, shooting down twelve confirmed aircraft.

Posted to Schutzstaffel 15 on graduating from gunnery school, Gottfried Ehmann was assigned to be the gunner for Flieger Warda. Their first victory came on 30 October 1917 when they shot down a Nieuport 27 over Passchendaele. This was followed on 21 March 1918 with an RE8, and on 24 April 1918 a Bristol F.2b. Then four days later, during a reconnaissance mission, their Halberstadt CL.II came under attack and the pilot Unteroffizier Warda was wounded. Gottfried Ehmann managed to help the pilot land the aircraft and later that same night salvage the aircraft.

With his pilot Unteroffizier Warda out of action, Ehmann was teamed up with Vizefeldwebel Huffzky. In June 1918 they scored two more victories, followed in July by seven more. During this last period Ehmann was wounded and whilst on sick leave learned that he had been awarded the Golden Military Merit Cross. One month later he received the Württemberg Gold and Silver Military Merit Medals.

Some sources put Ehmann's final tally as high as seventeen, but the official score is believed to be twelve.

LEUTNANT RUDOLF VON ESCHWEGE

Like many other German aviators in World War One, Rudolf von Eschwege never received the awards and accolades that others, less worthy of them, did. Born on 25 February 1895 in Bad Homburg von der Hohe, near Hamburg, Eschwege enlisted at the beginning of the war with the Jäger-Regiment zu Pferde Nr.3 (*3rd Regiment of Mounted Rifles*) as a Fähnrich. By the beginning of 1915 he had fought in many of the opening campaigns, including the Battle of Mulhausen and at the River Yser, and had been promoted to Leutnant. On 1 April 1915, he was awarded the Iron Cross 2nd Class and within weeks had asked to be considered for transfer to the new German Army Air Service. He was accepted and sent for training. On graduation he was posted to FA.36 and awarded the Knight's Cross with Swords of the Order of the Zähringer Lion, an award that had caught up with him from his time with the mounted rifles.

After spending some months flying two-seater reconnaissance missions – forty-six in total – he was posted to FFA.66 on the Macedonian Front as a fighter pilot. This, on the face of it, may have appeared at the time to be what can only be described as a backwater, but Eschwege looked upon it as a challenge. In the last three months of 1916 he claimed three victims and at the beginning of 1917 was transferred to FA.30

based at Drama. The squadron had been equipped with the latest Albatros D.Is and Halberstadt D.II fighters, which were far superior to the Allied fleet of Farmans, BE12s, Nieuports and Sopwith 1½ Strutters flown by RFC and RNAS pilots. Within six months his tally had risen to twelve and was known to the Allied pilots as the 'Eagle of the Aegean'. During this time he had been awarded the Bulgarian Bravery Order 4th Class in the 2nd Grade in April, followed in June by the 4th Class of the Order in the 1st Grade. This was followed by the Knight's Cross with Swords of the Royal Hohenzollern House Order on 8 July. In addition, a proposal was sent to Karlsrhue, Germany, that Eschwege be awarded a higher Baden decoration: the Military Karl-Friedrich Merit Order. The official proposal was as follows:

> With a two-seater had 46 enemy flights and with a single-seater 152. In numerous aerial combats he defeated 11 of the enemy and forced one to land (confirmed by the Commanding General of the Air Force). He is the most successful single-seater pilot on the Balkan Front.

Whilst this proposal was on a desk in Karlsruhe, another proposal was being considered in Berlin for the Orden Pour le Mérite. The criterion at the time for the award was for the recipient to have at least twenty victories officially recorded. However, the Macedonian Front was not so active as the Western Front and as such aerial activity was less than a quarter. Consequently any victory scored on the Macedonian Front was worth at least three on the Western Front. This was recognised by the awarding of the Orden Pour le Mérite to Oberleutnant Hans Joachim Buddecke for less than half of the victories of that of Eschwege, who at the end of October had raised his tally to seventeen.

Because of his contribution to the Turks, they awarded Rudolf von Eschwege the Turkish War Medal – called the 'Iron Crescent' by the Germans – and the Turkish Pilot's Badge. Both these awards showed the high esteem in which he was held by the Turkish military leaders.

Amongst the later victories were a number of balloons and this was the cause of some concern to the Allies. The attacking of balloons from the 17th British Balloon Section was not only becoming a serious problem, but it was diminishing their number of balloons dramatically so they decided to lay a trap. On 21 November 1917, an unserviceable balloon was prepared with the observation basket packed with 500 pounds of explosives and a dummy observer. A wire from the explosives to the ground was run out at the same time as the balloon was raised; the trap was set. The first German aircraft to come along was that of Rudolf von Eschwege flying a Halberstadt D.II. Seeing the balloon with its observer in the basket, von Eschwege dived into the attack and as he closed to open fire the explosives were detonated from the ground and in one huge explosion his aircraft was blown apart. The wreckage, with von Eschwege still inside, plunged to the ground, fatally injuring the pilot.

Given a burial with full military honours, the 'Eagle of the Aegean' was laid to rest without the awards and honours that he fully deserved.

Leutnant Rudolf von Eschwege, 'Eagle of the Aegean' (twenty victories), was recommended for the Orden Pour le Mérite but died in action on 21 November 1917.

LEUTNANT WILHELM FRANKL

The son of a Jewish salesman, Wilhelm Frankl was born on 20 December 1893 in Hamburg. Even at this early time resentment against the Jews was festering in Germany and Wilhelm Frankl was to find that promotion was not going to be easy. After finishing school he joined his father as a salesman, but his sights were set higher than that – literally. On 20 July 1913 at the age of twenty, Frankl learned to fly at the local Jastaschule and gained his licence. In 1914 at the outbreak of war, he applied to join the German Army Air Service and was accepted. Even though he was a qualified pilot, he was trained as an observer and posted to FA.40 in Flanders. He carried out a number of reconnaissance missions during 1914 and was awarded the Iron Cross 2nd Class. During the early part of 1915 there were more reconnaissance missions, and on 10 May 1915 he scored his first victory by shooting down a Voisin with a carbine. For this incident, he was awarded the Iron Cross 1st Class, and later that year was promoted to Vizefeldwebel.

In the autumn of 1915, Frankl applied for training as a fighter pilot and was sent to Jastaschule in November 1915. On graduating in December, he was posted to Kek Vaux at the beginning of January 1916, flying Fokker Eindeckers. Within days of arriving he had scored his second victory, another Voisin, over Woumen. Nine days later he had another Voisin in his sights over the same area and added that to his tally. At the end of May he had taken his score to six and had been given a commission to Leutnant. Within a few days he was awarded the Knight's Cross of the Royal Hohenzollern House Order, and the Hanseatic Cross. On 10 July Frankl took his score to eight and two days later was given Prussia's high award – the Orden Pour le Mérite.

Wilhelm Frankl was posted to Jasta 4 on 1 September and by the end of the month had added three more victories to his tally, bringing it up to 13. By the end of 1916 Frankl had added another two; the year ended on a quiet note. 1917 started quietly, but in April it livened up. On 6 April Frankl claimed four more victims, one of them at night and the remaining three shot down later that same morning, all within a space of one hour. He scored one more on 7 April, bringing his total to twenty.

On the afternoon of 8 April 1917, Frankl took off on patrol and flew into a patrol of British fighters from 48 Squadron RFC. Heavily outnumbered, his Albatros D.III took a succession of machine gun bullets and was seen to break up in the air. The remains of his aircraft and his body crashed to the ground near Vitry-Sailly. His body was sent back to Germany and Leutnant Wilhelm Frankl was buried with full military honours in Berlin-Charlottenburg.

In the 1930s the Nazi party removed his name from the list of air heroes of World War One because he was Jewish. In 1973, his name was reinstated and Luftwaffe JG.74 was named after him.

OBERLEUTNANT HERMANN FRICKE

Hermann Fricke was born on 17 June 1890 in Wolfenbüttel, just outside Brunswick. Even in his teens he was interested in the new form of transport − aviation − but it wasn't until the summer of 1912 that Hermann Fricke first took to the air as an aircraft passenger from a small airfield near Munster. At the end of 1912, Fricke joined the Infanterie-Regiment Freiherr von Sparr (3 Westfälisches) Nr.16, but just prior to World War One, Fricke was promoted from Fahnenjunker (*cadet officer*) to Leutnant and had been assigned to 2. Hannoversches Infantrie-Regiment Nr.77. Fricke applied to join the German Army Air Service and was seconded to the military Jastaschule at Johannisthal on 1 July 1914.

Fricke never finished the course after being washed out by the instructors, but the urge to fly still remained so he requested to be allowed to take a crash course as an observer. On 9 September 1914 Hermann Fricke graduated as an observer and was posted to Etappen Flugpark 1. One month later he joined FFA.11 where he served until 10 November 1916. During this two-year period he was assigned to 7. Thüringisches Infantrie-Regiment Nr.96 as acting Kompanie Kommandant from 15 October to 6 November 1915. Because of his previous infantry experience, it had been decided to send him to the front line to understand better the role of assisting ground troops and to give the ground troops a better understanding of the role of the observer. Rejoining his unit Fricke was able to understand better the problems of the German infantry soldier. The principal one was: where were the Allied positions and what was their strength?

During battles on the Somme, Arras and Flanders, Fricke flew sortie after sortie taking aerial photographs of the ground struggle beneath his reconnaissance aircraft. Having an interest in photography he also began to to take aerial photographs of Allied positions. His efforts met with considerable success, which was recognised by the German High Command with the award of the Knight's Cross of the Royal Hohenzollern House Order.

Oberleutnant Hermann Fricke (Orden Pour le Mérite).

During the harsh muddy winter of 1916/17 the German High Command instructed the now Oberleutnant Fricke to establish a War Photography Office at their headquarters. Fricke was appointed to the command of a new unit: Reihenbildzug 2. He equipped his unit's aircraft with built-in Reihenbildner cameras. These cameras were capable of photographing a mile-long strip of the ground below using continuous strips of film rather than the heavy glass plates. The strips were joined together to form an invaluable aerial view of Allied positions.

Fricke's aerial photographic maps provided the German High Command with the means to deploy and direct their forces on the ground to good effect. By now Fricke had flown well over 160 combat sorties and his unit had photographed some 3,700 square miles of Allied positions with their aerial cameras.

Fricke's innovative aerial photographs gained him the award of the Orden Pour le Mérite on 23 December 1917 for outstanding combat service as an observer with Fliegerabteilung Nr.2. The award was made by the Kaiser personally during a field investiture.

During the last desperate push against the Allies in the spring of 1918, ten aircraft from Flieger Abteilung and five from Flieger Abteilung Artillerie, commanded by Oberleutnant Hermann Fricke, were fitted with the serial cameras and the designation Lb (Lichtbild: *photographic*) was added to the designation making them Flieger Abteilung 3Lb.

Fricke continued to fly to the end of World War One, then fought in the Freikorps for seven months helping to put down the Communists. He commanded a paramilitary aviation unit called the Flieger Abteilung des Freikorps Hülsen during June 1919. After being grounded he led Maschinengewehr (*machine gun*) Abteilung des Freikorps Hülsen until the end of the uprising.

Oberleutnant Hermann Göring in the cockpit of an Albatros D.V of Jasta 27 in 1917. He won twenty World War One victories.

Oberleutnant Göring (leader of the Richthofen Geschwader, 1918) alongside his all-white Fokker D.VII, Nr.F.5152/18.

Oberleutnant Hermann Göring

Next to the Red Baron, Hermann Göring was probably the most famous, and later infamous, German pilot to come out of World War One. It was not for his actions during World War One that his infamy spread, but for his part in World War Two.

Hermann Göring was born on 12 January 1893 in Rosenheim, Upper Bavaria. He was the son of Heinrich Göring, a very high-ranking army officer who had also been a Governor of German South West Africa. In his early school years Hermann Göring was an unruly, rebellious and undisciplined boy, so his parents looked towards sending him to a military academy. Using a great deal of his influence, Heinrich Göring and family friend Ritter von Epstein succeeded in getting Göring into one of the best military academies at Karlsruhe. From Karlsruhe he progressed to Lichterfelde, an army cadet college for future officers in the German army. Here college behaviour was based on medieval codes and the cadet society, into which Hermann Göring was elected, adhered strictly to them. In 1912 Hermann Göring graduated from Lichterfelde with brilliant results and was commissioned into 4. Badisches Infanterie-Regiment Prinz Wilhelm Nr.112 and posted to its head-quarters at Mülhausen, Alsace.

The outbreak of war brought Göring into action within hours of the declaration. The garrison town of Mülhausen was situated in Alsace-Lorraine which had been annexed from the French after the war of 1870 and it was also on the wrong side of the Rhine. The moment war was declared, the Prinz Wilhelm Regiment retreated across the Rhine to German territory. The regiment was moved to the Vosges region and it was here that Göring contracted rheumatic fever and was hospitalised.

Whilst in hospital, Göring was visited by his friend Bruno Loerzer. Loerzer had served with Göring in the regiment, but had transferred to the German Army Air Service and became a pilot. Göring reflected on the mud and cold that awaited his return and wrote to his commanding officer requesting a place at the Freiburg Jastaschule. After waiting over two weeks and receiving no reply, Göring obtained the papers and signed them himself, including a transfer paper to the Jastaschule. During this two-week period he had been flying with Loerzer at every opportunity, getting in all the training he could. His transfer was refused and he was ordered to return to his unit, which was something Göring had no intention of doing. Now this situation posed a very serious problem for Hermann Göring; he was open to a charge of desertion and forging papers. He immediately telegraphed his godfather, von Epstein, who moved in extremely high circles. Then suddenly Kronprinz Friedrich Wilhelm intervened and asked that Göring be posted to the German Fifth Army field air detachment. The charges were suddenly reduced to one of lateness and he was given a medical certificate saying that he was not fit for duty on the front line.

In the autumn of 1914, Göring completed his training with FEA.3 as a cameraman-observer, then joined Bruno Loerzer at FFA.25. They soon acquired a name for carrying out the most dangerous of missions and in March received the Iron Cross 2nd Class. Then in May 1915 Göring and Loerzer carried out one of their most dangerous missions. They had to carry out a reconnaissance of the fortresses in the Verdun area that were held by the French and to photograph them in detail.

Many others had tried but had failed. For three days Göring and Loerzer carried out flights over the Verdun area and came back with photographs so detailed that General Erich von Falkenhayn asked to see them personally. So delighted with the results were the High Command, that Kronprinz Wilhelm exercised his royal prerogative and invested both Göring and Loerzer with the Iron Cross 1st Class in the field. In June 1915 Göring was posted to Freiburg for pilot training, graduating in October. He was posted to FA.25, and on 16 November 1915 he opened his victory tally by shooting down a Maurice Farman over Tahure.

In 1916, he was posted from one unit to another; first to Kek Stennay flying Fokker E.IIIs, then in March to Kek Metz where on 30 July he shot down a Caudron whilst escorting bombers over Memang. He then went back to FA.25 on 9 July, and back again to Kek Metz on 7 September. From there he went to Jasta 7 and a few weeks later to Jasta 5 on 20 October. It was whilst on patrol on 2 November 1916 that he first encountered the British Handley-Page bomber. He swooped in to look at it and came under fire. He returned the fire killing one of the gunners, but then from out of the clouds swooped a flight of Sopwith Camels, who proceeded to rake Göring's aircraft from stem to stern. Göring felt the bullets rip into the fuselage and into his thigh. He passed out but came to as his aircraft plunged toward the ground. Managing to regain control of his aircraft, he steered it toward what looked like a cemetery just over the German lines. As good fortune would have it, it turned out to be an emergency hospital and within a very short time of crash landing, he was on the operating table.

After recuperating, Göring was posted to Jasta 26 at the beginning of February, now commanded by Bruno Loerzer. By the end of that month he had raised his tally to six and was attracting the attention of High Command. He increased his tally on 10 May when he shot down a DH4 of 55 Squadron RFC. One week later he was given command of Jasta 27 and by the end of October had raised his tally to fifteen. On 27 October Göring was awarded the Military Karl-Friedrich Merit Order, the Knight's Cross with Swords of the Royal Hohenzollern House Order, and the Knight's Cross 2nd Class with Swords of the Baden Order of the Zähringer Lion. By the end of the year his tally had risen to sixteen.

In 1918 he increased his tally steadily and by the end of June had taken his tally to twenty-two. At the beginning of June 1918, Göring was awarded the Orden Pour le Mérite. On 9 July he was given command of Jagdgeschwader 1 (JG.1) — the Richthofen Geschwader — and promotion to Oberleutnant. Now Göring did very little combat flying. At the end of the war, he was ordered to instruct his pilots to fly their aircraft to an Allied field. He knew that the Allies wanted the latest Fokkers; he ordered his pilots to follow their instructions, but to set fire to the aircraft the moment they were on the ground.

After the war Hermann Göring went to Denmark in a flight advisory capacity after fighting in the post-war revolution, but returned to Germany in the early 1920s.

Hermann Göring joined the Nazi Party and became Adolf Hitler's right-hand man. He progressed through the party as its strength grew and took over command of the newly formed Luftwaffe. Göring held a number of other posts throughout World War Two, but the Luftwaffe was dearest to his heart. During World War Two he received the Knight's Cross of the Iron Cross and the Grand Cross of the Iron Cross, the only person ever to receive it. He was promoted to Feldmarschall then later to Reichsmarschall, heir apparent to Hitler.

Captured by the Americans at the end of the war, Hermann Göring stood trial for war crimes and was convicted. He was sentenced to death by hanging, despite his pleas to be executed by firing squad. In the end he cheated everybody by committing suicide on 15 October 1946, using a phial of cyanide poison he had been concealing on his person since his capture.

OBERLEUTNANT ROBERT RITTER VON GREIM

The son of a police captain, Robert Greim was born on 22 June 1892 in Bayreuth, Bavaria. Between the ages of fourteen and nineteen he was an army cadet, and on 14 July 1911 he joined the regular army. He was immediately put forward for officer training and on 29 October 1912 joined Bayerisches Feldartillerie-Regiment Nr.8. He was commissioned Leutnant on 25 October 1913. When World War One began, Greim's regiment was one of the first in action and led an action in the Battle of Lorraine at Nancy-Epinal on the assaults of St Mihiel and Camp des Romains. For these actions he was awarded the Iron Cross 2nd Class and became the 1st Battalion Adjutant on 15 March 1915. At the end of April 1915, Greim was awarded the Bavarian Military Merit Order 4th Class with Swords.

Like many of the other would be pilots he too began to look at the newly formed German Army Air Service and applied for a transfer. Greim began training as an observer on 10 August 1915 and was posted to FFA.3b, in which he opened his victory tally by shooting down a Maurice Farman in October. He was posted to FA(A).204 as an observer during the Battle of the Somme. Greim applied for pilot training at the end of 1916 and, after graduating, was awarded his pilots certificate and badge. He was posted to FA.46b as a reconnaissance pilot on 22 February 1917, and one month later was sent to Jastaschule for single-seater fighter training. On completing his conversion training, he was posted to Jasta 34 on 4 April 1917, flying Albatros D.Vs, Fokker Dr.Is and Fokker D.VIIs. Greim had his aircraft marked with his own colour scheme of a red cowl, two red fuselage bands and a white-silvery tail.

Greim added to his tally on 24 May by shooting down a Spad south of Mamey, and the following day shot down a Caudron R4 south east of Rambaucourt. At the end of May, he was awarded the Iron Cross 1st Class and the Bavarian Military Merit Order 4th Class with Crown and Swords. In June 1917 Greim took over command of Jasta 34 and within weeks had increased his tally by shooting down another Spad and a Nieuport. The following five months were lean and no enemy aircraft were shot down.

By the end of 1917 Greim had raised his tally to seven. With his tally standing at nine, on 29 April 1918 he was awarded the Knight's Cross with Swords of the Royal Hohenzollern House Order. Greim continued to score and was given command of Jagdgruppe Nr.10 on 21 March 1918, and later Jagdgruppe Nr.9. On 2 July Jasta 34 was scoring steadily, but after a particularly heavy and intense dogfight Greim crashed his aircraft on landing; he suffered a broken cheekbone, a sprained ankle and concussion. The injuries were to put him out for a month. This, together with an outbreak of influenza, was to weaken Jasta 34 drastically.

On 16 July, fifty-nine Allied aircraft attacked the airfield destroying two aircraft and damaging all the others including two of the hangars they were in.

By the time Greim had recuperated at the beginning of August, the Jasta had been re-equipped and came back with a vengeance when they accounted for eight enemy aircraft on 8 August. Greim continued to score steadily, claiming his twentieth victory on 21 August. Two days later, flying with Vizefeldwebel Johann Pütz, they attacked two British tanks knocking them out with machine gun fire. This was a remarkable feat as tanks were a new aspect of war and feared by ground troops. By the end of August Jasta 34 had accounted for sixteen British aircraft.

By the end of October 1918, Greim had raised his tally to twenty-eight and was awarded the distinguished honour of the Orden Pour le Mérite. This was followed the Bavarian Knight's Cross of the Military Max-Joseph Order, allowing him to use the title Ritter von Greim, thus making him a Knight. He was also promoted to Oberleutnant.

At the end of the war he was with the Bavarian Air Service and later became an advisor to the Chinese Nationalist Air Force. In the early 1930s Greim became the Director of the Bavarian Sport Flyers Association, then in 1934 he joined the Luftwaffe with the rank of Major and took over command of the Richthofen Geschwader.

In 1938, he was promoted to the rank of General and during World War Two commanded Fliegerkorps V, for which he received the Knight's Cross of the Iron Cross on 1 July 1940. On 2 April 1943 he was awarded the Oak Leaves to this award, followed one year later by the Swords when he was Generaloberst commanding the Air Fleets in Russia. When he was captured by the Americans in 1945, he was in fact head of the Luftwaffe, a post given to him personally by Adolf Hitler, who also promoted him to General-Feldmarschall after he had been flown to Berlin by aviatrix Hanna Reitsch. Robert Ritter von Greim committed suicide on 24 May 1945 at a hospital in Salzburg, Austria.

LEUTNANT DER RESERVE WILHELM GRIEBSCH

Wilhelm Griebsch was born in Posen on 30 June 1887. During his school years he developed a passion for flying. At the age of twenty-one he entered technical college in Danzig and four years later, having gained his qualifications as an engineer, he went to Jastaschule at Berlin-Hohannisthal. Upon being awarded his pilot's certificate on 29 December 1913, Griebsch set his sights on flying in the German Army Air Service.

When World War One broke out in 1914 he immediately volunteered for the Air Service and, after initial army officer training, he left the training school with the rank of Leutnant der Reserve.

After completing his military flying training, Griebsch was assigned to FFA.41. Within a few months he was re-assigned to FA.250 as a reconnaissance pilot and was immediately in the thick of battle on the Western Front. He then began to fly as an observer with FA.250 and later with FA(A).213 where his technical knowledge proved invaluable. His particular speciality was long-range reconnaissance missions and he carried out the enormous total of 345 missions. Such was the enthusiasm in which he threw himself into the war, it is said that Griebsch carried out missions in every major campaign on the Western Front.

The outstanding information and technical details obtained by Griebsch whilst carrying out these missions proved of great value to the German High Command in their strategic ground battle plans and operations. Even though under enemy air attack, he continued to observe and record the Allied positions beneath his wings in detail, and still managed to fight back with his machine gun.

His outstanding record of successful missions as an observer brought him the Orden Pour le Mérite on 30 September 1918: one of the very few observers to be awarded the decoration. Most such decorations were awarded to fighter pilots.

Having spent almost four years in the midst of battle, Wilhelm Griebsch was taken off operational flying. He was sent back to Berlin to use his hard-won expertise at the Albatros Aircraft Co. in Berlin, where he spent the last few months of World War One.

After the war, still with a passion for flying, he obtained work at the Junkers Flugzeug-Werke in Dessau as a test pilot.

On 20 July 1920 Griebsch took off to flight test a new aircraft. It is said he had an injured left arm at the time and when at 1,900ft over Mosigkau a sudden problem developed and he was unable to control the aircraft. His aircraft fell out of the sky and crashed, killing him instantly.

OBERLEUTNANT JURGEN VON GRONE

The youngest son of an army officer, von Grone was born at Schwerin on 14 November 1887. Studying to became an advocate, he volunteered for a one-year enlistment with Garde-Feldartillerie-Regiment Nr.1.

When World War One began, von Grone was a Leutnant serving with Feldartillerie-Regiment Nr.11 on the Western Front. His unit was engaged in heavy fighting in the Namur sector of the front and the battle experience gained was put to good use by von Grone when he became an observer. He was posted to the Eastern Front in 1915 and, during heavy fighting, was wounded and hospitalised. On returning to duty he became commander of one of the new mobile anti-aircraft trains that the Germans had formed. He was awarded the Iron Cross 2nd Class, then the Iron Cross 1st Class.

In December 1915 he transferred to the Air Service as an observer and after completing his training was posted to FA.222. His specialist task as a reconnaissance observer was to photograph Allied troop movements and positions. By the summer of 1917 he had flown 130 combat reconnaissance missions and was promoted to command the Photographie Truppen of 7. Armee. On 10 September 1917 he was the first observer to photograph Paris from a height of 7,000m.

On 13 October 1918 Oberleutnant Jurgen von Grone was awarded the Orden Pour le Mérite for his outstanding contribution to the war effort. Part of his citation read:

Oberleutnant von Grone performed outstanding deeds during the large battles of 7th Army. Since the end of May he has made 50 long-range missions over enemy territory. The results of this long-range reconnaissance — up to 100 kilometres behind enemy lines — contributed substantially to our knowledge of enemy positions. Leutnant von Grone carried out numerous long-range flights, among them twelve over 100 kilometres behind the enemy front, despite enemy defences, up to 6,000 metres altitude under heavy air attack he prevailed. By reason of his above average performance I consider him worthy of the award of The Pour le Mérite'.

Signed
Hugo Sperrle, Hauptmann,
Commandant of Flyers, 7th Army.

Sperrle later became Feldmarschall in World War Two.

Jurgen von Grone survived World War One and was discharged from the army in 1920 with the rank of Hauptmann.

GENERAL DER KAVALLERIE ERNST VON HOEPPNER

Born in Toonin on the Pomerian island of Wollin on 14 June 1860, Ernst Hoeppner appeared to be destined for a military career from a very early age. On finishing his schooling, he joined the army as a cadet. On graduating, he was promoted to Sekondleutnant and assigned to Magdeburgisches Dragoner Regiment Nr.6 stationed at Stendal. In 1890 he was posted to the War Academy and upon graduating in 1893 was assigned the post of Squadron Commander of Dragoner Regiment Nr.14 in Colmar, Alsace. An appointment to the General Staff in 1902 heralded the start of a distinguished career. This was followed two years later by a promotion to Oberleutnant and a staff officer's position with 9. Armee Korps at Altona. In 1906 Hoeppner was given command of the Husaren-Regiment Nr.13 stationed in Diedenhofen.

Oberleutnant Hoeppner's organisational capabilities soon came to the fore, and this was rewarded in 1908 by his appointment to Chief of the General Staff of 7. Armee Korps and a promotion to Oberstleutnant. This position was to last until 1912 when he was given command of 4. Kavallerie Brigade in Bromberg, one of the most prestigious commands in the German army. This culminated in 1913, when the title 'von' was bestowed upon him, giving him the right to change his name to Ernst von Hoeppner and made him a 'Teutonic Knight'.

At the outbreak of war in 1914, von Hoeppner was Chief of the General Staff of 3. Armee, a position he was to hold until May 1915, when he took over command of 14. Reserve-Division of 1. Armee. Such was the rapid movement of senior officers at the time, as the army attempted to stabilise its organisational problems, that von Hoeppner was appointed Chief of the General Staff of 2. Armee within a few months. In June 1916 he was moved again when he took over command of 75. Reserve-Division. Again the German High Command could not make up its mind when they recalled von Hoeppner from the Eastern Front late in June 1916. His army was in a desperate situation at the time, with superior Russian forces threatening to break German defences at Lake Naroch. An earlier attempt to break the defences had failed, but now they had been breached; the Austro-Hungarian 4. Armee was virtually destroyed due to the incompetence of their commander, the Archduke Joseph Ferdinand.

In October 1916 von Hoeppner was promoted to General and appointed Kommandierender-General of the German Army Air Service. He immediately set to work to unify all the various units under one command structure. Because the German Air Force had started life as 'general units' consisting of six or less aircraft, its development had been ragged; specialised units came under the command of various structures. There were single-seater fighters, single-seater reconnaissance, single-seater artillery liaison, escort fighters and bombers, all needing to come under one command structure. Von Hoeppner set about it with a single-minded purposefulness and by the spring of 1917 had unified the entire German Army Air Service.

On 8 April 1917, the Kaiser recognised General Ernst von Hoeppner's achievements by awarding him the Orden Pour le Mérite. He was to stay at his post until the end of the war when he retired to his home on the island of Wollin. He died there on 25 September 1922 at the age of sixty-two.

Oberleutnant Erich Homburg

The son of a forester, Erich Homburg was born on 2 October 1886 in Rosenthal, Bavaria. After leaving school, he joined the army as a cadet with Reserve-Fieldartillerie-Regiment Nr.12. When war broke out in August 1914, Homburg had already been awarded a commission and was the regiment's ordnance officer as well as adjutant. The regiment moved to the Western Front and was immediately involved in fighting. After many months of intense and heavy fighting, Homburg was later awarded the Iron Cross 2nd Class.

During a lull in the fighting in the early part of 1915, he was offered a flight in a reconnaissance aircraft. Homburg was so taken with the flight and the relative freedom it afforded that he applied for a transfer to the German Army Air Service. In the spring of 1915, he was accepted and posted for flying training. On graduating in the autumn, Homburg was posted to FFA.34 as a reconnaissance pilot. He quickly developed an interest in communications and was assigned the post of communications officer. On 25 September 1915, he was awarded the Iron Cross 1st Class for his reconnaissance work.

During the next two years he created a reporting system that used ground-to-air radio and became the first flyer to use it. During this time he also turned his attention and skills to aerial photography and carried out flight strip photographic reconnaissance missions over the battles of the Somme, Verdun, Champagne and Romania. During the German offensive in Italy, Homburg was sent to carry out aerial photographic missions, which helped the campaign tremendously. At the beginning of August 1918 he returned to the Western Front and was given command of FA(A).260. On 13 October Homburg was awarded the Orden Pour le Mérite, one of the very few non–fighter pilots to receive the award. He was also promoted to Oberleutnant in recognition of the 239 tactical reconnaissance and photographic missions he had flown over enemy territory.

When Germany finally capitulated in 1918, Homburg managed to get every single one of his aircraft, every piece of equipment, and all his personnel back into Germany.

Homburg continued with his interest in aerial photography after the war, using the expertise gained in the war for peaceful purposes. The planning of new airfields for commercial use was one of the applications for which aerial photography was used. He was appointed Director of Air Transport-AG for Lower Saxony in 1926 at Hannover's city airport administration. In the early 1930s Homburg was appointed President of the Reichs Association of Regional Air Traffic Companies. He was also president of a number of sporting flying organisations, and his positions included Director of the Aviation Office in Hamburg.

At the onset of World War Two, Homburg returned to active service with the Luftwaffe, attaining the rank of Generalmajor on 1 November 1940.

OBERLEUTNANT HANS-GEORG HORN

Born on 28 April 1892 in the small town of Berbisdorf in Silesia, Hans–Georg Horn was the son of the local Lutheran pastor. After finishing his schooling he attended the military school at Danzig as a cadet. At the outbreak of war in 1914 he held the rank of Unteroffizier at the college, and was returned to the infantry regiment that was his parent unit. The regiment was moved to the Western Front and within days of arriving were in action. On 8 August 1914 Horn was involved in the storming of Maas Heights during the Battle of Longwy. One month later he fought at the Battle of Combres; his leadership during the battle earned him promotion to Leutnant and the Iron Cross 2nd Class.

On 17 July 1915, whilst leading his troops from the front, Horn was wounded during a charge on enemy positions. He returned to his unit after a week in hospital, but at the end of July was wounded again, this time badly. Whilst in hospital he was awarded the Iron Cross 1st Class, but a chance meeting with a pilot from the German Army Air Service was to change his whole attitude to the war.

At the end of October, just after being released from hospital, Horn applied for transfer to the German Army Air Service and was accepted. He was posted to FEA.10 on 5 December 1915 for training as an observer. On graduating in February 1916, he was posted to a defence squadron flying reconnaissance missions for the infantry.

The remaining year was spent flying mission after mission, then in January 1917 he was posted to Schutzstaffel 11 for two months, then to FA(A).221 in April. This move was to bring Horn into contact with some of the most intensive fighting of the war, including the battles at Verdun.

On 7 June 1917, Horn suffered another wound when his aircraft was hit by ground fire and Horn was hit in the left buttock. Despite the extensive damage to his aircraft, his pilot Unteroffizier Fritz Clausen managed to get the aircraft back to their airfield at Bisseghem.

Oberleutnant Hans-Georg Horn (Orden Pour le Mérite) with FF(A).221. He was the best observer in the German Army Air Service, with over 300 missions over enemy positions to his credit with his pilot Otto Jahnke (Military Merit Cross).

Leutnant Horn

After a couple of weeks in hospital, Horn returned to his unit to find Clausen had been assigned to Jasta 26 and he was assigned another pilot, Vizefeldwebel Otto Jahnke. He and Jahnke flew almost daily, and this was recognised by the German High Command on 15 July 1917, when he was awarded the Knight's Cross with Swords of the Royal Hohenzollern House Order. It was recognised that Horn was without doubt one of the best observers in the German Army Air Service, if not the best. This was borne out in November 1917 when, during the battles near Gheluvelt, Horn and his pilot flew six flights in the most horrendous weather conditions. The information they brought back enabled the infantry on the ground to make important advances, whilst saving the lives of many of their troops.

On 23 December 1917, Hans-Georg Horn was awarded the Orden Pour le Mérite, whilst Jahnke received the Military Merit Cross. Horn was one of only five observers to be honoured with the Orden Pour le Mérite. In May 1918, he was posted to 7. Infanterie-Division as a flying liaison officer for two months with the rank of Oberleutnant. He returned to his unit in August and was wounded later the same month; the wound ostensibly ended his active flying career. At the end of the war, he had accumulated over 300 missions over enemy territory. His flying days were not quite over, with the signing of the Armistice he was assigned to Kagohl 401 to fly reconnaissance missions for the border police. In November 1919 Hans-Georg Horn resigned from the army and returned to civilian life.

LEUTNANT DER RESERVE JOSEF CARL PETER JACOBS

The son of a middle-class businessman, Josef Jacobs was born in Kreuzkapelle, Rhineland on 15 May 1894. His interest in all things mechanical showed itself in 1912 when at the age of eighteen he learned to fly at the nearby Jastaschule at Hangelar. Two years later at the outbreak of World War One, Josef Jacobs enlisted in the German Army Air Service and was posted to FEA.9 to be trained as a military pilot. On graduating, he was posted to FA.11 as a reconnaissance pilot on 3 July 1915. On the same day, during a test flight in an LVG No.B315 accompanied by Oberleutnant Walter Lackner, their aircraft was fired upon by anti-aircraft guns and they were observed by an Allied fighter. For Jacobs the war had well and truly begun.

Within four months Jacobs rose from Flieger to Vizefeldwebel, and only then was he awarded his Pilot's Badge. For over a year he was engaged in reconnaissance missions over the lines, then early in 1916 FA.11 were assigned a number of Fokker E.III Eindeckers. He opened his victory tally unofficially on 1 February when he claimed a Caudron, but it was unconfirmed. The end of March brought promotion to the rank of Leutnant and the claim for a balloon, for which he was awarded the Iron Cross 2nd Class. But it was not the victory of the shooting of a stationery object in the sky that Jacobs wanted for his Ehrenbecher (*honour cup*), he wanted a 'Teutonic Knight's' victory of claiming an aircraft.

On 21 March 1916 the single-seater fighters of FA.7, 11 and 39 were amalgamated into a new unit called Fokkerstaffel-West. The new unit with its four aircraft were based at Le Faux Ferme, near Coucy, and placed under the command of Oberleutnant Erich Hoenmanns. Fokkerstaffel-Ost comprising five aircraft from FA.26 and 29 was also formed and it was based at St Erme under the command of Leutnant von Manteuffel.

With the arrival of the Fokker Eindeckers came a change in fortune for Jacobs; on 12 May 1916 he claimed his first victim. The following is an English translation of his report:

Airfield 13 May 1916

REPORT
on downing of a Caudron biplane southwest of Laon

On 12.5.16. toward 8:45 p.m. an enemy aircraft was fired on by anti-aircraft fire in the area Soisson-Laon. I started with my 100-hp Fokker E.III 608/15 shortly thereafter and met the aircraft, a twin-engined Caudron at 1800m near Pinon. Before the fight I fired a flare and opened fire on the Caudron when I was within 60-80m. After about 30 rounds a jam occurred, which I soon cleared however. Meanwhile the Caudron flew towards the front and made a right-hand turn toward Anizy-Eizy. Because my machine climbed during this time, I had the edge in speed when thereafter I pushed my nose down and having closed to about 80m, fired 30-40 rounds while turning, whereupon the Caudron headed towards Bourguignon in a steep glide. Prevented from firing by a second jam, I tried by turning and spiralling to prevent the Caudron from getting away. Near the village of Bourguignon the Caudron was within 50m from the ground and I thought that he would land on a clear grass field but once again he tried to escape in the valley. Once again I flung myself at him and at about 10m I fired some shots, whereupon the machine fell sideways down into a wood.

Jacobs
Leutnant of Reserve

On 25 October 1916, Jacobs was posted to Jasta 22 at the request of its commander Oberleutnant Honemanns, a long-time friend. Within weeks of his arriving at Jasta 22, he was posted temporarily to Jastaschule 1 as an instructor where he spent part of the winter. On returning to Jasta 22 on 8 January 1917, Jacobs was awarded the Iron Cross 1st Class and he celebrated by opening his victory score with the squadron by shooting down a Caudron R4 over Terny Sorny on 23 January. By the end of August, his tally had risen to five and he was appointed Staffelführer of Jasta 7. With the appointment came the award of the Knight's Cross with Swords of the Royal Hohenzollern House Order. By the end of 1917 Jacobs's tally had risen to twelve, and his Jasta was re-equipped with Fokker Dreideckers. Jacobs had his aircraft painted all black and it soon became known to Allied airmen.

Leutnant der Reserve Josef Carl Peter Jacobs
(Orden Pour le Mérite, with forty-eight
victories).

The end of 1917 with Jasta 7 was quiet; there was a lull in hostilities and Jacobs used the time to mould his Jasta into a fighting unit. Jacobs chose as his flying partner Oberflugmeister Kurt Schönfelder, who already had two 'kills' on the board. The lull didn't last and in April Jacobs claimed his latest victim: an RE8 of 7 Squadron RFC, over western Ostend. The fighting became intense and by the end of July both Jacobs and Schönfelder had increased their tally, and with it their friendship.

On 18 December during a dogfight with Sopwith Camels and Sopwith 1½ Strutters Jacobs had just dispatched one of the Camels into the ground and was lining up a second when he felt bullets thudding into the fuselage of his aircraft. He started to take evasive action but had a mid-air collision with another Fokker Dreidecker. His aircraft suffered horrendous damage to the engine section and spun out of control toward the ground. Jacobs considered jumping without a parachute but decided to try and stay with the aircraft. Gaining some semblance of control he nursed the damaged aircraft back toward his own lines and touched down on a battle-scarred field. Passing out from the impact, Jacobs came to amidst a pile of wreckage and found himself being pulled out by German soldiers. Miraculously unhurt, he spent the night being entertained by them before returning to his unit the following day.

Jacobs continued to score steadily and increase his tally, which had risen to twenty-four. On 26 June 1918, whilst on patrol with Schönfelder, they were attacked by three Sopwith Camels from 210 Squadron RAF. During the fight Jacob's saw Schönfelder's aircraft spinning out of control and into the ground.

On 18 July 1918 came the news that he had been awarded Prussia's prestigious award, the Orden Pour le Mérite. It came as a message which read:

18.7.18
Lt. d. Res. Jacobs
Commanding Officer Fighter Section 7

His Majesty has in recognition of your excellent accomplishment as a fighter pilot bestowed on you the Order of Merit.
It gives me great pleasure to inform you of this fact and to congratulate you on this, the supreme token of distinction from your highest War Lord

The Commanding General von Hoeppner

Leutnant Josef Jacobs was the last recipient of this prestigious order.

Jacobs gradually became Germany's greatest exponent of the Fokker Dreidecker and by the end of 1918 had disposed of forty-eight of the Allies aircraft. After the Armistice he, with Osterkamp and Sachsenberg, fought against communists in the Baltic.

In the early 1920s Jacobs became a flight instructor with the Turkish Army, helping them develop a formidable air force. In 1931 he became a director of the Adler Works, still maintaining his interest in aviation. Two years later he set up his own aircraft manufacturing plant at Erfurt although this was not a great success. Speed was still a passion and he became involved in the world of car and powerboat racing and bob-sledding.

Prior to the start of World War Two, Jacobs did not volunteer for the newly formed Luftwaffe but at the onset was commissioned a Major in the reserves. He was a reluctant officer in the Luftwaffe and his views on the National Socialist Party were well known and documented, as were his objections to the anti-Jewish policies. At one point he even moved his company away from Germany to Holland in order to prevent Göring becoming a major shareholder. Furious at this Göring made it clear that he would have Jacobs arrested. The military governor of Holland at the time was Friedrich Christiansen, a fellow holder of the Orden Pour le Mérite who told Jacobs of Göring's intent and helped him slip away. Jacobs spent the rest of the war in hiding.

At the end of the war, Josef Jacobs moved away from aviation and started a crane-operating company, but such was his love of aviation that he became one of the greatest sources of information on World War One aircraft and personnel for historians.

Leutnant Josef Jacobs died in Munich on 29 July 1978 at the age of eighty-four.

HAUPTMANN RUDOLF KLEINE

Rudolf Kleine was born on 28 August 1886 at Minden, Westphalia. His father was an Infantry Colonel in Infanterie-Regiment Nr.15, so it was no surprise that Rudolf Kleine wanted to join the army after leaving school. He joined the Corps of Cadets in 1901 and graduated as a Leutnant on 14 June 1905. He was assigned to Infanterie-Regiment Nr.65, in which he made rapid progress becoming the battalion adjutant in 1910. In the spring of 1913, Kleine decided that the infantry was losing its appeal and applied for transfer to the German Army Air Service and was accepted.

Hauptmann Rudolf Kleine held the Orden Pour le Mérite for six bombing missions against London, Harwich and Felixstowe. He was killed in action.

In September of 1913, Kleine was sent to the Herzog-Karl-Eduard Jastaschule at Gotha for training as a pilot and, upon graduating in June 1914, was awarded his oval silver pilot's badge and assigned to Air Battalion Nr.3 at Cologne. In August 1914 he participated in one of the first battles of the war by flying reconnaissance for the German Brigades who had been charged with capturing the fortress city of Liège. For his part in the action, Kleine was awarded the Iron Cross 2nd Class and promoted to Oberleutnant. For the next year Kleine carried out numerous reconnaissance missions over the enemy lines, feeding back important information. On one mission in July 1915, whilst carrying out another reconnaissance sortie over enemy lines, he was wounded in the arm and hospitalised.

After recovering he was promoted to Hauptmann and in December was posted to Ostend, Belgium, to take command of Kagohl 1. His appearance as commander of Kagohl 1, wearing the oval silver badge of a German military pilot, was unusual sight amongst Kagohl commanders as nearly all of them were observers.

For the next twelve months his squadron made numerous scouting and reconnaissance missions over the enemy lines, including a crucial one, carried out by Kleine himself, which reported the massing of French troops for the battle of champagne. The precise report given by Kleine helped the German infantry prepare for the assault, thus cutting their losses. For his part in this Kleine was awarded the Knight's Cross with Swords of the Royal Hohenzollern House Order and the Iron Cross 1st Class. On 23 August 1916, Kleine was given command of FFA.53, a position he held until 23 June 1917 when he took command of Kagohl 3.

His primary assignment was the bombing of London and it was to this end that he initially made himself unpopular with the German High Command. Kleine maintained that the bombing of London would serve no real purpose and would in fact hinder a possible peace plan. Kleine set about planning his first raid, but decided against London; instead he targeted the port of Harwich and the Royal Naval Air Station at Felixstowe. On 4 July 1917, twenty-five Gotha bombers took off towards England. By the time they reached the sea, seven of the bombers had engine problems and aborted the mission. The remaining bombers headed north toward the Suffolk coast where the group split into two flights. On reaching Harwich, one half of the flight unloaded their bombs; fortunately for the inhabitants, only two of the bombs actually dropped on the town, the remainder went into the sea. The other half of the flight attacked Felixstowe – this time with more success. A number of bombs fell on the Royal Naval Air Station, destroying one aircraft and severely damaging several others. British casualties were seventeen dead and twenty-nine wounded. All the German aircraft returned safely. Eighty-three British aircraft were scrambled from airfields in Kent and Essex, but not one made contact with the enemy Gothas.

During the next couple of months, Kleine planned and carried out six bombing missions on London and on 4 October 1917 was awarded the Orden Pour le Mérite.

On 12 December, during an attack on Ypres, his flight came under heavy attack from Allied fighter aircraft. Kleine's aircraft came under heavy machine gun fire; it was raked from stem to stern, which caused it to fall out of control to the ground. The bodies of Kleine and his men were recovered by German troops.

Hauptmann Hermann Köhl wearing his
Orden Pour le Mérite. He was commander of
Bogohl 7 and flew Gotha C-type bombers
against ammunition dumps with great
success. He died on 7 October 1938.

HAUPTMANN HERMANN KÖHL

The son of a Bavarian General, Hermann Köhl was born in Neu-Ulm, Bavaria, on
15 April 1888. It was only natural that he should follow in his army father's footsteps
and on leaving school he joined the army as a cadet. On graduating, he was commissioned as a Leutnant in the Württembergisches Pionier-Bataillon Nr.13 and was
posted to the Western Front at the outbreak of war in 1914. In October 1915, Köhl
was badly wounded in action and hospitalised. On returning to his unit in January
1915, he was awarded the Iron Cross 2nd Class.

Köhl then applied for transfer to the German Army Air Service much to the
annoyance of his father, who was not convinced that aeroplanes were for soldiers.
Köhl was accepted and posted to the Jastaschule at Aldershof, Berlin, where in spring
1915 he was awarded his Observer's Badge. For the first nine months of his new
career, Köhl was a reconnaissance observer assigned to FA.41 and flew a number of
missions in support of artillery and infantry. In March 1915 he was promoted to
Oberleutnant, followed in May with the award of the Knight's Cross of the
Württemberg Military Merit Order. The rest of 1915 was relatively quiet for Köhl
and FA.41.

At the beginning of 1916, everything changed and the unit was moved south
toward the Somme. Within weeks of arriving, Köhl was assigned to Kasta 22 of KG.4

whose primary function was to give cover for various Feldflieger Abteilungen. During one such mission in March, Köhl claimed one enemy aircraft shot down. Unfortunately there was no confirmation of this and, although normally the first 'kill' would have attracted the awarding of an Ehrenbecher, recognition was not forthcoming. His fellow officers, convinced that Köhl was correct, gave him a silver cigarette case which was suitably inscribed.

In August 1916 Köhl was given command of Kasta 22 followed some months later by an Ehrenbecher for another victory, this time confirmed. The Kasta trained together perfecting their bombing techniques until February of 1916, when they began their bombing raids. Initial raids were not great successes, but on the night of 6/7 November 1916 Köhl and his pilot, Leutnant Kalf, attacked a French ammunition depot at Ceresy. The resulting explosion was seen and heard for miles, and caused the French serious munition problems – albeit for only a short period. The success of the mission earned Köhl the Knight's Cross with Swords of the Royal Hohenzollern House Order.

During a mission on 15 December 1916, Köhl's aircraft encountered two Nieuport fighters and came under machine-gun fire. With a dead engine and other damage, pilot Unteroffizier Paul Rüger managed to land the aircraft in front of the German lines. On landing in the shell-ravaged ground the aircraft flipped over on to its back, trapping Köhl in the wreckage. Köhl ordered his pilot to save himself as the wreckage of the aircraft came under fire from British lines. The pilot went for help, returned some minutes later with German troops, and cut Köhl from the wreckage. After a few weeks in hospital Köhl returned to his unit only to be assigned to FEA.6 at Grossenhain in Saxony.

On 2 April 1917 Köhl was re-assigned to KG.4 and given command of Kasta 19. Then in May, after hearing speculative plans to carry out a night bombing raid on Paris, Köhl made two unauthorised scouting flights over the capital, much to the displeasure of the hierarchy. It is also mooted that Köhl carried out an unauthorised raid on Dover on the night of 2/3 September 1917, but there is nothing officially recorded.

Kagohl 4 was renamed Bogohl 4 and assigned to the Asiago-Piave Front in Italy in an attempt to support their struggling Austrian allies. Commanding Bomben-staffel 19, Köhl arrived at the airfield at Aviano on 15 December 1917, just in time for the airfield to be 'jumped' by two Sopwith Camels from 28 Squadron RFC. The two pilots, Captain William Barker VC and Lieutenant Harold Hudson, strafed the airfield, damaging four aircraft and a number of hangars. It is also said that as they flew away they dropped a large Christmas card with 'Merry Christmas' written on it.

The German High Command, incensed at the audacity of the raid, ordered a retaliatory strike on enemy airfields the following day; the main target was to be the airfield at Trevignano. The strike turned out to be a disaster and became known as the Aerial Battle of Istrana, named after the Allied airfield there. The Germans lost nine aircraft and inflicted little damage on the Allied airfield. The next few months consisted of night bombing raids on Allied airfields and met with limited success. In February all German aviation units were ordered back to the Western Front for a last ditch offensive.

Germany had negotiated a peace settlement with Russia, which released large numbers of German troops to the Western Front. On the opening day of the Kaiserschlacht (*Emperor's battle*), Köhl was given command of Bogohl 7. It was equipped with Gotha C-type bombers and Köhl concentrated on the railway stations and ammunition dumps. He gained considerable success when he attacked two of the French army's largest ammunition dumps with devastating effect. After the second attack, Köhl was recommended for the Orden Pour le Mérite. He was one of only two Bogohl commanders to be awarded the honour: the other being Ernst Brandenburg.

Köhl would have been given the award a year earlier had he not upset the High Command with his unauthorised flights over Paris and Dover. The award, given for over 800 operations, came just after one of the squadron's most dangerous missions: a low-level attack on the largest French ammunition depot. On the night of 20/21 May 1918, the squadron of Gothas flew at under 200ft to the French ammunition depot near Blargies, south-west of Amiens. The raid was a complete success, but it was a raid that came too late for Germany.

During a raid in July 1918, the squadron came up against some of the strongest Allied opposition in the air that they had ever encountered. During the attempt to retreat away from the target, Köhl's bomber was forced down behind Allied lines. Together with his pilot and observer-gunner, they set fire to the aircraft and attempted to reach their own lines. The three crew members were captured and sent to a POW camp. In September Köhl managed to escape and make his way back to Germany. By this time the war was over and Köhl left the army – but not aviation.

He joined the Junkers company and helped create new civil air routes in Europe and within Germany. But his sense of adventure was not dead and on 13 April 1928, after a 36½-hour flight across the Atlantic, his Junkers W.33 'Bremen' landed on Greenly Island, Labrador. Köhl was accompanied on the flight by another German, Baron von Hünfeld, and an Irishman, Commander J. Fitzmaurice. The three intrepid aviators were fêted in New York and Washington, putting German aviation firmly back on the map. Hermann Köhl died ten years later on 7 October 1938.

LEUTNANT OTTO KÖNNECKE

Born the son of a carpenter in Strasbourg on 20 September 1892, Otto Könnecke seemed destined to follow in his father's footsteps after qualifying from the Building Trade School at Frankfurt am Main in 1909. He was a carpenter's assistant for two years, then in 1911, volunteered for military service with the Eisenbahn-Regiment Nr.3 (*Railway Regiment No.3*) at Hanau. After two years he was transferred to FEA.4 at Metz and promoted to Unteroffizier. It was at Metz that Könnecke learned to fly and when war was declared the following year, he was a qualified NCO flying instructor.

Although there was a desperate need for pilots at the beginning of the war, there was an even greater need for instructors and he was to stay at Metz as an instructor until 3 December 1916. The German Army Air Service, at this point in the war, had lost a large number of pilots in France so pilots from Macedonia were sent to the

Western Front, and new and less experienced fighter pilots sent to take their place. Otto Könnecke was one of the inexperienced pilots, battlewise, who were posted to Jasta 25.

On 9 January Otto Könnecke claimed his first victory, but it was unconfirmed. The following month he opened his tally on 5 February when, over northwestern Moglia, he shot down a Henry Farman from Serbian Air Park No.30. The following day he raised his tally by shooting down another Farman from Serbian Escadrille F.98. He then, like the pilots before him, was posted back to the Western Front to join AFP.2 in March 1917 as a reconnaissance pilot, and in April he was assigned to Jasta 5. He joined up with two other NCO pilots, Fritz Rumey and Josef Mai, who later became known as the 'Golden Triumvirate' and between them scored 109 victories by the end of the war.

By the end of 1917, Otto Könnecke had raised his score to eleven. He flew his distinctive Albatros D.V with its green fuselage and tail edged in red, and a black and white checkerboard marker edged in red just ahead of the black cross on the fuselage.

Könnecke continued to score steadily and his tally rose until on 12 May his skill and dedication was recognised by the High Command and he was awarded the Golden Military Merit Cross. The following month, on 15 June, he was commissioned as a Leutnant. This was followed on 20 June with the Knight's Cross with Swords of the Royal Hohenzollern House Order; his tally stood at twenty-three. One month later he had raised his tally to thirty-two and with it came the coveted Orden Pour le Mérite.

Otto Könnecke finished the war with a victory score of thirty-five. In 1926, he joined Lufthansa as a pilot; in 1935 with the birth of the Luftwaffe he enlisted and became Commandant of Flying Schools with the rank of Major. He died in Germany on 25 January 1956.

LEUTNANT ARTHUR LAUMANN

Arthur Laumann was born in Essen on 4 July 1894. On the outbreak of war he volunteered and joined Feldartillerie-Regiment Nr.83. For the next two years Laumann fought on the Western and Eastern fronts; he was awarded the Iron Cross 2nd Class and a commission to Leutnant. During the year, Laumann wrote numerous requests for transfer to the German Army Air Service and in August 1917 this was granted.

Laumann was sent for training and, upon graduating, was presented with his certificate and pilot's badge and posted to FA(A).265 as a reconnaissance pilot. It is interesting to note that this unit was commanded by his brother.

In May, Laumann was posted to Jasta 66 as a fighter pilot, although he had not been given any training as such. It soon became apparent that he was a natural fighter pilot and he opened his account by shooting down a Spad 2 over Courelles. It was both a happy day for Laumann and a sad day for the Jasta as its commander, Rudolf Windisch, was shot down and killed. In the following two months, Laumann had raised his score to fifteen and taken command of Jasta 66. On 14 August 1918 he was posted to Jasta 10, part of JG.1, to replace another of Germany's top aces, Erich Löwenhardt, who had been killed.

Leutnant Arthur Laumann (Orden Pour le Mérite, with twenty-eight victories) had 'AL' painted on the side of his fuselage.

Laumann's Fokker D.VII was distinctive with a monogrammed 'AL' on the side of the fuselage. Laumann was rewarded on 29 September 1918 with the award of the Iron Cross 1st Class and the Knight's Cross of the Royal Hohenzollern House Order. His score was now twenty–eight and this achivement was recognised by the Kaiser who awarded him the Orden Pour le Mérite. Arthur Laumann stayed as commander of Jasta 10 until the end of World War One.

During the period between the wars Laumann worked as an instructor, but joined the Luftwaffe in 1935 and became commander of the new JG Richthofen squadron. He survived World War Two and became the German Air Attaché to Yugoslavia and Greece. He died of a stroke in Münster on 18 November 1970.

HAUPTMANN LEO LEONHARDY

Leo Leonhardy was born on 13 November 1880 in the small town of Rastenburg, East Prussia. After leaving school in 1895, he joined the army as a cadet and graduated as a Leutnant in 1900, joining the East Prussian Infantry. Prior to the outbreak of World War One, Leonhardy applied for transfer to the German Army Air Service. In autumn 1913, he was accepted and posted to the Jastaschule at Johannisthal for training as a pilot.

Ten days after starting his flying training, his aircraft collided in mid–air with another pupil's aircraft. Although Leonhardy managed to get his aircraft back on the ground, the resulting crash left him with horrendous injuries: including broken breastbone, nose and legs, a skull fracture, and two breaks in his spine. He was rushed to the hospital at Wiesbaden, where after numerous operations the doctors managed to restore him to health. After over a year in hospital, he was declared fit for active duty and posted to Idflieg (Inspectorate of Flying) in Berlin. Using his considerable manipulative skills, he managed to persuade the High Command that he was fit enough to return to active duty in the field.

In the summer of 1915, Leonhardy was posted to the Army Airfield of the Southern Army in Muncacz. Within weeks he was flying again – albeit secretly at first. After three months he applied for flying duties as an observer and was posted to FA.59 together with his confidant, Leutnant Kohlhepp, who had secretly worked with him during the previous months.

Leonhardy and his pilot flew numerous reconnaissance missions during 1916 for the artillery and infantry, for which he gained promotion to Oberleutnant and won the Iron Cross 2nd Class. In September 1916, Leonhardy was posted back to Jastaschule at Johannisthal for training as a pilot and, upon graduating in January 1917, was posted to FA.25. After flying a number of missions Leonhardy took command of Bogohl 6 in the summer of 1917. He was promoted to Hauptmann and awarded the Knight's Cross of the Royal Hohenzollern House Order.

Leonhardy planned a number of missions against the Allies, but the one on 18 February 1918 was to be memorable for him and his crews. The attack was on the Allied airfield at Malzeville, where his squadron dropped over 300 bombs which destroyed ten hangars and thirteen Nieuport fighters, together with a fuel and ammunition dump which supplied the airfield. In May 1918, the squadron led by Leonhardy carried out a raid on a French bomb and fuel dump at Etaples, causing considerable damage, for which he received the Iron Cross 1st Class. On 2 October after completing over eighty-three missions, Hauptmann Leo Leonhardy was awarded the Orden Pour le Mérite.

When war ended, Leonhardy was assigned the job of an observer again, this time it was to observe the destruction of German aircraft in accordance with the Versailles Treaty. He retired from military service in 1919, suffering from ill health. He died in Berlin on 12 July 1928.

HAUPTMANN BRUNO LOERZER

Bruno Loerzer was born in Berlin on 22 January 1891. At the age of seventeen he became a cadet with 4. Badisches Infanterie-Regiment Prinz Wilhelm Nr.112. Later he was accepted at military school and, after graduating, rejoined his old regiment in January 1913 with the rank of Leutnant. In the regiment Leutnant Bruno Loerzer met Hermann Göring and the two of them were to become inseparable lifelong friends throughout their military careers. However, Loerzer soon tired of the infantry and applied for Jastaschule where he was accepted. In August 1914, he began flying training and graduated in October; he was sent to FA.25 as a reconnaissance pilot. In the meantime, Göring was having problems with the authorities back at the regiment and was on the point of being court-martialled. On 28 October Göring decided to join his friend Loerzer as his observer. It appears that the regiment was glad to see the back of Göring and approved his transfer – unofficially. It was only

The twenty surviving Orden Pour le Mérite winners in 1925, left to right: Loerzer, Walz, Buckler, Bäumer, Köhl, Keller, Thuy, Osterkamp, Könnecke, Veltjens, Jacobs, Bongartz, Laumann, Sachsenberg, Leonhardy, Bolle, Klein, von Boenigk, Degelow, and Wüsthoff.

out of respect for Göring's father, the former Governor of German South West Africa, and the influence of his godfather Ritter von Epstein that the Army did not pursue the matter.

For the next seven months Loerzer and Göring flew mission after mission, and were awarded the Iron Cross 2nd Class on 7 March 1915. In April, General Erich von Falkenhayn, whose armies were being held back due to the chain of forts at Verdun, demanded some clear photographs of the fortresses. All missions to accomplish this failed but Loerzer and Göring volunteered for the mission. For the next three days, Loerzer cruised low over the forts, sideslipping and weaving with Göring taking photographs. General Falkenhayn was delighted with the result, so much so that Kronprinz Wilhelm exercised his royal prerogative and invested Loerzer and Göring with the Iron Cross 1st Class in the field.

By the end of June 1915, Loerzer asked to be transferred to a fighter squadron. He was transferred to FA.60 then to FA(A).203. On completion of his fighter training he was posted to Kek Jametz, where on 21 March 1916 he recorded his first victory. Ten days later he had raised his tally to two. He was badly wounded in the legs during a fight with Allied aircraft on 3 April 1916, which hospitalised him until January 1917. He was then posted briefly to Jasta 5 at the beginning of 1917 then to Jasta 17. Then at the end of 18 January 1917, he was given command of Jasta 26.

By the end of 1917 his personal tally had risen to twenty. Honours were to bestowed upon him before the year was out – among them the Knight's Cross with Swords of the Royal Hohenzollern House Order. On 12 March he was awarded the Orden Pour le Mérite and nine days later given command of JG.3 equipped with

Jasta 26 pilots on 5 February 1918, near Roulers. Pictured in front of a Fokker D.V, left to right, are: Vizefeldwebel Fritz Classen, father of Leutant Burchard; Unteroffizier Erich Buder, Vizefeldwebel Santjer; Monteau (mechanic); Offizierstellvertreter Otto Esswein; Second Lieutenant Cyril Ball (brother of Albert Ball VC who had been shot down by Esswein); Leutnant Dahm; Hauptmann Bruno Loerzer; Leutnant Helmut Lange; Unteroffizier Naubauer; Leutnant Willi Etzold; and Leutnant Burchard.

Fokker D.VIIs powered by BMW engines. This aircraft was to inflict heavy casualties on the Allied fighters right up to the end of the war.

Bruno Loerzer still continued to fly, usually with Jasta 26 alongside his younger brother, who before the war had been a pastor. In October 1918, he was promoted to Hauptmann and by the end of the war had raised his score of victories to forty-four.

During World War Two, Loerzer rose rapidly through the ranks to Leutnant-General of the Luftwaffe and was awarded the Iron Cross 1st Class and later the Knight's Cross of the Iron Cross. When he was promoted to Generaloberst, it was quite obvious to all that his long-term friendship with Feldmarschal Hermann Göring had a great influence on the decision. Bruno Loerzer died on 23 August 1960.

OBERLEUTNANT ERICH LÖWENHARDT

The son of a doctor, Erich Löwenhardt was born in Breslau on 7 April 1897. His education was at a military cadet school at Lichterfelde and on the outset of war he was posted to Infantrie-Regiment Nr.141. His regiment was moved immediately to the Eastern Front, where on 2 October 1914 he was commissioned in the rank of Leutnant. At the end of October he was wounded badly and was awarded the Iron Cross 2nd Class. On returning to his unit at the beginning of January 1915, he was assigned to duties in the Carpathian Mountains. It was whilst in action in the mountains that he saved the lives of five wounded soldiers. For this he was awarded the Iron Cross 1st Class and transferred to the Alpine Corps. In October of 1915, he requested a transfer to the German Army Air Service as an observer. After training and serving nearly a year as an observer Löwenhardt requested pilot training and was posted to FA(A).265 early in 1916. After nearly a year as a reconnaissance pilot, he undertook fighter training early in 1917 and was posted to Jasta 10 in March of that year.

A week after arriving at Jasta 10, Löwenhardt scored his first victory when he destroyed a French observation balloon belonging to 58 Cie over Reicourt. By September he had raised his tally to five and was slightly wounded in a dogfight with a British fighter. He managed to force land his aircraft near Roulers. On 6 November, with his tally raised to eight, his aircraft's lower wing broke whilst in combat and again he had to make a forced landing near Winkel St Eloi.

The new year started well. On 5 January he destroyed another observation balloon, bringing the number of balloons he had destroyed to five. Another two balloons followed on 12 and 15 March, together with a BF2b on 18 January. By the end of March he had raised his tally to fifteen. One week short of his twenty-first birthday he was appointed commander of Jasta 10, becoming one of the youngest commanders in the German Army Air Service. On 11 May with his tally at twenty, he was awarded the Knight's Cross with Swords of the Royal Hohenzollern House Order. On 31 May Löwenhardt was awarded the Orden Pour le Mérite.

Löwenhardt continued his destruction of Allied aircraft and by the end of July 1918 his tally had risen to forty-eight. During the months of June and July, he had been acting commander of JG.1, an incredible responsibility for a man who was still only twenty-one years old.

Oberleutnant Erich Löwenhardt (Orden Pour le Mérite, with fifty-four victories) was killed in action on 10 August 1918.

On 8 August 1918, a patrol led by Löwenhardt encountered a patrol of Sopwith Camels. Löwenhardt himself accounted for three whilst the rest scattered. This brought his total to fifty-one. On the next day two more victories upped it to fifty-three.

On 10 August, in a dogfight with SE5as from 56 Squadron RAF, he shot down a SE5a, but collided with Leutnant Alfred Wenz, a member of Jasta 11 whose patrol had joined up with that of Jasta 10. Both pilots took to their parachutes but Löwenhardt's failed to open and he was killed.

LEUTNANT JOSEF MAI

Josef Mai was born in a small town just outside Berlin on 3 March 1887. After an uneventful childhood he joined the army at the beginning of the war. In May 1915 he applied to join the German Army Air Service and was accepted. He began training as a pilot almost immediately and graduated on 28 July 1916. He was posted to Kasta 29 of KG.5, flying two-seater reconnaissance missions until he started his fighter pilot training in February 1917. On completing the course he was promoted to Offizierstellvertreter and assigned to Jasta 5 under the command of Oberleutnant Hans Berr. Within weeks he had claimed his first two victories: the first a Sopwith Camel over Rumaucourt, the second a DH5 over Selvigny. He was awarded the Iron Cross 2nd Class, followed by the Iron Cross 1st Class after his fifth victory at the end of November 1917.

Whilst at Jasta 5 he was joined by two other NCOs, Otto Könnecke and Fritz Rumey, they became known as the 'Golden Triumvirate' who, at the end of the war, had a combined score of 108 confirmed victories. All these 'kills', bar one, were achieved whilst they were serving with Jasta 5, thus making the squadron one of the most successful in the German Army Air Service.

In June 1918, the three NCOs were awarded the Golden Military Merit Cross, known as the Pour le Mérite für Unteroffizieres. The three pilots continued to score steadily as did many of the other pilots, who being officers began be awarded high honours for their achievements, including the coveted Orden Pour le Mérite.

Right through to September 1918, Josef Mai increased his score to thirty, ten of which were Sopwith Camels and another ten were Bristol Fighters, which was far more than many other holders of the Orden Pour le Mérite had achieved. The Jasta had seen a number of prominent pilots pass through, including Heinrich Gontermann and Paul Bäumer, both of whom were awarded the Orden Pour le Mérite.

Josef Mai was promoted to Leutnant and his name put forward for recommendation of the Orden Pour le Mérite. Könnecke and Rumey had both been given commissions and had been awarded the Orden Pour le Mérite, amongst other high awards. Why Josef Mai appears to have been held back is not known, there does not appear to be any reason why he should have been. He was one of the Jasta's top pilots and one of the highest scoring pilots and well liked. The war came to an end before the award could be processed.

Josef Mai died in Germany at the age of ninety-four on 18 January 1982.

Leutnant Josef Mai (second left) with Jasta 5 pilots, and Lieutenants Scholz and Wookey (sixth and eighth from left) of 11 Squadron RFC who were shot down over Boistrancourt on 17 October 1917.

Leutnant Josef Mai (Golden Military Merit Cross, with thirty victories).

OberLeutnant Carl Menckhoff

Born on 4 April 1883 at Herford, Westphalia, Carl Menckhoff joined the German Army at the age of twenty in 1903. His time in the army was short lived, within six weeks he was taken ill with acute appendicitis and invalided out. He returned to Herford where he stayed for the next eleven years. When war broke out in 1914 he immediately volunteered and joined Infantrie-Regiment Nr.106 at Leipzig. Such was the demand for men at the time that his training was a matter of collecting his uniform, cleaning his rifle and heading for the front line at Alsace-Lorraine, and ultimately the Battle of the Marne. Menckhoff was an aggressive soldier and rapidly made his mark. Toward the end of his first year as a soldier, he was selected for a mission behind the lines dressed in a French uniform, for which he was awarded the Iron Cross 1st Class. Within months he was seriously wounded during a battle and returned once again to Herford to recuperate.

His recovery was extremely slow and, when finally recovered, he was deemed to be unacceptable for infantry duties. Carl Menckhoff immediately applied for flying duties and was accepted. During his training it was discovered that his aggression on the ground was matched by his aggression in the air. He took to flying naturally and was a good pilot, but on the ground his maverick and cavalier attitude toward army discipline and etiquette caused problems. He may have been a good fighter, but he was not a good soldier; he was allowed to remain in the German Army Air Service because his instructors maintained that his exceptional flying ability outweighed his indifference toward the drillbook and army etiquette. The fact that Germany was in desperate need of pilots also may have had something to do with it.

Oberleutnant Carl Menckhoff (Orden Pour le Mérite, with thirty-nine victories) died in Switzerland in 1948.

His first posting was to the Eastern Front where he gained a great deal of flying knowledge but very little combat experience. Early in 1916, he was recalled for duty as an instructor, but his aggressive nature soon made it clear that he would be far better employed with a fighting squadron. He was posted to Flamers for a special short course in air combat, then early in 1917 he was posted to Jasta 3 in Flanders with promotion to Vizefeldwebel. Within days he had scored his first victory: a Nieuport XXIII of 29 Squadron RFC. Two more followed by the end of the month and by September he had raised his tally to twelve. On 28 September he was shot down and wounded in a dogfight by aircraft of 56 Squadron RFC. After recovering from his wounds he returned to Jasta 3 and by the end of 1917 had raised his tally to eighteen. In February 1918, he was awarded a commission and given command of Jasta 72. He was also awarded the Knight's Cross with Swords of the Royal Hohenzollern House Order. This was followed on 23 April 1918 by the award of the Orden Pour le Mérite.

The following four months saw Carl Menckhoff's tally rise to thirty-nine, then three days after his thirty-ninth victory he met his equal when he encountered Lieutenant William Avery of 95th Aero Squadron, USAS. After a short fight, Menckhoff was forced down behind Allied lines and taken prisoner. Following inter-rogation, he was transferred to Camp Montoire, near Orleans, where he joined an ever-growing number of pilots from the German Army Air Service. His impatience was fuelled by his aggression and tired of waiting for repatriation he escaped on 23 August and headed for Switzerland. One week later he crossed the border, remaining there till the end of the war. Seeing the state of Germany after the war, Carl Menckhoff decided to stay in Switzerland and set up business there. He remained in Switzerland until his death in 1948.

LEUTNANT GEORG MEYER

Like a large number of his contemporaries, Georg Meyer was one of Imperial Germany's top aces during World War One; he was also one of those aces who never became a household name. Unlike the Richthofens, the Udets and Boelckes, Georg Meyer stayed away from the limelight.

Born in Bremen on 11 January 1893, he started his military service in the infantry in 1911, serving in Infanterie-Regiment Nr.75. At the outbreak of war he joined the Guard Ersatz Division and fought at the front for the next two years. On 1 February 1916 he transferred to the Air Service and underwent training as a pilot, first at Johannisthal, then to Altenburg, and finally Hannover. On successfully completing the course in August, he was posted to FFA.69 in Macedonia together with his observer Oberleutnant Harmjanz. At the end of 1916 he was transferred to FA(A).253 where on 7 February 1917 he claimed the first of twenty-four victories when he shot down a Nieuport over Lemmes.

Two months later Meyer carried out the initial fighter pilot's course and was posted to Jasta 22 for further training. Taken under the wing of Josef Jacobs he was trans-ferred to Jasta 7 to complete his training. He claimed two victories in August, followed by another in September for which he received the Iron Cross 1st Class. He had already received the Iron Cross 2nd Class whilst serving with the infantry.

Leutnant Meyer was posted to Jasta 37 on 25 March 1918 and less than one month later became Staffelführer on 14 April. One month later he received the Hanseatic Cross of Bremen, followed by the Knight's Cross with Swords of the Royal Hohenzollern House Order. During the 'Black Day' of the German Army – 8 August 1918 when the German lines were broken on almost all fronts – Georg Meyer downed three aircraft and a balloon. In September he added five more to his tally, three more in October and his final one on 4 November; this brought his total to twnety-four confirmed victories. His name was submitted for the Orden Pour le Mérite on 5 November but before it could be granted the war ended.

After surviving the horrors of war Georg Meyer was killed in a motorcycle accident on 15 September 1926.

Unteroffizer Erich Mix

Mix was born on 27 June 1898 and enlisted in the infantry in 1916. He served with the infantry for a year then transferred to the German Army Air Service. After training he was posted to Royal Saxon Jasta 54 in June 1918 with the rank of Gefreiter.

He opened his First World War victory score by shooting down a French Salmson 2A2 over Tricot on 11 June 1918. By 30 October 1918 he accounted for two balloons and one unidentified enemy aircraft; this brought his victories to four. He was promoted to Unteroffizer on 10 September and later commissioned. His awards are believed to be the Iron Cross 1st and 2nd Class.

During the 1930s Mix enlisted in the Luftwaffe and on the outbreak of World War Two was an officer in JG.53. He was promoted to Major on 1 December 1939, and put in command of JG.2 where he began to fly ME109s on combat missions. On 17 September 1939 he reopened his First World War victory tally by downing a French Bloch 131 – this was not confirmed – but his next two victories on 21 September over a French Morane 406 and on 22 November over another Morane 406 were confirmed. This made his tally six confirmed and one uncon-firmed. He was awarded the Iron Cross 2nd Class on 29 September 1939.

On 19 May 1940 during the battle of France, he destroyed three enemy aircraft on the ground with a low-level strafing run at Cambrai; his official total victories now stood at eight. On 21 May he downed another Morane 406 then he himself was shot down by a Morane 406 over French lines, but he was able to make his way back to his unit. On 26 May 1940 he was awarded the Iron Cross 1st Class.

On 9 September he downed a Hurricane over the Channel but it was not until 7 July 1941 that he had his last official victory: a Blenheim V1 of 139 Squadron over Holland.

On 26 September 1941 he was placed in command of JG.1, then in August 1942 he became Kommodore of JG.1. In March 1943 he became Jagerführer at Bretagne. On 1 April 1944 he was promoted to Oberst.

Erich Mix survived World War Two and died in 1971. He was an unusual ace airman having victories in both world wars: five in World War One and six in World War Two.

Leutnant Max Ritter von Müller

Born on 1 January 1887 in Rottenburg, Lower Bavaria, Max Müller rose from relative obscurity to become one of Germany's top fighter aces of World War One. After serving an apprenticeship as locksmith, Müller joined the in army in 1912 as a driver where it was discovered that he had a natural mechanical aptitude. He soon came to the notice of his superiors and was assigned as chauffeur to the Bavarian War Minister. By this time Müller had acquired an interest in aviation and, it is said, that every time he opened the door for the minister he asked to be transferred to the Bavarian Army Air Service. His persistence was rewarded.

He was posted to the army Jastaschule at Schleissheim on 1 December 1913. After four months of training, he qualified as a pilot and received his certificate and Bavarian Pilot's Badge on 4 April 1914. With the situation deteriorating by the day, the German Army was mobilised, which included the air service. Müller was posted to FA.1b as a reconnaissance pilot and carried out several missions with his observer Leutnant Peter Muller (no relation). On 18 August 1914, whilst carrying out a reconnaissance mission in an Otto aircraft, he was attacked by a French Farman and was shot down. His aircraft fortunately came down in German-held territory and he was rescued from the wreckage; it was discovered he had broken both legs on impact. His observer was also rescued and had suffered minor injuries. Upon recovery Müller was back in the air, this time with the rank of Offizierstellvertreter and the Iron Cross 2nd Class.

At the beginning of January 1915 Müller was awarded the Bavarian medal of the Military Merit Cross 3rd Class with Crown and Swords. In April he was also awarded the Iron Cross 1st Class.

Müller was chosen to fly an extremely dangerous photographic mission on 13 December 1915 and was awarded the Bavarian Bravery Medal in Silver. The photographic missions were flown at such low levels that his aircraft was hit several times by ground fire, but the information he brought back regarding the French positions was invaluable. By May the following year he had made over 160 missions as a reconnaissance pilot. By now he was one of the most experienced reconnaissance pilots in the German Army Air Service, but he wanted to be a single-seater fighter pilot, so he applied for a transfer to a fighter squadron. He was transferred to single-seater training at Mannheim, where on 18 May 1916, after graduating, he was posted to Kek B of FFA.32.

Müller remained at Kek B until 1 September 1916 when he was posted to Jasta 2 under the command of the legendary Oswald Boelcke. It is testament to the regard in which Müller was held that he was one of the first pilots to be selected by Boelcke. On 10 October, he scored his first victory when he shot down a FE2b of 11 Squadron RFC. Within two weeks his tally had risen to five The formation of a new Jasta, Nr.28, prompted the move of a number of experienced pilots, including Max Müller and Leutnant Ray, to form the backbone of the squadron. By the end of June 1917, Müller's tally had risen to eighteen, making him the top-scoring fighter pilot in the Jasta.

His performance had not gone unnoticed and 28 June 1917 the King of Württemberg conferred the Military Merit Medal in Gold on Leutnant Max Müller.

The following month he was awarded one of the most exclusive awards of World War One, the Member's Cross with Swords of the Royal Hohenzollern House Order. On 26 August the unprecedented step of promoting him to a Leutnant in the regular army was taken. Usually these promotions were in the reserve and this was the first time this had ever occurred.

Max Müller went from strength to strength; by the beginning of September 1917 he had raised his tally to twenty-seven and with it came the Orden Pour le Mérite, making him the most decorated pilot (next to Manfred von Richthofen) in the German Army Air Service. Almost immediately came another high award, the Bavarian Gold Bravery Medal, which was normally only awarded to non-commissioned officers, but Müller had been recommended for it as an NCO and it had taken so long to be processed. Nevertheless the award was given to him, making him the only aviator to hold both the Bavarian Silver and Gold Bravery Medal. Max Müller was given the Gold Bravery Award not for one single act of bravery, but for his performance between April 1917 and June 1917, when he shot down twelve enemy aircraft.

A well-earned leave resulted in him asking to rejoin his old squadron Jasta 2, also known as Jasta Boelcke, to assist his old friend Erwin Böhme in bringing it into shape. His request was granted and he was posted to Jasta 2 on 3 November 1917. On 6 January 1918, following the death of the commanding officer Leutnant Walter von Bülow-Bothkamp, and with his own tally standing at thirty-six, Müller took over command of Jasta 2. Three days later in Albatros D.Va Nr.5405/17 over Moorslede,

Leutnant Max Ritter von Müller (Orden Pour le Mérite and top Bavarian ace, with thirty-six victories).

he and his patrol attacked an RE8 of 21 Squadron RFC, flown by Captain G.F.W. Zimmer and his observer 2nd Lieutenant H.A. Somerville. As he attacked, two SE5as flown by two very experienced fighter pilots, Captains F.O. Soden and R.L. Childlaw-Roberts, jumped him at the same time from above and behind. Müller's aircraft shuddered from the machine-gun assault and spun towards the ground in flames. As the searing flames reached his cockpit, the brave Müller, who was not wearing a parachute, jumped to a quick death.

After the war Müller was posthumously awarded the Knight's Cross of the Military Max-Joseph Order, which conferred a knighthood on him that was backdated to 11 November 1917. Leutnant Max Ritter von Müller was thirty-one years old.

OBERLEUTNANT ALBERT MÜLLER-KAHLE

This future holder of the Orden Pour le Mérite was born on 29 June 1894, the son of a Lutheran pastor. When World War One began he enlisted as a cadet in Fussartillerie-Regiment Nr.20 but the next year applied to join the German Army Air Service. Accepted, he underwent training as an artillery spotter and observer.

Serving with FA(A).202, FA(A).215, FFA.47 and FA.6, he saw active service on the Western Front in sectors at Douai, Somme and along the North Sea coast. Müller-Kahle became very proficient in calling in artillery fire on specific targets.

Oberleutnant Albert Müller-Kahle (Orden Pour le Mérite), with the observer who directed the heavy guns (Pariskanone) which bombarded Paris in March 1918.

The Germans began to use heavy artillery mounted on railway trucks and Müller-Kahle was able to direct their fire on important strategic targets such as the coal mines at Béthune.

So proficient did Müller-Kahle become in artillery spotting that he was selected early in 1918 to become an observer for the new long-range guns named the Kaiser Wilhelm Geschutz, designed by Professor Rausenberger of Krupps, to bombard Paris.

These monster guns (eight in total) weighed 142 tons and had a barrel length of 130ft. At 07:15 on 23 March 1918 these guns opened fire on Paris with Müller-Kahle in the air acting as artillery fire adjuster. The Geschutz guns were fired 110km from behind German lines. Müller-Kahle climbed to 5,000m then flew to within 39km of Paris and directed fire. Coming under heavy anti-aircraft fire and machine guns from British fighters, he managed to complete his spotting and return to base. It was estimated that over 400 of the giant projectiles were fired into Paris. Müller-Kahle's spotting for the guns did not last long as it was considered dangerous to the security of the gun emplacements. Agents in the city itself carried out the spotting after the initial attack by means of a coded telephone circuit that operated via Switzerland.

Albert Müller-Kahle was awarded the Knight's Cross with Swords of the Royal Hohenzollern House Order on 11 October 1917. The following month, whilst with FA.6, came the Knight's Cross 2nd Class with Swords of the Saxon Albert Order.

One year later he was awarded the prestigious Orden Pour le Mérite. He survived the war and became a Generalmajor in the Luftwaffe during World War Two.

LEUTNANT MAX RITTER VON MULZER

Max Mulzer was born on 9 July 1893 in Bavaria, the son of a cavalry officer. He enlisted in the army as a Fähnrich in 1910 and graduated as an officer cadet on 10 July 1914 from the Könighiches Bayern Kadettenkorps and joined Cheveaulegers-Regiment Nr.8. He was commissioned on 13 December 1914 as a Leutnant, and fought in some of the earliest battles around Alsace and Nancy. Later his regiment was moved north and was in action on the Somme, Arras and Flanders, but his eyes were on the future. Mulzer asked to be transferred to the Bavarian Army Air Service to train as a pilot and on 20 August 1915 his request was approved. He was posted to the army's Jastaschule at Schleissheim, where after four months' training, he graduated obtaining his flying certificate and Bavarian Pilot's Badge.

He was posted to FFA.4b on 13 December 1915 and after two months was transferred, along with Oswald Boelcke and Max Immelmann, to FFA.62 where training as a fighter pilot began. On 13 March 1916, he scored his first victory, albeit an unconfirmed one, when he shot down a Morane Saulnier and was awarded the Iron Cross 2nd Class. For this he received the Ehrenbecher dem Sieger im Luftkampfe (*honour goblet to the victor in air battle*). Although this was an award that could not be worn, it was recognised in the same vein as an decoration or medal and was entered on the recipients war record. Mulzer made up for the unconfirmed 'kill' on 30 March when he shot down and had confirmed a Vickers FB5 Gunbus from 11 Squadron RFC over north Wancourt.

Leutnant Max Ritter von Mulzer (Orden Pour le Mérite, with ten victories). He was the first Bavarian airman to be awarded the Orden Pour le Mérite.

On 1 May 1916, after four months of frontline flying, Mulzer was awarded his Bavarian Pilot's Badge. This was a perfect example of the way that the German Army Air Service made a pilot earn his wings.

At the beginning of June Mulzer was posted to join Kek Nord in Russia where he quickly made his presence felt by scoring three more victories in a matter of ten days, bringing his tally to six. For this he was awarded the Iron Cross 1st Class. On 18 June, after scoring his fourth victory, his friend and mentor Max Immelmann was killed. It fell to Max Mulzer to carry Immelmann's Ordenskissen (*orders cushion*) at his friend's funeral.

In June Max Mulzer was posted to Doui to join FFA.32, then temporarily with Kek 'B', where he increased his tally to eight. The eighth victory brought Mulzer the Orden Pour le Mérite, the first Bavarian to be honoured with Prussia's highest award. On 26 September, he was further honoured when he received the Knight's Cross of the Military Max-Joseph Order. This in effect made him a Knight and allowed him to change his name to Max Ritter von Mulzer. By the beginning of August, von Mulzer had raised his tally to ten. At the beginning of September he was assigned to the AFP.6 at Valenciennes to test a number of new aircraft.

On 26 September 1916, von Mulzer took off to test Albatros D.I Nr.4424/16 but, during the test flight, the aircraft side-slipped at low altitude and crashed. Max von Mulzer died from his injuries.

LEUTNANT ULRICH NECKEL

Ulrich Neckel was born in Bavaria on 23 January 1898. His early childhood was like many others of his age at the time: mundane. Neckel though was always seeking adventure and at the age of sixteen, when World War One began, he volunteered for the army. He was sent for training as an artillery man with the Holstein Feldartillerie-Regiment Nr.24. On completing the training in January 1915, he was sent to the Eastern Front and was in action immediately. Within six months he had been awarded the Iron Cross 2nd Class for distinguishing himself under fire. The terrible conditions at the Eastern Front were beginning to take their toll on Neckel and made him think of ways to escape the cold and the mud. In September 1916 he applied for transfer to the German Army Air Service and was accepted. He was posted to the Jastaschule at Gotha in November 1916 and graduated as a pilot in February 1917.

After joining the Air Service to get away from the Eastern Front, he was posted back to the same front to join FA.25. After flying a number of reconnaissance missions he applied for training as a fighter pilot and in August was sent to Jastaschule at Valenciennes. On graduating in September, he was posted to Jasta 12 and promoted to Gefreiter. Neckel opened his tally on 21 September 1917 when he shot down a Sopwith Pup from 46 Squadron RFC over eastern Monchy-le-Preux. By the end of the month he had increased his score to two after shooting down a DH5 of 41 Squadron. His total stood at three by the end of the year.

Leutnant Ulrich Neckel (Orden Pour le Mérite with Jasta 12, with thirty victories) died of tuberculosis on 11 May 1928.

Such was Ulrich Neckel's success in the first quarter of 1918 that he was commissioned to Leutnant and awarded the Iron Cross 1st Class. At the end of April his tally had risen to ten. Neckel continued to be a thorn in the side of the Allies and had taken his score to twenty by the end of July. At the beginning of September he was transferred to Jasta 19 and increased his tally in that month to twenty-four. Neckel was awarded the Knight's Cross with Swords of the Royal Hohenzollern House Order on 24 August and was given command of Jasta 6 in JG.1 on 1 September.

When the Armistice came in November, Leutnant Ulrich Neckel's score stood at thirty. Not long after the war he contracted tuberculosis and, after a very long illness, died in Italy on 11 May 1928.

LEUTNANT LANDWEHR FRIEDRICH NIELEBOCK

The son of an army officer, Friedrich Nielebock was born in Weissenwarthe, northern Germany, on 4 July 1882.

When World War One began in 1914 Nielebock was doing his volunteer reserve duty with a foot artillery regiment at Lauenburg. He realised that his artillery training and experience could be put to best use in the air as an artillery spotter and reconnaissance observer. Nielebock then had a couple of weeks as a balloon observer with Feldluftschiffer Abteilung Nr.29 (*field airship unit*), but then applied to go to observer school with the German Army Air Service. After one month's observer training Nielebock joined FA(A).250; he was wounded on 24 January 1918.

The very nature of Leutnant Nielebock's job meant that he kept a low profile throughout his career as did most of the observers. The high-profile fliers were the fighter pilots, but the job of the observation pilots and observers was equally important and, in some cases, more so. On 2 June 1918, Leutnant Nielebock was awarded the Orden Pour le Mérite and his citation, written by his commander Hauptmann Schäffer, is a record of his service and bravery in combat. It is seen here in its entirety because it is one of the finest examples of a citation written during World War One.

Since the beginning of the war, interrupted only for his training as an aerial observer, Leutnant Nielebock has been continuously in the Field actively engaged with the combat troops at Ypres and Wytschaette salients. His aerial accomplishments, shown in 18 months of activity on the Flanders Front, are to be praised. Up until now he has carried out 280 successful missions. He is an artillery observer and in that capacity has carried out 196 fire missions, of which 134 had positive effect. Furthermore, he found and reported by radio 728 artillery battery positions and 331 other important targets. These were accomplished under heavy fire from flak by both day and night. His performance in the battles of recent days is deserving of special recognition. In two days of total reliance on his information, the Staff Headquarters of the 18th Reserve Corps took measures that were decisive for the success of the subsequent battles.

On April 18 (1918), based on his report, the regrouping of the enemy artillery behind the gas barrage could be detected. From other reconnaissance sources there were no useful information whatsoever. His findings provided the basis of our orders to attack. After constant rains, the weather on Kemmel Mountain unexpectedly cleared and Leutnant Nielebock was able to report on the new artillery positions in time. Since they had been thought to be much closer to the Front than they were, orders for all of our artillery for the next morning had to be revised in a few hours. This usually impossible deed was only accomplished through his untiring dedication.

Multiple flights on the same day are no exception to him and when there are possibilities for effective reconnaissance, he flies until the fuel tank is empty. Not only Leutnant Nielebock's work as an artillery observer deserves recognition but so does his work in the development of cooperation between the fliers and the artillery. His recommendations in this area have led us to maximum use of both arms. He has given us many new ideas to execute, especially an excellent method of delivering important target information along the main front in connection with the Group 'Wytschaette'. Leutnant Nielebock carried out his orders with great daring. Air battles and damage to his machine were common. In four instances he had to make emergency landings on account of battle damage. On January 24, 1918, he was wounded in air battle, but after three weeks, still on a cane, reported as fit for service with the unit.

Schäffer, Hauptmann und Abteilungsführer

Fliegerabteilung A 250

Leutnant Friedrich Nielebock survived the war and returned to gain professional qualifications in the building trade and became a director of a large company.

Leutnant Friedrich Nielebock held the Orden Pour le Mérite, which was awarded for bravery in combat as an observer directing deadly artillery fire.

Leutnant Friedrich Theodor Noltenius

The son of a Professor of Medicine, Friedrich Theodor Noltenius was born in Bremen on 8 January 1894. With his family's background there was only one profession for him to enter and on leaving school he entered university to study to become a doctor. Then came the interruption that was to put his career on hold: World War One. On 4 August 1914 he joined the Feldartillerie-Regiment Nr.13 and was immediately posted to the Eastern Front. From December 1914 until December 1915, Noltenius fought on the Eastern Front; during this period he was awarded the Iron Cross 2nd Class and a promotion to Unteroffizier. The regiment was then transferred to France where they saw action until November 1917. On 5 October 1916 Noltenius was given a commission and during battle in April 1917 he was wounded and awarded the Iron Cross 1st Class for his part. This was followed three months later by the award of the Knight's Cross of the Württemberg Military Merit Order.

Leutnant Noltenius applied for transfer to the German Army Air Service and was accepted. On 3 November he started his training at FEA.1 at Altenburg, and then progressed to advanced training at FEA.10 at Boblingen at the beginning of 1918. On graduation he was sent to AFP.7 in preparation for posting to a combat unit. During this period he spent time with FA(A).234 before being posted to Jastaschule II at Nivelles at the end of June 1918. On completion of his training he was immediately posted to Jasta 27 of JG.3. What is remarkable about Noltenius is that in the next four months he accounted for twenty-one enemy aircraft which indicates that he was a natural pilot and, in the short period of time that he was fighting, he possessed the ability to adapt this skill to that of a fighter pilot.

The Jasta took possession of Fokker D.VIIs early in August and, by the end of the month, had claimed three victories. But not all was plain sailing. Maybe it was jealousy on the part of the older pilots, but by the end of September Noltenius had increased his score by ten, bringing his total of 'kills' to thirteen in just two months. Disputes with other pilots over claims resulted in Noltenius being transferred to Jasta 6 of JG.1 on 27 September 1918, but within a month he was in a head-on clash with the Jasta's Staffelführer, Ulrich Neckel. The problem was that when Jastas flew together and got involved in fights with Allied aircraft, some of the victories were shared, or deemed to be squadron victories. Some claims were even settled by the throw of a dice between the claiming parties and sometimes the more senior pilots pulled rank. It appears that the latter happened on six separate occasions with Noltenius and he objected. Within two weeks he was on the move again, this time to Jasta 11, where he remained until the Armistice. By this time he had increased his score to twenty-one, a truly remarkable tally in such a short time. He was put forward for the prestigious award of the Orden Pour le Mérite, but it was too late for it to be awarded; however, three days before the Armistice he was awarded the Knight's Cross with Swords of the Royal Hohenzollern House Order.

After the war Noltenius fought against the Spartacists, a group of German left-wingers who formed the nucleus of the German Communist Party. However, he later resumed his medical studies to become a doctor. He moved to South America in 1923 where he stayed for ten years. On his return to Germany in 1933 he started flying again only to lose his life in a crash in 1936.

OBERLEUTNANT ZUR SEE THEODOR OSTERKAMP

Born the son of a forestry worker in Duren in the Rhineland on 15 April 1892, Theodor Osterkamp was studying forestry when war was declared. Rather than be conscripted into the army, Osterkamp enlisted in the Naval Flying Corps in August 1914. His initial request was to be trained as a pilot, but the need for observers was greater. On completion of his training on 24 March 1915, he was posted to II Marine Feldflieger Abteilung (*naval field flying unit*) in which he flew operational missions along the Belgian coast for the next two years. During this period he was promoted to Vizeflugmeister and transferred to I Marine Feldflieger Abteilung. His success was rewarded with the Iron Cross 2nd Class and his commission on 13 July 1916 to the rank of Leutnant der Reserve der Matrosenartillerie (*lieutenant of reserves of naval artillery*).

The repetitive missions began to make Osterkamp look toward the single-seat fighter pilots, who appeared to have excitement (misplaced, as he soon found out) surrounding them all the time. In February 1917, Osterkamp applied for fighter pilot training. In March he was accepted and began his training, graduating on 14 April. He was posted to Marine-Feld-Jagdstaffel Nr.1 (MFJ.1) the same week and opened his score on 30 April when he shot down a Sopwith Camel over Oostkerke. At the end of July 1917, Osterkamp had raised his tally to five and on 20 August was rewarded with the Iron Cross 1st Class and the Knight's Cross of the Royal Hohenzollern House Order. A Spad from Esc. Spa.31 fell under his guns on 24 September, raising his tally to six. In October he was given command of MFJ.2 and promotion to Oberleutnant zur See.

His baptism under fire was one that didn't exactly inspire confidence. Whilst on a solo familiarisation flight in a new Fokker E.V Eindecker, he was jumped by three Spads; the end result was that he had to bale out. Fortunately he landed unhurt behind his own lines. At the beginning of 1918, Osterkamp spent time reorganising the MFJ.2, making it more efficient and this was reflected in the way that victories started to come the unit's way. By the end of July 1918, Osterkamp's personal tally had risen from six to nineteen, and by the end of August was standing at twenty-three. For this he received the Orden Pour le Mérite on 2 September. His war against the Allies ended in 1918, but he continued to fight in the Baltic area until 1920.

In 1935, Theodor Osterkamp joined the Luftwaffe as it started to build. He was given command of Jagdfliegerschule Nr.1 in 1939, a post he held until the following year when he took over command of JG.51. Almost immediately he was in action against the French and in the months of May and July shot down a total of six Allied fighters, which included three Hurricanes and a Spitfire. For this he was awarded the Knight's Cross of the Iron Cross on 22 August 1940. He became Commander of Fighters in northern France and later in Sicily he held the rank of Leutnantgeneral. He also became very critical of the High Command and the way they were operating the war in the air; because of his outspokenness, he was retired in 1944. It was probably the tremendous respect that the Luftwaffe pilots and ground crews felt for him that prevented an alternative fate befalling him.

HAUPTMANN PAUL FREIHERR VON PECHMANN

Paul Pechmann was born on 28 December 1899 at Gauchsmühle, near Nurnberg. He began his military career by enlisting in Fussartillerie-Regiment 7 stationed in Cologne. He was promoted to Leutnant in 1914 but realised that life as an infantryman was not for him and applied for transfer to the new air service that was being formed. In June 1915 he started training as an observer and after a year he was posted to the Flieger Abteilung Artillerie at Wahn. He went with this unit to the front but then transferred to FFA.6. After he had completed several missions he was finally awarded his Observer's Badge. He then saw service as an artillery observer with FA.215 and FA.217 on the Flanders section of the Western Front. During his three years' service with these units, his outstanding abilities brought him several decorations, including the Knight's Cross of the Royal Hohenzollern House Order.

In the summer of 1917 he was promoted to Oberleutnant and given command of FA.33 followed by command of FA(A).217. On 31 July 1917 Pechmann was awarded the Orden Pour le Mérite. The prestigious award was presented to him personally by Kaiser Wilhelm II in a special ceremony not far from the front line. Included in the citation for the decoration were the words: 'For having carried out over 700 operational sorties against the enemy.'

Although he had qualified as a pilot, Pechmann's Orden Pour le Mérite was awarded for services as an observer with FA.215 and FA.217. He was the first artillery and reconnaissance flier to gain this prestigious award.

Pechmann remained in service with his unit on the Western Front and was flying during the Battle of Cambrai when the British made use of tanks. Pechmann's unit was responsible for re-supplying the hard-pressed German forces – which they did with distinction.

Like many of his contemporaries amongst the observers, Pechmann's contribution to the air war was one that was always going to be overshadowed by the flamboyant single-seat fighter pilots. But he, like his fellow observers, did their job and did it well.

Pechmann was never one to shirk from duty and would never order one of his men to do something that he himself would not do. During one very foggy morning he ordered his pilot to take off on a very important low-level reconnaissance mission. Accompanied by two fighters, who incidently could not see him, they came under very intense ground fire. Pechmann had ordered his pilot to fly very low because of the weather, and it was not until they returned that they counted 125 holes in his aircraft.

During the latter days of the war, Pechmann carried out supply drops to beleaguered troops, but finally spares and fuel for his aircraft ran out and they could do no more.

After World War One Pechmann remained in the German Army Air Service but retired in 1920 as a Hauptmann.

Leutnant Fritz Pütter (Orden Pour le Mérite, with twenty-five victories with Jastas 9 and 68) died of injuries on 10 August 1918.

LEUTNANT FRITZ PÜTTER

Fritz Pütter was born in Duelmen, Westphalia, on 14 January 1895. World War One was declared on 4 August 1914 and on 24 August Fritz Pütter joined the Westphalian Infantry Regiment. After scant training he was sent to the Eastern Front and was immediately involved in heavy fighting. Early in 1915 Pütter was involved in an incident of heroism that not only earned him the Iron Cross 2nd Class, but a battle-field commission to Leutnant. On 12 October 1915, he was transferred to Infanterie-Regiment Nr.370. It was then that he began to be interested in the German Army Air Service and in February 1916 he applied for a transfer. He was accepted and posted to FEA.8 at Graudenz on 20 May 1916.

On completion of his flying training on 9 December 1916, he was posted to FA.251 as a reconnaissance pilot. After two months of flying reconnaissance missions, Pütter requested a transfer to fighter pilot duties. He was sent to Jastaschule and on graduating was posted to Jasta 9 on 17 March 1917. He opened his tally on 14 April when he shot down a French observation balloon whilst on patrol over east Suippes. By the end of the year he had increased his tally to five – all French observation balloons.

On 12 January 1918, Pütter scored his first victory over another aircraft when he shot down a Spad, but finished the day by adding another balloon to his tally. By the end of January he had added another two aircraft and two balloons to his tally, bringing the total to ten. Pütter was awarded the Iron Cross 1st Class in February although the month itself was one of the quietest the Jasta had known. Pütter was posted to Jasta 68 on 3 February as Commandant and spent the month familiarising himself with the aircraft and pilots. However, things were to change in March and, by the end of the month, Pütter had shot down another six aircraft: his tally was fifteen. For this he was awarded the Knight's Cross with Swords of the Royal Hohenzollern House Order.

Pütter continued to score steadily against the Allies and by the end of May had raised his tally to twenty-five. On 31 May he was awarded the Orden Pour le Mérite. Disaster struck on 16 July when he encountered enemy aircraft and engaged them. During the ensuing dogfight the tracer ammunition in his Fokker caught fire. Although very badly burned, he managed to limp back to his base where he was rushed to hospital. Later he was transferred to a burns hospital in Bonn where he died of his injuries on 10 August.

Hauptmann Wilhelm Reinhard

Born in Düsseldorf in 1890, Wilhelm Reinhard started his army career with Badisches Fussartillerie-Regiment Nr.14 in 1908. In 1914, when the regiment went to war, Reinhard had been promoted to Leutnant, but he was unfortunately wounded in action on 11 November; for this he was awarded the Iron Cross 2nd Class. Returning to the front, Reinhard continued to fight and in March 1915 was awarded the Order of the Zähringen Lion and a promotion to Oberleutnant for continual bravery under fire.

The following month Reinhard applied for transfer to the German Army Air Service. His application was accepted and he was assigned to observer school on 6 June 1915. After graduating he was posted to FA(A).205 on 24 August 1915. For the next six months Reinhard flew missions along the front. In March 1916 he applied for pilot training and was accepted. He was sent to FEA.6 in Grossenhain for training, completing the course in June 1915. He was then posted to the Balkans to serve with FA.28 as a reconnaissance pilot. For almost a year Wilhelm Reinhard served on this bleak front, along with the remainder of the almost-forgotten FA.28. Then at the end of May 1917 he was reprieved and assigned to Jastaschule in Leipzig for initial training as fighter pilot. From there he went to Jastaschule in Warsaw to convert to single-seat fighter aircraft. It was at Warsaw that he finally received his Bulgarian Pilot's Badge.

On graduating he was assigned to Jasta 11 on 10 July 1917, which was now part of JG.11 in Flanders and under the command of the legendary Rittmeister Manfred Freiherr von Richthofen. Wilhelm Reinhard's arrival came at a time when the role of leader seemed to be changing almost weekly; the following day, on 11 July, the new commander of Jasta 11, Kurt Wolff, was injured during combat. Admitted to hospital, Kurt Wolff joined his Geschwaderführer Manfred von Richthofen who had a few days earlier been wounded in the head. Reinhard was sent for and told that he was to take over as temporary leader of Jasta 11. He had been selected because of his experience, maturity and rank, even though he did not have one 'kill' to his credit. However, he rectified this problem on 22 July when he shot down a Sopwith 1½ Strutter. There was one slight drawback though: two other pilots Leutnant Karl Deilmann and

JG.1 Staffelführer on 21 March 1918. Left to right are: Leutnant Kurt Wüsthoff, Hauptmann Wilhelm Reinhard, Rittmeister Manfred von Richthofen, Oberleutnant Erich Löwenhardt and Oberleutnant Lothar von Richthofen.

Vizefeldwebel Heinrich Küllmer each claimed to have shot down the same aircraft. It wasn't until Richthofen returned from hospital and resumed leadership that the problem was resolved: the victory was given to Reinhard.

Over the following months Reinhard continued to score steadily and with the victories came more awards. By September 1917 his tally had risen to six, but then he was wounded in the thigh and hospitalised. In the meantime newly promoted Oberleutnant Kurt Wolff returned to take over command of Jasta 11 on 11 September. This was a very short command as Kurt Wolff died four days later when he was shot down in a fight.

It wasn't until November that Reinhard was fit enough to return to his Jasta; during this period the Jasta was under the command of Oberleutnant Kurt-Bertram von Döring. When Reinhard did return, the new commander was Lothar von Richthofen. He was no longer required as commander of Jasta 11, but Jasta 6 required a new commander as theirs, Leutnant Hans Adam, had just been killed.

Wilhelm Reinhard was now the most senior officer in the Geschwader after Manfred von Richthofen. Jasta 6, under the steady command of Reinhard continued to score steadily despite the atrocious weather conditions that plagued the area throughout the winter.

On 21 April 1918, two flights took off after reports that Allied aircraft had been seen in the vicinity. The first flight was led by Leutnant der Reserve Hans Weiss, the other by Manfred von Richthofen. When all the aircraft returned with the exception of Richthofen, concern swept through the Jasta. Three aircraft were sent out immediately to look for the Geschwaderführer, but they found nothing. When it was confirmed two days later that his aircraft had been shot down and Manfred von Richthofen killed, Oberleutnant Karl Bodenschatz produced a handwritten note from Manfred von Richthofen stating that in the event of his death Oberleutnant Wilhelm Reinhard was to take his place.

In the following months Reinhard led by the example set by Richthofen from the front and by June 1918 had taken his tally to twenty. It was at this time that Reinhard went on leave, part of which would be spent at Aldershof testing new aircraft. On 3 July Reinhard watched Oberleutnant Hermann Göring testing a Dornier-designed Zeppelin-Lindau D.I fighter. After landing the aircraft Göring asked Reinhard if he would like to put the aircraft through its paces. Reinhard took off and after a few manoeuvres at around 1,000ft, there was a sharp crack and the wing struts broke, causing the wings to collapse. The crippled aircraft spun into the ground killing Wilhelm Reinhard instantly.

Hermann Göring replaced Wilhelm Reinhard as commander of Jagdgeschwader Freiherr von Richthofen Nr.1, as it was now called. Reinhard had been proposed for the Orden Pour le Mérite, but with his tragic and untimely death the award was never approved.

OBERLEUTNANT LOTHAR FREIHERR VON RICHTHOFEN

Younger brother of the famous Red Baron, Lothar von Richthofen was born on the Richthofen family estate at Breslau on 27 September 1894. Prior to the outbreak of World War One he joined a cavalry regiment and when war broke out was serving with Dragoner-Regiment Nr.4. Spurred on by the example of his elder brother, he transferred to the German Army Air Service in the autumn of 1915. Serving as an observer with KG.4 he was determined to be a fighter pilot and gained his pilot's certificate in 1916.

On 6 March 1917 he had his first operational posting as a pilot to Jasta 11, commanded by his brother Manfred. He scored his first victory on 28 March 1917 when he shot down FE2b No.7715 of 25 Squadron RFC. Remarkably, his victory total began to increase almost daily. On 11 April he shot down two aircraft, another two on 13 April ,and two more on 14 April. By 30 April he had downed another nine aircraft; his tally came to sixteen confirmed kills. He was awarded the Iron Cross 1st Class to add to his Iron Cross 2nd Class.

The first day of May dawned and Lothar continued his pursuit of Germany's opponents. A FE2d of 25 Squadron went down beneath his guns, bringing his total to seventeen confirmed victories. On 10 May he was awarded the Knight's Cross with Swords of the Royal Hohenzollern House Order. By 13 May another seven aircraft were shot down to bring his score of kills to twenty-four. But the 13th proved unlucky for him as he was badly wounded in combat and hospitalised. However, his luck returned on the following day. Lying in hospital he was awarded Prussia's highest honour for bravery in combat, the Orden Pour le Mérite. A short five months afterwards the same award was given to his brother Manfred.

Lothar returned to flying duty on 15 September 1917 and took command of Jasta 11. Six weeks later on 9 November he was back in combat and shot down a BF2b of 8 Squadron near Zonnebecke. On 23 November he added his twenty-sixth kill to his score by bringing down another BF2b. It was three months into 1918 before he scored again. On 11 March he shot down a BF2b of 62 Squadron, followed the next day by two more BF2bs.

The next day was 13 March and again the number proved unlucky for Lothar when he was severely wounded in combat. Some consolation was that he was promoted to Oberleutnant whilst in hospital. He was also awarded the Bavarian Military Merit Order 4th Class with Swords. Returning to Jasta 11 on 19 July he shot down his thirtieth aircraft – a Camel of 73 Squadron – on 25 July. Ten more enemy aircraft went to his credit during August – three of them in one day (8 August). His final victories came on 12 August when he brought down two Camels of 98 and 209 Squadrons: his total stood at forty confirmed victories.

However, again he was badly wounded and did not return to combat. Lothar survived the war and returned to flying after the Armistice, but died in a flying accident on 4 July 1922.

Oberleutnant Lothar Freiherr von Richthofen (Orden Pour le Mérite, with forty victories) being helped out of his Albatros D.III Scout, 1917.

LEUTNANT DER RESERVE PETER RIEPER

Born on 13 April 1887, near Hannover, Peter Rieper qualified as a doctor in 1912. The following year he enlisted in the army reserve and in August 1914 transferred to the regular army, serving with Feldartillerie-Regiment Nr.74 as an NCO.

He was wounded in action whilst serving with his regiment. When fit for duty he requested training as a balloon observer for which his artillery training and experience were valuable skills. His request was granted and after training he qualified in the dangerous balloon observer role. Serving with Ballonzug Nr.19 as an artillery spotter and intelligence gatherer he quickly found out just how dangerous being a balloon observer was. Seated alone in a wicker basket slung under a tethered balloon, the observer made an easy target for enemy aircraft. His only contact with the ground was by telephone cable that often broke, leaving the observer useless. If attacked the observer could – if uninjured – make a quick exit by a static line parachute attached to the basket.

By 1916 he was promoted to Leutnant der Reserve Ballon-Beobachter (*balloon observer*) but had a close call in spring when his balloon was attacked by four enemy fighters. Rieper was busy directing artillery fire on an enemy rail marshalling yard and failed to notice the approaching fighters. Armed with only a Mauser rifle, he returned fire but was no match for aircraft machine guns. Luckily for Peter Rieper, the German ace Max Immelmann came to his rescue and saw off the four fighters. Rieper's accurate artillery spotting resulted in the destruction of the marshalling yard.

Fate caught up with him on 3 June 1918 when aloft near Villers-Cottert Allied gunfire opened up and his balloon began to burn – riddled with machine-gun fire. In the barrage of fire Peter Rieper was badly wounded in the shoulder and decided to take to his parachute. Leaping from the doomed balloon with seconds to spare, he landed in front of German lines with such force that he broke his leg. Badly wounded he was taken to hospital but was declared as unfit for further service at the front.

A month later on 7 July 1918 he was awarded the Orden Pour le Mérite – the only German balloon observer to do so. He survived the war and went into business.

OBERLEUTNANT FRIEDRICH RITTER VON RÖTH

Friedrich Röth was born in Nurnburg on 29 September 1893 to a military family. He started his military career at the outbreak of war by volunteering to join Bayerisches Feldartillerie-Regiment Nr.8. Because of his background, he was immediately promoted to Unteroffizier. In his regiment's first action Röth was seriously injured and spent almost a year in hospital. It was during his time in hospital that he received his commission to Leutnant on 29 May 1915. It was also at this time that he considered a career move to the German Army Air Service. After recuperating Röth applied for pilot training, and after just a few weeks was severely injured in a flying accident during training. The accident put him back in hospital for almost a year, but he was able to qualify as a pilot in February 1917.

Röth was assigned to FA(A).296b on 1 April 1917 and carried out a number of reconnaissance sorties. In June 1917 he was awarded the Bavarian Military Merit

Oberleutnant Friedrich Ritter von Röth (Orden Pour le Mérite, with twenty-eight victories).

Leutnant Fritz Rumey (Orden Pour le Mérite, with forty-five victories) was killed in action on 27 September 1918.

Order 4th Class with Swords; then began a series of moves to different Jastas. On 10 September he was posted to Jastaschule 1, then to Jasta 34 on the 17th, and to Jasta 23 on 4 October. He was awarded the Iron Cross 1st Class on 1 November for his dedication to his role as a reconnaissance pilot.

January 1918 turned Röth from a reconnaissance pilot into an aggressive attacking pilot: on 25 January he attacked and shot down three reconnaissance balloons all within ten minutes of each other. For this dangerous mission he was to be awarded the Knight's Cross of the Military Max-Joseph Order; he thus had the honour of changing his name to Friedrich *Ritter von* Röth. During the following month another award was made: the Knight's Cross with Swords of the Royal Hohenzollern House Order.

On 24 April 1918, Röth took command of Jasta 16. By this time he had raised his tally to ten: nine of which were balloons, the other being an RE8 of 16 Squadron RFC. He was promoted to Oberleutnant on 19 August and, having reached twenty-two victories, was awarded the Orden Pour le Mérite on 9 September. On the cessation of hostilities Röth's tally had risen to twenty-eight, of which twenty were observation balloons – all scored in multiples of two or three during probing missions over enemy lines.

Germany's defeat was something that Röth could not come to terms with. He had been convinced that Germany was unbeatable and that right was on their side throughout the conflict. On New Year's Eve 1918 at the age of twenty-five, he committed suicide.

LEUTNANT FRITZ RUMEY

Fritz Rumey was born in Königsberg, Bavaria, on 3 March 1891. In 1911 he volunteered to join the Infanterie-Regiment Nr.45 as an infantryman. Three years later, at the outbreak of World War One, his regiment was mobilised and sent to the Russian Front. Rumey was detached to Grenadier-Regiment Nr.3 and was immediately in action. In the following twelve months he distinguished himself to the extent that he was awarded the Iron Cross 2nd Class. It was not long before he realised that there was another kind of war going on: the war in the air.

At the beginning of 1915, Rumey volunteered for transfer to the German Army Air Service and on August 5 was posted to Jastaschule. After training and gaining his certificate, he was posted to FA(A).219 as an observer.

After over a year of flying as an observer on reconnaissance missions, Rumey applied for training as a pilot and was posted to Jastaschule on the Western Front early in 1917. On completion of his training, Rumey was posted to Jasta 2 in May 1917 and then to Jasta 5 on 10 June with the rank of Vizefeldwebel. At the end of June he was promoted to the rank of Leutnant. He celebrated this promotion by opening his tally on 26 June by shooting down the British pilot Lieutenant E.C. Eaton of 65 Squadron. For this he received the Bavarian Military Merit Cross 2nd Class with Swords on 7 July. During one combat mission against the British on 25 August 1917 he was wounded and only just managed to get his aircraft back to the base. After two weeks he was back in the air and by the end of the year had raised his tally to five.

By the end of May 1918, Rumey's tally had risen to twenty-one and he had been awarded the Bavarian Military Merit Cross in Gold. His efforts had not gone unnoticed and with his tally at twenty-nine, he was awarded Prussia's distinguished Orden Pour le Mérite. Rumey continued to wreak havoc amongst the British squadrons until 27 September 1918 when, in the midst of a dogfight over Neuville-St Remy, the top wing of his Fokker D.VII collided with the wing of an SE5a flown by Captain G.E.B. Lawson of 32 Squadron RAF. With his aircraft spinning towards the ground, Fritz Rumey took to his parachute, but it failed to deploy and he was killed. Captain Lawson managed to guide his badly damaged SE5a to the ground and survived. Fritz Rumey was just twenty-seven years old.

OBERLEUTNANT ZUR SEE GOTTHARD SACHSENBERG

Gotthard Sachsenberg was born on 6 December 1891 in Rossau. His childhood, like many others, was uneventful. However, in 1913 at the age of twenty-two, he joined the Imperial German Navy as a sea cadet. One year later Germany was at war and Sachsenberg immediately volunteered for aviation duties in the Naval Air Service. Like others before him he wanted to be a pilot, but the need for observers was great. After training he was posted to MFA.2, where after ten missions he was awarded the Iron Cross 2nd Class as a Fähnrich. Then in January 1916 his promotion to Leutnant came through and with it a new posting to training school, this time as an instructor.

In the meantime Sachsenberg had applied for pilot training which was approved. He was posted to Jastaschule at Mannheim for training in February and, after graduating in April, returned to his old unit MFA.2 flying Fokker E.IIIs from Mariakerke. Sachsenberg had no success as a fighter pilot that year, mainly because of a lull in the fighting in that area, but he continued to carry out observation duties. In May 1917, after taking command of MFJ.1 in February, the war suddenly escalated and he scored his first victory: a Belgian Farman over Dixmude. On 20 August after six victories, he received the Knight's Cross with Swords of the Royal Hohenzollern House Order.

By the end of 1917 he had raised his tally to eight and was awarded the Iron Cross 1st Class, House Order of Albert the Bear, and the Knight's Cross 1st Class with Swords. The beginning of 1918 saw the war hotting up and by the end of August, Sachsenberg's tally had risen twenty-four and he was awarded the Orden Pour le Mérite. Other honours came his way: the Friedrich Cross 1st and 2nd Class of Anhalt; Friedrich-August Cross 1st and 2nd Class of Oldenburg, and the Hanseatic Cross of Hamburg. At the end of the war his tally stood at thirty-one; the last victory was scored when he flew with the Marine Freikorps MJGrI in the Baltic.

Oberleutnant zur See Gotthard Sachsenberg died on 23 August 1961 at the age of sixty-nine.

LEUTNANT KARL EMIL SCHÄFER

Karl Emil Schäfer was born on 17 December 1891 in Kregfeld, Bavaria. In 1909 he served a year's compulsory service in the army with Jäger-Regiment Nr.10. After leaving the army Schäfer went to Paris and was there when World War One broke out. After some difficulties he managed to return to Germany and was immediately assigned to Reserve-Jäger-Regiment Nr.7. The regiment went into action within weeks of his joining and in September he won the Iron Cross 2nd Class as well as promotion to Vizefeldwebel. Within days of receiving the award and the promotion, he was badly wounded during a particularly intensive push forward and was hospitalised for six months. It was whilst in hospital that he considered a move to the German Army Air Service.

On release from hospital he rejoined his unit and after re-establishing himself was granted a commission in May 1916 to Leutnant. He was also awarded the Iron Cross 1st Class and the Military Merit Order 4th Class with Swords from Bavaria. He then asked to be transferred to the German Army Air Service for training as a pilot. His request was approved and after only two months' training he was awarded his pilot's certificate.

On 30 July, 1916, Schäfer was sent to the Eastern Front where he joined KG.2, Staffel 8. For the next six months Schäfer flew reconnaissance missions, then the unit was moved to the Western Front and Schäfer joined Kasta II of KG.3.

On 22 January he scored his first victory when he shot down a French Caudron over west Pont-à-Mousson. It was the start of a rapid but short career. He was posted

Leutnant Karl Emil Schäfer in the cockpit of Albatros D.I, Nr.D1724.

Leutnant Karl Emil Schäfer (Orden Pour le
Mérite, with thirty victories) was killed in
action on 5 June 1917. He served with KG3,
Jasta 11 and Jasta 28.

to join Manfred von Richthofen's Jasta 11 on 21 February 1917 and made his mark
by shooting down eight aircraft in the following month of March – five of them in
two days. By the end of April he had raised his tally to twenty-three and had been
awarded the Knight's Cross with Swords of the Royal Hohenzollern House Order
and the Orden Pour le Mérite. Schäfer was also given command of Jasta 28.

During the following month of May, Schäfer raised his tally to twenty-nine. On
4 June he shot down a DH4 from 55 Squadron RFC, bringing his tally to thirty. Just
after 16:00 on 5 June 1917, he and other members of Jasta 28 engaged FE2d fighters
of 20 Squadron RFC. After a short but vicious fight, Schäfer was shot down by FE2d
No.A6469, flown by Lieutenant H.L. Satchell and his observer T.A. Lewis. Karl Emil
Schäfer was twenty-five years old.

HAUPTMANN EDUARD RITTER VON SCHLEICH — 'THE BLACK KNIGHT'

Eduard Schleich was born in Munich, Bavaria, on 9 August 1888. Little is known of
his early life, but his military career began in 1906, when he joined Bayerisches
Infanterie-Regiment Nr.11 as an infantryman. He worked his way up the promo-
tional ladder to become a Feldwebel in 1908 and the following year he was promoted
once again to Fähnrich. Two years later he received his commission and was placed
on the reserve list. In 1914 he was called up to join his old regiment and within
months was in the thick of the action. On 25 August 1914, he was severely wounded
during one battle and was returned to Munich to recuperate and convalesce. It was
while convalescing that he decided upon a career change and applied to transfer to

the German Army Air Service. He was accepted and in May 1915 was posted to FEA 1 at Schleissheim for training. On 11 September 1915, on completion of his flying training, he was awarded his Bavarian Pilot's Badge; this was to be the cause of certain problems later.

Schleich's first posting was to FA.2b in October of 1915 and he teamed up with observer Leutnant Hans Adam. After a number of reconnaissance flights, he was wounded during an encounter with Allied fighters in February 1916. In September 1916, after recuperating, he was suddenly and unexpectedly put in command of Fliegerschule I, where he became a flying instructor. Early in February 1917, he was transferred to a Bavarian escort unit, Schutzstaffel 28, as its commanding officer. The elation didn't last long; because of the shortage of aircraft he was unable to lead his unit, but had to 'fly' a desk. Within weeks he had written furious letters to Kommandeur der Flieger at 5. Armee headquarters requesting transfer to a fighter unit. Although he had been an instructor, Schleich was posted to fighter training school at Famars, near Valenciennes. His instructor, Leutnant Boheme, announced after two weeks' instruction that he could teach him no more and suggested that he posted to a fighter unit.

He was posted to Jasta 21 on 21 May 1917 with the rank of Oberleutnant and was again given command, albeit only temporary, of the squadron – without having scored a single victory. He scored his first victory on 25 May, when on patrol over Moronvilliers he shot down a Spad VII. For a first victory this was a notable one. His opponent was none other than Sous-Lieutenant René Pierre Dorme of the French Air Service, who at the time had forty-three victories to his credit. Dorme's gold watch was later dropped over a French airfield – together with a note from Jasta 21 stating Dorme had died bravely for France.

After his second victory on 17 June – a Sopwith 1½ Strutter – he was given command of the squadron permanently. It was then that the problems started. There still existed in Germany a feudal system and the fact that Jasta 21 was a Prussian unit that had just been designated a Saxon unit (now commanded by a Bavarian) caused a source of embarrassment to the senior members of the old military guard who still held positions of high authority. His command was put under the microscope and any infringement, no matter how minor, was jumped upon by the higher powers.

In the following four months Schleich raised his tally to twenty-five, but his command came under attack for the lack of results from his other pilots. After one incident concerning three of his pilots, which earned him a severe reprimand, he assembled all his pilots and threatened them that, unless they showed more offensive spirit, they would be removed from the squadron and sent away in disgrace. Within days the pilots starting scoring victories and the pressure from above eased. However, the success was not without its losses.

In July, the squadron had moved to Chassogne-Ferne, near Verdun, and during one skirmish with the enemy Schleich's friend Leutnant Limpert was killed. Out of respect for his friend, Schleich had his Albatros D.Va painted jet black. The black fighter with its white band round the fuselage became well known by Allied fighter pilots and soon earned him the nickname 'The Black Knight'.

Schleich, although a commanding officer, was not averse to having his own extremely foolish moments. One such incident happened after a Spad had been forced down intact. Schleich had the aircraft painted in German markings and headed for the front, where he actually joined up with a French squadron on patrol. It took quite a few minutes before the French pilots realised what was happening. Before they could react, Schleich had headed back for his own lines only to be fired upon by German anti-aircraft fire. Fortunately their aim was bad and he landed back safely at his own airfield. The Kommandeur der Flieger was not amused and severely reprimanded him for the escapade.

The rest of the squadron was performing well – among them were Leutnant Emil Thuy and Leutnant Karl Thom who were both later awarded the Orden Pour le Mérite. Just after achieving his twenty-fifth victory, Schleich fell ill with dysentery. He was rushed to hospital in a serious condition. Some months later he was told that Prussian bureaucracy had taken advantage of his enforced absence and had removed from command. They decreed that no Bavarian should serve in a Prussian unit – let alone command one. It was at times like these that one wonders whom the Germans were actually fighting!

On 23 October 1917, Schleich was given command of Jasta 32, an all-Bavarian squadron, with his tally at thirty-five. He was awarded the Orden Pour le Mérite on 4 December 1917 in recognition of his services, but did not receive the customary Royal Hohenzollern House Order that usually went with it.

The following month he was given command of Jastaschule I and in March command of Jagdgruppe Nr.8 which consisted of Bavarian Jastas 23, 34 and 35. It was not until the end of 1918 that he learned that he had been awarded the Knight's Cross of the Military Max-Joseph Order, the Saxon Knight's Cross, the Albrecht Order 2nd Class and the Bavarian Military Merit Order 4th Class with Crown and Swords. With these awards came promotion to Hauptmann and the title of nobility: Eduard Ritter von Schleich. He remained in control of Jagdgruppe Nr.8 until the end of the war and ended his war by being a member of the Armistice Committee.

In the 1920s he joined Lufthansa and stayed until the rise of Nazism when he joined the Luftwaffe in 1933. He even visited Britain in the black uniform of the Waffen SS. During the war he rose to the rank of Generaloberst, commanding combat units. He later took up a post in occupied Denmark, before becoming General de Flieger in Norway. He was taken prisoner at the end of the war by the Allies and interned in a POW camp for high-ranking officers. It was there that he died following a short illness.

Fregattenkapitän Peter Strasser

Born on 1 April 1876 in Hannover, Peter Strasser was to follow in the traditional footsteps of his family. After leaving school Strasser joined the navy as a cadet at the age of 15, receiving his initial training on the training ships *Stein* and *Moltke*. Upon graduating he was sent to the Navy School in Kiel. Further training on the specialised instruction ships *Mars* and *Blücher* on gunnery completed his training and he was promoted to Leutnant zur See.

In 1897 Strasser was posted to the cruiser *Hertha* and toured East Asia for two years. He returned to a shore base, before being posted again to the gunboat *Panther*

Fregattenkapitän
Strasser

Fregattenkapitän Peter Strasser (Orden Pour le
Mérite), assisted by a Zeppelin commander,
raided England 1915. He was killed in action on
5 August 1918 when Zeppelin L70 was shot
down by Lieutenant Peter Cadbury.

as gunnery officer from 1902 to 1904. After a period at a shore base, Strasser was
posted to the battleship SMS *Westfalen*, where his skill as a gunnery officer was proven
when he won the Kaiserpreis for the best gunnery officer in the service. Strasser, a
dedicated professional seaman, was a fair but strict disciplinarian, and his gunnery
crews were amongst the best. In 1910 he was posted to the battleship SMS
Mecklenburg, where his reputation went before him. He won the Kaiserpreis for the
next three years, during which time he had applied for a transfer to the naval aviation
wing. This had been refused on the grounds that he was too valuable a gunnery
officer to be lost to the new aviation wing.

But in September 1913 it all changed. Strasser was ordered to report to naval headquarters in Berlin on 1 September 1913. After reporting to the adjutant, he was
shown into the office of a senior naval officer. After hearing a breakdown of his
career read out to him, he was told of the death of Leutnantkommander Matzing in
the crash of the Zeppelin LZ.1 in the North Sea. He was then told that he was to
be put in command of the naval Zeppelins. Strasser pleaded that he had no
knowledge of airships, but it was pointed out to him that all the most experienced
airshipmen had died in the crash and new men had to be trained. It was a dedicated
disciplinarian that the navy wanted, knowing it was going to need an officer of
strength and character to command.

Less than a month after taking command, his strength of character was put to the
test when the airship LZ.2 exploded in mid-air, killing all the crew. By interrogating
all the witnesses Strasser found the cause and arranged for modifications to be made

to the one existing airship and all future ones. At the outbreak of war in 1914, the Naval Air Division found itself with just one airship, the LZ.3. Strasser immediately requested the building of new ones; he pointed out to the High Command the advantage of being able to fly above any blockade imposed by the British and to bomb London from the air.

On 19 January 1915, the first air raid on Britain took place. The LZ.3, LZ.4 and LZ.6 (carrying Strasser) lifted off shortly before 11:00. Not long after take-off, LZ.6 had to return to base due to engine trouble, but the remaining two airships attacked the Norfolk region of Britain and bombed Great Yarmouth. Although very little damage was done, the fact that Britain had been bombed from the air made the British painfully aware that they were no longer invulnerable. Strasser was promoted to Korvettenkapitän for his part in the organisation and partial success of the raid. From this meagre beginning, Strasser was to command a fleet of airships that carried out over 200 sorties and over 1,000 reconnaissance flights against the Allies.

Strasser was promoted to Fregattenkapitän on 20 August 1917 and received the award of the Orden Pour le Mérite. He continued to lead his men in attacks against Britain. On 5 August 1918 he led his entire squadron of airships on a raid over London. As the squadron approached Yarmouth, Strasser – in the biggest and newest airship, the LZ.70 – suddenly saw a DH4 aircraft (flown by Lieutenant Peter Cadbury RNAS) appear out of the dense cloud in front of them. The guns of the DH4 suddenly opened up and incendiary and tracer bullets ripped into the gas bags and fuel tanks of the LZ.70. Strasser and his crew were helpless as flames spewed from the sides of the giant airship; seconds later it exploded in a mass of burning fuel and tangled metal. The wreckage of the giant airship and its doomed crew plunged into the dark waters of the North Sea that was to become their grave.

The remaining airships saw that they had been discovered, aborted their mission and returned to Nordholz. In four short years Peter Strasser had taken an idea and turned it into a reality. It was to disrupt Britain's way of life during the war years in a way never before dreamed of and, in doing so, tied up thousands of soldiers and hundreds of pieces of artillery that tried to combat the airborne threat.

LEUTNANT KARL THOM

Born on 19 May 1893 in Freystadt, West Prussia, Karl Thom was one of many young men whose life was altered dramatically by war. After leaving school at the age of fourteen, he had a succession of jobs until he was eighteen when he joined the army in 1911, volunteering for three years' military service. He was assigned to Husaren-Regiment Nr.5. Three years later war broke out and Thom, now an experienced soldier, was posted to Jäger-Regiment zu Pferde Nr.10 on 4 September 1914 and promoted to Unteroffizier. The regiment was soon in action and, in one particularly aggressive action, Thom was seriously injured and received the Iron Cross 2nd Class. After being released from hospital in June 1915, he applied for transfer to the German Army Air Service and was accepted.

In September Karl Thom was sent to pilot training school; he graduated as a pilot in January 1916. He was posted to FA.216 operating patrols in the Vosges sector

Leutnant Karl Thom (Orden Pour le Mérite, with twenty-seven victories) survived World War One but went missing in action on the Russian Front during World War Two.

Left to right: Leutnant Luthringer, Leutnant Schmuckle and Leutnant Thom.

where Thom carried out reconnaissance missions. On 16 May 1916 he crashed on landing and was badly injured. After release from hospital, Thom was promoted to Vizefeldwebel on 24 July, and he was posted to Romania in October to join FA.48 as a reconnaissance pilot. At the end of October he was shot down and captured, but managed to escape and made his way back to his unit. For this he was awarded the Iron Cross 1st Class. Karl Thom yearned for more action and a chance to go hunting himself instead of continually being the hunted. On 24 April, after a number of requests, he was posted to Jastaschule and trained as a fighter pilot. On graduation he was posted to Jasta 21 on 15 May.

Karl Thom opened his score on 22 August 1917 when he shot down a French AR2 over south Avocourt. Two weeks later he gained his second when he shot down a Caudron over Foret-de-Hesse. At the end of September, his tally had risen to twelve and he was awarded the Golden Military Merit Cross. Thom had added two more 'kills' to his tally when he attacked a balloon on 23 December and was injured by defending Allied fighters. He managed to get his crippled aircraft back to base and was hospitalised for a month as a result of his injuries. He returned to Jasta 21 on 24 January 1918 and was promoted to Offizierstellvertreter. His tally remained static for several months as there was little action. Then in June, activity in the area became hectic. By the beginning of August he had raised his tally to twenty-seven and was awarded the Member's Cross with Swords of the Royal Hohenzollern House Order. Four days later he was wounded again when his patrol ran into a swarm of RFC SE5s.

At the end of August he was commissioned in the rank of Leutnant, but was still in hospital and remained there until the beginning of October. On 1 November, five days before he returned to Jasta 21, he was awarded the esteemed Orden Pour le Mérite. Thom stayed with Jasta 21 until the Armistice. He was badly injured in a crash the day before the war ended.

During World War Two, Karl Thom joined the Luftwaffe and held posts in Eastern Germany. He was reported missing whilst visiting the Russian Front and is thought to have been taken prisoner. He was never seen again.

OBERST HERMANN VON DER LEITH-THOMSEN

Born in Flensburg, Prussia, on 10 March 1867, Hermann von der Leith-Thomsen was the son of a wealthy farmer. His early years consisted of schooling and helping his father on the farm. At sixteen he joined the army as a cadet and, upon graduating in 1889, was posted to Pionier-Bataillon Nr.9 as a Leutnant. During the following years, his organisational skill were honed to such an extent that he was sent to the Prussian War Academy in 1909. Upon graduating, Leith-Thomsen was given the position of Chief of the Technical Section of the German Greater General Staff, a position he held until the outbreak of World War One.

In May 1914, he was promoted to Oberleutnant and assigned as General Staff Officer with the Inspection of the Air and Ground Transportation System. Leith-Thomsen was not a desk soldier and on 26 August 1914 took part in the Battle of Tannenberg where General Ludendorff's army totally annihilated part of the Russian army. Leith-Thomsen distinguished himself to the extent that he was awarded the

Oberst von der Hermann Leith-Thomsen
(Orden Pour le Mérite), Chief of the
General Staff to the Commanding General
Air Strike Forces. He died in 1942 whilst
serving with the Luftwaffe.

Iron Cross 2nd Class. One month later he was assigned to the General Command of
Reserve Corps 24 as a staff officer. With Reserve Corps 24 he took part in the Battle
of Ypres and in the winter campaign in the Carpathian Mountains.

The newly formed German Army Air Service was beginning to make its presence
felt but it was still raw and needed the steady hand of someone with good organisational skills and the ability to cut red tape. Oberleutnant Hermann von der Leith-
Thomsen was just the man. At the beginning of 1915 he was appointed Chief of the
Field Flying Systems of the German Army Air Service, responsible only to the
Commanding General of Air Strike Forces. One year later he was appointed Chief
of the General Staff to the Commanding General of the Air Strike Forces.

Prior to Leith-Thomsen appointment in the German Army Air Service, it had
only about 100 pilots and 150 aircraft, but in the two years under his guidance the
number of pilots grew to over 5,000. General Erich Ludendorff paid tribute to Leith-
Thomsen: 'It is due to Major Leith-Thomsen's strong creative powers that Germany
should be grateful for developing its Air Strike Forces so successfully.' On 8 April
1917, Hermann von der Leith-Thomsen was awarded the Orden Pour le Mérite and
promoted to Oberstleutnant. At the end of the war, he took part in the deactivation
of the German Army Air Service under the Treaty of Versailles and for a short period
was Head of the War Ministry Aviation Department.

In 1935, with war clouds once again looming on the horizon, Leith-Thomsen
offered his services and was given the rank of Generalmajor personally by Adolf Hitler.
He was assigned to the Luftwaffe section of the War Department and immediately put

Leutnant Emil Thuy (Orden Pour le Mérite, with thirty-five victories) served with FFA.53, Jasta 21 and Jasta 28.

his organisation skills to work. Two years later he was promoted to Generalleutnant and in 1939 to General der Flieger. Leith-Thomsen died of a heart attack on 5 August 1942 at the age of seventy-five.

LEUTNANT EMIL THUY

Born on 11 March 1894 in Hagen, Westphalia, Emil Thuy was the son of a local schoolteacher. His early childhood was uneventful, but like many others, it was to change completely in 1914 with the outbreak of war. Emil Thuy was one of the first in his town to volunteer for front-line duty and was duly enlisted in Rheinland Pionier-Regiment Nr.3. Immediately after very basic training his regiment was sent to the Western Front. In October 1914 Thuy was badly wounded in action and returned to Germany. Whilst in hospital it was realised that he was unfit for further service and Thuy was discharged from the army.

On release from hospital he applied for the German Army Air Service and was accepted. On completion of his training he was awarded his certificate and Pilot's Badge and, on 10 July 1915, was posted to FFA.53 as a reconnaissance pilot with the rank of Gefreiter. He was awarded the Iron Cross 2nd Class on 7 August, possibly because of his previous war experiences. After further combat training he scored his first victory on 8 September and was promoted to Unteroffizier in the same month. Thuy was awarded the Iron Cross 1st Class on 10 November, followed by promotion to Vizfeldwebel the following month.

Leutnant Emil Thuy at Jasta 21 with Fokker
D.VII Nr.262/18.

On 26 March 1917 he received his commission to Leutnant. In November his request for fighter pilot training was granted and he was sent to Jastaschule. Thuy graduated on 28 January 1917 and was posted to Jasta 21. He opened his tally on 16 April when he shot down a Caudron over north Berry-au-Bac. His tally had risen to fifteen by 24 September. On 26 September he was made commander of Jasta 28. Emil Thuy was awarded the Knight's Cross with Swords of the Royal Hohenzollern House Order on 6 November 1917.

By the end of 1917, Thuy's tally had risen to seventeen. On 2 February 1918, he and his unit were attacked by Allied fighters and, although wounded, Thuy was able to make his way back to his airfield. His wounds hospitalised him for several weeks but on 21 February he was back in command of the Jasta.

By the end of May he had raised his tally to twenty-one and was awarded the Knight's Cross of the Military Merit Order of Württemberg. On 6 June 1918, he became the leader of Jagdgruppe Nr.7, which comprised Jastas 28, 33, 57 and 58. On 30 June he was awarded the Orden Pour le Mérite. He reached twenty-two victories on 20 June, and finally thirty-five on 14 October 1918.

At the end of the war Thuy remained in aviation by training pilots at flying schools. As the Luftwaffe began to reform, he became an instructor at a Luftwaffe Jastaschule near Smolensk, Russia. Emil Thuy was killed on 11 June 1930 in a flying training accident.

HAUPTMANN ADOLF RITTER VON TUTSCHEK

Adolf von Tutschek was born in Ingolstadt, Bavaria on 16 May 1891. His father and grandfather were both military men so it was no surprise when in 1910, at the age of nineteen, he joined Bayerisches Infanterie-Regiment Nr.3 as a cadet. After serving his time as a cadet he was commissioned in 1912. When war broke out he was assigned to Bayerisches Infanterie-Regiment Nr.40 and was immediately in action on the Western Front. One year later his regiment was in action on the Eastern Front where he was wounded on 2 May. For this and other actions he had been involved in, he was awarded the Iron Cross 1st Class and the Bavarian Military Merit Order 4th Class with Swords. He was discharged from hospital in June and within days was back in action with his regiment. On 31 January 1916 he was awarded the Military Max-Joseph Order for playing a major part in a seventeen-day stand against superior Russian forces. Tutschek had volunteered in August to lead his men to capture a key Russian position and, after bitter hand-to-hand fighting, he and a rapidly dwindling handful of survivors held out until reinforcements arrived to relieve them.

He was recalled to headquarters on 17 January 1916 and promoted to Oberleutnant, then ordered back to the Western Front at Verdun. He was gassed on 26 March 1916 and hospitalised for several months. During this period he was awarded another Bavarian Military Merit Order 4th Class with Swords and it was while lying in hospital that his thoughts turned to other aspects of his military career. One of the services that intrigued him was the German Army Air Service. He applied for a transfer and was accepted, although his own regiment were not at all keen on losing an experienced infantry officer.

Hauptmann Adolf Ritter von Tutschek (Orden Pour le Mérite, with twenty-seven victories) was killed in action on 15 March 1918.

Adolf Ritter von Tutschek reported to Schleissheim as a student pilot on 25 July 1916. Three months later, at the end of October 1916, after qualifying as a pilot, he was posted to FA.6B to train firstly as a two-seater pilot then later as a single-seater fighter pilot.

Another award was made to him on 17 January 1917 when he received the Bavarian Military Merit Order 4th Class with Crown and Swords. On completion of his single-seater training, he was posted to Jasta 2 (Boelcke) on 25 January. In just over a month he opened his score and raised his tally to three. At the end of April 1917 he was given command of Jasta 12, not for his flying prowess and record, but because of his experience in command as an infantryman. By the middle of July he raised his tally to thirteen, for which he was awarded the Knight's Cross with Swords of the Royal Hohenzollern House Order. In less than two months his tally had risen to twenty-one and he was awarded the Orden Pour le Mérite on 3 August 1917.

One week later whilst on patrol, von Tutschek came under attack from aircraft of 8 Naval Squadron. He was severely wounded in the ensuing dogfight over Fresnoy when he was shot down by Flight Commander C.D. Booker. He survived the crash and after recuperating was promoted on 6 December 1917 to Hauptmann. He was given a staff job at Kogenluft which lasted a year before he demanded to go back into action. He was given command of the newly formed JG.11, comprising Jastas 12, 13, 15 and 19, on 1 February 1918: it was a short-lived command.

On 15 March 1918, whilst flying in his green Fokker Dr.I Nr.404/17, he was shot down and killed by Lieutenant H.B. Redler of 24 Squadron, flying in a SE5a.

Adolf Ritter von Tutschek was nearly twenty-seven years old when he died and had twenty-seven victories to his credit.

Oberleutnant Ernst Udet

Probably one of the most charismatic German pilots of World War One, Ernst Udet was born in Frankfurt-am-Main on 26 April 1896, The son of a wealthy landowner, Ernst Udet had a natural flair for anything mechanical and had his own motorcycle. He applied to join the Army at the age of seventeen but was rejected several times before he was finally able to persuade the authorities to accept him. On 7 August 1914, whilst German troops occupied Liège, Ernst Udet reported to the German Automobile Club with his motorcycle to play his part as a messenger. On 21 August 1914, he joined the Army and was assigned to 26 Württemburg Reserve Division as a motorcycle messenger.

For the next few months, Udet rode his motorcycle backwards and forwards behind the lines delivering messages. On one particularly bad night, when the sound of guns appeared to be encircling him, he swerved to miss a shell-hole in the road and crashed. After ten days in hospital he was sent to Belgium to catch up with his division, but could not find them. In Liège he was given the job of delivering messages and it was there that he met Leutnant von Waxheim, a pilot who was to influence Udet's life.

Orders came for Udet to be sent home and on his arrival he immediately volunteered for the Pilot's Reserve Detachment in Schleissheim. His meeting with von

Waxheim had convinced him that Air Service was where his future lay. Whilst waiting for a response to his request, he trained as a pilot at his own expense, sending further applications to Darmstadt and Döberitz. A few weeks later orders came through for him to go to Darmstadt for pilot training. After completion of his training, Udet was posted to FA(A).206 as a Gefreiter. Leutnant Bruno Justinus was assigned as his observer and three weeks later, after a spell of patrols in which they never saw an Allied aircraft, they spotted a French monoplane attacking a railway station. As they approached they realised that the Frenchman was in trouble and was gliding toward the ground. Udet tucked in behind and noticed that the aircraft had a machine gun mounted behind the propeller. The French aircraft, encouraged by Udet, made a forced landing and, before the pilot could set fire to his aircraft, it was captured by German soldiers. The pilot, it was discovered later, was Roland Garros; the capture of his aircraft, together with the gun and device to enable the pilot to fire through the propellor arc, was to alter the course of air-to-air fighting dramatically. Udet received the Iron Cross 2nd Class for the incident.

On 18 March 1916, Udet was posted to FA.68, which later became Kek Habsheim, and scored his first victory when he shot down a Farman F40 whilst defending Mulhausen during a raid by French aircraft. It is claimed that he attacked twenty-two hostile aircraft – flying on his own in Fokker D.III Nr.356/16. On September 28 he was posted to Jasta 15; by the end of the year he had raised his tally to two. At the beginning of January 1917, he was awarded the Iron Cross 1st Class and at the end of the month received his commission to Leutnant.

In May 1917 he recorded his sixth victory and requested a transfer to Jasta 37. This was agreed and he was transferred on 19 June. Five months later Udet received a telegram saying that his friend Leutnant Gontermann had been killed and that he was to take command of Jasta 37. Two weeks later he was awarded the Knight's Cross with Swords of the Royal Hohenzollern House Order. By this time he had raised his tally to fifteen confirmed victories.

On 23 March 1918, Udet was posted to Jasta 11 as commanding officer until 8 April. Three days before his twenty-second birthday a telegram arrived:

> His Majesty the Emperor has been gracious enough to bestow upon you the Pour le Mérite in recognition of the twenty planes shot down by you.

The next day he was given command of Jasta 4.

Udet's aircraft was a distinctive Fokker D.VII with a red fuselage: the upper surfaces of the top wing had red and white candy stripes. Written on the upper tail surface, for any attacker from the rear to read, was the inscription 'Du noch Nicht!' (*Not you yet!*). His aircraft also carried the initials of his fiancée – 'LO'. With his tally of victories standing at forty, he was shot down during a dogfight with Breguet aircraft and escaped with slight injuries. As his aircraft spun earthwards, Udet scrambled out of the cockpit only to find that his parachute harness had caught on the control column. After struggling for what seemed an eternity he broke free; his parachute opened some 300ft from the ground. He landed heavily in a shell hole and was rescued by German infantry.

Oberleutnant Ernst Udet (Orden Pour le Mérite, with sixty-two victories).

In the following two months Udet raised his tally to sixty confirmed victories and was awarded the Lübeck Hanseatic Cross and the Hamburg Hanseatic Cross. On 26 September 1918, with his tally at sixty-two, he was badly wounded in the thigh – putting an end to his combat flying days.

After the war Udet became a test pilot and a movie stunt pilot, flying all over the world. At the onset of World War Two he was persuaded to join the Luftwaffe and attained the rank of Generaloberst. He was later given the post of GOC Aircraft Production and immediately set about developing a new fighter bomber. However, in his rapid rise up the ladder of promotion, he had made enemies – none so deadly as Generaloberst Ehard Milch. Milch began to undermine Udet's authority and cause him many problems.

On 17 September 1941 Ernst Udet died. The German propaganda machine announced that he had died whilst testing a new aeroplane and Hitler announced that Udet would be given a state funeral. In reality – Udet had committed suicide by shooting himself with a Mexican Colt revolver that he had brought back from America during his stunt pilot days. It was the political infighting within the Luftwaffe and the fact that his position was completely undermined that caused him to take his own life.

His coffin was placed on the catafalque in the Air Ministry's Hall of Honour in the Wilhelmstrasse and then taken by gun carriage via the Louisenstrasse to Invaliden Cemetery, where he was buried with full military honours.

LEUTNANT JOSEPH VELTJENS

Joseph Veltjens was born on 2 June 1894 in a small village west of Düisberg in Saxony. An uneventful childhood led to him joining the army at the age of twenty when he enlisted in the Kaiserin-Augusta Garda-Regiment Nr.4 on 3 August 1914. Three months later he was attached to Leib-Grenadier Regiment Nr.8 and later transferred to 8. Korps-Kraftwagen Kolonne. During this period Veltjens received a number of rapid promotions that culminated in the rank of Vizefeldwebel and the award of the Iron Cross 2nd Class.

At the end of October 1915, Veltjens applied for transfer to the German Army Air Service and was accepted. He was sent to Jastaschule and at the end of December 1915, he was awarded his pilot's certificate and badge. On 10 May he was posted to FA.23 as a reconnaissance pilot where, after carrying out a large number of missions, he was commissioned at the end of 1916 to Leutnant in recognition of his skills in this field of flying.

At the beginning of 1917, he applied to Jastaschule for training as a fighter pilot and was accepted. On completion of the course he was posted to Jasta 14; in the following month, on 14 April, he scored his first victory by shooting down a Spad over Craonne in his Albatros. With his tally at five, he was posted to Jasta 18 on 15 August. By the end of 1917 he had raised it to nine and had been awarded the Knight's Cross 2nd Class with Swords from Saxony.

On 20 March 1918, Veltjens was posted to Jasta 15, where on 18 May he took command and shot down a French Breguet XIV bomber over Cauny. This brought his tally to thirteen and with it came the Iron Cross 1st Class, the Knight's Cross 2nd Class with Swords of the Albert Order of Saxony, and the Knight's Cross with Swords of the Royal Hohenzollern House Order on 20 May. Veltjens continued to score victories freely and by the end of August 1918 had raised his tally to thirty-one. His efforts were recognised and he was awarded the Orden Pour le Mérite.

At the end of the war Joseph Veltjens had a total of thirty-five 'kills' to his credit.

During World War Two, Veltjens joined the Luftwaffe with the rank of Colonel, flying transport aircraft, and at one time was Göring's emissary to Finland. He died in 1943 when the Junkers Ju52-3m that he was flying was shot down over Yugoslavia by resistance fighters.

LEUTNANT WERNER VOSS

The eldest son of an industrial dyer, Werner Voss was born in Krefeld on 13 April 1897. He was expected to enter the trade of dyeing which had been the tradition of the Voss family for generations, but Werner Voss had other ideas; he was to enter another trade concerned with another different kind of dying – and one that would see him meet his demise at the early age of twenty.

Werner Voss was a member of the Krefeld Militia and liked nothing better than to wear the dashing uniform of the Krefeld Hussars two evenings a week for two months during the summer. When war broke out he was assigned to Westfälisch Husaren-Regiment Nr.11 and was sent to the French border of Lorraine. Within

Leutnant Joseph Veltjens (Orden Pour le Mérite, with thirty-five victories).

Jasta 15 pilots celebrating their unit's laurel victory wreath. Leutnant Veltjens stands fourth from left.

days of reaching the border, France declared war on Germany and Voss found himself in the last battle in which cavalry were to play a vital role. Elsewhere in Germany cavalry units were being disbanded – it was decided they were of no more use and the Hussars were turned into infantrymen. Voss had no liking for this and applied for pilot training in the German Army Air Service. In August 1915 he was accepted and, by this time considered a veteran, promoted to Unteroffizier and awarded the Iron Cross 2nd Class – he was just eighteen years old.

Voss was sent to pilot school where it was discovered that he was a natural pilot and on completion of his course in February 1916, was posted to FEA.7 as an instructor. One month later he was promoted to Vizefeldwebel and posted to KG.4 initially as an observer but on receiving his Pilot's Badge took over the controls of an Aviatak two-seater fighter/bomber. In September he was promoted to the rank of Leutnant and posted to Jasta 2 in November, where he was to fly with the legendary Baron Manfred von Richthofen. One month later, after scoring two victories (Nieuport Scout and a DH2), he was awarded the Iron Cross 1st Class. By the end of February 1917 his tally of victims had risen to twelve and in March he was awarded the Knight's Cross with Swords of the Royal Hohenzollern House Order. Voss was becoming a household word in Germany and on 8 April 1917, with his tally now at twenty-four, he was awarded the Orden Pour le Mérite.

May 1917 saw Werner Voss posted to Jasta 5, where by the end of June he had taken his tally to thirty-four. He was promoted to Kompanie Kommandant of Jasta 29 for the month of July and then to Jasta 14 as acting Commander – he was just twenty years old. At the end of July he was appointed Staffelführer of Jasta 10; his tally now

Leutnant Voss (forty-eight victories) standing by his Fokker Dr.I Dreidecker with a face painted on the engine cowling.

stood at thirty-four. Voss was flying a Fokker Dr.I marked with the distinctive chrome yellow cowling of Jasta 10. Voss's aircraft cowling had a face painted on it.

During August and September, Voss increased his tally to forty-eight, but then on 23 September 1917 he became engaged in what was to later become known as one of the most famous dogfights of the war.

On patrol he came on a flight of British SE5s of 56 Squadron but, unknown to him and also unfortunately, the flight consisted of a number of top 'Aces', including McCudden, Rhys-Davids, Barlow, Muspratt, Cronyn, Childlaw-Roberts and Bowman. For over ten minutes, Werner Voss almost single-handedly fought the British flight, inflicting damage – some serious – on all of the opposing aircraft. It was 2nd Lieutenant Arthur Rhys-Davids who finally managed to get his machine gun sights on the tailplane of the elusive Voss – a burst from his machine guns sent Voss's Fokker Dreidecker Nr.103/17 plunging earthwards. Voss was buried by British soldiers on the spot where he crashed and died. Major James McCudden said of Voss afterwards: 'His flying was wonderful, his courage magnificent and in my opinion he is the bravest German airman whom it has been my privilege to see fight.'

Leutnant Werner Voss was just twenty years old.

HAUPTMANN FRANZ WALZ

Franz Walz was born on 4 December 1885 in a small hamlet south of Mannheim, Bavaria. At the age of twenty, he volunteered for the army and joined Bayerisches Infanterie-Regiment Nr.8 on 5 July 1905. It soon became obvious that he was a natural leader and three years later in 1908 was promoted to Leutnant. His interest soon moved beyond the infantry to the newly created German Army Air Service. In 1912 Walz applied to be transferred to the German Army Air Service, a request that was approved some months later. Walz was posted to the German Army's Jastaschule at Schleissheim where he graduated some four months later.

At the outbreak of war in 1914, Walz took command of FFA.3, a reconnaissance unit, and in November 1914 was promoted to Oberleutnant. The following year he carried out over 200 reconnaissance sorties on the Western Front. This was rewarded in December 1915 by the command of Kagohl 1's Kasta 2, a two-seater reconnaissance aircraft squadron. On 9 April 1916, Franz Walz opened his score when he shot down a French Caudron whilst on a reconnaissance patrol over Douamont. He increased his tally on 21 May when he shot down a Nieuport. By the end of June Walz had raised his score to five, and had flown over 300 reconnaissance sorties. On 29 July he shot down an enemy aircraft but was wounded in the foot during a reconnaissance mission the next day. After managing to return to base he was hospitalised for the next few months.

On his return to Kagohl 1 on 5 September, he was awarded the Knight's Cross with Swords of the Royal Hohenzollern House Order. Walz was given command of Jasta 2 on 29 November, followed by promotion to Hauptmann on 20 January 1917. He increased his tally to seven on 14 May, and was again posted to command Jasta 34 the following month. It soon became obvious that his skills were as a reconnaissance pilot, not a fighter pilot, so it was decided to utilise them elsewhere.

On 25 August 1917 he was posted to FA.304b in Palestine. Here, he and his squadron carried out reconnaissance flights and missions, culminating on 22 July 1918 with the award of the Turkish Silver Liakat Medal. One month later, on 9 August, he was awarded the prestigious Orden Pour le Mérite. This award was usually associated with fighter pilots, but was awarded to Franz Walz because of the 500 sorties he had successfully carried out. The following month on 15 September he was awarded the Osmanie-Orden 4th Class with Swords, together with the Iron Cross 2nd Class and 1st Class. Three other Bavarian awards and one Austro-Hungarian award showed the respect felt for Walz – even though he was not a household name in Germany. After receiving his award on 15 September, he was captured by the British when his aircraft was forced down. He was released on 1 December 1919 after the war had finished.

Franz Walz returned to Germany and served with the Reichswehr and state police. In 1939, at the onset of World War Two, he joined the Luftwaffe and had reached the rank of Generalleutnant by 1 April 1944. He was captured by the Russians at the beginning of 1945 and died as a prisoner of war in Breslin, Silesia, in December 1945.

LEUTNANT RUDOLF WINDISCH

Born in Dresden on 27 January 1897, Rudolf Windisch was one of the few German pilots who did not come from an upper class background. He entered military service in 1912 before the war had started, joining the Infanterie-Regiment Nr.177. Within weeks of the war starting, Windisch was wounded though not seriously. He

Leutnant Rudolf Windisch (Orden Pour le Mérite, with twenty-two victories).

Leutnant Windisch with his observer Oberleutnant Maximillian von Cossel. Both engaged in cloak and dagger operations behind Russian lines.

then applied – whilst on sick leave – to be transferred to aviation school and on 22 January 1915 was assigned to the Military Pilot's School at Leipzig. On graduating on 10 June, he was promoted to Unteroffizier and assigned to FEA.6 as an instructor. He soon became bored with teaching, although it was a responsible and safe post. He had already tasted action as an infantryman and had been wounded. Windisch applied for a combat posting and on 1 May 1916 was sent to FFA.62. One month later the whole unit was moved to the Russian Front. It wasn't long before he had made his mark with a number of daring reconnaissance flights over the front and for which he was awarded the Iron Cross 2nd Class, together with a promotion to Vizefeldwebel.

On 25 August he scored his first victory and opened his tally by shooting down an observation balloon. For this he was awarded the Iron Cross 1st Class followed some weeks later by the award of the Prussian Crown Order 4th Class with Swords. Windisch was the only pilot ever to receive the order during the war. The award rose out of a special mission carried out by Windisch and his observer Oberleutnant Maximillian von Cossel. On 2 October 1916, Windisch landed his aircraft behind the Russian lines to drop off von Cossel, whose brief it was to blow up a strategic railway bridge near Rowno–brody. The following day, 3 October, Windisch returned to pick up his observer – the mission completed. For this extremely daring mission, both men were presented to the Emperor on 18 October and also received the Honour Cross with Swords from the Principality of Waldeck and the St Henry Medal in Silver from Saxony.

After a brief leave, Windisch was sent to KG.2 on the Western Front on 24 November. On 5 December, he was commissioned in the rank of Leutnant. He continued reconnaissance patrols until 20 February when he was posted to Jasta 32 as a fighter pilot. After further training he started to make his mark against Allied fighters. An AR2 on 18 September followed by a Spad on the 27th brought his tally to three. His fourth victim, a Spad on 1 November 1917, brought him the Knight's Cross 1st Class with Swords of the Albert Order of Saxony.

By the end of November Rudolf Windisch's tally had risen to six. He was posted to Jasta 50 on 10 January 1918 for just two weeks, then to Jasta 66 as commanding officer. By the end of May 1918, he had raised his tally to twenty-two during which time he was awarded the Knight's Cross with Swords of the Royal Hohenzollern House Order, the Austrian-Hungarian Bravery Medal in Silver 2nd Class and the Saxon St Henry Medal in Gold. On the day of his twenty-second victory, he was shot down and taken prisoner by the French. Under the assumption that he was a captive and a POW, the Orden Pour le Mérite was awarded to him, but it was never collected.

When the war was finally over and repatriation of prisoners commenced, efforts were made to locate Leutnant Windisch – but he was never seen again. The story of his disappearance is shrouded in mystery. A number of explanations were given, including one that he was shot trying to steal a French aeroplane, but this was never confirmed. To this day it is still a mystery what happened to Leutnant Rudolf Windisch.

LEUTNANT KURT WINTGENS

The son of an army officer, Kurt Wintgens was born in Neustadt on 1 August 1894. At the age of 19 he became a cadet with Telgraphen-Battalion Nr.2 in Frankfurt and was sent to military academy to begin his career but war broke out. He immediately rejoined his unit and was soon in action against Allied forces. By the end of 1914 he had been awarded the Iron Cross 2nd Class. Aviation was the new challenge amongst young German officers and Kurt Wintgens was not slow to see the advantages and excitement it had to offer. He applied to be transferred to the aviation section and was accepted as an observer. Because of his experience in telegraphy. he was attached to AOK.9 (Armee-Oberkommando Abteilung). His first experiences were on the Western Front then Poland. In March 1915 he was accepted for pilot training and within four months had qualified as a pilot, showing exceptional skills that had him posted to FFA.67, flying Fokkers, then to FFA.6b. On 1 July 1915 he opened his score when he shot down a Morane Parasol east of Luneville. The claim was unconfirmed – had it been it would have been the first German fighter 'kill' in history. A second claim of another Morane Parasol on 4 July was also unconfirmed.

Four days later he was posted to FFA.48 and given a roving commission. On 15 July 1915, another Morane Parasol came into his gunsights and moments later fell in flames – this time it was confirmed. Kurt Wintgens had opened his score. On 9 August 1915 he accounted for a Voisin over Gondrexange, raising his tally to two. He fell ill with influenza and various other minor ailments which subsequently curtailed his flying.

On his return to flying in January 1916 he resumed scoring by shooting down a Caudron G.IV. By the end of June 1916 he had raised his tally to eight and was

Leutnant Kurt Wintgens in a studio pose wearing spectacles and his Orden Pour le Mérite round his neck. He was shot down in flames on 25 September 1916 by the French ace Lieutenant Hurteaux of Escadrille No.3.

awarded the Orden Pour le Mérite – only the fourth German pilot to be so honoured. He was posted to FA.23's Kek Vaux and then to Jasta 4 when it was amalgamated. Three weeks later came another award, the Iron Cross 1st Class. This was quickly followed by the Knight's Cross with Swords of the Royal Hohenzollern House Order and the Bavarian Military Merit Order 4th Class with Swords. His tally had risen by the end of September to nineteen and he received the Knight's 2nd Class with Swords of the Saxon Albert Order.

On 25 September 1916, whilst flying escort to a two-seat reconnaissance aircraft, he fought off an attack from aircraft from French Escadrille 3. In doing so fell under the guns of the French ace Lieutenant Hurteaux and was shot down in flames. It is believed that the observer in the German two-seat aircraft that Wintgens protected so valiantly was Joseph Veltjens who was later to become a pilot and an ace. Kurt Wintgens was twenty-two years old when he died.

OBERLEUTNANT KURT WOLFF

Kurt Wolff was born on 6 February 1895 in the village of Greifsweld, Pomerania. At the age of seventeen he became a cadet with the Eisenbahn-Regiment Nr.4, where he served as an Unteroffizier in the field. On 17 April 1915, after seeing action in the war, he was promoted to Leutnant. But his eyes were on other things and he asked to be transferred to aviation. Although his regiment was reluctant to let him go, the need for fighter pilots was greater and in July 1915 he was transferred.

Leutnant Wolff.

Oberleutnant Kurt Wolff (Orden Pour le
Mérite, with thirty-three victories) was killed in
action on 15 September 1917 by Flight Sub-
Lieutenant N.M. McGregor.

His first flight was nearly his last. His instructor misjudged a landing in their LVG
and crashed. The instructor was killed but Kurt Wolff suffered nothing more than a
dislocated shoulder. It did not deter him and he made rapid progress, receiving his
Pilot's Badge in December. His first posting was to a Kampfgeschwader unit at
Verdun where, in an Albatros Scout, he was quickly in action against ground troops.
After some months his unit was moved to the Somme where they were soon in the
thick of the action against Allied ground troops.

On 5 November 1916, he was posted to Jasta 11, where although he carried out
a number of sorties against Allied aircraft, he failed to score one victory. Command
of the unit was taken over by Manfred von Richthofen and – under his guidance –
the unit began to take toll of enemy aircraft. Within a couple of weeks he had secured
his first victory, BE2d No.5856 of 16 Squadron RFC, over Givenchy on 6 March
1917. Within seven weeks he had taken his tally to twenty-seven. On 26 April, he
was awarded the Knight's Cross with Swords of the Royal Hohenzollern House
Order and one week later, on 4 May, the Orden Pour le Mérite. His run of luck
temporarily ran out when on 11 July, after taking command of Jasta 29, he clashed
with a Sopwith Triplane of 10 Squadron RNAS, and was shot in the hand. Managing
to fly his Fokker Dreidecker with one hand – he was able to return to base. The
injury kept him on the ground for two months, but on 11 September he returned
to flying duties. The following day, orders came through announcing his promotion
to Oberleutnant. On 15 September, in his Fokker Dreidecker with other members

of his Jasta, he encountered Sopwith Camels from 10 and 70 Squadrons RNAS over Moorslede. After a brief dogfight, his Fokker Dr.I Nr.FI102/17 fell to the guns of a Sopwith Camel, flown by Flight Sub-Lieutenant N.M. McGregor, and crashed just north of Wervicq. He was just twenty-two years old.

LEUTNANT KURT WÜSTHOFF

The son of a local businessman, Kurt Wüsthoff was born in Aachen on 27 January 1897. Even at an early age it was discovered he had a natural aptitude for anything mechanical, so it was no surprise when he joined the army and immediately applied for the German Army Air Service at the age of sixteen. He was accepted and sent to the military pilot's school at Leipzig. After four months he was awarded his pilot's certificate and badge. Because he was too young to be sent to the Front, Wüsthoff was posted to FEA.6 at Grossenhain as an instructor. After much pressurising of his superiors, he succeeded in getting posted to KG.1 in the Flanders Sector. For the next eighteen months, Wüsthoff flew in such places as Bulgaria, Romania and Macedonia as a bomber/reconnaissance pilot, then at the beginning of June 1917, after being promoted to Vizefeldwebel, he was posted to Jasta 4 in France. It was here that he scored his first victory, when he attacked and shot down a Sopwith 1½ Strutter from 45 Squadron RFC over Vormezeele. Ten days later he brought down an observation balloon over Wytschaete. For this he was awarded the Iron Cross 2nd Class.

Leutnant Kurt Wüsthoff (Orden Pour le Mérite, with twenty-seven victories) died from injuries on 23 July 1926.

At the end of July, with his tally standing at six, he was awarded the Iron Cross 1st Class. Wüsthoff was commissioned on 1 August 1917 and later that month, after scoring his seventh victory, was awarded the Knight's Cross with Swords of the Royal Hohenzollern House Order. Wüsthoff continued to take toll of Allied fighters and by the end of November his tally stood at twenty-six. On 26 November he was awarded the Orden Pour le Mérite. He was acting commander of Jasta 4 in December until the end of February 1918 when he was promoted to Staffelführer. Wüsthoff was then assigned to the staff of JG.1 until 16 June when he was given command of Jasta 5. The following day whilst flying Leutnant Georg Hantlemann's Fokker D.VIII he was jumped by fighter aircraft from 23 and 24 Squadrons RFC and shot down near Cachy. He was badly wounded in both legs and was taken to a French hospital.

Wüsthoff was released from the prison hospital in 1920 and returned to Germany on crutches. He maintained that the French doctors had deliberately neglected to give him proper treatment and he was taken to Dresden so that German doctors could look after him. After a number of operations over a period of two years, he was finally able to leave hospital and walk unaided. He secured a job with an Austrian car manufacturer and returned to his first love: flying. On 18 July 1926, he attended an airshow that had been set up to raise funds for a memorial to Max Immelmann; during an aerobatic display he crashed and was badly injured. Five days later he died from his injuries.

6

VICTORY TOTALS
OF GERMAN AIRMEN

As always, partly due to the confusion of battle, the number of victories claimed and given can vary widely. Many victories were shared and many were unconfirmed. Lists of victories therefore can also vary.

80	Rittmeister Manfred von Richthofen
62	Oberleutnant Ernst Udet
54	Oberleutnant Erich Löwenhardt
48	Leutnant Werner Voss
45	Leutnant Fritz Rumey
44	Hauptmann Rudolf Berthold
43	Leutnant Paul Bäumer
41	Leutnant der Reserve Josef Carl Peter Jacobs
41	Hauptmann Bruno Loerzer
40	Hauptmann Oswald Boelcke
40	Leutnant Franz Buchner
40	Oberleutnant Lothar Freiherr von Richthofen
39	Leutnant Heinrich Gontermann
39	Oberleutnant Carl Menckhoff
36	Leutnant Julius Buckler

36	Leutnant Max Ritter von Müller
35	Leutnant Gustav Doerr
35	Leutnant Otto Könnecke
35	Hauptmann Eduard Ritter von Schleich
35	Leutnant Emil Thuy
35	Leutnant Joseph Veltjens
33	Leutnant Heinrich Bongartz
33	Leutnant Heinrich Claudius Kroll
33	Oberleutnant Kurt Wolff
32	Oberleutnant Theodor Osterkamp
31	Leutnant Paul Billik
31	Rittmeister Karl Bolle
31	Oberleutnant zur See Gotthard Sachsenberg
30	Leutnant Karl Allmenröder
30	Leutnant Carl Degelow
30	Leutnant Josef Mai
30	Leutnant Ulrich Neckel
30	Leutnant Karl Emil Schäfer
29	Oberleutnant Harald Auffahrt
29	Hermann Frommerz
28	Leutnant Walter Blume
28	Leutnant Walter von Bülow-Bothkamp
28	Leutnant Arthur Laumann
28	Oberleutnant Friedrich Ritter von Roth
27	Oberleutnant Fritz Otto Bernert
27	Leutnant Otto Fruhner
27	Leutnant Hans Kirchstein
27	Leutnant Karl Thom
27	Hauptmann Adolf Ritter von Tutschek
27	Leutnant Kurt Wüsthoff
26	Leutnant Oliver Freiherr von Beaulie-Marconnay
26	Oberleutnant Oskar Freiherr von Boenigk
26	Oberleutnant Eduard Ritter von Dostler
26	Leutnant Max Nather
25	Leutnant Georg von Hantelmann
25	Leutnant Fritz Pütter
24	Leutant Erwin Böhme
24	Leutnant Georg Meyer
23	Leutnant Hermann Becker
22	Oberleutnant Hermann Göring
22	Leutnant Hans Klein
22	Leutnant Pippart
22	Leutnant Werner Preuss
22	Vizefeldwebel Karl Schlegel
22	Leutant Rudolf Windisch

21	Leutnant Hans Adam
21	Oberleutnant zur See Friedrich Christiansen
21	Leutnant Fritz Friedrichs
21	Leutnant Fritz Hohn
21	Leutnant Friedrich Theodor Noltenius
20	Vizefeldwebel Friedrich Altemeir
20	Oberleutnant Hans Bethge
20	Leutnant Rudolf von Eschwege
20	Leutnant Wilhelm Frankl
20	Leutnant Hans von Freden
20	Leutnant Walter Goetsch
20	Hauptmann Wilhelm Reinhard
20	Oberleutnant Otto Schmidt
19	Vizefeldwebel Gerhard Fiesler
19	Leutnant Otto Kissenberth
19	Leutnant Kurt Wintgens
19	Vizeflugmeister Alexandre Zenses
18	Leutnant Hartmuth Baldamus
18	Leutnant Franz Hemer
18	Vizefeldwebel Oskar Hennrich
17	Leutnant Walter Boning
17	Leutnant Ernest Hess
17	Leutnant Franz Ray
17	Leutnant Hans Rolfes
17	Vizefeldwebel Josef Schwendmann
16	Leutnant Hans Boehning
16	Leutnant Ludwig Hanstein
16	Leutnant Rudolf Klimke
16	Leutnant Karl Odebrett
16	Leutnant der Reserve Hans Weiss
15	Vizefeldwebel Christian Donhauser
15	Leutnant Albert Dossenbach
15	Vizefeldwebel Albert Haussmann
15	Leutnant Alois Heldmann
15	Oberleutnant Max Immelmann
15	Leutnant Johannes Klein
15	Leutnant Otto Loffler
15	Leutnant Victor von Pressentin
15	Leutnant Theodor Quant
15	Leutnant Julius Schmidt
15	Leutnant Kurt Schneider
14	Leutnant Ernst Bormann
14	Vizefeldwebel Rudolf Franke
14	Offizierstellvertreter Edmund Nathanael
14	Leutnant Franz Piechurek

14	Leutnant Karl Plauth
14	Vizefeldwebel Emil Schape
14	Leutnant Georg Schlenker
14	Vizefeldwebel Wilhelm Seitz
14	Leutnant Paul Straele
14	Leutnant Rudolf Wendelmuth
13	Vizefeldwebel Karl Bohnenkamp
13	Oberleutnant Hans Joachim Buddecke
13	Leutnant Siegfried Buttner
13	Leutnant Heinrich Geigl
13	Vizefeldwebel Robert Heibert
13	Vizefeldwebel Reinhold Jorke
13	Leutnant Johann Janzen
13	Vizefeldwebel Christel Mesch
13	Vizefeldwebel Otto Rosenfeld
13	Oberflugmeister Kurt Schönfelder
13	Oberleutnant Erich-Rüdiger von Wedel
12	Vizefeldwebel Erich Buder
12	Oberleutnant Theodor Cammann
12	Leutnant Diether Collin
12	Vizefeldwebel Gottfried Ehmann
12	Offizierstellvertreter Otto Esswein
12	Vizefeldwebel Sebastian Festner
12	Leutnant Walter Höhndorf
12	Vizefeldwebel Max Kuhn
12	Vizefeldwebel Friedrich Manschott
12	Leutnant Hans Mueller
12	Oberleutnant Franz Schleiff
12	Leutnant Richard Wenzel
11	Leutnant Heinrich Arntzen
11	Leutnant Raven Freiherr von Barnekow
11	Leutnant Joachim von Busse
11	Leutnant Xaver Dannhuber
11	Oberleutnant Rittmeister Kurt-Bertram von Döring
11	Leutnant Heinz Dreckmann
11	Vizefeldwebel Willi Gabriel
11	Oberleutnant Stephan Kirmaier
11	Leutnant Hans von Keudell
11	Leutnant Alfred Lindenberger
11	Leutnant Fritz Loerzer
11	Leutnant Hermann Pfeiffer
11	Leutnant Hugo Schäfer
11	Leutnant Renatus Theiller
10	Oberleutnant Ernst Freiherr von Althaus
10	Offizierstellvertreter Paul Aue

10	Vizefeldwebel Dietrich Averes
10	Oberleutnant Hans Berr
10	Leutnant Franz Brandt
10	Vizefeldwebel Fritz Classen
10	Leutnant Martin Dehmisch
10	Leutnant Wilhelm Frickhart
10	Leutnant Justus Grassmann
10	Leutnant Rudolf Mattaei
10	Leutnant Max Ritter von Mulzer
10	Vizefeldwebel Alfons Nagler
10	Leutnant Wilhelm Neuenhofen
10	Oberleutnant Hans Schuez
10	Leutnant Werner Steinhauser
10	Leutnant Erich Thomas
10	Leutnant Paul Turck
10	Offizierstellvertreter Bernhard Ultsch
10	Leutnant Paul Wenzel
10	Leutnant Joachim Wolff

Part Two

German Aircraft Manufacturers and their Aircraft

GERMAN AIRCRAFT MANUFACTURERS OF WORLD WAR ONE

This part covers only the major German aircraft manufacturers of World War One. There were over fifty in total; to cover all the companies would require several volumes or one massive tome.

German aircraft manufacturers, like their Allied counterparts, were in their infancy at the beginning of World War One. There were a number of small manufacturing enclaves producing small sports-type aircraft, but nothing that could be construed as a military type.

As World War One progressed so did the standard and quality of German and Allied aircraft production. Two decades later World War Two would find these two protagonists using the lessons they had learned and the strides they had made in aviation, once again locked in aerial combat.

After the wars of German unification (1864–1871), the German Empire appeared, to all intent and purposes, to be one country, but was in fact under the control of two states: Prussia and Bavaria, with Prussia being the dominant state. This unusual situation had come about when, in order to create the German Empire, Bismarck granted Bavaria and its ruling dynasty, the Wittlesbachs, certain privileges as long as they recognised and supported the Prussian House of Hohenzollern as the ruling dynasty of the German Empire. This gave Bavaria an independent railway system and postal service, diplomatic independence and military autonomy.

The manufacture of aircraft in these early years was dominated by Prussia, with the Bavarian and Austro-Hungarian manufacturers very much smaller. Naval aviation in both states, however, was kept separate from the army, mainly because of the deep-seated rivalry that existed between the two factions. The Bavarians and Austro-Hungarian military hierarchy relied on one major aircraft manufacturer in the early years, whilst the Prussians spread their investments amongst a number of manufacturers. This, of course, reduced the chance of expensive and disastrous failures – which in the early years proved to be the case.

In 1908 the German Air Fleet League was formed in an attempt to promote military aviation. Within six months it had attracted 3,000 members. Among them were: Ernst Bassermann, leader of the National Liberal Party in the Imperial Parliament; Dr Richard Brosien, director of the Rheinische Kreditbank; Leutnantgeneral Stephan von Nieber (retired), former commander of the Airship Battalion. The league, together with the Imperial Automobile Club and the Berlin Society for Aviation, joined the German Airship Association (later the German Aviators Association) which was the controlling body of Germany's civil aviation. It was this association that was beginning to deal with the issuing of pilot's licences, flight and airfield regulations; in short, everything that had to do with heavier-than-air flight. In 1909 the Prussian Ministries of the Interior and Public Works granted the association full official powers, thus placing the control of German aviation in their hands.

The German War Ministry watched these developments with great interest, but did not participate. However, as time went by they became increasingly interested and awarded a subsidy of 15,000 marks to the technical committee. They, in turn, gave three inventors – Hans Grade, Richard Schelies and Hermann Dorner – 5,000 marks to build an aircraft. The results were disappointing but the War Ministry was not put off and ordered its research unit to build the army its own aircraft using the designs that had been submitted by W.S. Hoffmann at a meeting of the German Air Fleet League in the previous year.

Progress in building the aircraft was hampered by the lack of an engine. The German engine manufacturers came up with nothing that was anywhere near suitable, so in disgust the War Ministry purchased a French engine. The first flight on 1 March 1910 was carried out by Hauptmann Wolfram de le Roi and after a brief hop, in which the aircraft reached a height of 3.5m, it crashed causing minor damage. The second flight on 18 March 1910 went the same way as the first, except this time the damage was irreparable. The cost to the Prussian Army had been over 42,000 marks. It has to be remembered that at the time there were no aviation experts around and almost everything was done by guesswork, tempered with a lot of luck.

The first German aircraft company was formed in October 1908 on a field near the town of Darmstadt by August Euler. Euler's interest in aviation stemmed from his association with three French aircraft manufacturers: Blériot, Farman and Delagrange. Euler, who built bicycles and automobiles, was also an agent for German and French metal firms and it was through this he had got to know the French aviation manufacturers.

Euler applied to build the French Voisin under licence but the French government refused permission, which, although a setback to Euler, did not stop him. On

12 December 1908 he wrote to the commander of the 18. Armee Korps in Darmstadt asking for a field and hangar in exchange for training some of the officers as pilots. The request was passed to the War Ministry who granted the request on the conditions that he would pay for the construction of the hangar, pay for any damage caused to the surrounding roads during its construction, keep the military informed of his progress at all times, and allow the army access to his company at any time. He was also not allowed to demand payment from the army for any damages sustained, although he would be liable for any damage he or his company caused. In return, he could have the field for five years, free of charge. The local commander also gave him a verbal agreement that no other aircraft manufacturer would be allowed to use the field during this time.

When Euler found that he could not hire sufficient labour to build the hangar, he negotiated with the 21. Nassau Pionier Battailon to provide the necessary men and tools as long as he provided the transport, materials and housing. The hangar was completed on 19 April 1909 at a cost of 2,400 marks.

In 1909 the Prussian Army gave the government permission to sell their airfield at Johannisthal to a private company called the Johannisthal Flugplatz GmbH. The army then subsidised the company to the tune of 20,000 marks a year. This, of course, enabled the army to keep control of the airfield for their own purposes as and when they wanted. The company, in order to maintain the field and the hangars, leased out sections to other manufacturers as the subsidy they received from the army was insufficient for their needs. Later the War Ministry increased the subsidy to 40,000 marks.

The first real dealings the army had with the aircraft manufacturers concerned the training of officers as pilots. The reason for this was that they wanted their own fully trained pilots before they purchased any aircraft. The manufacturers reluctantly agreed because the civilian market was almost non-existent and this was one way of generating revenue.

The Rumpler aircraft manufacturing company also started building aircraft well before World War One started. The first aircraft to come from their factory was the Rumpler Eindecker, which was based on the Taube design. A flimsy looking machine, as indeed most of the early aircraft were, the Eindecker was powered by a 100hp Mercedes D.I engine and saw a great deal of service in the initial stages of the war on reconnaissance missions.

At the same time that Rumpler started manufacturing the Flugmaschine Wright GmbH (*Wright Flying Machine Co.*) appeared on the same field at Johannisthal, near Berlin. The company had been established by the Motorluftschiff Studiengesellschaft (*Motor Airship Study Co.*) with a working capital of 500,000 marks, which was an extraordinary amount of money at the time, to enable the Wrights' patented machine to be built.

With the threat of World War One looming, a number of these aircraft manufacturers started to look toward producing an aircraft that could be used for military purposes. Among these were three brothers, Alfred, Walter and Ernst Eversbusch, who established an aircraft manufacturing plant with the financial aid of the Bavarian government. The government decided to come to the aid of the brothers because they were concerned that unless they contributed to the manufacture of the aircraft, they would have no say in the equipment that would be used by Bavarian aircrews.

Initially the Bavarian Government's intention was to approach the Albatros company and to acquire the rights to build their aircraft in Bavaria, but negotiations fell through. Then the Bavarian Flying Service stepped in and, at their instigation, the Pfalz company approached Gustav Otto, a financier who helped finance the new company and assisted in the development of the business. They also acquired the rights to build the Otto biplane. The Pfalz Flugzeug-Werke was built at Speyer am Rhein in July 1913. The first aircraft to be produced there was not one of their designs, but the Otto pusher biplane which was powered by a 100hp Rapp engine. Later, Alfred Eversbusch managed to obtain a licence from the French Morane-Saulnier company to manufacture the L-type Parasol monoplane.

Another company, LFG, had its roots back in 1906, when a company by the name of Motorluftschiff Studiengesellschaft had been created at the instigation of Wilhelm II to carry out the manufacture of airships. The company changed its name a few years later to LFG Bitterfeld, from which sprang another company by the name of Flugmaschine Wright GmbH. This company went into liquidation in 1912, but was revived by a number of top financiers, including Alfred Krupp. To avoid being confused with the aircraft company LVG, the name *Roland* was added to the chosen name for the company of LFG, creating the company LFG Roland.

Although Siemens-Schuckert's first excursion into the world of aviation was in 1907, the company actually started life back in 1847 manufacturing telegraph equipment. It was known as Siemens-Halske OH then it merged with the Schuckert Werke and became the famous Siemens-Schuckert company.

The year 1914 saw the outbreak of war and the German government requested that all companies respond to the war effort. Siemens-Schuckert reactivated the aviation department under the control of Dr Walter Reichel, who was assisted by Dr Hugo Natalis and designer/pilots Franz and Bruno Steffen. The company's first effort was a single-engined monoplane that had been built for Prince Friedrich Sigismund of Prussia and was based on a design by Swedish aircraft builder Villehad Forssman. Two of the Siemens-Schuckert Bulldogs, as they were known, were built in 1915 and submitted to the Idflieg for testing. One aircraft was fitted with a 100hp Siemens-Halske Sh.I rotary engine, the other with a 100hp Mercedes S.I. Both the aircraft were rejected on the grounds of poor performance and, even worse, handling qualities. This highlighted Idflieg's role inasmuch as they would not accept substandard aircraft no matter how desperate the war situation.

The Automobil und Aviatik AG & Hannoversche Waggonfabrik AG, or the Aviatik company as it became known, was a well-known German aircraft manufacturer before World War One. At the beginning of the war, a number of Aviatik B.I and IIs, built before the war, were pressed into service with the German Army Air Service as unarmed reconnaissance aircraft. Like most of the early aircraft, the pilot flew the aircraft from the rear cockpit, whilst the observer sat in front.

As the need for aircraft intensified, the first of the Rumpler biplanes appeared in 1914: the Rumpler B.I. A small number were built and supplied to the German Army for training purposes and reconnaissance duties.

Another of the manufacturers that was beginning to make its mark was the Fokker company. The name Fokker is synonymous with aviation in both First and Second World Wars and the company produced some of Germany's finest military aircraft. Development of Fokker aircraft started in 1911, when Anthony Fokker produced the first of his many aircraft, the Spyder. With very little interest being expressed in Holland, Anthony Fokker moved to Germany registering his company, Fokker Flugzeug-Werke GmbH, in the Trade Register in Berlin on 22 February 1912.

Fokker's Jastaschule was initially the most successful part of his company; the authorities moved his school to Schwerin-Görries in Mecklenburg and supplied him with a large number of students. They also started to purchase his aircraft as by now the war had started and German aviation, in terms of aircraft, was extremely thin on the ground.

All the aircraft manufacturers came under the control of the Flugzeugmeisterei (*Air Ministry*) and Idflieg. Desperate as the situation with aircraft had become, the Inspectorate would not be pressured into accepting aircraft that did not measure up to their strict rules of requirements. Anthony Fokker discovered this to his cost and, because of his alien status, almost lost his liberty. It was only his high-level connections that prevented this.

One of the first manufacturers to attempt to build a large bomber was the Union Flugzeug-Werke GmbH of Berlin-Teltow. A designer by the name of Karl Bomhard was joined by Dr Josef Sablatnig and George König and together produced the Union Arrow Biplanes. Later two more designers, Baurat Rittberger and Karl Schopper, joined the company and it was they who designed the Union G.I bomber. Despite several setbacks, caused mainly by engine production difficulties, the aircraft carried out a couple of tests before it was destroyed when it shook apart because of excessive vibration as it was about to land. Fortunately the crew survived but it was the end of the road for the company.

Not all the manufacturers started life building aircraft. The Junkers Flugzeug-Werke started life not as an aircraft manufacturer, but as a manufacturer of gas water-heaters for bathtubs. One of their aeronautical engineers, Dr Hugo Junkers, was one of the most innovative engineers of his time and who, during his lifetime, was awarded more than 1,000 patents covering an extremely wide variety of fields. His involvement in aviation is legendary and for some years he had been looking at the concept of producing an all-metal monoplane aircraft. At the beginning of December 1915 the Junkers J.1 – also known as the E.I – appeared. The first test flight, carried out on 12 December by Leutnant Friedrich Mallinckrodt at Döberitz, was a resounding success. The thin sheet-metal covering the aircraft gave rise to the name 'Tin Donkey'.

One of the largest German aircraft manufacturers of World War One was Luftverkehrs GmbH (LVG) located at Johannisthal, Berlin. In 1907 the German General Staff approached the company with a view to building a 'military' non-rigid airship. The Type-M, as it was called, was completed but was not a success. This was followed by a much larger version which by all accounts was very successful, but for some unknown reason the project was dropped. Two years later the company was approached again, this time to build three aircraft. The use of the old Parseval airship hangar at the base gave the company all the room they needed to produce some of Germany's finest two-seater aircraft. The first aircraft produced in 1912 were of the standard Farman type. Then in 1912, a Swiss aeronautical engineer Franz Schneider joined LVG from the French Nieuport company and started building aircraft that had been designed by LVG. Two years and three aircraft later, which at best could only be described as mediocre, the company went back to its original business of electrical manufacture.

One of the most famous German aircraft of World War One was the twin-engined Gotha bomber built by the Gothaer Waggonfabrik company. The origins of the company went way back before World War One, when one of the first aircraft they built was of Taube (*dove*) design and given the designation LE.3. Originally built for the civilian market, a number of these aircraft saw service at the beginning of World War One after being requisitioned by the German Army as scouts. Only a small number were built.

One class of German aircraft stood out more than most; these were the R-Planes. The R stood for *Riesenflugzeug* or 'Giant Aircraft', and were specifically designed and built as bombers. They were, however, not the success that had been hoped for, but they did lead the way for future large bombers to be built.

GERMAN AIRCRAFT MANUFACTURERS OF WORLD WAR ONE

The manufacturers highlighted in bold were the main builders of German aircraft during this period.

Albert Rinne Flugzeug-Werke — Rummelsburg bei Berlin
Allgemeine Electrizitäts GmbH — **Hennigsdorf bei Berlin**
Ago Flugzeug-Werke GmbH — Johannisthal bei Berlin
Albatros Werke GmbH — **Johannisthal bei Berlin**
Friedrichshafen bei Berlin

Ludwig-Alter-Werke — Darmstadt
Automobil und Aviatik AG — **Leipzig-Heiterblick**
Bayerische Flugzeug-Werke AG — München
Bayerische Rumpler Werke GmbH — Augsburg
Daimler Motorengesellschaft Werke — Sindelfingen
Deutsche Flugzeug-Werke GmbH — **Lindenthal bei Leipzig**
Euler Werke — Frankfurt am Main, Niederrad
Fokker Flugzeug-Werke GmbH — **Schwerin-Gories**
Mecklenburg

Flugmaschine Fabrik Franz Schneider — Seegefeld bei Spandau
Flugmaschine Rex GmbH — Cologne
Flugzeugbau Friedrichshafen GmbH — **Manzell**
Warnemünde

Flugzeugwerft Lübeck Travemünde GmbH — Travemünde-Privall
Germania Flugzeug-Werke GmbH — Leipzig-Mockau

Goedecker Flugzeug-Werke	Mainz Gonsenheim
Gothaer Waggonfabrik AG	**Gotha**
Halberstädter Flugzeug-Werke GmbH	**Halberstadt**
Hannoversch Waggonfabrik AGe	**Hannover-Linden**
Hansa und Brandenburgische **Flugzeug-Werke GmbH**	**Priest bei Brandenburg am Havel**
Hanseatische Flugzeug-Werke (Karl Caspar AG)	Hamburg Fühlsbüttel
Jeannin Flugzeugbau GmbH	Johannisthal bei Berlin
Junkers Flugzeug-Werke AG	**Dessau**
Junkers-Fokker Werke	
Kaiserlich Marinewerft Reichwerft	Danzig Kiel Wilhelmsavhen
Kondor Flugzeug-Werke GmbH	Essen
Linke-Hoffman Werke AG	Breslau
Luftfahrzeug GmbH (LFG)	**Berlin-Charlottenburg**
Luftfahrzeugbau Schütte-Lanz	Mannheim-Rheinau Zessen bei Königswursterhausen
Luft Torpedo GmbH	Johannisthal bei Berlin
Luftverkehrs GmbH	**Johannisthal bei Berlin**
Märkische Flugzeug-Werke GmbH	Golm-in-der-Mark
Mercur Flugzeugbau GmbH	Berlin
Naglo Boots-Werft	Pichelsdorf-Spandau, Berlin
National Flugzeug-Werke GmbH	Johannisthal bei Berlin
Nordeutsche Flugzeug-Werke	Tetlow bei Berlin
Oertz Werke GmbH	Reiherstieg bei Hamburg
Ostdeutsche Albatros Werke GmbH	Schneidemühl
Otto Werke GmbH	München
Pfalz Flugzeug-Werke GmbH	**Speyer am Rhein**
Rumpler Flugzeug-Werke GmbH	**Johannisthal bei Berlin**
Sablatnig Flugzeugbau GmbH	**Berlin**
Schwade Elugzeug und Motorenbau	Erfurt
Siemens-Schuckert Werke GmbH	**Berlin** **Nürnberg**
Union Flugzeug-Werke	Tetlow bei Berlin
Waggonfabrik Josef Rathgeber	München-Moosach
Zeppelin Werke, Lindau GmbH	Reutin Seemo
Zeppelin Werke Staaken GmbH	**Staaken bei Berlin**

The next section is a brief history of the highlighted manufacturers and the part they played in World War One. Each company history is followed by the specifications of selected aircraft that they built, to give an example of the variety of craft available.

ALLGEMEINE ELECTRIZITÄTS GESELLSCHAFT (AEG)

In 1914 a two-seat unarmed reconnaissance aircraft, the AEG B.I, appeared in the skies over France; it was the first military aircraft produced by AEG. The B.I was selected for reconnaissance and artillery-spotting duties almost from the outset of war. It was unusual because it had a tricycle undercarriage and a wing span of over 50ft. Powered by a 100hp Mercedes D.I. engine, the B.I had a top speed of 63mph. As with all wartime weapons, necessity became the mother of invention, and within months the B.I had been superseded by the B.II, which was fitted with a more powerful Mercedes engine. The tricycle undercarriage had been replaced, thus making the aircraft a standard 'tail dragger'.

A venture into the development of twin-engined bombers gave AEG a new impetus, when early in 1915 the AEG I(KI) appeared. Powered by two 100hp Mercedes D.I engines and carrying a crew of three, the aircraft did not prove to be the success it had been hoped for and only one was built. In July 1915 a slightly larger version of the G.I appeared, the G.II. Powered by two 150hp Benz Bz.III engines, the aircraft carried an aircrew of three and was armed with two machine guns and carried 200kg of bombs externally. Between fifteen and twenty of these aircraft were built and were used by the Kampfgeschwadern.

The AEG B.III appeared in June 1915, fitted with a 120hp Mercedes D.II engine and a reduced wing span of 42ft 11½in. Once again the aircraft was used for unarmed reconnaissance missions with a top speed of 68mph. One month later, in March 1915, the first armed AEG appeared in the shape of the AEG C.I. Fitted with a 150hp Benz Bz.III engine, the C.I was virtually a B.II fitted with a more powerful engine and carrying a Bergmann machine gun in the observer's position.

Crew of an AEG G.I standing beside their aicraft.

AEG G.II with a triple-tail.

The AEG C.II appeared in October 1915 and was a slightly smaller version of the C.I. The fuselage was 3ft shorter and the wing span had been reduced by 2ft which reduced the weight of the aircraft by some 50lb. The aircraft was equipped with bomb-carrying equipment which enabled it to carry four 10kg bombs. Powered by the 150hp Benz Bz.III engine with its distinctive rhinohorn exhaust, the aircraft had a top speed of 86mph.

This was followed at the end of 1915 by the radical design of the AEG C.III, in which the pilot was seated behind the observer. Powered by a 150hp Benz Bz.III engine, the aircraft only reached the experimental stage and only one was ever made. Amongst a number of other things, there were serious problems with the pilot's visibility during flying and landing.

By the end of the year a third type of bomber had appeared, the AEG III. This was the first of the bombers to have balanced control surfaces and was powered by two eight-cylinder 220hp Mercedes D.IV engines. It carried an aircrew of three and was armed with two manually operated machine guns and 300kg of bombs. It had a range of 700km (435 miles) with a top speed of 98mph.

Early in February 1916, manufacturers were asked to produce a new two-seat fighter/reconnaissance aircraft and AEG produced the C.V. Powered by a 220hp Mercedes D.IV engine, the C.V had a top speed of 103mph and could climb to 3,280ft in less than 5 minutes. One was built and entered for competition, but the Albatros C.V proved to be a far better aircraft and was selected.

At the beginning of 1916 the German Army High Command started a programme – designated the R-plane – which was designed to replace airships with long-range bomber/reconnaissance aircraft. Accordingly a number of aircraft manufacturers were approached, which included AEG.

Other aircraft companies such as Siemens-Schuckert, Albatros, Aviatik had been working on such an aircraft since mid-1914. AEG staff had some considerable experience in building bombers, but nothing on the scale of the R.I that was to eventually appear.

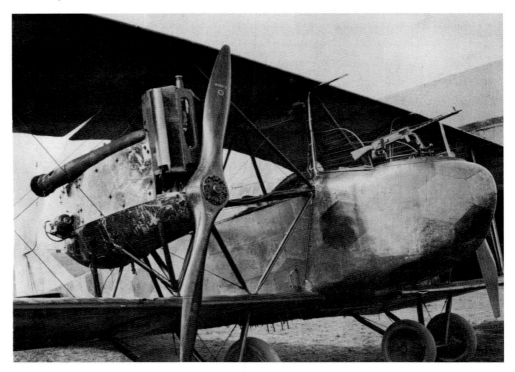

Excellent close-up shot of the nose and engine section of an AEG G.IV.

In charge of the project was former Deutsche Flugzeug-Werke (DFW) test pilot Oberleutnant Brückmann, with Chief Engineer Ing. Sander, his assistants Dipl.Ing. Werner Zorn and Professor Oesterlein. The aircraft was a real *tour de force* and consisted of a number of revolutionary designs including an all-steel fuselage, mixed steel and duraluminium wings and electrically operated tailplane trim controls.

The R.I was powered by four 260hp Mercedes D.IVa engines, the first of which were started by a single Bosch inertia starter and then 'clutch-starting' the remaining three engines. On the prototype model each engine had its own radiator; these were later replaced by two large radiators which consisted of four separate units mounted on the centre-section struts. They also had four-bladed propellers which – surprisingly – were later replaced by two-bladed ones.

The first flight took place on 14 June 1918 and a number of problems manifested themselves. The most serious was that with the engines throttled right back and with the elevator full down, the nose of the aircraft continued to rise. To enable the aircraft to make a safe landing, all available weight had to be moved forward.

Allocated the designation of R.21, the bomber carried out a number of other test flights and it was decided that the propellers were not suitable. They were returned to the propeller factory and were fitted with additional glued sections. The propellers were returned to AEG with the warning that it would be at least ten days before the glue had set properly. Impatient to get the aircraft into the air again Oberleutnant Brückmann had the propellers fitted within four days of their return. Zorn warned

Brückmann that it was unsafe to fly the aircraft. On 3 September 1918 the aircraft took to the air, but within one hour tragedy struck. One of the propellers flew apart, this caused the cardan shaft to tear loose and shatter the centre-section structure. The result was that the AEG R.21 broke apart in the air, killing all seven members of the crew.

Test pilot Max Fiedler who was flying a Rumpler C.I. chase plane as an escort described the accident:

> I recall being slightly over the R.21 at about 6,000 feet when Brückmann, celebrating the event, waved a cognac bottle as the R.21 swung to the left and then a right bank. There was a flutter and suddenly the wings folded back. It was a terrifying sight.

Production was immediately halted until the problems were sorted out, but the main problem had been identified very soon after the accident.

AEG received a contract for a second R.I, designated the R.II, but the project was never completed.

In December 1916 two models of the AEG C.VII appeared, the difference between the two was that one had straight wings, whilst the other had a heavily swept upper wing and a large spinner on the airscrew. Only one of each was built.

Another single model was built in 1917, the AEG C.IV N: a single-engined night bomber. Based on the design of the C.IV, the C.IV N had a wing span of 50ft 2in, was powered by a 150hp Benz Bz.III engine and had a flight duration of four hours. It was not a great success and only one was built. This was followed by the C.VIII, an experimental two-seater with multi-spar wings and radiators situated either side on the fuselage that closely resembled ears. Powered by a 160hp Mercedes D.III engine, the C.VIII had a top speed of 106mph and could climb to 3,280ft in 3.8 minutes.

AEG J.I.

An investigation into the field of single-seater fighters in March 1917 produced the AEG D.I. Powered by a 160hp Mercedes D.III engine, this stocky little fighter was capable of a top speed of 137mph. It was built in limited numbers and one was flown in combat by Leutnant Walter Höhndorf, who was killed in the aircraft on 5 September 1917.

Two further prototypes were produced, differing only in the fact that they had 'ear'-type radiators fitted either side of the fuselage. There was even a triplane version, the AEG Dr.I, but it proved to have no more performance value than the previous three models.

The arrival of the triplane prompted AEG to produce an experimental version, the AEG C.VIII Dr. Similar to the C.VIII in design, even down to the unusual tail surfaces, the aircraft proved to be no better than the C.VIII and development was not pursued.

Early in 1918 another experimental single-seater triplane was produced, the AEG P.E. (Panzer Einsitzer). It had an armoured aluminium-sheet-covered fuselage and tubular wing spars. Powered by a 195hp Benz Bz.IIIb engine, the fighter was capable of a top speed of 103mph. It was armed with twin Spandau forward-firing machine guns and capable of carrying four small bombs. Just before the Armistice another fighter aircraft appeared from the factory – the AEG DJ.I. Derived from the AEG P.E., the DJ.I was powered by the V.8 195hp Benz Bz.IIIb engine which was, like the DJ.I's fuselage, was covered in armoured aluminium. It had a top speed of 112mph and a climb rate 830ft per minute. It was designed as an armoured single-seat ground attack fighter, whose British equivalent was the Sopwith Salamander, but the war ceased before it could be put into production and the main protagonists were at peace, albeit for just a short time.

AEG J.IA on a tail stand; it is interesting to note the skis.

SPECIFICATIONS

AEG C.IV

Wingspan	44ft 2in
Length	23ft 5½in
Height	11ft
Weight Empty	1,760lb
Weight Loaded	2,464lb
Maximum Speed	98mph
Ceiling	16,400ft
Duration	4hrs
Armament	One forward-firing synchronised Spandau machine gun
	One manually operated Parabellum machine gun in observer's position
Engine	One 160hp Mercedes D.III – six-cylinder, in-line, water-cooled

AEG J.II

Wingspan	44ft 2in
Length	23ft 7½in
Height	11ft
Weight Empty	3,201lb
Weight Loaded	3,828lb
Maximum Speed	93mph
Ceiling	16,400ft
Duration	2½hrs
Armament	One forward-firing synchronised Spandau machine gun
	One manually operated Parabellum machine gun in observer's position
Engine	One 160hp Mercedes D.III – six-cylinder, in-line, water-cooled

AEG Dr.I. (Dreidecker)

Wingspan	30ft 10in
Length	20ft
Height	7ft 6in
Weight Empty	1,562lb
Weight Loaded	2,134lb
Maximum Speed	106mph

Ceiling	14,600ft
Duration	4–5hrs
Armament	One forward-firing synchronised Spandau machine gun
Engine	One 160hp Mercedes D.III – six-cylinder, in-line, water-cooled

AEG C.VIII Dr (Dreidecker)

Wingspan Upper	36ft 9in
Middle	35ft 5in
Lower	25ft 1in
Length	22ft 8in
Height	7ft 6in
Weight Empty	1,562lb
Weight Loaded	2,134lb
Maximum Speed	103mph
Ceiling	14,000ft
Duration	4–5hrs
Engine	One 160hp Mercedes D.III – six-cylinder, in-line, water-cooled

AEG DJ

Wingspan	36ft 9in
Length	21ft 8in
Height	7ft 6in
Weight Empty	2,600lb
Weight Loaded	3,106lb
Maximum Speed	103mph
Ceiling	13,920ft
Duration	4–5hrs
Engine	One V-8 195hp Benz Bz.IIIb, in-line, water-cooled
Armament	Twin Spandau machine guns and provision for four small bombs

ALBATROS WERKE GMBH

The Albatros Werke produced their first aircraft in 1912: the Albatros L.3, a single-seat scout type. This was followed by the L.9, a single-seat scout type designed by Claude Dornier.

The first of the reconnaissance/trainers, the B.I, appeared in 1913. The aircraft was initially used as a trainer, but with the outbreak of war it was used both as a trainer and reconnaissance aircraft. Powered by a 100hp Mercedes D.II engine, the B.I had a top speed of 65mph and a flight duration of four hours. Only a small number were built before being replaced by the B.II. The B.II, like the B.I, had an extremely strong slab-sided fuselage made up of four spruce longerons covered with plywood. Like all the early aircraft, the pilot sat in the rear cockpit, which gave him a very limited view for take-offs and landings. Used for training and reconnaissance duties, the B.II was replaced by the B.III with only minor modifications.

The arrival of Allied fighter aircraft prompted the development of a faster reconnaissance aircraft. Albatros produced the (OAW – Ostdeutsche Albatros Werke) C.I powered by the 150hp Benz engine, but only two were built. A second Albatros, the (OAW) C.II built in 1916, powered by a straight-eight Mercedes D.IV engine, was produced; this time only one was built.

Early in 1915 the company embarked on a singularly ambitious project, a four-engined bomber. Designed by Konstrukteur (*designer*) Grohmann, the Albatros G.I had a wingspan of 89ft 6½in, a wing area of 1,485sq.ft and a fuselage length of 39ft 4¼in. It was a very large aircraft. On the lower wing, four 120hp Mercedes D.II engines in nacelles were mounted driving four tractor propellers. The first flight took place on 31 January 1916 and was flown by a Swiss pilot Alexander Hipleh. The G.I

Unknown pilots in front of an Albatros B.I.

Albatros B.II in flight.

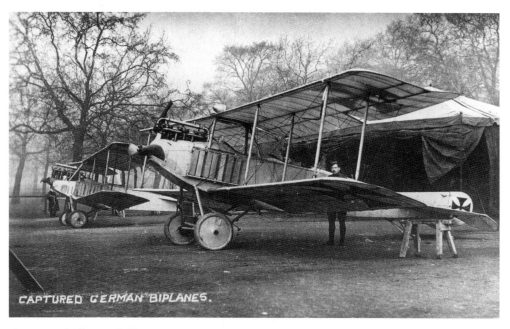

A captured Albatros B.III.

Albatros C.I in flight wearing Swiss markings.

became the forerunner of the G.II and G.III, although the two latter aircraft were twin-engined bombers.

A completely different design early in 1916 produced the Albatros C.II. Called the Gitterschwanz (*trellis-tail*), the design was of the pusher type looking very similar to the De Havilland DH.2. Powered by a 150hp Benz Bz.III engine, the C.II did not measure up to expectations and only one was built. This was quickly followed by the Albatros C.IV which reverted back to the original basic design. A 160hp Mercedes D.III engine was fitted into the C.III fuselage to which a C.II tail assembly and undercarriage were fixed. Again, only one of these aircraft was made.

A purely experimental model, the Albatros C.V Experimental, was built at the beginning of 1916. It had a wing span of 41ft 11½in supported by I-struts in an effort to test the interplane bracing. Powered by an eight-cylinder 220hp Mercedes D.IV engine, the C.V Experimental supplied a great deal of information to Albatros Werke. The C.VI followed soon afterwards; it was based on the C.III airframe and powered by a 180hp Argus As.III engine giving the aircraft a top speed of 90mph and carrying enough fuel for a 4½-hour flight duration. In 1917 a night bomber version, the C.VIII N, was evolved. Bombs were carried beneath the lower wings, but it was only powered by a 160hp Mercedes D.III engine; only one was built.

At the same time that the night bomber was being built, a two-seat fighter/reconnaissance aircraft, the Albatros C.IX, was being built. With a straight lower wing and a considerably swept upper wing, it presented an unusual aircraft configuration – only

Albatros C.VII. This was originally built out of many parts from Albatros C.V.

three were built. This was followed by the Albatros C.XIII and again it was for experimental purposes and only one was built. A return to the original design of the two-
seater reconnaissance produced the Albatros C.XIV. There was one difference: the
C.XIV had staggered wings and again only one was built. The C.XIV was later
modified into the C.XV. It was too late for appearance of this aircraft in any numbers
as the end of the war came.

The air supremacy of the German Army Air Service during 1916 had been
gradually eroded by the rapid development of Allied fighter aircraft. In a desperate
attempt to regain air control, Albatros Werke was approached to design and build a
fighter that would do just that. Looking at the highly manoeuvrable Nieuport that
was causing some of the problems, the company's top designer Robert Thelen set to
work and produced a design that combined speed and firepower. If the aircraft
couldn't out-manoeuvre the Nieuport, the Albatros could catch it and blast it out of
the sky. That is precisely what the designed Albatros did.

The first of the Albatros series, the D.I, was powered by a 160hp Mercedes engine
or the 150hp Benz, which was enclosed in a semi-monocoque plywood fuselage.
The cylinder heads and valve gear were left exposed as this gave assisted cooling and
greater ease of access for the engineers who had to work on the engine. Engine
cooling was achieved by mounting two Windoff radiators, one on each side of the
fuselage and between the wings, and a slim water tank mounted above and toward
the rear of the engine at an offset angle to port. The extra power given to the aircraft
enabled the firepower (twin fixed Spandau machine guns) to be increased without
loss of performance.

The fuselage consisted of ⅜in thick plywood formers and six spruce longerons. Screwed to this frame were plywood panels and the engine was installed with easily removable metal panels for both protection and ease of maintenance. The upper and lower wings and the tail surfaces were covered with fabric. The fixed tail surfaces, upper and lower fins, were made of plywood. The control surfaces were fabric covered over a welded steel-tube frame with a small triangular balance portion incorporated in the rudder and the one-piece elevator.

The undercarriage, a conventional streamlined steel-tube, V-type chassis, was fixed to the fuselage by means of sockets and sprung through the wheels with rubber shock cord.

The Albatros was a very satisfactory aircraft to fly, but it was discovered to have a major drawback during combat. The top wing, because of its position to the fuselage, obscured the pilot's forward field of vision. The problem was solved by cutting out a semi-circular section of the top wing in front of the pilot, and by lowering the wing so that the pilot could see over the top.

The first Jasta to receive the Albatros D.I was Jasta 2 on 17 September 1916, which was commanded by the legendary Oswald Boelcke. Three weeks later Boelcke was killed when his Albatros was involved in a mid-air collision with his wingman Erwin Böhme as they both dived to attack the same British aircraft, a DH2 of 24 Squadron RFC.

In the middle of 1916 the German Naval High Command decided that it would be a good idea to have a single-seat fighter floatplane as a defence aircraft. The Albatros D.I was used as the basis of the Albatros W.4 although the latter was considerably larger in overall dimensions, the wing span being increased by 1m (3ft).

Albatros D.II Nr.910/16 belonging to Leutnant Max Böhme of Jasta 5.

Late in 1916 the Albatros D.III appeared with subtle but noticeable changes to previous marks. But by the summer of 1917, this too had been superseded by the Albatros D.V and D.Va just as the SE5s and SPADs (Société Pour Aviation et ses Dérièves) of the Allies started to regain control of the skies. The same problem seemed to dog the Albatros throughout its lifetime: the lower wing had a tendency to break up in a prolonged dive. In one incident, Sergeant Festnter of Jasta 11 carried out a test flight in an Albatros D.III when at 13,000ft the port lower wing broke up and it was only his experience and a great deal of luck that prevented the aircraft crashing into the ground. Even the legendary Manfred Freiherr von Richthofen experienced a similar incident on 24 January 1917 whilst testing one of the new Albatros D.IIIs that had recently arrived at Jasta 11.

Tests were carried out and it was discovered that the single spar was positioned too far aft causing vibrations which increased as the dive continued. This eventually resulted in the structure of the wing collapsing under the erratic movement. A temporary stopgap was achieved by fitting a short strut from the V-interplane to the leading edge. Instructions were then given to pilots not to carry out long dives in the Albatros, which, as one can imagine, drastically reduced the faith pilots had in the aircraft, especially when under combat conditions.

A large number of Jastas were being supplied with the Albatros III and IV, and once again superiority in the air passed to the Germans. The rapidly becoming famous 'Aces' were flying the Albatros IIIs and IVs, among them Werner Voss and Prinz Friedrich Carl of Prussia, who commanded a Flieger Abteilung unit and kept an Albatros at Jasta 2 for his personal use. The superiority of the Albatros IIIs and IVs, however, was shortlived with the arrival of the Sopwith Triplane and the SPAD S.VII, and later the SE5 and Sopwith Camel. The Germans quickly realised that each time they came up with a supposed superior design the Allies countered it with an even better one. The Allies also had the advantage of being able to turn to a variety of aircraft manufacturers, whereas the Germans were limited in choice.

Albatros Werke were pressured into improving the Albatros, and the Albatros D.V was developed. The D.V had a major change to the shape of the fuselage. The D.III fuselage, with its flat sides, was replaced with an elliptical fuselage. The aileron cables were routed through the top wing instead of the lower wing but the wing structures were the same. Fitted with a six-cylinder in-line, water-cooled 200hp Mercedes D.IIIa engine, the increased speed of the D.V started to redress some of the balance of air power, but not enough to make any substantial difference. Even the appearance of the D.Va, although a superior aircraft to the D.V, did nothing to improve German air superiority.

Albatros Werke was not being idle – the Albatros marque was being developed and an experimental model, the D.IV, was produced. With the fuselage of a D.Va and the wings of a D.II, the experimental fighter was powered by a specially geared version of the 160hp Mercedes D.III engine, which allowed the engine to be completely enclosed in the nose. There were a number of insurmountable problems with the engine and the project was scrapped. Two months later in August 1917, another experimental fighter appeared, the D.VII. It was powered by a V-8 195hp Benz Bz.IIIb engine, which gave the aircraft a top speed of 127mph and a rate of climb rate of nearing 1,000ft per minute. Again, only one model was built.

Ernst Udet standing in front of his Albatros D.III.

The appearance of the Albatros Dr.I in 1917 was to assess the possibilities of producing a triplane. After many tests the aircraft was deemed to be no better than the D.V. and did not proceed. However, at the beginning of 1918 another triplane appeared: the Albatros Dr.II. The heavily staggered triple wings were braced with very wide struts and ailerons were fitted to all the wingtips. It was powered by a V-8 195hp Benz Bz.IVb engine, with frontal-type radiators which were mounted in the centre section between the upper and middle wings. Speed of the aircraft was affected considerably because of the drag caused by the radiator's position.

A two-seater reconnaissance/bomber appeared at the beginning of 1918, the Albatros J.II. It was powered by a 220hp Benz Bz.IVa engine which gave the aircraft a top speed of 87mph. The J.II was armed with twin fixed downward-firing Spandau machine guns and one manually operated movable Parabellum machine gun in the rear cockpit. The downward-firing guns protruded through the floor of the fuselage between the legs of the undercarriage. Four examples were built but it arrived after the Junkers J.1 and the success of the J.1 overshadowed the J.II to the extent that no more were built.

A number of prototypes made their appearance early in 1918, the first being the Albatros D.IX. It was powered by a 180hp Mercedes D.IIIa giving it a top speed of 96mph. Only one was built. A second model appeared, the Albatros D.X, powered by a V-8 195hp Benz Bz.IIIb engine. This gave the aircraft a top speed of 106mph. At a fighter competition at Aldershof, it initially outperformed all the other competitors, but was unable to sustain the performance throughout. Again, only one model was built.

The Albatros D.XI which followed was the first Albatros aircraft to use a rotary engine. Fitted with the Siemens-Halske Sh.III of 160hp, it was installed in a horseshoe-shaped cowling with extensions pointing toward the rear. These exten-

Captured Albatros D.Va. The troops in the background belonged to the USAS.

sions assisted in the cooling by sucking air through the cowling. Two prototypes were built: one with a four-bladed propeller, the other with a twin-bladed model.

Two prototype Albatros D.XIIs followed both fitted with different engines, but fitted with a Böhme undercarriage, which for the first time featured compressed-air shock absorbers. Neither aircraft was considered for production.

The Albatros D.V model was the most famous of all the Albatros aircraft. It was supplied to various Jastas in May 1917 in an attempt to bolster flagging morale. Pilots were encouraged to emblazon their aircraft to personalise them. Manfred von Richthofen and Eduard Ritter von Schleich earned their nicknames from their respective red and black Albatros D.Vs. By May 1918 there were 131 Albatros D.Vs and 928 D.Vas in operational service, but it was too late – the war was over by November.

Specifications

Albatros C.III

Wingspan	38ft 4¼in
Length	26ft 3in
Height	10ft 2in
Weight Empty	1,872lb
Weight Loaded	2,976lb
Maximum Speed	87mph
Ceiling	11,000ft
Duration	4hrs
Engine	One 150hp Benz Bz.III – six-cylinder, in-line, water-cooled
Armament	One fixed forward-firing Spandau machine gun One manually operated Parabellum machine gun in observer's position

Albatros Dr.I. (Dreidecker)

Wingspan	28ft 7in
Length	24ft
Height	7ft 11in
Weight Empty	2,600lb
Weight Loaded	3,106lb
Maximum Speed	103mph
Ceiling	13,920ft
Duration	4–5hrs
Engine	One 160hp Mercedes D.III – six-cylinder, in-line, water-cooled
Armament	Twin Spandau machine guns

Albatros Dr.II. (Dreidecker)

Wingspan	32ft 10in
Length	20ft 3in
Height	11ft
Weight Empty	1,487lb
Weight Loaded	2,013lb
Maximum Speed	103mph
Ceiling	13,920ft
Duration	4–5hrs
Engine	One V-8 195hp Benz Bz.IVb – in-line, water-cooled
Armament	Twin Spandau machine guns

Albatros D.III.

Wingspan	29ft 8¼in
Length	24ft ½in
Height	9ft 9¼in
Weight Empty	1,454lb
Weight Loaded	1,949lb
Maximum Speed	108mph
Ceiling	18,000ft
Duration	2hrs
Engine	One 160hp Mercedes D.IIIa – six-cylinder, in-line, water-cooled
Armament	Twin Spandau machine guns

AUTOMOBIL UND AVIATIK AG

The Automobil und Aviatik AG was a well-known German aircraft manufacturer before World War One. At the beginning of the war, a number of pre-war Aviatik B.I and IIs were pressed into service with the German Army Air Service as unarmed reconnaissance aircraft. Like most of the early aircraft, the pilot flew the aircraft from the rear cockpit, whilst the observer sat in front. Powered by 100hp Mercedes D.I. engines, both the B.I and B.II had a top speed of 85mph and a flight duration of two and a half hours.

Early in 1915 Aviatik produced the C.I reconnaissance aircraft, only this time the observer was armed with a Parabellum machine gun which was mounted on rails either side of the cockpit. This unusual arrangement was not the best as it gave a very restricted line of fire when it was necessary to use the machine gun and also when carrying out observation duties. Thoughts turned to reversing the seating arrangements, but the idea had already been pre-empted by other aircraft manufacturers like Albatros, Rumpler and LVG who were mass-producing far superior designs.

The design of the Aviatik C.I was of the conventional box girder construction, made up of four spruce longerons held together with stranded steel cables. The fuselage was covered with curved aluminium panels over the engine area, whilst fabric covered the remainder of the fuselage. The wings had a span of 41ft and were of the normal rectangular shape covered with fabric.

The C.I was powered by a six-cylinder, in-line, water-cooled 160hp Mercedes D.IIIa engine, which gave the aircraft a top speed of 88mph, a ceiling of 11,480ft and a flight duration of three hours. Originally the radiators were mounted on either side of the fuselage, but on an improved model they were mounted just below the leading edge of the top wing on the front section struts. The manifold exhaust was led over the top wing which restricted the pilot's view. The undercarriage was of the normal V-type, the struts being joined by a short horizontal tube which also served as an anchorage for the rubber cord shock absorbers. It was additionally strengthened with stranded steel cables which cross braced the undercarriage between the front legs.

A C.Ia model was produced with the seating arrangement of pilot and observer reversed, but when the C.II appeared shortly afterwards the seating was as before, with the pilot sitting in the back. Forty-three of this type were ordered before it was superseded by the C.III which appeared at the beginning of 1916. The airframe of the C.III was the same as the C.I and C.II, but with a few additional refinements. The manifold exhaust system was changed so that it ejected horizontally to starboard instead of directly over the top. A new aerofoil-shaped radiator was installed in the starboard side of the upper wing centre-section. The forward section was streamlined and a large nose cone fitted. The pilot's cockpit was fitted with a streamlined headrest which provided an extra degree of comfort. These refinements added a further 11mph to the aircraft's top speed.

Aviatik B.I. It was one of the German Air Services' earliest unarmed two-seater reconnaissance aircraft.

The brief appearance early in 1917 of the Aviatik C.V showed an excursion into a new way of thinking. The gull-shaped wings of the aircraft provided the crew with an excellent upward and uninterrupted field of vision. The aircraft was powered by a 180hp Argus As.III engine, which was neatly cowled and streamlined into the fuselage. Surprisingly, only one of the aircraft was built.

The appearance of the Aviatik C.VI model was in fact one that was built under licence by Deutsche Flugzeug-Werke (DFW). This was one of the most successful of all the two-seat reconnaissance/artillery observation/photographic aircraft produced by Germany during World War One, and large numbers of the aircraft were made. The C.VI was powered by a six-cylinder, in-line, water-cooled 200hp -Benz Bz.IV engine, which gave a top speed of 96mph, a climb rate of 340ft per minute and a flight duration of three and a half hours.

If there was a C.VII model then it was probably only on the drawing board, because the next model to make an appearance was the Aviatik C.VIII. Looking very much like the Halberstadt CL.II, the C.VIII had a plywood-covered fuselage tapering down to a narrow tail.

This was quickly followed by three C.IX prototypes which were built for test purposes. One of the prototypes had ailerons on all four wingtips; another had ailerons on the top wing only – with the remaining prototype's airframe being tested to destruction.

The first Aviatik fighter aircraft appeared late in 1916 in the shape of the Aviatik D.II. The whole forward section of the fuselage was a steel tube, whilst the aft section was of plywood. It was fitted with a 160hp Mercedes D.III engine. Only one of the aircraft was built. One year later, two prototype Aviatik D.IIIs powered by a V-8 195hp Benz Bz.IIIb engine (top speed of 108mph) appeared and took part in the D-type competition at Aldershof.

An Aviatik D.IV was produced soon afterwards but there is little information on this aircraft available. In mid-1918 Aviatik produced another fighter, the D.VI. This also took part in the D-type competitions at Aldershof and like the D.IIIs, performed extremely well. Powered by a V-8 195hp Benz Bz.IIIb engine and with a large car-type radiator on the nose, the D.VI was fitted with a four-bladed propeller. Only one D.VI was built and the information gained was passed to the next generation fighter, the Aviatik D.VII.

There was very little difference between the Aviatik D.VI and the D.VII, except for the re-designing of the tail surfaces. The aircraft was armed with twin Spandau machine guns.

The Aviatik company venture into the fighter world was not a very successful one, but their development of the two-seat reconnaissance/artillery spotting aircraft was second to none and large numbers of these aircraft became the mainstays of the Flieger Abteilung of the German Army Air Service.

Aviatik C.I seen here with its pilot.

Aviatik C.Ia in the snow. The German sentry in the background with his brightly striped sentry-box keeps a wary eye on the aircraft.

Aviatik C.III. Note the Maltese crosses on the wheels.

Aviatik D.I powered by a 185-hp Austro-Daimler engine.

Aviatik D.I at Egna, Italy, after being shot down.

SPECIFICATIONS

Aviatik C.I

Wingspan	41ft ¼in
Length	26ft
Height	9ft 8¼in
Weight Empty	1,650lb
Weight Loaded	2,732lb
Maximum Speed	88mph
Ceiling	11,480ft
Duration	3hrs
Engine	One 160hp Mercedes D.IIIa – six-cylinder, in-line, water-cooled
Armament	One manually operated Parabellum machine gun mounted on rails

Aviatik C.III

Wingspan	38ft 5¼in
Length	26ft 6¼in
Height	9ft 8¼in
Weight Empty	2,156lb
Weight Loaded	2,948lb
Maximum Speed	100mph
Ceiling	14,760ft
Duration	3hrs
Engine	One 160hp Mercedes D.IIIa – six-cylinder, in-line, water-cooled
Armament	Two manually operated Parabellum machine guns mounted on rails

Aviatik (Berg) D.I

Wingspan	26ft 3in
Length	22ft 6in
Height	8ft 2in
Weight Empty	1,345lb
Weight Loaded	1,878lb
Maximum Speed	115mph
Ceiling	20,175ft
Duration	2½hrs
Engine	One 200hp Austro-Daimler – in-line, water-cooled.
Armament	Two fixed forward-firing 8mm Schwarzlose synchronised machine guns.

Deutsche Flugzeug-Werke GmbH (DFW)

One of the first pure military aircraft produced by the DFW factory was the DFW B.I biplane, or to give it its correct designation the DFW Type M.D 14 B.I. Developed in 1914 as a reconnaissance and training aircraft, it originally had a welded steel tube fuselage and was powered by a 100hp Mercedes D.I engine. Later versions had an all-wood plywood covered fuselage and fitted with the more powerful 180hp Benz Bz.III engine. The B.I had a wingspan of 45ft 11½in, a length of 27ft 6½in and a top speed of 75mph.

The B.II, powered by a 120hp Mercedes D.II engine, was produced at the beginning of 1915 and had a wingspan of 41ft 4½in – some 4½in shorter than that of the B.I, but with the same length of fuselage. Like the B.I, the B.II was used as a reconnaissance aircraft as well as for training purposes. The German fighter ace and holder of the Orden Pour le Mérite, Oberleutnant Kurt Wüsthoff, trained in one of the B.II training aircraft at the Leipzig-Lindenthal flying training school near Berlin.

A venture into the single-seater fighter market with the DFW Floh (flea) ended when the tiny aircraft crashed on its initial test flight early in 1915. One of the reasons given for the accident was the appalling lack of visibility from the cockpit. Powered by a 100hp Mercedes D.I. engine, it had a wingspan of 20ft 4in, and a fuselage length of 14ft 9½in. The DFW Floh looked completely out of proportion.

At a request by the Idflieg DFW were asked to join the R-plane programme and develop a heavy bomber. Their first bomber was the DFW R.I designed by Hermann Dorner and took a year to make. These were unique in their construction inasmuch as the four eight-cylinder, in-line 220hp Mercedes D.IV engines were internally mounted, each driving a separate propeller. They were mounted in an unusual manner: the two tractor types were fitted above and slightly ahead on the two pusher-type engines. The first radiators were triangular shaped and were mounted between the centre-section struts, but these were soon replaced by four Windhoff radiators fitted to the fuselage in the centre section gap.

The first flight took place on 5 September 1916, the first of twelve flights before the aircraft was delivered to the Army Air Park at Döberitz. After further testing by Army pilots, the R.I was flown via Königsberg to Alt-Auz to join RFA 500 (Riesen Flugzeug Abteilung). On 13 June 1917 the R.I carried out its one and only successful mission when it dropped 680kg of bombs on Schlok, in retaliation for an earlier Russian attack.

Departing on its second mission in September 1917, the R.I experienced a problem when one of its four engines failed. The pilots, instead of continuing on three engines, turned the aircraft round to return to the field. Overheating on a gear box caused the second engine to be stopped, the result being that the aircraft was now too heavy to be kept in the air. Searching for a place to land, the crew of the giant aircraft, which was now running on the two remaining engines, spotted a training field and put the aircraft down. Unfortunately they failed to spot a deep trench running across the field and the aircraft crashed as the wheels plunged down into the trench. The aircraft spilled its load of bombs and fuel onto the field then exploded. One of the crew was killed.

In September 1916 the prototype DFW C-Type was produced. This was the fore-runner of what was to be one of the most successful of all the two-seater German reconnaissance aircraft of World War One: the DFW C.V. Only one C-Type was built and powered by a 150hp Benz Bz.III engine. This was quickly followed by the DFW C.I and C.II and the only difference between the two aircraft was that the pilot flew the aircraft from the rear cockpit in the C.I, but in the C.II flew it from the front seat. Otherwise they were identical in every other detail and a number of these aircraft were built and delivered to the German Army. Powered by 150hp Benz Bz.III, the C.I and C.II had a wingspan of 36ft 9in, a fuselage length of 23ft 7½in, an operating ceiling of 13,120ft and a top speed of 87mph. There was only one gun: a manually operated Parabellum machine gun mounted in the rear cockpit.

A second DFW R.II was built at the end of 1916 after an order from the Idflieg. Basically the same as the R.I, except that the overall dimensions were increased slightly, the R.II was powered by four eight-cylinder in-line Mercedes D.IVa engines. The fuselage of the first R.I was made up of spruce longerons covered in plywood, but because of the twisting forces that the fuselage was subjected to during flight, the R.II longerons were reinforced with steel tube frames and cables.

The first of the R.IIs made its maiden flight on 17 September 1917 and although the flight was very successful there were still problems with vibration despite the strengthened engine mounts. This problem was later solved by encasing the trans-mission shafts with stiffener tubes. A second of six R.IIs ordered was built in February 1918, but there were problems, and modifications had to be made before it was accepted by the Army. A third was built later but none ever saw active service.

An attempt to develop a pusher aircraft, a DFW C.III pusher biplane powered by a 150hp Benz Bz.III, amounted to nothing. The aircraft looked almost identical to the French Breguet pusher biplane.

The DFW C.IV was developed at the end of 1916 and featured single-bay wings. The C.IV was powered by a 150hp Benz Bz.III engine, with the radiator mounted beneath the upper leading-edge. The aircraft was armed with two machine guns: a fixed forward-firing Spandau and a manually operated Parabellum mounted in the rear cockpit. A number were developed for the German Army.

An attempt to develop a single-seat fighter surfaced again in 1917 with the DFW D.I. The prototype was very similar to the DFW Floh; the only difference being a 160hp Mercedes D.III engine with a car-type radiator mounted at the nose. Only one was built. A second modified prototype appeared some months later fitted with twin Spandau machine guns. Again only one was built. A third DFW D.I. modified prototype appeared at the end of 1917. Almost identical to the second modified D.I, only the ailerons were removed from the lower wingtips. The development of these models led to the production of the DFW Dr.I Dreidecker designed for the D-type competition at Aldershof, Berlin, in January 1918, but it was not a success.

The DFW F.34 appeared in April 1918. Looking very similar to the Albatros fighter, it was powered by a 160hp Mercedes D.III engine that gave it a top speed of 110mph and a climb rate of 1,100ft per minute. It was armed with twin fixed forward-firing Spandau machine guns, but very little is known of its whereabouts after its sudden disappearance.

Kite balloon in flames after being shot down by a Fokker fighter. In the foreground is a DFW C.V.

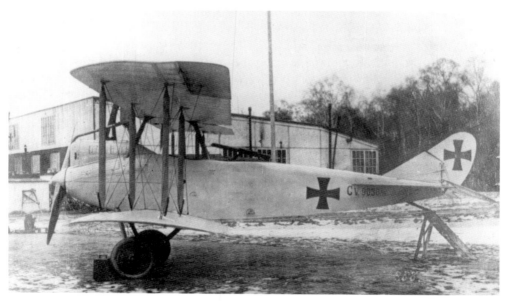

A DFW C.V with a fully cowled engine. These cowlings were often removed during missions.

A third DFW heavy bomber, the R.III, was on the drawing board at the end of September 1918. The aircraft had a separate navigator's steering section in front of the wings, whilst the dual cockpit was situated directly under the trailing edge of the wings. It had a double-decked fuselage capable of carrying 2,500 kg of bombs, eight machine guns, a wireless cabin, a bomb aimer's position and eight sleeping bunks. One unusual feature was the replacement of the normal tail skid with a faired tail wheel, but before production could begin the war came to an end and the Armistice was declared.

SPECIFICATIONS

DFW C.II

Wingspan	36ft 9in
Length	23ft 7½in
Height	9ft 3in
Weight Empty	1,595lb
Weight Loaded	2,717lb
Maximum Speed	87mph
Ceiling	13,120ft
Duration	2hrs
Engine	One 150hp Benz Bz.III – six-cylinder, in-line, water-cooled
Armament	One manually operated Parabellum Machine gun mounted in the observer's cockpit

DFW C.V

Wingspan	43ft 6½in
Length	25ft 10½in
Height	10ft 8in
Weight Empty	2,134lb
Weight Loaded	3,146lb
Maximum Speed	97mph
Ceiling	16,400ft
Duration	3½hrs
Engine	One 200hp Benz Bz.IV – six-cylinder, in-line, water-cooled
Armament	One fixed forward-firing Spandau Machine gun One manually operated Parabellum Machine gun mounted in the observer's cockpit

The bullet-riddled remains of a DFW C.V after being shot down at Pilckem Ridge in 1917.

Probably mail or supplies being loaded aboard a DFW C.Va whilst senior officers look on.

DFW R.I

Wingspan	96ft 9½in
Wing Area	1,988 sq.ft
Length	57ft 9in
Height	21ft 4in
Weight Empty	12,434lb
Weight Loaded	18,440lb
Maximum Speed	81mph
Ceiling	16,400ft
Duration	6hrs
Engine	Four 220hp Mercedes D.IV – eight-cylinder, in-line, water-cooled
Armament	Bombs

FOKKER FLUGZEUG-WERKE GMBH

The name Fokker was synonymous with aviation in both the First and Second World Wars and produced some of Germany's finest military aircraft. Development of Fokker aircraft started in 1911, when Anthony Fokker produced the first of his many aircraft: the Spinne (*spider*). This was followed in April 1914 by the Fokker M.5 which developed into two models: the M.5K and M.5L, both powered by a 50hp Gnôme engine. The K stood for the short wingspan version, the L for the long-span model. Performance was disappointing, so a reconditioned 70hp Gnôme engine was purchased and installed in the M.5L. The difference in performance was immediate and, together with the new comma-shaped rudder, made the aircraft an attractive proposition to the Army. A number of both the M.5K and M.5L models were purchased by the military and were in operation as reconnaissance aircraft when war began. There was one further M model, the Fokker M.5K/MG which mounted a Parabellum machine gun for testing synchronisation gear.

Fokker had developed a number of aircraft prior to World War One, but on the day war was declared against Britain, all German aircraft manufacturers were informed by telegram that their aviation material was under the control of the Army. Fokker was immediately inundated with requests by the German Navy and various other operational units to buy his existing aircraft. In fact, had the Allies offered to buy his aircraft, there is no doubt that Fokker would have sold them to the highest bidder. Fokker off-loaded all of his aircraft, spare parts and junk, with the exception of an M.5L Grüner Vogel (*green bird*) belonging to Leutnant Hans von Buttlar's squadron. He also accepted orders for aircraft from the Army and Navy as well as Austria – orders that he had no hope of fulfilling, and for this he received a severe reprimand from the Idflieg.

The Fokker works consisted of a number of tumbledown shacks and huts, so Fokker and his staff set to work to repair, enlarge and equip these workshops for production. The main factor that was against Anthony Fokker was that he was an alien in a country that was at war, and as such could expect no special entitlements.

Criticised by the Allies for allying himself with the Germans, Anthony Fokker wrote to a friend:

During my travels I have heard much criticism because I tied my fate to the Germans. The Allies blamed me for not having placed myself at the disposal of the Entente. These critics did not consider that my own country preferred French aeroplanes to mine, that England and Italy hardly bothered to respond, and that due to the wide-spread corruption I was unable to get started in Russia. Only Germany prepared a good reception for me, even if it was not entirely with open arms.

The Idflieg approached Fokker with the suggestion of developing a two-seat aircraft for the purposes of artillery spotting: the Fokker M.6. Based on the airframe of the M.5, the M.6 had a wingspan of 36ft, a fuselage length of 22.6ft and was powered by an 80hp Oberursel U.O rotary engine. The aircraft completed its initial tests and was sent to Schwerin to be evaluated by military pilots. On its second flight, the pilot, Oberleutnant Kolbe, and observer Hauptmann Ruff were confused by the fuel cocks. The engine stopped in mid-air and the aircraft crashed whilst Kolbe was attempting to land. It was completely destroyed and Kolbe killed. The observer was lucky to escape with minor injuries. Only one aircraft was built.

The M.6 was followed by an unusual model, the Fokker M.7 sesquiplane (one and a half wings). With the exception of the wings the rest of the aircraft was an M.5, only the fuselage was adapted to carry an observer in tandem with the pilot. The M.7 was powered by an 80hp Oberursel U.O engine. Production started in January 1915 and twenty were built, all going to German Naval Air Stations for reconnaissance purposes.

At one of the seaplane stations permission was sought from the Reichsmarineamt (the German admiralty) to convert one of the M.7s into a twin-float seaplane. The wingspan was increased and the interplane struts were inclined inwards to provide stronger bracing bays of equal length.

Fokker Spinne.

Anthony Fokker performing a loop from low altitude in a Fokker M.5L. A Spinne and an M.II can be seen in front of the hangar.

The wooden floats were taken from the unsuccessful W.2 and fitted to the aircraft by a strut system that was far stronger than that of the W.2. The M.7, now designated the Fokker W.3, underwent a series of trials, none of which were successful. The aircraft appeared to be extremely reluctant to take off, so the project was abandoned. The W.3 reverted back to an M.7 and was sent to Marine-Landflieger Abteilung, Johannisthal, for training purposes.

At the Fokker workshops Colonel von Eberhardt of Idflieg was delighted with Fokker's progress. After seeing a design for a new aircraft, the Fokker M.8, Eberhardt ordered a number of aircraft to form the nucleus of an observation squadron, and within days Fokker and his staff were at work developing the Fokker M.8.

The first aircraft came off the production line in July 1914 and within days was in action on reconnaissance duties. This was the first truly successful aircraft built by Fokker and was the production model of the recently demised M.6. There were a number of modifications including large apertures, with side windscreens, cut into the sides of the fuselage under the wings. This was done to give both the pilot and the observer a good downward field of vision. The tandem seating favoured in the M.6 was replaced by side-by-side seating in a single large cockpit, which was ideal for observation and artillery spotting purposes, but no good in an attacking or defensive role.

In September, a Fokker M.8, was forced to land near St Omer and was captured intact by the Allies. A number of Allied pilots flew the aircraft and were impressed with its handling qualities

Two Fokker squadrons, FFA.40 and FFA.41 (consisting of six aircraft in each), were formed for the purposes of artillery spotting and reconnaissance. Designated the Fokker A.I, the M.8 was flown by selected pilots only, one of them being Leutnant Otto Parschau, who was later to be awarded the Orden Pour le Mérite. Another of the pilots was Leutnant Oswald Boelcke, destined to be one of the top aces of the Imperial German Army Air Service. Powered by an 80hp Oberursel rotary engine, over thirty of the aircraft were supplied to the army.

The Fokker factory was not only supplying aircraft to the German Army, but also to the Austro-Hungarian Army Air Service. In September 1915, Fokker supplied two aircraft: the Fokker M.10E, a single seat artillery spotter powered by an 80hp Oberursel U.O rotary engine; the Fokker M.10Z, a two-seat reconnaissance/trainer powered by a 100hp Oberursel U.I rotary engine.

The addition of a machine gun brought the aeroplane into the realms of a fighting machine. No longer relegated to the role of the observer or the 'carrier-pigeon', aircraft were now recognised as an essential part of the war machinery. One of the major problems that faced the pilots was the fitting of forward-firing guns. This was easily the most effective method of attacking a foe, although invariably the propeller got in the way. Many of the Allied aircraft were of the pusher type, meaning the engine and propeller were behind them. This gave the pilot an unobstructed view of his opponent and enabled his observer, who sat in front of the pilot, to carry out an attack without the fear of hitting the propeller and shooting themselves down.

One of the first Allied aircraft to be designed for offensive missions was a two-seat biplane with a pusher engine, the Vickers FB5, or Gunbus as it was more commonly known. The first of these aircraft began to arrive at the beginning of 1915 and were issued to 5 Squadron RFC in France. As usual with such problems, necessity became the mother of invention and this was no exception. A well-known pre-war French aviator and stunt pilot, Roland Garros, a member of Escadrille MS.23, realised the problems facing pilots and gunners alike and designed a forward-facing gun mounting on his own Morane Parasol. He had a Hotchkiss machine gun mounted directly in front of the cockpit and wedges of armoured steel screwed to the backs of each blade to deflect any bullets fired that did not pass between them. It worked to a certain degree and in the first part of April he shot down and destroyed three German aircraft.

On 18 April 1915, Roland Garros – flying a Morane Parasol – was attacking the railway station at Courtrai, when his aircraft was hit by a Mauser rifle bullet fired by a German soldier named Schlenstedt. The Mauser bullet severed the fuel line and the aircraft was forced to crash land behind German lines. That Mauser bullet was ultimately the instrument of one of the most important influences on the art of aerial fighting during World War One. Although Roland Garros tried to destroy his aircraft he was unsuccessful and, together with his aircraft, was captured.

It did not take the Germans long to realise whom they had captured and the prize they had in his aircraft. The wreckage of his Morane Parasol was passed to Hauptmann Foerster who took it to Doeberitz, where Simon Brunnhuber was ordered to make a working copy of the interruptor firing mechanism. This he did and high-ranking officers watched with great interest as the engine and propeller were set up and the machine gun was fired. It is not certain whether or not the steel of the deflecting plates was of armoured plated quality or that the armour piercing bullets used were of superior quality, but the propeller disintegrated and the whole test bed was shattered. All those who were watching were lucky to escape without injury. It was then decided to pass the whole project over to Anthony Fokker, the Dutch aircraft designer. After examining the method used to fire the machine gun and recognising its limitations, he decided that instead of making copies of it he would improve on it.

A synchronised machine gun with an interrupter mechanism had earlier been designed by a Swiss LVG engineer by the name of Franz Schneider, and patented in July 1913. Schneider questioned Anthony Fokker's patent saying it was based on his design. Fokker maintained that Schneider's design was based on the blocking of the machine gun when a propeller blade was in front of the barrel. A two-bladed propeller revolved at 1,200 times a minute, which meant that it passed in front of a machine gun muzzle 2,400 times in a minute. Fokker's design was worked by a camshaft and lever, which fired the machine gun the instant there was no blade in front of the gun barrel. The Parabellum gun fired 600 times in minute, so his design was based on a method to make the propeller cam shaft fire the machine gun when there was no blade in the way. In all probability, the actual design was more than likely conceived by another member of Fokker's design team, Heinrich Luebbe.

Fokker and his engineers Luebbe, Leinberger and Heber got to work and seventy-two hours later they had designed and built the mechanism. Every time the propeller blade lined up with the muzzle in front of the firing machine gun, a cam, actuated by the engine, stopped the gun firing. The system was tested and fitted to a Fokker M.5K Eindecker for final testing. A young Leutnant Oswald Boelcke was assigned to carry out the testing and after normal tests took it on a mission. After the third mission Boelcke had scored a victory. (The first M.5K victory was by Leutnant Wintgens on 1 July 1915.) The Germans were delighted and ordered not only the interrupter firing gear system, but the Fokker M.5K aircraft, which was redesignated the E.I (E for Eindecker).

With the arrival of the Fokker Eindecker and its interrupter-firing mechanism came a new threat to the Allies. By the end of the summer of 1915, the German pilots were attacking the British and French aircraft with devastating results. They had acquired air supremacy.

Anthony Fokker at this time was under a great deal of criticism not only from his own countrymen, but from the Allies about his close ties with Germany. Fokker's defence was that at the onset of the war, his aircraft had been requisitioned by the German Army, together with all the spare engines and equipment. He said he was blamed for not placing himself at the disposal of the Allies, but argued that Holland preferred to buy French aircraft, and England and Italy declined to respond to his proposals. Russia was so corrupt that it would have been impossible to deal with them and the only country who even offered to respond to him (although it was not entirely with open arms) was Germany. It is said that the British government later offered him a substantial sum of money to work for them.

The need to arm reconnaissance aircraft prompted Fokker to carry out a most unusual experiment. He took two M.7 fuselages, each with its own tail section, and in between fitted a nacelle with two 80hp Oberursel rotary engines, one pusher and one tractor. In the nacelle between the engines sat the pilot. The two fuselages and the nacelle were joined together by a biplane structure. In the front of the fuselage sat two gunners, which was ideal for a frontal attack, but made no provision for defence if attacked from the rear. After a number of test flights, carried out by Fokker himself, the idea was scrapped because there were too many problems to make it a worthwhile project.

Fokker brought out another experimental aircraft at the end of 1915, the Fokker M.16E. This was a single-bay two-seater aircraft with the top wing level with the top of the fuselage. Powered by a 120hp Mercedes D.II engine the aircraft was a model for the next version, the two-seater Fokker M.16Z. This was a complete redesign of the M.16E and was powered by a 200hp Austro-Daimler engine. It was fitted with a forward-firing Schwarzlose machine gun for the pilot and a single manually operated Schwarzlose machine gun for the observer. Thirty of these aircraft were built and sold to the Austro-Hungarian Army Air Service.

A single-seater version was also built at the end of 1915, the Fokker M.17 E/1. Powered by a 100hp Oberursel U.I rotary engine, M.17 E/1 was armed with a fixed

Fokker E.I Scout fitted with a headrest to help the pilot sight his machine gun.

forward-firing Spandau machine gun. Only one was ever built. A modified version of the E/1, the E/2, appeared shortly after and a small number were sold to the Austro-Hungarians, with a designation of Fokker B.III, for unarmed scouting roles. Three more experimental versions were developed at the end of 1915 and the beginning of 1916: the Fokker M.17z, M.18z and M.20z. The only differences between the three models were modifications to the tail surfaces and the testing of new engines.

During the same period, a number of other experimental aircraft appeared: the Fokker M.22 was fitted with a re-designed cowling; followed by the W.4, a floatplane version of the Fokker M.7. Neither was put into production.

At the beginning of 1916, Fokker decided that all his experimental aircraft would carry the prefix 'V'. The first of these, the Fokker V.1 designed by Reinhold Platz, was a revolutionary model that had a steel-tube fuselage that was rounded out to the cowling. Although appearing to be of an orthodox structure, the wing surfaces moved and had no fins. The deep section wings were fully cantilevered and covered in plywood. Conventional ailerons were replaced by 1m-long differentially moving wingtips giving lateral control. A lifting surface fairing was fitted between the axle, a characteristic that was to persist with virtually all subsequent Fokker aircraft. Powered by a 100hp Oberursel U.I rotary engine, V.1 was fitted with twin forward-firing Spandau machine guns.

One of the finest aircraft series produced by Fokker was the Fokker D series. However, its beginnings were hardly auspicious for when the first of the series, the Fokker D.I (D for Dreidecker), was presented to the military for evaluation, it came in for some scathing reports. This infuriated Anthony Fokker; unfortunately for him, the reports came from two German Flying Corps officers, who besides carrying out their normal duties were both eminent aeronautical engineers. A number of recommendations were made and after all these had been implemented, three aircraft were ordered. After further evaluation by the air force there was an additional order for twenty-five Fokker D.Is with 120hp Mercedes engine. Some minor modifications were made and a further eighty were delivered.

The Austro-Hungarian Army Air Service purchased a number from Fokker, but the Ungarische Allgemeine Maschinefabrik AG (MAG) of Budapest began to build the Fokker D.I under licence. A number of the aircraft were used in Turkey and Mesopotamia. Tragedy struck the Fokker factory on 27 June 1916, when chief designer Martin Kreutzer flew a Fokker D.I on an acceptance flight. Shortly after taking off, the aircraft crashed and Kreutzer was dragged from the wreckage. Barely conscious the mortally injured Kreutzer managed to explain to his rescuers that a jammed rudder had caused the crash, but that didn't stop Anthony Fokker turning up and berating the dying man.

Kreutzer's place was taken by Reinhold Platz, who was instrumental in designing and producing the Fokker D.II. This design was closely followed by the Fokker D.III at the end of August 1916. One of the aircraft was given to Oberleutnant Oswald Boelcke, one of Germany's top aces. On the day after receiving the aircraft, 2 September 1916, Boelcke claimed his twentieth victim when he shot down a DH2 flown by Captain R. Wilson. Boelcke retained the aircraft and during the next two weeks claimed five more victims.

Although the aircraft was easy to fly and very manoeuvrable, it was noticeably slower than the Nieuport and no faster than the Sopwith 1½ Strutter. This was not good enough for Boelcke so when the Albatros D.I appeared, a considerably better aircraft, Boelcke quickly switched aircraft. The Fokker D.III, on Boelcke's recommendation, became a home-defence fighter.

The Fokker D.IV, also known as the Fokker M.20, was one of the aircraft designed by Anthony Fokker himself. Structural tests on the wings were carried out by German aeronautical engineers at Aldershof and serious weaknesses were found. The Idflieg insisted on improvements and again the structure of the wings became suspect. After a series of tests, it became apparent to the Idflieg that Fokker and his engineers relied heavily on guesswork when designing new aircraft. With the problems ironed out, an initial order for twenty of the aircraft was placed, which was later increased to thirty.

The Fokker D.IV had some initial success but the aircraft was not liked by the front-line pilots and when a new engine became available, the 160hp Mercedes D.IIIa, priority was given to the Albatros and Pfalz fighters. To add insult to injury, Anthony Fokker was ordered to build 400 AEG C.IV two-seater aircraft under licence. Complaining that the complexity of the aircraft's design would prevent him making hardly any profit, Anthony Fokker was told to study the soundness of the aircraft's structural design and learn from it. During construction of the AEG C.IV, the whole Fokker factory was under the supervision of Dr Koner, an expert on materials and production control. One wonders if the reason for that was a deliberate move to enable the Idflieg to keep a watchful eye on Fokker.

The Fokker V.1 was re-designed and fitted with conventional tail surfaces and an improved 120hp Mercedes water-cooled engine. The differentially moving wingtips for lateral control were retained. The new model was designated Fokker V.2.

At the beginning of 1917 a new design of aircraft appeared – the Fokker V.3. The new design had three wings, the middle and bottom spans were of identical length, whilst the top span was longer. The aircraft was powered by a 110hp Oberursel U.II engine. V.3 was to be the forerunner of the famous Fokker Dr.I. This was followed by V.4 which had hollow interplane struts between the wings to cure the wing vibration suffered by V.3. Then followed the V.5, V.6 and V.7; all were variations of V.3. The V.8, however, was of a most unusual design and said to have been built expressly on the instructions of Anthony Fokker. It was a triplane with an extended fuselage, with a pair of wings mounted just aft of the cockpit. Powered by a 120hp Mercedes D.II engine, the aircraft had two very short test flights, but was totally impracticable and scrapped.

The V.9, V.10 and V.11 that followed reverted back to biplanes. V.11 was judged at the first of the D-type competitions to be the best in its class and although just the prototype very little modification was required before the aircraft was put into production. It was powered by a 160hp Mercedes D.III engine and had a climb rate of nearly 600ft per minute.

The appearance of two Fokker F.I fighters, Nrs 102/17 and 103/17, on 16 August 1917 at Manfred von Richthofen's fighter wing at Courtrai caused a stir. The leader of Jasta 10, Leutnant Werner Voss visited the squadron on 29 August to test fly the aircraft and was delighted with the results. Making his first operational flight in Nr.103/17 the following day, he shot down a British aircraft.

Between 30 August and 23 September, Voss claimed twenty-one aircraft shot down, but on the last day whilst on patrol he spotted a lone SE5a. Diving in to attack, he failed to notice to other SE5As of B Flight, 56 Squadron RFC, led by Captain James B. McCudden. Three aircraft now went after Voss and, although he fought like a fury, his aircraft was shot down by 2nd Lieutenant Rhys-Davids, flying one of the other SE5as. The British acknowledged the skill and daring of Voss, saying that such a foe should have been taken alive.

Richthofen, still recovering from a head wound received on 6 July, insisted on being one of the first of his Jasta to fly the aircraft. It was well known that he had very little faith in the reliability of the rotary engine, but he took to the F.I instantly. The following month six new Fokker Dreideckers arrived, their designation having been changed to Fokker Dr.I.

One of the major problems that faced the pilots of the Fokker Dr.I was the cramped leg room in the tiny cockpit, subsequently the majority of the pilots were relatively short. Nearly all the pilots of the Richthofen Jagdgeschwader flew the Fokker Dr.I until April 1918, when it was replaced by the Fokker D.VII biplane.

Throughout this period the red Fokker Dr.I Dreidecker of Manfred von Richthofen scoured the skies looking for opponents and with this created a great deal of legend. Some reports said that his aircraft was fitted with triple machine guns, other said he was invincible and in league with the devil. In fact Richthofen's aircraft was a perfectly standard Fokker Dr.I, the only difference being that Richthofen had at least two spare aircraft available all the time. The aircraft was initially powered by a 110hp Oberursel UR.II engine, which was later replaced by the Thulin-built Le Rhône nine-cylinder rotary engine.

Fokker V.3.

Hauptmann Adolf Ritter von Tutschek of JG.2 about to start the engine on his Fokker Dr.1 Dreidecker.

Fokker D.VIIs under construction in the factory.

The V.13 prototype was converted into the Fokker D.VI at the beginning of 1918. Powered by a 110hp Oberursel UR.II engine the aircraft underwent a series of tests, but was disappointing. However, twenty-seven of the aircraft were ordered, but soon relegated to home-defence duties. Seven aircraft, that were part of a later order, were sold to the Austro-Hungarian Army Air Service. A total of sixty Fokker D.VIs were supplied to the German Air Army Service.

A number of V models appeared during the year, including V.17 the first monoplane of the V series. The majority of the components came from the now-defunct Dr.I. The wings were fitted mid-fuselage which gave a poor downward/forward visibility. This was followed by the V.18 which was a biplane powered by a 160hp Mercedes D.III engine. After a number of tests it was destroyed in an aerial collision with the V.13 during trials at Aldershof. It was followed by the V.20, V.21 and V.22, the latter becoming the production model D.VII. This was one of the best German fighter aircraft of the war, over one thousand were built and at least 800 of these were in operational use. It was one of those aircraft that lent itself to being open to variations and a large number were made, both experimental and production.

V models continued to appear: the V.23, V.24, V.25, V.26 and V.27, all of which contributed to the development of production aircraft. The V.26 went into production as the E.V model, which was re-designated the Fokker D.VIII. By 1 November 1918 eighty-five D.VIIIs were operational on the Western Front and a further twenty-five in service with the naval coast-defence units.

The remaining V series of aircraft – V.28, V.29, V.30, V.31, V.33, V.34, V.36 and V.37 – never went into production and were experimental versions. The Fokker aircraft company was one of the most prolific of manufacturers of World War One and left an indelible mark on the world of aviation.

SPECIFICATIONS

Fokker D.VII

Wing Span	29ft 3½in
Length	22ft 11½in
Height	9ft 2¼in
Weight Empty	1,540lbs
Weight Loaded	1,870lbs
Engine	One 160hp Mercedes D.III – six-cylinder, in-line, water-cooled.
Maximum Speed	116mph
Service Ceiling	22,900ft
Duration	1½hrs – later reduced to 1hr
Armament	Twin fixed forward-firing Spandau machine guns synchronised to fire through the propeller arc. They could also be fired independently.

Fokker Dr.1 Dreidecker

Wing Span	23ft 7in
Wing Area	201½sq.ft
Length	18ft 11in
Height	9ft 8in
Weight Empty	893.2lbs
Weight Loaded	1,289.2lbs
Engine	One 110hp Oberursel UR II of Thulin-built Le Rhône nine-cylinder rotary
Maximum Speed	103mph
Service Ceiling	20,000ft
Duration	1½hrs – later reduced to 1hr
Armament	Twin fixed forward-firing Spandau machine guns synchronised to fire through the propeller arc. They could also be fired independently.

Fokker E.V

Wing Span	27ft 4½in
Length	19ft 3½in
Height	9ft 2¼in
Weight Empty	891lbs
Weight Loaded	1,241lbs
Engine	One 110hp Oberursel U.II rotary
Maximum Speed	127mph
Service Ceiling	18,900ft
Duration	1½hrs – later reduced to 1hr
Armament	Twin fixed forward-firing Spandau machine guns synchronised to fire through the propeller. They could also be fired independently.

FLUGZEUGBAU FRIEDRICHSHAFEN GMBH (MANZELL SITE)

The Friedrichshafen FF.29 seaplane was one of the first aircraft built by Flugzeugbau Friedrichshafen GmbH and was used for coastal patrol work. Powered by a 120hp Mercedes D.II engine, it carried no armament, but on occasion carried a very small bomb load. It was superseded by the FF.29a which had modified floats and tail surfaces. The FF.29a was also the first and last winged German aircraft ever be carried on a submarine.

During the early stages of World War One the German Army quickly overran Belgium, and the port of Zeebrugge fell into German hands – becoming a base well suited to operations by U-boats. A handful of officers in the Imperial German Navy based at Zeebrugge began to look into the possibilities of operating aircraft from submarines, although at that time there was no operational requirement to do so.

Rather it was a case of personal initiative, circumstance and the availability of a Friedrichshafen FF.29, a twin-float, single-engined seaplane.

The base commander, and U-boat captain, Oberleutnant zur See Friedrich von Arnauld de la Periere also, unusually, was an aviator. Together with Oberleutnant zur See Walter Forstman, commander of U-12, they became 'Ace' U-boat commanders, seized with offensive spirit, and determined to find out whether the radius of action of a seaplane could be extended by using the submarine as a seaplane transporter. The nearest point on the enemy coast, North Foreland in Kent, lay some seventy-three miles away.

Despite it being midwinter, on 6 January 1915, the seaplane, with its 57ft wingspan, was lashed down athwartships on the foredeck of U-12 and the unlikely combination sailed to carry out trials. The bows were trimmed down; the aircraft was subsequently floated off and taxied away – all within the protection afforded by the long breakwater of Zeebrugge Mole. It was decided to continue with the trials immediately. The strange and vulnerable combination, with the aircraft lashed athwartships and U-12's two heavy Korting oil engines leaving a tell-tale plume of smoke, headed for the open sea. Despite a heavy swell, the situation was just about manageable. Some thirty miles offshore, the U-boat's commander flooded the forward tanks and floated the aircraft off and it was able to take off successfully. With von Arnauld de la Periere and his observer Herman Mall aboard, they flew along the coast of Kent undetected before returning to Zeebrugge direct, rather than making the agreed rendezvous with U-12 in weather which had deteriorated further. At the debrief, Forstman and von Arnauld considered the whole exercise a complete success but agreed that after the difficulties in getting the aircraft launched, the seas needed to be calmer and the aircraft more secure on deck.

The remarkable trial conducted in wartime – virtually in the Allies' backyard – was designed to establish a strike capability with small bombs, if not at the heartland then at least the coastal towns of the enemy. Soon the Friedrichshafen FF.29 had been adapted to carry 12kg bombs, and during the year, twenty-six raids were flown against British and French targets.

On Christmas Day 1915, a Friedrichshafen FF.29 flew along the River Thames to Erith on the outskirts of London and dropped two bombs. It was fortunate that they fell without causing injury and damage. Three British aircraft chased the FF.29 without success and it returned safely. The German airmen, or 'Zeebrugge Fliers' as they were called, had more problems from their aircraft than they did from the British. On many occasions their seaplanes were forced to land with fouled ignitions or fuel line stoppages and because of the limited range of the aircraft, many of the more important targets were beyond reach. Understandably, the frustrations of the aircraft crews created morale problems, but the problems were recognised by the U-boat officers because they too shared the dangers of operating relatively new and untried weapons – because of this, a bond sprang up between the whole crew.

Combined trials of aircraft and submarine had continued sporadically, but high-level support was not forthcoming. No doubt this was a correct decision given the vulnerability of the combination and the unreliability endemic in these early aeroplanes. A report to the German High Command on the future of submarine-launched aircraft was thoroughly investigated, and the decision was made that the project be dropped. Von Arnauld was told: 'U-boats operate in the sea, aircraft in the air there is no connection between the two.' The days of experimenting with aircraft and submarine were over.

At the beginning of 1915, the Friedrichshafen company, in response to a request for a heavy bomber, produced the Friedrichshafen G.I. This was a twin pusher-engined bomber with a biplane tail that carried a crew of three: a pilot, gunner and bombing officer/gunner. Only a limited number were built but it paved the way for further models.

The almost identical G.II followed but had a mono tail. One additional modification was to put flaps behind the wheels to prevent stones being flung up into the pusher airscrew. Engines were two Benz Bz.IV pusher types, and the aircraft had a wingspan of 66ft 7½in, a fuselage length of 36ft 3in and a height of 11ft 9¾in. It was a reasonably successful aircraft and a number were built to join the Gotha bombers of the Bombengeschwader force. The information and results that came back from the front, later helped develop the G.III.

The company continued to develop flying boats and in May 1915 produced the Friedrichshafen FF.31. Only two of these aircraft were built and these were of the pusher type. Looking very similar to a floatplane version of the British DH2 Gunbus, the FF.31 carried a single manually operated Parabellum machine gun. The two aircraft, Nrs. 274 and 275, had a wingspan of 55ft 3½in, a length of 33ft 4in and a top speed of 61mph. They were powered by a 150hp Benz Bz.III engine and used by the German Navy.

One of the most successful of all of Friedrichshafen's seaplanes was the FF.33. There were seven variants of the aircraft; the 33e being the most memorable. The seven aircraft were split into two categories: the FF.33b, 33e, 33j and 33s, being unarmed reconnaissance patrol seaplanes; the remaining three (33f, 33h and 33l) were armed patrol fighters that were used for escort purposes. The FF.33/33a was designed so that the pilot sat in the rear cockpit but the design of the FF.33b reversed the seating positions, placing the pilot in the forward cockpit. A 160hp Maybach engine was fitted in the 33b, with the radiators placed either side of the fuselage adjacent to the front cockpit. Only five of this variant were built.

The FF.33e was almost identical except for the floats, which were considerably longer and the tail float removed. The FF.33e was powered by a 150hp Benz Bz.III engine with the radiator system located against the leading edge of the upper wing. Approximately 188 of the FF.33e seaplanes were delivered to the German Navy, the most famous of these being the *Wölfchen* which was carried aboard the German auxiliary cruiser SMS *Wolf*.

From November 1916 to December 1918 the SMS *Wolf* and her 'cub' scoured the Indian and Pacific Oceans looking for prey. The FF.33e *Wölfchen* would be lowered into the water and would take off on a reconnaissance flight sending back information by radio. If a likely merchant ship was found, the pilot of the *Wölfchen* would identify the nationality and drop a message printed in English onto the deck, ordering the vessel to alter course and steam toward the German cruiser *Wolf*. The underlying threat was that if she didn't do what she was told, she would be bombed. Then, as if to drive the point home, the *Wölfchen* would drop a bomb about 20yds from the bow of the merchant ship. A number of ships were captured in this manner and prize crews put aboard. The Armistice put an end to the raider's roaming of the sea.

Experimentation with the pusher engine continued with the Friedrichshafen FF.34. With twin fuselages and powered by a 240hp Maybach Mb.IV engine, the aircraft had a 60ft 4½in wingspan, a length of 35ft 8in, a height of 13ft 5½in and carried a single manually operated Parabellum machine gun. It was also one of the first German aircraft to carry a radio transmitter. Only one of the aircraft was built. The fuselage was later retained and re-modelled as the FF.44.

In 1915 Friedrichshafen built a twin-engined torpedo carrying aircraft – the FF.35. Powered by two 160hp Mercedes D.III engines which drove pusher airscrews, it had a 77ft 10in wingspan, a fuselage length of 44ft 3½in, had a top speed of 71mph and carried an armament of one torpedo and two manually operated Parabellum machine guns. Only one was ever built.

One of the first land versions of the FF.31 – the FF.37 – appeared at the beginning of 1915 and again only one was built. Like most of the aircraft manufacturers at the time, the company were always experimenting with variations of production models, seeking to improve performance figures.

Another variation that came from the FF.33c was the FF.39, a two-seat, single-engined reconnaissance seaplane that carried a radio transmitter. Powered by a 200hp Benz Bz.IV engine, the FF.39 had a wingspan of 56ft 1½in and a fuselage length of 38ft 1in. It had a top speed of 85mph, a flight duration of five hours and carried one machine gun, a manually operated Parabellum in the rear cockpit. Fourteen of these aircraft were supplied to the German Navy.

FF.33e *Wölfchen* being lowered into the water from the seaplane carrier SMS *Santa Elena*.

Experiments with a three-seater reconnaissance seaplane resulted in the Friedrichshafen FF.40. It had a single 240hp Maybach engine mounted in the fuselage, which drove two tractor airscrews between the wings. It had a wingspan of 68ft 11in, a length of 40ft 9½in, a height of 14ft 5½in and carried one manually operated Parabellum machine gun mounted in the nose section. Only one of the aircraft was built.

The results from the tests of the FF.40 led to the production of nine FF.41s in February 1916. These were twin-engined, three-seater, reconnaissance seaplanes of which two versions were built – with a single tail and a compound tail. Encased in metal housings, the two 150hp Benz Bz.III engines drove tractor airscrews. With a wingspan of 72ft 1in, a fuselage length of 43ft 6½in and a height of 15ft 5½in, the FF.41 had a top speed of 78mph and a range of 360 miles. It carried one torpedo and had a single manually operated Parabellum machine gun in the front cockpit. It is not known if it carried a radio transmitter.

A deviation from large reconnaissance seaplanes resulted in the appearance of the Friedrichshafen FF.43, a single-seat fighter. With a top speed of 101mph and a climb rate of over 500ft per minute, the fighter seemed destined to be put into major production, but for some unknown reason only one was ever built. Another single-seat fighter appeared shortly afterwards, the Friedrichshafen D.I powered by a 160hp Mercedes D.III engine. Again like its stablemate, the FF.43, only one was built.

The appearance of the Friedrichshafen G.III, together with the Gotha, formed the backbone of the German bomber force that carried out bombing raids on Paris and London. The G.III had a wingspan of 77ft 9½in, a fuselage length of 42ft and was powered by two six-cylinder in-line, water-cooled 260hp Mercedes IVa engines, which gave a maximum speed of 84mph and a flight duration of five hours. It carried

FF.33e *Wölfchen* on the deck of her mother ship SMS *Wolf*.

three manually operated Parabellum machine guns mounted in the nose and rear cockpits. The bomb load was up to 3,300lb.

Information gained by previous designs created the FF.44, a two-seat reconnaissance aircraft, which in reality was the FF.34 re-built with a normal fuselage. It was powered by a 240hp Maybach Mb.IV engine fitted with reduction gears. The FF.44 had a wingspan of 60ft 4½in, a fuselage length of 35ft 7½in and a height of 13ft 11½in. It had a flight duration of five hours and carried a single manually operated Parabellum machine gun mounted in the rear cockpit.

In 1917, in an attempt to take the offensive, Friedrichshafen built the FF.48. This two-seater fighter seaplane was fitted with machine guns for both the pilot and observer. For a fighter it was quite a large machine, with a wingspan of 54ft 4in, a length of 36ft 9in and a height of 14ft 5½in. The FF.48 was powered by a direct-drive 240hp Maybach engine, which gave a surprising top speed of 95mph and a climb rate of over 500ft per minute. Only three examples of this aircraft were built.

May 1917 saw the appearance of the FF.49c, the successor to the FF.33j. The FF.49c was fitted with a 200hp Benz Bz.IV engine. The FF.49c was probably one of the most reliable and rugged of all the German seaplanes, and on a number of occasions it made open-sea landings to rescue downed aircrews. It was equipped with a radio transmitter and receiver, and armed with one fixed forward-firing Spandau machine gun and a manually operated Parabellum machine gun in the rear cockpit.

A number of these seaplanes were carried on the German seaplane carriers like the SMS *Santa Elena*. One incident concerning an FF.49c from the ship was to lay testament to its strength and durability. The aircraft, flown by Hans Sommermann with his observer Georg Pätzold, took off on a reconnaissance patrol over the English Channel/North Sea together with another seaplane. During the flight they discovered a new enemy minefield and set to plotting its position. When they realised that their fuel gauges were showing low, they tried to return to their mother ship without success. After six hours flying, both aircraft ran out of fuel and put down on the water. Putting out their sea anchors the two aircraft waited to be rescued, but during the night freshening winds and a heavy sea caused one of the aircraft to slip her anchor.

Sommermann and Pätzold stayed with their aircraft amid stormy seas for the next five days. On the sixth day, close to collapse from hunger and thirst, they saw fishing boats nearby and fired red distress flares. The flares were ignored so in desperation they hacked away a wing panel to which they tied a piece of white fabric and waved it frantically in the direction of the trawlers. One of the trawlers (later found to be Swedish) steamed toward them and took the two grateful airmen aboard and took them to Sweden. Both owed their lives to the ruggedness and strength of the FF.49c which – even after the terrific battering it took in the storm tossed seas of the North Sea – still remained afloat.

Their companions had been rescued two days earlier by a Dutch ship, after they had attracted its attention by ingeniously signalling SOS with their machine gun.

The success of the FF.49c prompted the designers to modify one aircraft as a single-engined bomber. Powered by a 200hp Benz Bz.IV engine, the FF.49b, as it was redesignated, carried no armament other than bombs, and a radio transmitter and receiver. With a wingspan of 56ft 11½in, a fuselage length of 37ft 10in and a height of 14ft, the aircraft had a top speed of 95mph and a flight duration of 5½ hours. The pilot's position was also reversed with him flying the aircraft from the rear cockpit. Twenty-five of these models were built.

Another land-based fighter appeared in June 1917, the Friedrichshafen D-Type Vierdecker (*quadruplane*). Looking very much like the Albatros and built purely as an experimental model, the 160hp Mercedes D.III-powered aircraft crashed on its first flight.

Shortly afterwards, the Friedrichshafen C.I land-based aircraft arrived. Although it appeared as new model, it was in fact an FF.33L seaplane fitted with a conventional undercarriage. Only one was built. At the same time as the appearance of the C.I, a new model did actually appear: the Friedrichshafen N.I, a single-engined, two-seater night bomber powered by a 260hp Mercedes D.IVa engine. The design was such that the wings were swept back considerably, which resulted in the pilot having to look over a very extended nose. This made night landings a nightmare. Only one of the aircraft was built.

At the end of June 1917, three twin-engined torpedo-carrying seaplanes were built, powered by two 260hp Mercedes C.IVa engines. Designated the Friedrichshafen FF.53, they were not the success hoped for and the information gathered was used to build the FF.59a. There were two versions of the aircraft, the FF.59a and FF.59b which eventually resulted in the production of the FF.59c.

When the FF.59c appeared at the beginning of 1918 little more than a modified FF.39. The inboard bracing cable had been removed, which enabled the rear gunner to shoot forward, albeit somewhat riskily, and a 200hp Benz engine fitted; to all intents and purposes, it was still an FF.39. It was fitted with transmitting and receiving radio equipment which was now becoming more and more a normal part of aircraft

FF.49c being hoisted aboard the SMS *Santa Elena*.

FF.49c after coming to grief during landing.

equipment. The FF.59c had a wingspan of 58ft 5in, a fuselage length of 37ft 1in, a height of 13ft 11½in, a top speed of 88mph and a flight duration of over five hours.

Spurred on by the success of the FF.33 model – especially that of the FF.33e *Wölfchen*, which illustrated the ease by which a seaplane could be carried and operated from a ship – the FF.64 was produced. Designed as a two-seat reconnaissance aircraft, the wings could be folded back without compromising its structural strength and could be easily stored aboard ship. It was powered by a 160hp Mercedes D.III engine and carried a manually operated Parabellum machine gun in the rear cockpit. The FF.64 was fitted with a radio transmitter and receiver. Only three were built.

At the same time as the FF.64 was being developed, an experimental single-wing seaplane was designed. Based loosely on the Brandenburg W.29, the FF.63, as it was known, had only two test flights before it was scrapped.

Another G class bomber was built at the end of May 1918, the Friedrichshafen G.IV (FF.55). Based on the design of the previous G bombers, the G.IV had the front cockpit removed giving it a 'sawn off' look. It had a twin tail and was armed with only one rear gun. It had a wingspan of 74ft 2in, a fuselage length of 39ft 4½in and powered by two 260hp Mercedes D.IVa engines. An unknown number were built. There was a G.V (FF.62) built, but no details of the aircraft can be found.

An extremely large experimental triplane was built during 1918 and was one of the first seaplanes to have an enclosed cockpit. Powered by four 160hp Mercedes D.III engines, the Friedrichshafen FF.60 as it was designated, carried a crew of four: two pilots, an observer/gunner and a gunner. It had been designed for long-distance patrols, but only one was built before the Armistice came. No specifications are available.

The Friedrichshafen company was one of the major manufacturers of seaplanes during World War One and produced some of the world's finest naval aircraft of that period.

SPECIFICATIONS

Friedrichshafen FF.33e

Wingspan	54ft 11½in
Length	34ft 3½in
Height	12ft 2½in
Weight Empty	2,217lb
Weight Loaded	3,636lb
Maximum Speed	74mph
Ceiling	13,100ft
Duration	5–6hrs
Engine	One 150hp Benz Bz.III – six-cylinder, in-line, water-cooled.
Armament	One manually operated Parabellum Machine gun mounted in the observer's cockpit

Friedrichshafen FF.49b

Wingspan	56ft 11½in
Length	37ft 9½in
Height	13ft 11½in
Weight Empty	3,150lb
Weight Loaded	4,613lb
Maximum Speed	95mph
Ceiling	13,100ft
Duration	5–6hrs
Engine	One 200hp Benz Bz.IV – six-cylinder, in-line, water-cooled
Armament	None

Friedrichshafen G.II

Wingspan	66ft 7½in
Length	36ft 3in
Height	11ft 9¾in
Weight Empty	4,840lb
Weight Loaded	6,934lb
Maximum Speed	95mph
Ceiling	16,100ft
Duration	5–6hrs
Engine	Two 200hp Benz Bz.IV – six-cylinder, in-line, water-cooled
Armament	One manually operated Parabellum machine gun in the nose, a second in section aft of the cockpit

G.II built by Daimler, with the pilot standing up in the cockpit.

Close-up of the port engine and fuselage whilst the crew service the aircraft

Captured G.IVb on display in Hyde Park during 1918.

GOTHAER WAGGONFABRIK AG (GOTHA SITE)

One of the most famous German aircraft of World War One, the twin-engined Gotha bomber was built by the Gothaer Waggonfabrik company. The origin of the company was before the war, when one of the first aircraft they built was of Taube (*dove*) design, the LE.3. Originally built for the civilian market, a number of the aircraft saw service at the beginning of World War One, being requisitioned by the German Army as scouts. Powered by a 100hp Mercedes D.I engine, the LE.3 had a wingspan of 47ft 7in, a fuselage length of 32ft 9½in, a top speed of 60mph and a climb rate of 2,000ft per minute. Only a small number of were built.

Another of Gotha's aircraft that saw service at the beginning of the war was the LD.1a, which was developed from the civilian version LD.1. Manufactured specifically as an unarmed scouting and reconnaissance aircraft, LD.1a was powered by a 100hp Oberursel U.I engine, giving a top speed of 71mph. The aircraft had a wingspan of 47ft 7in, and a fuselage length of 24ft 4in. An unknown number were built.

Gotha also produced a seaplane version of the reconnaissance aircraft, WD.1. It was fitted with twin-floats and a small single float mounted under the tail section. Powered by a Gnôme 100hp engine, WD.1 had a wingspan of 46ft 3½in, a fuselage length of 33ft 9½in, a top speed of 61mph and a maximum operating ceiling of 8,200ft. Five WD.1s were supplied to the German Navy.

The development of the Gotha LD.2 in August 1914 brought another unarmed reconnaissance aircraft to the Gotha range. Although similar in design and with almost the same specifications, it was powered by a 100hp Mercedes engine with the radiators fixed on either side of the fuselage, just in front of the cockpit. A small number were built and were used for a time at the front, before being replaced by the improved model LD.6a. Prior to the appearance of LD.6a, Gotha produced a small scout aircraft, the Gotha LD.5, which was almost half the size of the other models. Powered by a 100hp Oberursel U.I engine, the aircraft was intended to be a fast reconnaissance model, but after testing it was realised that there were a number of stability problems and it was not a practical or viable proposition. Only one was built.

LD.6a on the other hand was a standard-size long-distance reconnaissance aircraft, capable of carrying a small bomb load. It had balanced tail surfaces and of traditional wood and fabric construction. Powered by a 150hp Benz Bz.III engine which had radiators mounted either side of the fuselage in front of the observer's cockpit. LD.6a had a wingspan of 40ft 8½in, a fuselage length of 27ft 7in and a top speed of 78mph.

At the beginning of March 1915, the last of LD series was produced, the Gotha LD.7. Like all the previous LD models, it was designed specifically for reconnaissance duties. Its specifications were almost identical to that of the LD.6a, with the exception of the engine which was a 120hp Mercedes D.II engine. An unknown number were built; it is thought to be less than twenty.

A second seaplane version appeared during 1915, the Gotha WD.2. Very similar in design to LD.6a, eleven WD.2s were supplied to the navy. WD.2 was fitted with a 150hp Benz Bz.III engine which gave a top speed of 70mph and an operational ceiling of 9,840ft. The wingspan was 51ft 2½in and the length was 34ft 5½in. No armament was carried.

One version of WD.2 was sent to Turkey, and was one of the first reconnaissance aircraft to be fitted with a machine gun mounted on top of the centre section. To operate the gun the observer had to stand up in his cockpit. A limited number were sent.

A radical new design, the Gotha WD.3, appeared in July 1915. It was a twin-boomed aircraft with a central nacelle that housed not only the 160hp Mercedes D.III engine with a pusher airscrew, but also contained cockpits for the pilot and observer. The observer's position was in the extreme front of the nacelle and was armed with a manually operated Parabellum machine gun. WD.3 was also one of the first seaplanes to have a radio transmitter. With a wingspan of 51ft 2½in and a wing area of 583sq.ft, the aircraft presented an unusual sight. A number of problems were discovered during tests and only one was built.

Another experimental seaplane was built around the same time, the Gotha WD.5. This model was not a new variation but a modified WD.2. The 150hp Benz Bz.III engine was replaced with a 160hp Mercedes engine with two narrow strip radiators attached to the front centre-section struts. The model was sent to Haltenau Naval Air Station for tests, but was declined as a reconnaissance aircraft. The Commanding Officer Kapitänleutnant Langfield decided that he would keep the aircraft and use it as his personal transport.

A unique design by Oskar Ursinus was developed by Gotha at the beginning of 1915, the Gotha Ursinus GUH G.I. This was a landplane version of what became a seaplane version the following year. The design was unique as the fuselage was raised above both wings and engines. The aircraft carried a crew of three: pilot, observer and gunner. The gunner's position in the nose of the aircraft gave him an uninterrupted field of fire. The engines, two 150hp Benz Bz.IIIs, were mounted so close together that the tips of the propellers were almost touching. The idea was that in asymmetric flight should one of the engines fail then control of the aircraft

Gotha G.IIs in front of the airship hangar at Gontrode.

Gotha G.IV after a landing mishap.

could thus be maintained easily. Several of the land version models were built, but information on them is sparse.

At the end of 1915 a twin-engined torpedo seaplane was built and designated the Gotha WD.7. Powered by two 120hp Mercedes D.II engines, WD.7 had a wingspan of 52ft 6in, a fuselage length of 37ft 1in, and a height of 11ft 9½in. Top speed was 85mph, with an operational ceiling of 13,120ft. Eight of the aircraft were built and assigned to flying schools for training pilots and observers prior to their moving on to larger operational aircraft.

Another aircraft appeared at the same time, the Gotha WD.8. This was a single-engined version of WD.7 fitted with a 250hp Maybach Mb.IV engine which gave a top speed of 81mph and an operational ceiling of 14,760ft. It had been designed as an armed reconnaissance aircraft and fitted with a manually operated Parabellum machine gun in the observer's rear cockpit. Only one was built.

In February 1916 Gotha produced another armed reconnaissance seaplane, the Gotha WD.9. Only one was supplied to the German Navy fitted with a 160hp Mercedes D.III engine. A similar version, fitted with a 150hp Benz engine, was supplied to the Turkish government. The aircraft had a wingspan of 49ft 2½in, a fuselage length of 32ft 2in, a height of 12ft 5½in and a top speed of 85mph. Both aircraft carried a manually operated Parabellum machine gun in the observer's rear cockpit.

With the relative success of WD.7 model, Gotha produced another twin-engined torpedo-carrying reconnaissance aircraft, the Gotha WD.11. This model was considerably bigger and had a wingspan of 73ft 10½in, a fuselage length of 44ft 1in and a

Gotha G.V bomber being loaded with bombs for a raid on England.

height of 15ft 2in. It was powered by two 160hp Mercedes D.III engines which drove two pusher airscrews and gave a top speed of 75mph with a climb rate of nearly 300ft per minute. The WD.11 carried one torpedo and had a manually operated Parabellum machine gun mounted in the observer's cockpit in the nose. Thirteen of this model were delivered to the German Navy.

Gotha continued to build seaplanes and in 1916 produced WD.12. This was an unarmed reconnaissance aircraft powered by a 160hp Mercedes D.III engine, with a fuselage length of 32ft 9½in, a top speed of 88mph and a flight duration of five and a half hours. Only one WD.12 was supplied to the German Navy, six were supplied to Turkey.

The seaplane version of the Gotha Ursinus GUH – the UWD – appeared in 1916. This version was almost identical, except that it was powered by two 160hp Mercedes D.III engines and the undercarriage was replaced with floats. Only one of this model was built and was not as successful as the land version.

The first of the prototype Gotha bombers appeared in 1916, the G.II and G.III. Both versions were identical externally and in specifications, the only difference being internal ones. They had a wingspan of 77ft 9½in, a fuselage length of 38ft 8in and a wing area of 967sq.ft. They were powered by two 260hp Mercedes D.IVa engines which gave a top speed of 92mph. Only a small number were built and flown on the Western Front, one unit being Bogohl 3 based at Ghent, Belgium.

In September 1916 the first Gotha bomber appeared, the Gotha G.IV. Trials had earlier been carried out with G.II and G.III and the results brought about the development of the bomber. There was one very unusual feature incorporated into the

Gotha G.IV and G.V bombers over London in 1917.

Gotha G.IV known as the 'sting in the tail'. The rear gunner's position in the aircraft enabled him not only to fire upwards and backwards, but downwards as well. This was achieved by the gunner firing through a specially designed tunnel in the bottom of the fuselage. This defensive method was extremely effective as a number of Allied fighter pilots were to find out to their cost.

The G.IV bomber arrived just as the German military hierarchy were about phase out Zeppelins for bombing raids. The Zeppelin had serious limitations. Because of their size they were easily spotted, they were slower and when hit with incendiary bullets they invariably caught fire dramatically, unlike Gotha G.IV.

In April 1917, thirty of G.IV bombers were delivered to Nr.3 Heavy Bomber Squadron, based at St Denis Westrem and Gontrode, which was under the command of Hauptmann Ernst von Brandenburg. The first series of raids, carried out between

25 May and 22 August 1917, were relatively successful and the squadron suffered very few casualties. One of the reasons for their success was that the Gotha G.IV was powered with two 260hp Mercedes engines and was able to operate at a height of 15,000ft. This allowed them to drop their bombs and, because of the inadequate British early warning system, be on their way back to base before Home Defence fighters could scramble and reach the Gotha's operational height.

The Gotha G.IV had a wingspan of 77ft 9½in, a fuselage length of 38ft 11in and a wing area of 966.6sq.ft. Powered by two six-cylinder, in-line, water-cooled 260hp Mercedes D.IVa engines, G.IVa had a top speed of 87mph with an operational ceiling of 21,320ft and a range of 350 miles. Its armament was two manually operated Parabellum machine guns mounted in the front and rear cockpits, and a bomb load that varied from 660lb to 1,100lb, depending on the mission and whether it was a daylight or nighttime raid. The Gotha G.V which followed afterwards was almost identical.

Another export model was Gotha WD.13, an armed patrol seaplane which was an upgraded version of WD.9. Although the German Navy carried out a series of trials with this aircraft, none were acquired, but in 1917 the Turkish government purchased over eight of the aircraft. Powered by a 150hp Benz Bz.III engine, which gave a top speed of 82mph, it was armed with a manually operated Parabellum machine gun fitted in the observer's rear cockpit.

Of all the seaplanes built by Gotha only WD.11 and WD.14 were built with production numbers in mind. Thirteen WD.11 reconnaissance seaplanes were built, whilst sixty-nine models of WD.14, which had been designed and developed as an attack torpedo aircraft, were produced. Developed from WD.7 and WD.11 proto-types, WD.14 had a wingspan of 83ft 8in, a fuselage length of 47ft 5in, and a height of 16ft 5in. It was powered by two 200hp Benz Bz.IV engines mounted on the lower wings.

The fuselage of WD.14 consisted of a basic rectangular braced box girder, made up of spruce longerons and spacers. The torpedo was slung beneath the fuselage and between the floats. The pilot's and torpedo-man's cockpit, were one and the same situated under the wings. It was of a side-by-side configuration, with access available to the nose cockpit for the torpedo-man to enable him to aim and release the torpedo. Once the torpedo had been released, the torpedo-man's role reverted to that of gunner. There were two manually operated Parabellum machine guns mounted in the rear and nose cockpits.

Torpedo attacks using the WD.14 were carried out. However, the aircraft was substantially underpowered for the weight of the torpedo and the armament that it was supposed to carry. This made it extremely difficult aircraft to handle and only some of the top pilots were able to use it to its full capability. The attacks bore no result and a decision was made to use the aircraft for long-range reconnaissance missions over the North Sea in place of vulnerable airships. In place of the torpedo, jettisonable fuel tanks were fitted which enabled the aircraft to stay aloft for up to ten hours. Initially they were reasonably successful then it was discovered that in the event of one of the engines failing, WD.14 was unable to fly on one engine, and having to carry out emergency landings on the sea, other than in calm weather, proved disastrous. The aircraft were relegated to the role of minesweepers, but even at that they were relegated to escorting coastal convoys.

Toward the end of 1917 another variation of an earlier model appeared, the Gotha WD.15. Derived from WD.12, the WD.15 was an enlarged version with a plywood covered fuselage and fin. Only two aircraft were built and both were powered by a 260hp Mercedes D.IVa engine. The aircraft had a wingspan of 56ft 5in, a fuselage length of 36ft 9in, a top speed of 95mph and an operating ceiling of 13,780ft. These two WD.15s were the last single-engined aircraft that Gotha delivered to the German Navy.

The results acquired from using the Gotha WD.14 as a long-range reconnaissance aircraft were put to use with the development of the Gotha WD.20. Only three of these aircraft were built and they were developed purely as long-range reconnaissance aircraft with additional fuel tanks in place of the torpedo carried by previous aircraft. The WD.20 had a wingspan of 73ft 8½in, a fuselage length of 47ft 5in, a top speed of 80mph and a flight duration of ten hours. Its only armament was two manually operated Parabellum machine guns: one mounted in the nose, the other in the observer's cockpit just aft of the wings.

As the production of the G.V bomber series came to an end, a number of modified versions suddenly appeared. The G.Vb was a modified version of the G.Va and fitted with additional wheels on the undercarriage and a compound tail assembly. It was powered by two 260hp Mercedes D.IVa engines that drove two pusher airscrews, giving the aircraft a top speed of 84mph. A small number were built but were not successful. This was followed by a prototype model, the G.VI.

Probably the world's first asymmetric aircraft, the G.VI's fuselage was offset to the portside and had a 260hp Mercedes D.IVa engine mounted in the nose which drove a tractor airscrew. Another 260hp Mercedes D.IVa engine, driving a pusher airscrew, was mounted in a nacelle in the starboard housing. A number of test flights were made but the aircraft crashed attempting to land and was destroyed; no more were made.

At the same time as G.IV was making its test flights, another prototype came off the production line, the Gotha G.VII. This was a small twin-engined aircraft that had been developed for ultra-long-range photo-reconnaissance missions. When a special photographic unit (the Reihenbildzug) was formed, four of these aircraft were supplied. A month later a production model based on the G.VII prototype was launched. The G.VII production model bore little or no resemblance to the prototype and was supplied to the military late in 1918, too late to make any significant difference to the outcome of the war. With a wingspan of 63ft 3in, a fuselage length of 31ft 7½in, and a wing area of 689sq.ft, the G.VII had ailerons at all four wingtips and slightly swept wings to compensate for the removal of the nose section.

Another version of G.VII, the G.VIII, was built the only difference being a longer wingspan of 71ft 3½in. There were a further two models built, Gotha G.IX, which was built by LVG, and Gotha G.X. The G.X was another twin-engined photo-reconnaissance aircraft, but powered by two 180hp BMW (Bayerische Motor Werke) engines. Little is known about either aircraft and no details are available.

The wreckage of a Gotha G.V bomber being recovered from the sea off Sheerness.

Later, in 1918, two more long-range reconnaissance aircraft were built – Gotha WD.22. Similar in design and construction to WD.14, WD.22 was powered by four engines: two 160hp Mercedes and two 100hp Mercedes D.Is. The engines were mounted in tandem in twin nacelles, the two forward engines driving tractor airscrews, the two rear engines pusher airscrews. With a wingspan of 85ft 3½in, a fuselage length of 47ft 3in, a wing area of 1,588sq.ft and a top speed of 82mph, WD.22 promised a lot but delivered very little.

Not to be deterred, Gotha, in 1918, came up with three of the largest aircraft built during World War One, Gotha WD.27. They were so large that they came into the category of the R aircraft – Riesenseeflugzeug (*giant seaplane*). With a wingspan of 101ft 8½in, a fuselage length of 57ft 9in and a wing area of 2,084sq.ft, the WD.27 was a giant of a seaplane. It was powered by four 160hp Mercedes D.III engines, which were mounted in tandem in twin nacelles that turned spinnered pusher and tractor airscrews. The giant aircraft had a top speed of 84mph.

SPECIFICATIONS

Gotha LD.2

Wing Span	47ft 7in
Length	24ft 7½in
Height	9ft 8¼in
Weight Empty	1,617lbs
Weight Loaded	2,479lbs
Engine	One 100hp Mercedes D.I – six-cylinder, inline, water-cooled
Maximum Speed	65mph
Service Ceiling	20,900ft
Duration	1½hrs – later reduced to 1hr
Armament	None

Gotha WD.II

Wing Span	73ft 10½in
Length	44ft 1in
Height	15ft 1¼in
Weight Empty	5,361lbs
Weight Loaded	7,883lbs
Engine	Two 160hp Mercedes D.III – six-cylinder, in-line, water-cooled
Maximum Speed	75mph
Service Ceiling	22,900ft
Duration	5hrs
Armament	One manually operated Parabellum machine gun mounted in the nose
	One torpedo carried under the fuselage between the floats

Gotha G.V

Wing Span	77ft 9¼in
Length	40ft 1in
Height	14ft 1in
Weight Empty	6,028lbs
Weight Loaded	8,745lbs
Engine	Two 160hp Mercedes D.IV – six-cylinder, in-line, water-cooled
Maximum Speed	87mph
Service Ceiling	21,320ft
Duration	5hrs
Armament	Two manually operated Parabellum machine guns mounted in the nose and rear of the aircraft
	Six 110lb bombs

Gotha WD.14

Wing Span	83ft 8in
Length	47ft 5in
Height	16ft 5in
Weight Empty	6,930lbs
Weight Loaded	10,212lbs
Engine	Two 200hp Benz Bz.IV – six-cylinder, in line, water-cooled
Maximum Speed	84mph
Service Ceiling	21,320ft
Duration	8hrs
Armament	Two manually operated Parabellum machine guns mounted in the nose and rear of the aircraft Six 110lb bombs

HALBERSTÄDTER FLUGZEUG-WERKE GMBH

One of the first aircraft built by the Halberstadt company to be used in the war was the Halberstadt B. Powered by an 80hp Oberursel U.O engine, this small biplane – produced in 1914 – was used purely for training purposes. It is thought only a handful was built.

Developed from the B model was the two-seater Halberstadt B.I, the first of the purpose-built military aircraft to be constructed and was used for reconnaissance purposes. Like most of the early aircraft, the pilot flew the aircraft from the rear cockpit, leaving the observer in the front cockpit to try and carry out his duties from a usually poor view. The B.II and B.III were almost identical to the B.I, but different engines were tried. The B.I and B.II were fitted with a 100hp Mercedes D.I engine, whilst B.III was fitted with a 120hp Mercedes D.II engine.

A new series appeared in late 1915, the Halberstadt C.I. This was a more compact version of the B.II and fitted with a rotary engine. The crew positions were reversed and a manually operated Parabellum machine gun fitted in the observer's rear cockpit. Only two were built as a weakness in the rudder was discovered.

The one and only twin-engined model appeared at the end of 1915, the Halberstadt G.I. Powered by two 160hp Mercedes D.III engines, which gave it a top speed of 95mph, the G.I had a flight duration of four hours. It had a wingspan of 50ft 10½in, a fuselage length of 29ft 6½in and was armed with two manually operated Parabellum machine guns and carried a bomb load of 440lb. Only one of the aircraft was built as it proved not to be satisfactory.

Another model appeared in February 1916, the Halberstadt D.I. Like the B series, D.I was similar in most ways and differed only in not having staggered wings and having the radiators mounted on either side of the fuselage just below the pilot's cockpit. D.II and D.III models which followed were almost identical with the exception being the change of engines from 100hp Mercedes D.I engine to 120hp Mercedes D.II engine.

The first of the fighter aircraft – the Halberstadt D.IV – appeared. Powered by a 150hp Benz Bz.III engine with a Rhino horn exhaust, D.IV had a top speed of

108mph and a flight duration of 1½hours. It had a wingspan of 28ft 10½in, a fuselage length of 23ft 11½in, and a wing area of 259sq.ft. It was capable of carrying one or two fixed forward-firing Spandau machine guns. A small number were made, but it was the prototype for the Halberstadt D.V fighter which followed.

Based on a standard D.III airframe, the D.V, was fitted with either a 120hp Argus D.II or 120hp Mercedes D.II engine. It had a wingspan of 28ft 10½in, a fuselage length of 23ft 11½in, a top speed of 108mph and a climb rate of over 1,000ft per minute. It was armed with one fixed forward-firing Spandau machine gun. All the pilots who flew the aircraft were delighted with it. A large number of these aircraft were built and a number were supplied to the Turkish government.

The first of the purpose-built two-seat long-range reconnaissance aircraft were built at the end of 1917. The Halberstadt C.III was constructed in the conventional manner of spruce wood and fabric covered in plywood. It was powered by a 200hp Benz Bz.IV engine that gave a top speed of 103mph. It carried an armament of one fixed forward-firing Spandau machine gun and one manually operated Parabellum machine gun mounted on a Scarf-type gun ring in the observer's rear cockpit.

The C.III had a wingspan of 40ft ⅜in and a fuselage length of 25ft 3¼in. Only six of these machines were completed and supplied to the German Army.

The design of a two-seat fighter in May 1917 created another type of aircraft for the Halberstadt company, the Halberstadt CL.II. It was created out of a need to protect the C-type photo-reconnaissance aircraft that were becoming increasingly important to the success of German infantry. A new flight was created, the Schutzstaffeln (*protection/escort flights*), and it was into this flight that the CL.II was introduced.

Powered by a 160hp six-cylinder, in-line, water-cooled Mercedes D.III engine, that gave a top speed of 103mph, an operational ceiling of 16,700ft and a flight duration of three hours. With a wingspan of 35ft 4in, a fuselage length of 23ft 11½in, and a wing area of 297sq.ft, the CL.II was a relatively small aircraft for a two-seater. It carried a quite formidable armament in one or two fixed forward-firing Spandau machine gun, a manually operated Parabellum machine gun mounted in the rear of the two seater cockpit, as well as 22lb of bombs and a number of anti-personnel grenades.

A large number of Halberstadt CL.IIs were supplied to the German Army and were used during some of the major offensives. During a British Court of Inquiry into the success of the German counter-offensive during the Battle of Cambrai, evidence was produced that the appearance of German close-support aircraft, like the Halberstadt CL.II, flying at low-level and firing into both the front trenches and the rear sections, was a major cause of the British infantry being thrown into confusion. It was this confusion, the Court of Inquiry found, combined with the morale boost given to the German infantry by these aerial attacks, that was one of the main contributors to the German troops' counter-offensive success.

With these successes, the name Schutzstaffeln was changed to Schlachtstaffeln (*battle flights*) and the flight section was expanded. With the expansion came the need for more aircraft and the Halberstadt CL.IV was produced. Very similar to the CL.II, the CL.IV's fuselage was three inches shorter, the horizontal tail surfaces were of a larger span and had a higher aspect ratio. The engine was the same as the CL.II but

Halberstadt CL.II.

Halberstadt CL.II undergoing repairs to its wings inside the factory.

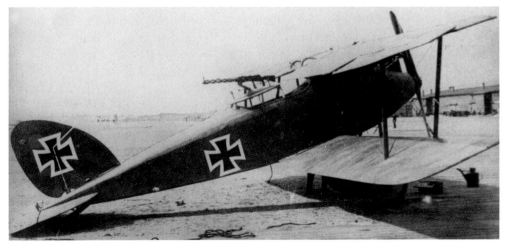

Halberstadt CL.II – a side view showing the rear gun and its ring-mounting.

the aircraft was now more manoeuvrable, which was necessary for its new role. The success of the Schlachtstaffeln flights resulted in missions that went ahead of infantry advances, with the intention of 'softening up' the Allied lines with low-level strafing attacks. The fuselage of the CL.IV was covered in plywood which, because of the low-level attacks carried out by the crews, left them exposed to small-arms fire. A number of crews were wounded or killed in this manner.

In March 1918, when the German Army made its final attempt to crush the Allies, thirty-eight Schlachtstaffeln had been created and were equipped with mostly Halberstadt CL.II and CL.IV aircraft. Some of the aircraft were fitted with two fixed forward-firing Spandau machine guns, one manually operated Parabellum machine gun in the rear of the large cockpit and a number of anti-personnel grenades mounted in boxes on the sides of the fuselage. There were a small number of flights which had been equipped with Hanover CL.IIIas. The failure of the offensive forced the CL.II and CL.IVs into a defensive role, which they carried out with distinction.

Toward the end of 1918, with the Americans firmly established in the war, the need for photo-reconnaissance aircraft resulted in the production of the Halberstadt C.V. Earlier in the year the Halberstadt company had developed a long-range, high-altitude reconnaissance aircraft and, unusually for manufacturers at this time, had carried out extensive tests on the prototype. They in fact tested it to destruction. The fuselage and tail section resembled that of the CL.IV, but that was the only resemblance. The large cockpit was replaced by conventional twin-cockpits and the dimensions of the aircraft were considerably larger than those of the CL.IV.

The aircraft had a wingspan of 44ft 8¾in, a fuselage length of 22ft 8½in, and was powered by a six-cylinder, in-line, water-cooled Benz Bz.IV engine. This gave a top speed of 106mph, an operational height of nearly 17,000ft and a flight duration of three and a half hours. With a crew of two (pilot and observer/gunner) the C.V carried one fixed forward-firing Spandau machine gun and one manually operated Parabellum machine gun in the rear cockpit.

The Halberstadt aircraft throughout the war performed as well as most other aircraft of their type, but never received the recognition by historians that they deserved.

SPECIFICATIONS

Halberstadt CL.II

Wing Span	35ft 4in
Length	23ft 11½in
Height	9ft
Weight Empty	1,701lb
Weight Loaded	2,493lb
Engine	One 160hp Mercedes D.III – six-cylinder, in-line, water-cooled
Maximum Speed	103mph

Front three-quarter port-side view of the Halberstadt CL.IV. This was possibly the prototype.

Rear view of the Halberstadt C.V.

Service Ceiling	16,700ft
Duration	3hrs
Armament	One or two fixed forward–firing Spandau machine guns
	One manually operated Parabellum machine gun in rear observer's cockpit
	Four 22lb bombs

Halberstadt C.III

Wing Span	40ft ⅜in
Length	25ft 3¼in
Height	9ft 8¼in
Weight Empty	1,870lb
Weight Loaded	2,882lb

Engine   One 200hp Benz Bz.IV – six-cylinder, in-line,
                                    water-cooled
Maximum Speed   103mph
Service Ceiling   16,700ft
Duration   3hrs
Armament   One fixed forward-firing Spandau machine gun
                                One manually operated Parabellum machine gun
                                    in rear observer's cockpit

Halberstadt C.V

Wing Span   44ft 8¾in
Length   22ft 8½in
Height   11ft
Weight Empty   2,046lb
Weight Loaded   2,730lb
Engine   One 200hp Benz Bz.IV – six-cylinder, in-line,
                                    water-cooled (with high compression cylinders)
Maximum Speed   106mph
Service Ceiling   16,700ft
Duration   3½hrs
Armament   One fixed forward-firing Spandau machine gun
                                One manually operated Parabellum machine gun
                                    in observer's rear cockpit

HANNOVERSCHE WAGGONFABRIK AG

One of the major contributors to the German Army Air Service during World War One was Hannoversche Waggonfabrik company. Builders of some of the finest two-seater reconnaissance aircraft of the time, the company actually started life as a manufacturer of railway rolling stock. With the outbreak of World War One, the German government pressed all manufacturers of machinery into war service. In 1915, the Hannover company were ordered to manufacture aircraft under licence from other aircraft manufacturers. A branch of the company was created under the name of Hannover-Linden and some of the first aircraft produced by Hannover were the Rumpler C.Ia, Aviatik C.I and Halberstadt D.II.

As the company became more and more proficient at producing other manufacturers' aircraft, Hermann Dorner, Hannover's chief designer, decided it was about time that they produced one of their own. At the beginning of 1917, the Flugzeugmeisterei requested a new type of two-seater aircraft that could be used both as a fighter and for reconnaissance. It was to be powered by a 160hp to 180hp engine and fit into the existing CL category of aircraft. The CL-type of aircraft had been assigned to escort duties – Schutzstaffeln.

With this requirement in mind, Hermann Dorner produced the first of the Hannover aircraft, the Hannover CL.II. Because Hannover had built the Aviatik C.I, the designation given to the Hannover's aircraft was the CL.II. The prototype CL.II was powered with an Argus As.III engine, which gave a top speed of 103mph, an operational ceiling of 24,600ft and a flight duration of three hours. It had a wingspan of 38ft 4in, a fuselage length 24ft 10½in and a height of 9ft 2½in.

The fuselage was of conventional construction and consisted of four main spruce longerons with plywood formers covered in thin plywood skinned with a doped fabric. The tail section was unusual. The vertical fin of the tail was integral with the fuselage and constructed in the same manner. The lower tailplane was constructed and covered in a similar manner, but on top of the tail fin was another tailplane, this being constructed of steel tubing and covered in doped fabric, as were the elevators.

The aircraft was greatly respected by the Allies as it was capable of absorbing a great deal of punishment and more than capable of giving as good as it got. The Hannover CL.II was armed with one fixed forward-firing Spandau machine gun and one manually operated rearward-firing Parabellum machine gun. A total of 439 of these aircraft were built.

The CL.III appeared later in 1917 and was almost identical except for the installation of a 160hp Mercedes D.III engine. Within months this engine was replaced by a 180hp Argus As.III engine, as it was decided that the Mercedes engine was desperately needed for single-seat fighters. The new aircraft with the Argus As.III engine were designated CL.IIIa. A total of 80 CL.IIIs and 587 CL.IIIbs were built, which brought the total of Hannover two-seat fighter/reconnaissance aircraft supplied to the German Army to over 1,000.

As with all the aircraft manufacturers at the time, variations were made and prototypes appeared. The Hannover CL.IIIb was almost identical to the CL.IIIa but with longer wings. Only the one model was built.

At the beginning of 1918, Hannover produced the C.IV. This was a high-altitude reconnaissance aircraft powered by a 245hp Maybach Mb.IV engine. This gave a top

Rear three-quarter view of the Hannover CL.II.

speed of 100mph, an operational ceiling of 29,520ft with a flight duration of three hours. The C.IV had a wingspan of 41ft 2½in, a fuselage length of 25ft 7½in and was armed with one fixed forward-firing Spandau machine gun and one manually operated rearward-firing Parabellum machine gun. The wings, because of their extended length had a V-centre strut arrangement, instead of the usual single I-interplane strut.

The prototype was tested by the military but showed no improvement on the existing Rumpler C.VII (Rubild) model. Only one was built.

Just before the Armistice, Hannover produced another model, the CL.V. There were in fact two variants of this model: one with a biplane tail configuration and one without. Both variants were powered by 185hp BMW.IIIa engines that gave a top speed of 115mph, an operational ceiling of 29,520ft with a flight duration of three hours. The biplane tail model had a wingspan of 34ft 7¾in, the monoplane tail version had a wingspan 34ft 5in. Fuselage length was the same for both (23ft 3⅝in), as was the height (9ft 6¼in). Armament for both models was the same as for all the previous versions.

Fifty Hannover C.V aircraft were built, but none went into service as Armistice was declared and their need gone. The Hannover two-seat reconnaissance aircraft was one of the most respected of the two-seat aircraft in the war. Both sides recognised its qualities and gave it the respect it deserved.

SPECIFICATIONS

Hannover CL.II

Wing Span	38ft 4½in
Length	24ft 10½in
Height	9ft 2¼in
Weight Empty	1,577lb
Weight Loaded	2,378lb
Engine	One 180hp Argus As.III – six-cylinder, in-line, water-cooled (with high compression cylinders)
Maximum Speed	103mph
Service Ceiling	24,700ft
Duration	3hrs
Armament	One fixed forward-firing Spandau machine gun One manually operated Parabellum machine gun in rear observer's cockpit

Hannover CL.III.

Hannover C.IV

Wing Span	41ft 2½in
Length	25ft 7½in
Height	9ft 2¼in
Weight Empty	2,112lb
Weight Loaded	3,069lb
Engine	One 245hp Maybach Mb.IV – six-cylinder, in-line, water-cooled (with high compression cylinders)
Maximum Speed	100mph
Service Ceiling	29,520ft
Duration	3hrs
Armament	One fixed forward-firing Spandau machine gun
	One manually operated Parabellum machine gun in rear observer's cockpit

Hannover CL.V

Wing Span	37ft 7¾in (first version); 34ft 5in (second version)
Length	23ft 3⅝in
Height	9ft 6¼in
Weight Empty	1,584lb
Weight Loaded	2,376lb
Engine	One 185hp BMW.IIIa – six-cylinder, in-line, water-cooled
Maximum Speed	115mph
Service Ceiling	29,520ft
Duration	3hrs
Armament	One fixed forward-firing Spandau machine gun.
	One manually operated Parabellum machine gun in rear observer's cockpit

HANSA-BRANDENBURGISCHE FLUGZEUG-WERKE GMBH

The Hansa-Brandenburg company were well known for production of seaplanes rather than land-based aircraft. One of their first aircraft, however, was the Brandenburg D, a two-seat observation aircraft that was built specifically for the German Army in 1914. Only twelve aircraft were delivered.

Later came the Brandenburg FD (B.I); four aircraft were sent to the flying schools at Hanseatische Flugzeug-Werke and Caspar Hamburg-Fuhlsbüttel, three to the Austrian Army and five to the German Army. During their short but active roles, they contributed greatly to the development of the German Air Arm.

The fuselage was constructed of a steel tube with a plywood-sheet covering, the wings were made of ash covered in fabric. The engine, with its rhinohorn manifold exhaust, was a 110hp Benz Bz.III. The wings of the Brandenburg FD were distinctive because the interplane struts were inward-sloping, a feature that was to be seen later on nearly all Austro-Hungarian Brandenburg C-types.

Prior to World War One, the Brandenburg company had been working on a design for a floatplane; the result, which appeared just after war had started, was the Brandenburg W. With a wingspan of 54ft 2in and a fuselage length of 30ft 10in, the aircraft was powered by a 150hp Benz Bz.III engine which gave it a top speed of 56mph. The floats of the aircraft were extremely crude and looked more like modified dinghies – but a total of twenty-seven were supplied to the Imperial German Naval Air Arm.

In 1915, the Brandenburg NW appeared – designed for reconnaissance duties and fitted with radio. Some were fitted with bomb racks that carried 5kg bombs. Based on the design of the Brandenburg W, the NW model showed a great deal of refinement and, whether deliberately or by accident, showed a remarkable resemblance to Heinkel's three-bay Albatros seaplanes. The floats on the NW model were of an elongated wedge shape and had a greater stabilising effect on the aircraft whilst taxiing. The NW model was powered by a 160hp Mercedes D.III engine which gave a top speed of 56mph. The floatplane carried no armament but had a flight duration of four hours. Thirty-two Brandenburg NWs were supplied to the German Navy.

Later the same year the development of the NW model was taken a step further by the creation of the Brandenburg GNW. This two-seat unarmed reconnaissance floatplane had an improved rate of climb, although the top speed was almost the same. Sixteen of the aircraft were delivered to the German Navy at the end of 1915.

The delivery in May 1916 of the Brandenburg LW caused a slight stir, when its designer Ernst Heinkel claimed that it was the first reconnaissance floatplane to be armed with a defensive weapon. Based on the design of the C.I land aircraft designed and built for the Austro-Hungarian Army Air Service; only one was ever built. Toward the end of 1916, a new model appeared, the Brandenburg KW. It was powered by a 200hp Benz Bz.IV engine, which gave a top speed of 83mph. Unfortunately, it was deemed to be underpowered and relegated to training duties.

One floatplane that was not relegated was the Brandenburg GW. It had been designed as a torpedo-carrying strike aircraft and carried a single torpedo weighing 1,595lb. Twenty-six were supplied to the Navy, all of which operated from the seaplane station at Angernsee in Courland, France. Powered by two 160hp Mercedes D.III engines which gave a top speed of 64mph, it had a wing span of 70ft 9in, a wing area of 1,103sq.ft and a length of 41ft 3in. The GW carried a single Parabellum machine gun as armament.

The decision to build another large flying boat resulted from the success of the torpedo trials with the GW, and heralded the arrival of the Brandenburg GDW. It had a wingspan of 80ft 4in, a length of 51ft 10in, a height of 16ft 4½in and an all-up weight of 10,672lb. Loaded, the GDW was a very large aircraft. Powered by two 200hp Benz Bz.IV engines, the aircraft could reach a top speed of 81mph. The torpedo that the aircraft had been designed to carry weighed 4,015lb, but bigger does not necessarily mean better and only one of the aircraft was ever built. After initial tests it was relegated to training duties.

The next aircraft from Brandenburg was in complete contrast to the GDW. This was the Brandenburg CC, a small single-seater floatplane fighter that had initially been built for the Austro-Hungarian Navy. The initials CC stood for Camilo Castiglioni, who was the financier behind Brandenburg. The small floatplane was powered by a 150hp Benz Bz.III engine which gave a top speed of 109mph, and a climb rate of 650ft per minute. It had a wingspan of 30ft 6in, a length of 25ft 3in and was armed with two Spandau machine guns. A large number of the aircraft were supplied to the Austro-Hungarian Navy and twenty-six were supplied to the German Navy. The Austro-Hungarian ace Leutnant Gottfried Banfield had a great deal of success flying the Brandenburg CC.

A slightly larger version of the Brandenburg CC model appeared in the middle of 1916, the Brandenburg FB 1915. With a wingspan of 52ft 6in, a length of 33ft 2in and powered by a 165hp Austro-Daimler engine, this fighter, although enthusiastically received by the Austro-Hungarians, was not liked by the German Navy. Only six were supplied to the German Navy, but a considerable number were supplied to the Austro-Hungarian Navy who were delighted with the aircraft and used them extensively during operations in the Adriatic.

In 1916 Ernst Heinkel designed a single-seat scout aircraft for the Austrian Army, which featured an unusual wing bracing system. The struts were in the form of four V-struts that were joined in the centre of the wing. This gave a star effect configuration. Built under licence by the Phönix and Ufag factories, the Brandenburg KDW (Kampf Doppeldecker Werke) was converted to a seaplane after a demand for a seaplane-station fighter. There were handling problems largely due to the blanketing of the small rudder by the deep fuselage. Like previous fighter aircraft, the fuselage consisted of four spruce longerons with plywood formers and spruce spacers. The fuselage was then covered with plywood. The tail surfaces were constructed of steel tubing covered in fabric. The wings were of wooden construction covered in fabric. It was powered by a six-cylinder in-line, water-cooled 160hp Maybach Mb.III engine, which gave a top speed of 106mph. Fifty-eight of the aircraft were built; thirty-eight were fitted with a single Spandau machine gun and the last twenty fitted with twin Spandau machine guns.

Whilst the development of the KDW was taking place, Ernst Heinkel was already working on a replacement. The seaplane fighters at the time were vulnerable to attack from the rear as all their guns were forward-firing, Heinkel was asked to design a two-seat fighter that had both forward and rearward firing capabilities; the result was the Brandenburg W.12. The elevated rear machine gun gave a superb field of fire all round the aircraft, including over the top of the wing. Based on the fuselage of the KDW it tapered upward from behind the engine mountings to give the rear gun the improved field of fire. The wings were made of spruce covered in fabric with plywood ribs. The upper wing a one piece structure, whilst the lower was of two pieces with heavy spruce struts between them. The ailerons were of steel tubing covered in fabric. Powered by a six-cylinder, in-line, water-cooled 160hp Mercedes engine or a six-cylinder, in-line, water-cooled 150hp Benz Bz.III engine, the W.12 had a top speed of 100mph and a flight endurance of three and a half hours.

It was in a W.12, on 17 December 1917, that Oberleutnant zur See Christiansen attacked and destroyed the British non-rigid airship C.27.

With the need for seaplanes firmly established in the expansion of the German naval flying services, an aircraft with longer flight endurance was required. The Brandenburg W.12 had served well but a larger aircraft was needed. This led to the development of the Brandenburg W.19. It had a wing span of 45ft 3½in (10ft longer than W.12), a fuselage length of 34ft 11½in (3½ft longer than the W.12), and was powered by a six-cylinder, in-line, water-cooled 260hp Maybach Mb.IV engine. The aircraft's flight endurance was around five hours and the first three of the fifty-five delivered aircraft were fitted with one fixed forward-firing Spandau machine gun and one manually operated Parabellum machine gun in the rear cockpit. The remaining fifty-two aircraft were fitted with twin fixed forward-firing Spandau machine guns and one Parabellum in the rear cockpit.

The respect that some German and Allied fliers had for each another was never more apparent than on 4 June 1918 when a patrol of British F2A flying boats from Felixstowe and Yarmouth were attacked by German Brandenburg W.19 and W.29 seaplanes. In the ensuing fight a number of aircraft on either side were shot down and one of them, flown by Lieutenant Robertson, was floating wrecked and upside down on the water. One of the German seaplanes alighted alongside and the pilot asked Robertson whether he wanted to be picked up and taken as a prisoner-of-war to Zeebrugge or to take his chance on being picked up by the Royal Navy. Robertson politely declined the offer of assistance, and with that the German pilot saluted his fallen adversary, took a picture of him and took off. Robertson was later rescued by the Royal Navy.

Two more land-based aircraft were produced during 1917, both of which were prototypes. The Brandenburg L.14 was a single-seat fighter produced as a development for the Austrian-built Brandenburg D.I. Powered by a 200hp Hiero engine, with a wingspan of 33ft 6in, a fuselage length of 23ft 1½in and a top speed of 102mph, only one of this type was built. The Brandenburg L.16 was a purely experimental model triplane. It was developed to test a variety of radiators and their positions for the 185hp Austro-Daimler engine.

Friedrich Christiansen, now firmly established as one of Germany's top seaplane commanders, approached Ernst Heinkel and suggested that an even faster and more manoeuvrable seaplane fighter was needed. Heinkel looked at the success of the W.12

Brandenburg (HB) W.20 moored on the River Havel. This model was originally designed to be carried aboard a U-boat but this was never realised.

Brandenburg (HB) C.I of the Austro-Hungarian Air Service, seen here on the Gardolo Airfield at Trient in 1917. Note the wooden slats on the ground on which the aircraft was placed.

Brandenburg (HB) C.I running up prior to take off.

Brandenburg (HB) C.I on the Italian Front in the process of being serviced by the ground crew.

Brandenburg (HB) L.16 running up prior to take off.

and decided to produce a monoplane version of the aircraft. To all intents and purposes the W.29 was just a W.12 with the top wing removed. The wing was extended by another 9ft and differed in thickness. The bracing struts were almost twice as thick at the roots as the wing had been turned from a high-speed section to a high-lift section. Construction of the aircraft was as the W.12: spruce longerons for the fuselage and covered in fabric, the wing spruce main spars with plywood ribs covered with fabric. Seventy-eight of the aircraft were built and supplied to the German Navy, the first forty were fitted with only one fixed forward-firing machine gun, but with radio. The remaining aircraft were fitted with twin fixed forward-firing Spandau machine guns and one manually operated machine gun in the rear cockpit, but the radios were removed. Powered by a six-cylinder, in-line, water-cooled 150hp Benz Bz.III engine, the W.29 was capable of a maximum speed of 109mph, could operate at a height of 16,400ft and had an flight endurance of around four hours.

In one incident Christiansen's W.29s attacked two F2A flying boats from Felixstowe shooting both down: the first crashing into the sea, the second being destroyed as it lay helplessly on the water after making an emergency landing.

The Brandenburg works produced a number of the finest reconnaissance and fighter aircraft, predominantly seaplanes, of World War One, but was also one of the least recognised.

SPECIFICATIONS

Brandenburg (HB) D

Wingspan	43ft 1in
Length	27ft 9in
Height	9ft 8½in
Weight Empty	2,240lb
Weight Loaded	3,836lb
Maximum Speed	62mph
Ceiling	3,350ft
Duration	1½hrs
Engine	One 110hp Benz Bz.II
Armament	None

Brandenburg (HB) W.33

Wingspan	52ft 0in
Length	36ft 5in
Height	11ft½in
Weight Empty	3,124lb
Weight Loaded	4.510lb
Maximum Speed	108mph
Ceiling	3,290ft

Duration	1½hrs
Engine	One 245hp Maybach Mb.IV
Armament	Two fixed forward-firing Spandau machine guns
	One manually operated Parabellum machine gun mounted in the observer's cockpit

Brandenburg (HB) L.16. (Dreidecker)

Wingspan	29ft 6½in
Length	23ft 8in
Height	12ft 2in
Weight Empty	1,628lb
Weight Loaded	2,057lb
Maximum Speed	118mph
Ceiling	9,290ft
Duration	1½hrs
Engine	One 185hp Austro-Daimler
Armament	Two fixed forward-firing Spandau machine guns.

Brandenburg (HB) W.29

Wingspan	44ft 3½in
Length	30ft 8½in
Height	9ft 10¼in
Weight Empty	2,200lb
Weight Loaded	3,286lb
Maximum Speed	109mph
Ceiling	16,400ft
Duration	4hrs
Engine	One 150hp Benz Bz.III – six-cylinder, in-line, water cooled
Armament	One fixed forward-firing Spandau machine gun (for the first forty)
	Two fixed forward-firing Spandau machine guns (for the last thirty-eight)

JUNKERS FLUGZEUG-WERKE AG

The Junkers Flugzeug-Werke started life not as an aircraft manufacturer, but as a manufacturer of gas water-heaters for bathtubs. Dr Hugo Junkers was one of the most innovative engineers of his time and during his lifetime, was awarded more than 1,000 patents covering an extremely wide variety of fields.

Hugo Junkers had for some years been looking at the concept of producing an all-metal monoplane aircraft and at the beginning of December 1915 the Junkers J.1, also known as the E.I, appeared. The first test flight, carried out on 12 December by Leutnant Friedrich Mallinckrodt at Döberitz, was a resounding success. Powered by a 120hp Mercedes D.II engine, J.1 had a top speed of 100mph, which was somewhat slower than the streamlined appearance gave. It was probably this, coupled with the thin sheet-metal covering of the aircraft, which gave rise to the name 'Tin Donkey'.

The J.1 had a wingspan of 42ft 5⅝in, a fuselage length of 24ft 4⅝in and a height of 10ft 3¼in. Only one aircraft was built, but it was enough to impress the Flugzeugmeisterei who asked Hugo Junkers to produce an armoured biplane.

In 1916 a second all-metal monoplane was built. The Junkers J.2 also known as the E.I. Only six were built powered by a 120hp Mercedes D.II engine, which gave a top speed of 90mph. The sixth model was fitted with the more powerful 160hp Mercedes D.III engine, but the performance difference was marginal. The J.2 had a wingspan of 36ft 1in, a fuselage length of 23ft 11½in and a height of 10ft 3in.

At the end of 1916, together with Professor Madelung, Hugo Junkers designed an armoured biplane covered in a corrugated metal sheet which was riveted to the duraluminium framework of Junkers J.1. The factory designation was J.4 but the military designation is always given as J.I. This has given rise to confusion when J.1 has been discussed.

The first J.1 (J.4) models had a hexagonal-shaped fuselage which was constructed of alloy, the rear section of the fuselage being covered in fabric. The nose section, which enclosed the engine and cockpits, was armoured and made of 5mm chrome-nickel sheet. It was this section that joined the rear fabric-covered part of the fuselage. The tailplane and elevators were of standard construction. Later models of this aircraft had a corrugated metal skin covering the entire fuselage.

J.1 (J.4) was powered by a six-cylinder, in-line, water-cooled 200hp Benz Bz.IV engine with a rhinohorn-type exhaust, which gave a top speed of 96.875mph and an endurance of two hours. It was armed with two fixed synchronised forward-firing Spandau machine guns and one manually operated Parabellum machine gun mounted in the rear cockpit. The upper wingspan was 52ft 6in, the lower wingspan 38ft 9in. The fuselage length was 29ft 10½in and the height was 11ft 1½in.

Two hundred and twenty-seven Junkers J.1s (J.4) were built in total, the first of them arriving at Flieger Abteilung (Infanterie) units at the end of 1917. Because of the weight of the armour plating, the crews found the aircraft difficult and extremely cumbersome during landings and take-offs. This, however, was weighed against the extra protection the armour plating provided, which more than compensated for the other problems. J.1 (J.4) was used extensively for low-level reconnaissance missions, as well as ammunition and ration supply drops to front line troops.

Encouraged by the acceptance of his aircraft by aircrews, Hugo Junkers started on what may be the most ambitious project of his First World War aeronautical career: the Junkers R.I. Powered by four 260hp Mercedes D.IVa engines which drove two propellers of 16ft 5in diameter, the projected speed of the aircraft was 112mph. Projected is the operative word. Although two models – the R.I and the R-plane project – were ordered by the Idflieg, none were ever constructed.

A great deal of experimentation using wind tunnels was carried out, but the project was so huge that even when the Fokker company were ordered to merge with

Junker J.7 in its now familiar corrugated metal skin.

An excellent overhead shot of the Junkers J.9 (D-I).

Junkers Cl.I after crashing during landing. The pilot stands relaxed by his damaged aircraft. The state of the ground on the airfield gives some idea of the conditions under which aircraft in World War One had to be operated.

Junkers progress was extremely slow. This was mainly due to the fact that Anthony Fokker was used to making wooden aircraft in mass production, whilst Junkers made all-metal aircraft which took longer to construct. In addition the two parties were not personally compatible. The Armistice put paid to any more progress and the parts that had been assembled were destroyed.

Whilst the development work was being carried out on the R.I projects, work continued on producing the smaller Junker models. The J.3 was scheduled to be the first to be completely covered in corrugated metal, but for some unknown reason, the airframe was never completed. There was no J.4, 5 or 6, but J.7 was built at the beginning of 1917. J.7 was the prototype for J.9, or D.I, model that went into production at the beginning of 1918.

Still continuing with the monoplane theme, the J.7 was the subject of a number of variants: some with ailerons, some without. Powered by a 160hp Mercedes D.III engine with a car-type radiator at the nose, the J.7 had a top speed of 105mph.

A matter of only months later, the Junkers J.8 appeared. This all-metal aircraft was a two-seat prototype of what was ultimately one of the mainstays of the Schlachtstaffeln, the J.10 (CL I). It was powered by a 180hp Mercedes D.IIIa engine, which gave it a top speed of 100mph and a climb rate of almost 1,000ft per minute. It had a wingspan of 39ft 6in, a fuselage length of 25ft 11in, and a height of 7ft 8½in. It was armed with twin synchronised fixed Spandau machine guns and one manually operated Parabellum machine gun mounted in the rear cockpit. Forty-seven Junkers J.10s were built and all were in action until the end of the war.

The German Navy, impressed with J.10, requested a seaplane version. Three aircraft were converted and allocated designation J.11 (CLS.I). These were almost identical to the J.10 with the exception of an additional fin fitted on the fuselage in front of the tailplane and floats instead of an undercarriage. It was powered by a 200hp Benz engine which gave a top speed of 112mph. It had a wingspan of 41ft 10in, a fuselage length of 29ft 4½in, and a height of 9ft 8in. The armament was the same as the J.10.

Although Junkers' contribution to First World War aviation was not as great as some of the other aircraft manufacturers, they became one of the most prominent during World War Two.

SPECIFICATIONS

Junkers J.I

Wing Span	42ft 5⅝in
Length	24ft 4⅝in
Height	10ft 3¼in
Weight Empty	1,980lb
Weight Loaded	2,222lb
Engine	One 120hp Mercedes D.II – six-cylinder, in-line, water-cooled
Maximum Speed	100mph

Service Ceiling	12,000ft
Duration	1¼hrs
Armament	None

Junkers J.I (J.4)

Wing Span	52ft 6in
Length	29ft 10½in
Height	11ft 1½in
Weight Empty	3,885lb
Weight Loaded	4,787lb
Engine	One 200hp Benz Bz.IV – six-cylinder, in-line, water-cooled
Maximum Speed	96.875mph
Service Ceiling	26,520ft
Duration	2hrs
Armament	Two fixed forward-firing Spandau machine guns One manually operated Parabellum machine gun in rear observer's cockpit

Junkers J.10 (CL.I)

Wing Span	39ft 6in
Length	25ft 11½in
Height	7ft 8½in
Weight Empty	1,562lb
Weight Loaded	2,310lb
Engine	One 180hp Mercedes D.IIIa – six-cylinder, in-line, water-cooled
Maximum Speed	100mph
Service Ceiling	16,520ft
Duration	1½hrs
Armament	Two fixed forward-firing Spandau machine guns One manually operated Parabellum machine gun in observer's rear cockpit

LUFTFAHRZEUG GMBH (LFG)

The company Luftfahrzeug GmbH (LFG) began in 1906 when Motorluftschiff Studiengesellschaft was created at the instigation of Kaiser Wilhelm II to carry out the manufacture of airships. The company changed its name a few years later to LFG Bitterfeld from which sprang another company, Flugmaschine Wright GmbH. The company went into liquidation in 1912, but was revived by a number of top financiers, including Alfred Krupp. The new company name was LFG but, to avoid confusion with the company LVG, *Roland* was added, making it LFG Roland.

The first factory opened up at Aldershof, but was destroyed by a mysterious fire on 6 September 1916, alleged to have been caused by the British Secret Service. The company then moved to Charlottenburg where it continued to manufacture aircraft.

One of the first military aircraft to be produced by LFG Roland was the C.II, a two-seat reconnaissance model. The C.I had been built by Albatros, so when LFG produced its own aircraft, its designation automatically started with C.II. The fuselage of the C.II was considered by some to cause problems in control because the top wing had been fitted directly to the top of the fuselage. To investigate the problem an airframe was mounted on a flat-top railway waggon and a series of fast runs made on a long stretch of straight track.

The first prototype of C.II was produced in October 1915, the brainchild of Dipl.Ing. Tantzen, but was lost on the second test flight due to engine failure. A second model was produced, but problems were discovered in the directional stability which was found to be due to the thin wings which tended to distort after long periods of flight.

The first production models were supplied to various Flieger Abteilungen for reconnaissance missions. The only armament carried was a manually operated Parabellum machine gun mounted in the observer's rear cockpit. One of the Flieger Abteilung units was FA.4 commanded by Hauptmann Eduard Ritter von Schleich. A number of Allied airmen who came in contact with these two-seat reconnaissance aircraft had tremendous respect for them. Some of the German aircrew said the aircraft resembled a whale and gave it the nickname of Walfisch.

The exact number of LFG Roland C.IIs that were built and supplied to the army is not known, but is believed to be several hundred. A number of these aircraft were built under licence by Linke-Hoffman company.

The design of the fuselage of the C.II was a departure from the traditional method. It was of a semi-monocoque construction and built on a skeleton of spruce longerons and plywood formers. The fuselage was covered with thin plywood strips which was spirally wound to the frame then glued and pinned. This was covered in fabric and doped. The unbalanced control surfaces were constructed of steel tube and covered in doped fabric, whilst other control surfaces were made of wood and covered in doped fabric.

The aircraft had a wingspan of 33ft 9½in, a fuselage length of 25ft 3½in and a height of 9ft 6in. Powered by a six-cylinder, in-line, water-cooled 160hp Mercedes D.III engine, the C.II had a top speed of 103mph, a relatively slow climb rate of 500ft per minute and a flight duration of four to five hours. Later models were armed with a fixed forward-firing, Parabellum machine gun.

A number of Jastas were supplied with the aircraft, including Jasta 27 which at the time was commanded by Oberleutnant Hermann Göring. One unit whose aircraft consisted entirely of LFG Roland C.IIs was Marine Feldjagdstaffel 2. The unit's aircraft were wiped out by a British bombardment a few months after receiving the Rolands. The aircraft were replaced with Albatros D.IIIs.

An improved model of the C.II was produced early in 1916 powered by a 200hp Benz Bz.IV engine. Only one model was built and was destroyed when the factory at Aldershof was burnt down.

LFG Roland C.II with pilot and observer standing in front of the aircraft.

LFG Roland D.II preparing to take-off.

Excellent side-view shot of the LFG Roland D.II.

Not to be deterred by the fire, the company, after moving to Charlottenburg, decided to produce a single-seat fighter: the LFG Roland D.I. The success of C.II had given rise to the development of new aircraft. Looking like a slimmer, more rakish model of C.II, the D.I was powered by a 160hp Mercedes D.III engine which gave a top speed of 105mph. The shape of the D.I gave rise to its name of Haifisch (*shark*) in contrast to the C.II Walfisch, upon which it was based.

D.I and D.II were powered by identical engines; another engine was tried later, the 180hp Argus As.III, which produced D.IIa. This gave a top speed of 105mph and a climb rate of 800ft per minute. Both D.I and D.II had minor differences in their construction, but in the main they were identical. With a wingspan of 29ft 4in, a fuselage length of 22ft 9in, and a height of 10ft 2⅜in, both aircraft were armed with two fixed forward-firing Spandau machine guns. Over three hundred of the aircraft were built, but surprisingly the vast majority of were built by the Pfalz Flugzeug-Werke under licence.

In October 1916 D.III appeared as a replacement for the D.IIa, but this was at the same time as the superior Albatros fighter and only a small number were built. Its specifications were the same as the D.IIa.

The C series continued to be built but with no C.IV model. A prototype two-seater based on the D.II design was produced. The C.V model was powered by a 160hp Mercedes engine and armed with one fixed forward-firing Spandau machine gun and one manually operated Parabellum machine gun mounted in the observer's cockpit. Only one aircraft was built.

The first, and the last, of the LFG Dreideckers was built at the beginning of 1917: the single-seat LFG Roland D.IV. It had a number of unusual features including a tailplane that could be adjusted for incidence prior to flight and it had ailerons fitted to both upper and lower wings. It was powered by a 160hp Mercedes D.III engine and was not one of the most elegant looking of the triplanes built. During its second flight test at the beginning of September 1917, the aircraft crashed on take-off. Fortunately the damage was repairable and within a week it had been rebuilt, but by the beginning of October the project had been dropped because it showed no advantages over the Roland D.III and D.V biplanes. It is not known how many were built.

The success of the D.I model prompted the navy to request a single-seat seaplane. A converted D.I, the LFG WD, was produced. Powered by a 160hp Mercedes engine, it had its first flight on 29 June 1917. It was not the success hoped for and only one prototype was built. There had been an earlier seaplane built by LFG, the LFG W, an Albatros C.Ia two-seat reconnaissance model which LFG built under licence. Only one of this type was built.

Continuing with the D series, a development of D.III was produced: the D.V model. The fuselage, although based on previous models, was considerably slimmer. It was powered by a 160hp Mercedes engine. Only one prototype was built.

The last of the original design two-seaters, the C.VIII, was built at the end of 1917. Based on the design of C.III, it was powered originally by a 260hp Mercedes D.IVa engine, but later by a 245hp Maybach Mb.IV engine. It carried one forward-firing Spandau machine gun and one manually operated Parabellum machine gun mounted in the rear cockpit.

LFG Roland D.IIs of Jasta 25 in the Balkans. The Jasta was under the command of
Hauptmann Burkhardt at the time.

One of the best fighter aircraft from the LFG stable was the LFG Roland D.VIa.
With its distinctive 'clinker-built' fuselage and droopy nose, it presented a sleek racy
look which was backed up with good performance. The fuselage was constructed in
the same manner as a small boat, with slightly tapered strips of spruce wood over-
lapping each other by two-thirds. It had a large horn-balanced rudder and overhung
balanced ailerons. Powered by a six-cylinder, in-line, water-cooled Benz Bz.IIIa
engine, the D.VIa could reach a top speed of 114mph and a climb rate of about
1,000ft per minute. The prototype D.VI production models were designated D.VIas
and marked the 1,000th LFG Roland aircraft built. The LFG Roland D.VIa had a
wingspan of 30ft 10in, a fuselage length of 20ft 8¾in and a height of 9ft 2½in. A
number of the aircraft became operational with Jasta 23 – the remainder saw service
with the German Navy being used for seaplane defence duties.

Another of the three prototype models was a standard D.VIb, fitted with two-bay
wings with I-interplane struts. Only one was built.

Two prototypes of the LFG Roland D.VII appeared at the beginning of 1918; the
first, Nr.224/18, was fitted with a 195hp Benz Bz.IIIb direct-drive engine, which
gave it a top speed of 108mph. The second, Nr.3910/18, which had differently
shaped and balanced ailerons, was also fitted with a 195hp Benz Bz.IIIb engine,
although this model had reduction gears to decrease the airscrew speed. Only one of
each model was built.

Three D.IX prototypes appeared just after the D.VIIs and were markedly different. The first version Nr.3001/18 was fitted with a 160hp Siemens-Halske Sh.III geared rotary engine that drove a four-bladed airscrew. It had overhung balanced ailerons. This was the first time a rotary engine had been used by LFG. The second prototype had much larger tail surfaces and a 210hp Siemens–Halske IIIa geared rotary engine. The third version was almost identical to the second, the only difference being the fitting of a large horn-balanced rudder. All three versions were fitted with twin fixed forward-firing Spandau machine guns.

The D.X series began with D.XIII – there appears to have been no D.X, X.I or X.II. The aircraft was no more than a re-engined D.VII with a V-8 195hp Korting engine with reduction gearing.

The arrival of the LFG Roland D.XIV, Nr.300/18, coincided with the installation of a power plant, the 170hp Goebel Goe.IIIa rotary engine. Four new versions of the LFG Roland D.XV, the first two using the D.VI airframe, were produced in May 1918. The first, Nr.3004/18, incorporated the D.IV 'clinker-built' fuselage. The wings had considerable stagger and were braced by twin-struts, but no bracing cables were used. It was powered by a 160hp Mercedes D.III engine, and had a wingspan of 28ft 4½in and a fuselage length of 20ft 7in.

The second D.XV version, Nr.3006/18, used the D.VI airframe and was powered by a 180hp Mercedes D.IIIa engine. The wings were braced by single I-struts and, like the first version, without the use of cables. This was also the last of the LFG Roland fighters to use the 'clinker-built' fuselage.

The third version of the D.XV had slab-sided fuselage constructed of plywood. The wings were braced with N-struts made of tubular steel. The engine was a 185hp BMW.III giving a top speed of 105mph. The fourth version, which was almost identical, was fitted with a 200hp Benz Bz.IIIa engine which gave a top speed of 108mph.

The 2,000th-built Roland LFG D.IVb with its 'clinker-built' fuselage.

The second of the first version LFG Roland D.VII.

Inspired by the success of the Fokker E.V fighter, LFG Roland produced the D.XVI – a parasol fighter with a plywood covered fuselage and fabric covered wings. D.XVI was powered by a 160hp Siemens-Halske Sh.III rotary engine which drove a four-bladed airscrew. A second version was produced which had slightly differently shaped vertical tail surfaces. The engine was also changed to a 170hp Goebel Goe.III rotary.

Just before the Armistice, the last in a long line of LFG Roland fighters appeared – the D.XVII. A parasol fighter, it incorporated the same fuselage and power plant as the D.XV prototype. It was armed, as all the previous fighters were, with twin forward-firing synchronised Spandau machine guns.

There was one attempt at producing a bomber: the LFG Roland G.I. Although having two propellers, it was in fact a single-engined aircraft turning both the propellers through a complicated system of gears and shafts. The aircraft was also fitted with heavy duty tyres and had twin nosewheels. It was powered by a 245hp Maybach Mb.IV engine, had a wingspan of 98ft 9¼in, a fuselage length 52ft 2⅛in, and a top speed of 100mph. It carried a crew of two and was armed with one manually operated Parabellum machine gun mounted in the rear cockpit.

The same year, LFG put forward a design for a single-seat scout plane. The LFG V.19, or Putbus as it was called, was a long-wing monoplane built of aluminium and powered by a 110hp Oberursel rotary engine which gave the aircraft a top speed of 112mph. The V.19 was a very simply designed aircraft, with a wingspan of just 31ft, a fuselage that was just a tube of flat wrapped duraluminium and an empty weight of 1,056lb. The wings held all the fuel and had automatic shut-off valves that enabled the wings to be removed without first draining the tanks.

Although initially the V.19 Putbus appeared to be better than the W.20, this was proved wrong. The main problem was that it took ten times longer to assemble and disassemble, and required five waterproof containers to house it. The German Navy's submarine arm was told that it was ready for trials, but shortly afterwards came defeat for Germany and all such trials and experiments were shelved.

LFG contributed a great deal to the German war machine and left behind a legacy in the world of aviation.

SPECIFICATIONS

LFG Roland C.II

Wingspan	33ft 9½in
Length	25ft 3½in
Height	9ft 6in
Weight Empty	1,680lb
Weight Loaded	2,824lb
Engine	One 160hp Mercedes D.III – six-cylinder, in-line, water-cooled
Maximum Speed	103mph
Ceiling	14,600ft
Duration	4–5hrs
Armament	One manually operated Parabellum machine gun mounted in the observer's cockpit and one forward-firing synchronised Spandau machine gun

LFG Roland C.III

Wingspan	33ft 9½in
Length	25ft 3½in
Height	9ft 6in
Weight Empty	1,680lb
Weight Loaded	2,824lb
Engine	One 200hp Benz Bz.IV – six-cylinder, in-line, water-cooled
Maximum Speed	103mph
Ceiling	14,600ft
Duration	45hrs
Armament	One manually operated Parabellum machine gun mounted in the observer's cockpit and one forward-firing synchronised Spandau machine gun

LFG Roland D.II & IIa

Wingspan	29ft 4in (D.II); 29ft 2½in (D.IIa)
Length	22ft 9in (D.II); 22ft 9½in (D.IIa)

Height   10ft 2⅜in (D.II); 9ft 8in (D.IIa)
Weight Empty   1,573lb (D.II); 1,397lb (D.IIa)
Weight Loaded   2,098lb (D.II); 1,749lb (D.IIa)
Engine   One 160hp Mercedes D.III – six-cylinder, in-line,
                          water-cooled (D.II)
                       One 180hp Argus As.III – six-cylinder, in-line,
                          water cooled (D.IIa)
Maximum Speed   105mph
Ceiling   14,600ft
Duration   4–5hrs
Armament   Two forward-firing synchronised Spandau
                          machine guns

LFG Roland D.VIa & D.VIb

Wingspan   30ft 10in
Length   20ft 8¾in
Height   9ft 2½in
Weight Empty   1,450lb
Weight Loaded   1,892lb
Engine   One 200hp Benz Bz.IIIa – six-cylinder, in-line,
                          water-cooled
Maximum Speed   114mph
Ceiling   19,600ft
Duration   2hrs
Armament   Two forward-firing synchronised Spandau
                          machine guns

LFG Roland D.III

Wingspan   29ft 4in
Length   22ft 9in
Height   10ft 2½in
Weight Empty   1,577lb
Weight Loaded   2,114lb
Engine   One 180hp Argus As.III – six-cylinder, in-line,
                          water-cooled
Maximum Speed   105mph
Ceiling   14,600ft
Duration   1hr
Armament   Two forward-firing synchronised Spandau
                          machine guns

LFG Roland G.I

Wingspan	98ft 9¼in
Length	52ft 2⅛in
Height	12ft 2½in
Weight Empty	6,050lb
Weight Loaded	9,460lb
Engine	One 245hp Maybach Mb.IV – six-cylinder, in-line, water-cooled
Maximum Speed	100mph
Ceiling	16,600ft
Duration	4hrs
Armament	One manually operated Parabellum machine gun

Luftverkehrs GmbH (LVG)

Located at Johannisthal, Berlin, Luftverkehrs GmbH (LVG) was one of the largest German aircraft manufacturers of World War One. The use of the old Parseval airship hangar at the base gave the company all the space they needed to produce some of Germany's finest two-seater aircraft. The first aircraft produced in 1912 were of the standard Farman type. In 1912, a Swiss aeronautical engineer Franz Schneider joined LVG from the French Nieuport company and started building aircraft that had been designed by the LVG's own designers. The first of these aircraft, the LVG B.I, an unarmed, two-seat reconnaissance/trainer, was built in 1913. It was a conventional two-bay aircraft, the fuselage being of a simple box-girder construction with wire-bracing and made of spruce longerons and plywood-cross members covered in doped fabric.

In June 1914, six B.Is took part in the Ostmarkenflug (Ostmark flight trials), taking the first four places. With the onset of war the existing B.Is were immediately pressed into service and production lines started. To meet the demand, Otto Werke, Münich, were licensed to build the B.I. As with all the early aircraft, the pilot sat in the rear cockpit. Powered by a 100hp Mercedes D.I engine, the B.I had a top speed of 63mph. It had a wingspan of 47ft 8½in, a fuselage length of 25ft 7½in and a height of 10ft 6in.

The arrival of the improved version of the B.I – the B.II – some months later showed only minor improvements. A semi-circular cut-out in the upper wing (to improve the pilot's upward visibility) and a small reduction in the wingspan were the only noticeable differences. An improved engine (the 100hp Mercedes D.II six-cylinder, in-line, water-cooled) gave the aircraft a top speed of 65mph. B.II was the main production model and a considerable number were built at the beginning of 1915. They were used mainly for scouting/reconnaissance and training purposes.

As the war intensified, the casualty rate of the unarmed reconnaissance and scouting aircraft rose alarmingly, so it was decided to introduce a purpose-built armed reconnaissance aircraft. With the additional weight of guns and ammunition, it became necessary to install more powerful engines. With this in mind, Franz Schneider produced a C series of aircraft, the first being the LVG C.I.

In reality, the C.I was no more than a strengthened B.I airframe fitted with a 150hp Benz Bz.III engine and a ring-mounted manually operated Parabellum machine gun in the observer's cockpit. Later models were fitted with twin forward-firing fixed Spandau machine guns. A small number of the aircraft were built and shipped to the front, where they were employed on bombing duties with the Kampfgeschwadern, and scouting and photo-reconnaissance duties with a number of Flieger Abteilung units. In appearance the C.I was almost identical to the B.II, except for a number of minor physical changes.

A single-seat derivative of the C.I was built for the German Navy as a torpedo bomber. Experiments were carried out with a mock torpedo mounted beneath the fuselage between the undercarriage. No further details are available and no official designation was given to the aircraft.

Early in 1915, Franz Schneider came up with a revolutionary two-seat, monoplane fighter. Designated LVG E.I, the aircraft was fitted with both a fixed forward-firing Spandau machine gun and a manually operated Parabellum machine gun mounted on a ring. Powered by a 120hp Mercedes D.II engine, the prototype was flown to the front for operational evaluation by Leutnant Wentsch, but during the flight the wings collapsed. The pilot was killed and it was discovered that the lower wing struts had not been fixed properly. Only one aircraft was built.

An attempt to produce a bomber also appeared during 1915, the LVG G.I. Placed in the G series of aircraft, it was powered by two 150hp Benz Bz.III engines. Greatly underpowered for a bomber, the G.I was not a success and was scrapped.

The C.II, which appeared a few months later, was again almost identical to the C.I; the main was being the engine, a 160hp Mercedes D.III six-cylinder, in-line, water-cooled.

The ongoing problem of having the pilot flying the aircraft from the rear cockpit was resolved with the experimental model LVG C.III. The aircraft was in effect a C.II with the cockpits changed around and only the one model was built.

Derived from LVG C.III came LVG C.IV which was a slightly enlarged model, powered by a straight-eight 220hp Mercedes D.IV engine. The reduction gearing in the engine turned one of the largest propellers fitted to a single-engined aircraft. It was one of these aircraft that made the first daylight raid on London in November 1916. With a wingspan of 44ft 7in, a fuselage length of 27ft 10½in and a height of 10ft 2in, the C.IV was one of the best two-seat aircraft in the German Army.

One experimental single-seat aircraft, the LVG D.10 was also one of the most unusual. Given the name Walfisch, it had a wrapped-plywood strip fuselage which was not much longer than the aircraft's wingspan. This bulbous-looking aircraft was powered by a 120hp Mercedes D.II. Details of its performance are not known and only one was built.

Probably one of the most successful, and one of the biggest, of the German two-seat reconnaissance/scout aircraft of World War One was the LVG C.V. Although overshadowed by the Rumpler C.IV, the LVG C.V was a close second. The C.V was not as fast as the Rumpler, but what it lacked in speed and power it more than made up for in being a total 'all-round' aircraft: sturdy and stable and capable of absorbing punishment. It had a wingspan of 44ft 8in, a fuselage length of 26ft 5½in, and a

Aerial shot from underneath of the LVG C.I.

height of 10ft 6in. Powered by a six-cylinder, in-line, water-cooled 200hp Benz Bz.IV engine, the C.IV had a top speed of 103mph and a flight duration of 3½ hours. It was armed with one fixed forward-firing Spandau machine gun, and one manually operated Parabellum machine gun in the rear observer's cockpit.

A second single-seat fighter was built at the end of 1916, the LVG D.II (D.12). It had a monocoque-type fuselage with a headrest behind the pilot and was the second in a series of experimental D-types. The D.II was powered by a 160hp Mercedes six-cylinder, in-line, water-cooled D.III engine. The wings were braced by means of V- interplane struts.

At the beginning of 1917 an experimental single-seat fighter, the LVG D.III, was produced with semi-rigid bracing in the form of struts. Although the landing wires were removed, the flying wires remained. It retained the monocoque-type fuselage covered in plywood, but the wings were more suited to that of a two-seater recon-naissance rather than a fighter. The wingspan was 32ft 10in, the fuselage 24ft 8½in and the height 9ft 7in. Powered by a 190hp NAG.III engine, the D.III had a top speed of 109mph and a flight duration of two hours. Only one type was built.

Another fighter appeared from the LVG stable at the end of 1917, the LVG D.IV. A much smaller model than D.III, the D.IV had a single-spar lower wing braced with V-interplane struts. It had a wingspan of 27ft 11in, a fuselage length of 20ft 7½in, and a height of 8ft 10½in. The nose of the aircraft was considerably blunter than previous models and housed the V-8 direct-drive 195hp Benz Bz.IIIb engine which gave a top speed of 110mph. After participating in the second of the D-type competitions at Aldershof in June 1918, a small number were built and supplied to the army. The Armistice arrived before any more could be manufactured.

One of the finest two-seater aircraft to come out of the LVG factory was the LVG C.VI. Over 1,000 examples of this aircraft were built and although physically there was hardly any difference between the C.V and the C.VI, it was much lighter and far more compact. The aesthetic look was put aside in favour of serviceability and prac-ticability. The need for this type of aircraft at this stage of the war was one of necessity and C.VI fulfilled this need. Powered by a six-cylinder, in-line, water-cooled 200hp Benz Bz.IV engine, the aircraft had a top speed of 106mph, an operational ceiling of 21,350ft and a flight duration of three and a half hours. It was armed with a fixed forward-firing Spandau machine gun and a manually operated Parabellum machine gun mounted in the rear observer's cockpit.

Among the observers who flew numerous flights in the LVG C.VI was Hauptmann Paul Freiherr von Pechmann, who flew somewhere between 400 and 500 observation flights as an observer (the exact figure is not known, but some historians have placed it as high as 700). For these exploits he received numerous awards and medals, but the most significant was the Orden Pour le Mérite; he was one of only two observers to be awarded the highest of all Prussia's aviation awards.

Toward the end of 1917, the Idflieg had been noting the load-carrying capacity of Caproni bombers with great interest. With this in mind they instigated a programme of building similar aircraft. The only completed model at this time was the twin-engined LVG G.III Dreidecker, designed by Dipl.Ing. Wilhelm Hillmann. Constructed of wood and covered in plywood, it was the largest aircraft ever built by LVG and had a wingspan of 80ft 4¾in, a fuselage length of 33ft 7½in, and a height of 12ft 9⅝in. Powered by two 245hp Maybach Mb.IV engines, it gave a top speed of 81mph and a flight duration of five and a half hours. Its armament consisted of manually operated Parabellum machine guns mounted in the nose and dorsal positions. It also carried a limited bomb load. The aircraft was given the designation G.III by the factory, but official records list the aircraft as the G.I. Only one was completed.

The Luftverkehrs company made more than a passing contribution to Germany's war machine and was a major contributor to the world of aviation.

The experimental LVG D.III. The landing wires have been replaced with struts but the standard flying wires were retained.

A Schneider-built LVG of pre-1914 vintage being transported by road on a purpose-built truck.

SPECIFICATIONS

LVG B.II

Wingspan	39ft 9¼in
Length	27ft 3½in
Height	9ft 8in
Weight Empty	1,597lb
Weight Loaded	2,362lb
Engine	One 100hp Mercedes D.I or D.II – six-cylinder, in-line, water-cooled
Maximum Speed	65mph
Duration	4hrs
Armament	None

LVG C.II

Wingspan	42ft 2in
Length	26ft 7in
Height	9ft 7¼in
Weight Empty	1,859lb
Weight Loaded	3,091lb

Engine	One 160hp Mercedes D.III – six-cylinder, in-line, water-cooled
Maximum Speed	81mph
Duration	4hrs
Armament	One manually operated Parabellum machine gun

mounted in the rear cockpit

LVG G.III

Wingspan	80ft 4¾in
Length	33ft 7½in
Height	12ft 9⅝in
Weight Empty	5,920lb
Weight Loaded	9,020lb
Engine	Two 245hp Maybach Mb.IV – six-cylinder, in-line, water-cooled
Maximum Speed	81mph
Duration	5½hrs
Armament	One manually operated Parabellum machine gun in the nose and one in dorsal position

PFALZ FLUGZEUG-WERKE GMBH

Germany, prior to World War One, was a country made up of a number of minor kingdoms and principalities. Among them was the kingdom of Bavaria which, after Prussia, was the second most powerful state in the German Second Reich. Bavaria enjoyed considerable military privileges and at the onset of World War One had its own air service, War Ministry and General Staff. There was an underlying bitter rivalry between some of the states as became apparent when bravery awards were given. There were Jastas made up of only Bavarians or Prussians in the early stages of the war. Unlike the other states, Bavaria's armed forces only came under the command of Kaiser Wilhelm II in time of war.

With the threat of World War One looming, three brothers – Alfred, Walter and Ernst Eversbusch – established an aircraft manufacturing plant with the financial aid of the Bavarian government. The government was concerned that, unless they contributed to the manufacture of the aircraft, they would have no say in the equipment that would be used by Bavarian pilots. Initially the intention was to approach the Albatros company and to acquire the rights to build their aircraft in Bavaria, but negotiations fell through. The Bavarian Flying Service stepped in and at their instigation the Pfalz company approached Gustav Otto, a financier who helped finance the new company and assisted in the development of the business. They also acquired the rights to build the Otto biplane. The Pfalz Flugzeug-Werke was built at Speyer am Rhein in July 1913. The first aircraft to be produced there was not one of their own designs, but the Otto pusher biplane which was powered by a 100hp Rapp engine.

Later Alfred Eversbusch managed to obtain a licence from the French Morane-Saulnier company to manufacture the L-type Parasol monoplane. The first Parasol was built at the end of 1914 but only a few of were built. It is interesting to note that the cockpit had transparent sides, which was totally unnecessary because the downward view was excellent without them. The next model was later given a military designation of the Pfalz A.I and powered with an 80hp Oberursel nine-cylinder U.O rotary engine. Their role was for photo-reconnaissance and scouting missions. There was a Pfalz A.II, which was just an A.I with a 100hp Oberursel nine-cylinder U.I rotary engine fitted.

At the same time as acquiring a licence to build the Morane-Saulnier L-type, Pfalz also obtained permission to build the H-type, which was re-designated the Pfalz E.I and fitted with the 80hp Oberursel U.O nine-cylinder engine. Walter Eversbusch, the youngest of the three brothers, enrolled in the Morane-Saulnier flying school near Paris in the spring of 1914 from where he graduated with his flying licence. He became the company's test pilot but was killed on 1 June 1916 when he crashed one of the aircraft.

When the war began in August 1914, the company had produced only three Otto biplane pushers, which were immediately dispatched to Bavarian squadrons. It soon became obvious that the Otto was seriously underpowered, taking fifteen minutes to reach a height of 2,500ft; considering the aircraft only had an operational ceiling of 3,600ft it was not really that suitable for reconnaissance missions. There was another problem, the Otto bore a strong resemblance to French pusher-engined aircraft and was often shot at by German infantrymen. Fortunately for the pilots of these aircraft, by December the Otto had been replaced by Albatros B and LVG models.

As the war progressed large numbers of the Pfalz E.I were built but very few saw service on the front line as they were assigned to Bavarian flying schools as unarmed trainers. A small number of E.Is saw action in Macedonia, Syria and Palestine.

The first ten Pfalz E.Is were unarmed scouts, but with the development of gun synchronisation gearing, the remaining fifty were fitted with a fixed forward-firing Spandau machine gun. In total, sixty of these aircraft were built and sent to the front. The Pfalz E.II was produced some months later, but this was just an E.I with the 100hp Oberursel U.I nine-cylinder rotary engine fitted and with the synchronised Spandau machine gun. The E.II had a wingspan of 33ft 5in, which was slightly longer than that of the E.I. Such was the need for aircraft at this time that the E.II was already in service with a number of Bavarian squadrons before the Idflieg had finished the Typen-Prufung (*acceptance test*); the test wasn't completed until July 1916.

This was followed by the debut of Pfalz E.III, an armed version of A.II Parasol monoplane. Only six were built, four of which managed to make the front line to see service. It was powered by a 100hp Oberursel U.I rotary engine, had a wingspan of 36ft 9in and a fuselage length of 22ft 5½in.

The next in the E series was the Pfalz E.IV. Almost identical to the other E series fighters, E.IV was fitted with a 160hp Oberursel two-row U.III rotary engine. It had a wingspan of 33ft 5½in, a fuselage length of 21ft 8in, a top speed of 100mph and a climb rate of 1,300ft per minute. It carried twin synchronised forward-firing

Spandau machine guns. This feisty little fighter was built, surprisingly, in small numbers; no more than twenty-five were known to have been manufactured.

The last of the E series was the Pfalz E.V. Constructed on the standard E-type airframe, the E.V was powered by a 100hp Mercedes D.I engine, giving a top speed of 103mph. This was a deviation from the rotary engines which powered the previous E series aircraft. It was armed with a synchronised forward-firing Spandau machine gun and was only slightly different from the other Pfalz monoplanes by an enlarged and different shaped rudder.

The monoplane fighter was rapidly being replaced by more rugged and manoeuvrable biplane fighters. Pfalz, in response to this, produced the Pfalz D.4. The fuselage of an E.V was taken and broadened, whilst the rudder assembly came from another of the E series. The first version produced was an unmitigated disaster and was virtually uncontrollable. The second version modified but didn't resolve the problems. Only one of each was built.

At the end of 1916, with the E series of monoplane aircraft completed, Pfalz company was instructed to build the LFG Roland D.I under licence. Up to this point a total of 300 A and E-types of aircraft had been constructed by Pfalz. The reason that Pfalz had been asked to build the Roland was because the Roland factory had been destroyed by fire and Pfalz had just completed building the last of their E series of fighter/reconnaissance aircraft.

During the period of constructing the LFG, the Pfalz design office was working on a design for a biplane fighter of their own. Then, at the beginning of 1917, the first of the D series of Pfalz aircraft appeared. This was a biplane version of the E.V Eindecker and was given the name of Walfisch. This short, tubby little aircraft, thought to have been powered by a 100hp Mercedes D.I engine with a car-type radiator at the nose, was unusual in that it had almost an enclosed cockpit. From information gathered, it appears that it was never designed as a fighter, but to be used for reconnaissance missions. It is not known how many were built, but it is thought that there were only two.

The Pfalz C.I appeared in 1917. It was a Rumpler C.IV, built under licence by the Pfalz company. It had additional bracing struts from the tailplane to the fin and ailerons on all four wingtips. Powered by a 260hp Mercedes D.IVa engine, this two-seater reconnaissance aircraft was armed with one forward-firing Spandau machine gun and one manually operated Parabellum machine gun mounted in the observer's cockpit. The designation of the Rumpler C.IV as the Pfalz C.I was a perfect example of the rivalry that existed between the various states and principalities. The Bavarian leaders insisted on purchasing only Bavarian-built aircraft, so when Bavarian companies built aircraft from other states, which were given designations pertaining to Bavarian companies, the leaders felt justified in purchasing them. It was this petty-minded thinking that hampered the flow of materials and aircraft to the front.

By the summer of 1917 the first of the Pfalz fighters appeared, the Pfalz D.III. The fuselage was of a wooden semi-monocoque construction made up of spruce longerons and oval plywood formers. The fuselage was wrapped with two layers of plywood strip in a spiral fashion in opposing directions, and covered in fabric which was painted with dope. The vertical tail fin was part of the main fuselage and made of fabric-covered wood. The rounded rudder was made of welded steel tube construction covered in fabric. The D.III was powered by a six-cylinder, in-line, water-cooled Mercedes D.III engine which gave it a top speed of 102.5mph, a climb rate of almost 1,000ft per minute and an operational ceiling of 17,000ft with a flight duration of two and a half hours. It was armed with two synchronised, forward-firing Spandau machine guns.

The Pfalz D.VI was the next in the series and was one of the most elegant of Pfalz aircraft. The fuselage was constructed with the now familiar wrapped strip-plywood, which was covered in fabric and painted with dope. It was powered by a 110hp Oberursel U.II rotary engine which was completely enclosed in a metal cowl. It had a wingspan of 23ft 3in and a top speed of 110mph. No actual figures are available of the number built, but it is believed to have been around twenty.

Shortly after the D.VI model was dispatched to the front, the Pfalz D.VII appeared. There were two versions of this aircraft: one with the 160hp Siemens-Halske Sh.III geared rotary engine, the second was with a 160hp Oberursel UR.III rotary engine. A third engine was also tried in the D.VII, the 160hp Goebel Goe.III.

There were slight differences in the dimensions of each aircraft: the wingspan on the first version was 24ft 8in and 26ft 7in on the second. The fuselage length on the first version was 18ft 6½in, on the second it was 18ft 2½in. The top speed was 118mph and both were equipped with twin synchronised forward-firing Spandau machine guns.

At the same time as the D.VII was being constructed a triplane was being constructed. The Pfalz experimental triplane was a D.IIIa conversion fitted with a six-cylinder, in-line, water-cooled 160hp Mercedes D.IIIa engine. For some unknown reason it never flew and was scrapped. The information gained, however, was not lost and some months later came another triplane, the Pfalz Dr.I.

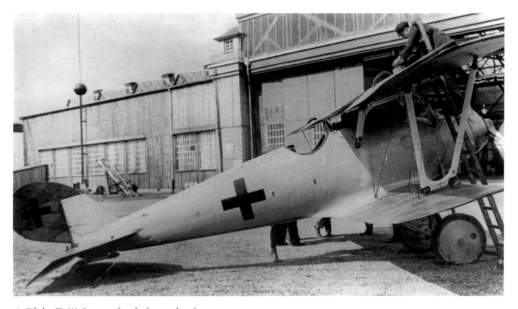

A Pfalz D.III Scout, fresh from the factory.

The Pfalz Dr.I was a stocky, powerful little aircraft with a wingspan of 28ft 1in and a fuselage length of 18ft ⅝in. The design of the fuselage was of the typical Pfalz construction: the Wickelrumpf, or wrapped-skin, which was built up on a light framework of stringers by a series of thin three-plywood strips and cloth tape. This type of construction improved the strength of the fuselage but it added to the weight. The aircraft was powered with the 160hp Siemens-Halske Sh.III rotary engine that gave it a top speed of 112mph and a climb rate of almost 1,500ft per minute. Despite the powerful engine its performance rating was not as good as the Fokker Dr.Is and, because of this, less than ten were manufactured.

A visit to the Pfalz factory on 12 December 1917 by Manfred von Richthofen accompanied by Leutnant Kreft, his technical officer, gave a ray of hope to the production of the aircraft. Pilots Hauptmann Willy Meyer, Ernst Schlegel and von Tutschek also visited the factory and flew the Pfalz Dr.I. But although they all praised the little fighter, no more aircraft were ordered.

In an attempt to find an improved version of the Pfalz Dr.I, the Dr.II and Dr.IIa were developed. The two aircraft were powered by the 110hp Oberursel UR.II and 110hp Siemens Sh.I engines respectively. Neither was successful and consequently were not put into production.

At the beginning of 1918, another single-seat fighter appeared, the Pfalz D.VIII. Three versions of this aircraft existed, each powered by a different engine: a 160hp Siemens-Halske Sh.III, a 160hp Oberursel U.III and a Goebel Goe.III. Of the three variants only the Siemens-Halske engined model was manufactured in any number, forty being built. The aircraft had a wingspan of 24ft 8in, a fuselage length of 18ft 6½in and a height of 9ft. The Siemens-Halske powered model had a top speed of 112mph and a climb rate of 1,200ft per minute. Almost identical to the

Pfalz D.IIIa seen here with the spinner removed.

Pfalz D.XII being serviced by ground crew whilst an armed guard stands watch.

D.VII, the aircraft was sent to the front line for evaluation with Jastas 5, 14 and 29. Reports came back saying that, although the aircraft was excellent to fly, its under-carriage had a tendency to collapse on landing. However, nineteen of the aircraft were still in operational service by the end of the year, but it never went into full production. Two modified versions were produced with different engines, but the confidence in the aircraft had gone and neither went into production.

One interesting experiment was carried out with the Pfalz D.VIII, using a Rhemag R.II engine which drove two counter-rotating propellers. On its first flight the aircraft crashed because it was excessively nose-heavy. The engine was then removed, repaired and shipped to Aldershof to be fitted to a Siemens-Schuckert D.IV, but before the tests could begin the war came to an end and the project was scrapped.

Although the Pfalz company had produced a number of excellent aircraft, with the exception of the Pfalz D.III, none of them had been particularly successful. The only other model that came anywhere near the D.III was the Pfalz D.XII. Looking similar to the Fokker D.VII, the D.XII was of a semi-monocoque design and was constructed of spruce longerons with plywood formers. The fuselage was wrapped with two layers of thin plywood strip, applied in opposite directions, covered in fabric and painted with dope. Powered by a 160hp Mercedes six-cylinder, in-line, water-cooled D.IIIa engine with a 'car-type' radiator mounted on the front, the D.XII had a top speed of 106mph, a climb rate of almost 1,000ft per minute and an operational ceiling of 18,500ft. The Pfalz D.XII had a wingspan of 29ft 6½in, a fuselage length of 20ft 10in and a height of 8ft 10½in. It was armed with two forward-firing synchronised Spandau machine guns.

When the first production models were sent to the front to replace the worn-out Albatros D.Vas and Pfalz D.IIIs, some of Germany's top pilots, including

Oberleutnant Ernst Udet and Leutnant der Reserve Hans Weiss, flew the aircraft and declared it as good as, if not better than, the already established Fokker D.VII. The Bavarian Jasta 4 commander Oberleutnant Eduard Ritter von Schleich reported that, although initially his pilots did not look too favourably on the replacement aircraft, their opinion changed rapidly after they had flown them in combat. Whether or not their recommendation carried any real weight is not known, but more than 300 Pfalz D.XIIs were supplied to Jastas 23, 32, 34, 35, 64, 65, 66, 77, 78 and 81. By the end of 1918 over 180 of the aircraft were still in operation on the Western Front.

Later in 1918 an improved model, the Pfalz D.IIIa, appeared: it had an improved engine (the 180hp Mercedes D.IIIa), the tailplane area had been increased and a modification to the wingtips of the lower wing. In all other areas it was the same as the D.III model. In total, over 800 of the Pfalz D.III and D.IIIa were built and according to the Inter-Allied Control Commissions figures at least 350 were still operational on the front line at the end of the war. It was undoubtedly the most successful fighter produced by the Pfalz factory.

Whilst still continuing to upgrade their existing aircraft, Pfalz produced an experimental model, the Pfalz D.XIV. Slightly larger than the D.XII it had a larger vertical fin and was powered by a 200hp Benz Bz.IV ü engine. This gave a top speed of 112mph and a climb rate of just over 1,000ft per minute. Only the one was built.

The results gained from this aircraft resulted in the production of the last of the single-seat fighters – the Pfalz D.XV. Its first official test flight was on 4 November 1918 and 180 were ordered. It is not known how many were actually built, but it is unlikely to have been the full complement as the Armistice came a week later. The D.XV was powered by a 180hp Mercedes D.IIIa engine; there were a number of models that were fitted with the 185hp BMW.IIIa engine, which gave a top speed of 125mph. The aircraft had a wingspan of 28ft 2½in, a fuselage length of 21ft 4in and a height of 8ft 10in.

Like a number of German aircraft, the Pfalz became one of the most respected fighter aircraft of World War One by both its pilots and by its opponents.

Pfalz D.XIV. This was a slightly larger version of the D.XII. It had a duration of ninety minutes and was armed with twin Spandau machine guns.

SPECIFICATIONS

Pfalz D.III

Wingspan	30ft 10¼in
Length	22ft 9½in
Height	8ft 9¼in
Weight Empty	1,532lb
Weight Loaded	2,056lb
Engine	One 160hp Mercedes D.III – six-cylinder, in-line, water-cooled
	One 180hp Mercedes D.IIIa – six-cylinder, in-line, water-cooled (D.IIIa)
Maximum Speed	102.5mph
Duration	2½hrs
Armament	Twin fixed forward-firing Spandau machine guns

Pfalz Dr.I

Wingspan	28ft 1in
Length	18ft ⅝in
Height	9ft 1in
Weight Empty	1,122lb
Weight Loaded	1,551lb
Engine	One 160hp Siemens-Halske Sh.III rotary engine
Maximum Speed	112mph
Duration	1½hrs
Armament	Twin Spandau machine guns

Pfalz E.I

Wingspan	30ft 5in
Length	20ft 8in
Height	8ft 5in
Weight Empty	759lb
Weight Loaded	1,177lb
Engine	One 80hp Oberursel U.O – nine-cylinder rotary engine
Maximum Speed	90mph
Duration	1½hrs
Armament	One Spandau machine gun

RUMPLER FLUGZEUG-WERKE GMBH

The Rumpler aircraft manufacturing company started building aircraft well before World War One. The first of their aircraft was the Rumpler Eindecker based on Taube design. A flimsy looking machine, as indeed most of the early aircraft were, the Eindecker was powered by a 100hp Mercedes D.I engine and saw a great deal of service in the initial stages of the war on reconnaissance missions.

As the need for aircraft intensified, the first of the Rumpler biplanes appeared in 1914, the Rumpler B.I. A small number were built and supplied to the German Army for training purposes and reconnaissance duties. B.I was powered by a 100hp Mercedes D.I engine which gave a top speed of over 90mph. It had a wingspan of 42ft 8in, a fuselage length of 27ft 6¾in and a height of 10ft 2⅛in.

Within a few months an improved version of the B.I appeared, the Rumpler 4A 13. Basically the design as the B.I, the 4A 13 was also powered by a 100hp Mercedes D.I engine, only the radiators were fitted either side of the fuselage beneath the pilot's cockpit. It also had a 'comma-type' balanced rudder fitted. The 4A 13 had a wingspan of 47ft 7in, otherwise all the remaining specifications were the same. A Rumpler 4A.14 was built the following month; it was identical to the 4A 13 with the exception of the engine, which was a 150hp Benz Bz.III.

The German Navy expressed an interest in the 4A 13 and ordered nine to be converted to seaplanes. Given the designation of Rumpler 4B 11, they were powered with a 100hp Benz Bz.I engine, which gave a top speed of 81mph, and were used for reconnaissance missions. Pleased with the success of the 4B 11 seaplanes, the German Navy ordered another eighteen. These were converted 4A 14s powered by a 150hp Benz Bz.III engine and given the designation 4B 12. Ten further models were ordered but these were powered by a 160hp Gnôme engine and given the designation of 4B 13.

Another flying boat was built in 1914 by Rumpler, the Rumpler 4E. This was a purpose-built model, unlike the others which were conversions of landplanes. Powered by a 120hp Austro-Daimler engine, 4E had a wingspan of 51ft 5in, a fuselage length of 29ft and a height of 11ft. Only the one was built.

One of the most famous and successful of all the two-seater reconnaissance aircraft built during World War One was the Rumpler C.I model. The first model appeared during 1915; by October 1916 over 250 C.Is and C.Ias were in service on all fronts. The C.Ia was only a C.I fitted with a 180hp Argus engine. The C.I was powered by a six-cylinder, in-line, water-cooled 160hp Mercedes D.III engine, with its back-sloping 'chimney' exhaust that protruded over the top wing. This was fitted into the nose of a slab-sided fuselage and constructed in a box-girder design with a rounded top section. The fuselage was constructed of four longerons that were made of pine facing toward the rear of the aircraft and four that were made of ash facing toward the nose. They were spliced together in the cockpit region. Ash was also used for the lateral and vertical spacers at the rear of the cockpit, whilst steel tubing was used for the front section. All the tail and fin surfaces were constructed of welded steel tube and covered in dope-painted fabric.

The exploits of the Rumpler C.I are a matter of record and they were used widely for photo reconnaissance missions. One problem did arise on those flights in

Rumpler C.I with French soldiers guarding it after it had been forced down.

Rumpler C.I Nr.6081/16 fitted with skis.

Captured Rumpler C.I in British markings.

Damascus in 1917: the heat. Many of the flights were a waste of time as the high temperatures affected the gelatine emulsion on the photographic plates.

There was no C.II, and the C.III was produced in limited numbers. It was powered a 220hp Benz Bz.IV engine and had a distinctive 'comma' shaped rudder and large angular balances on the ailerons. The top of the fuselage behind the observer's cockpit was shaped to be part of a streamlined headrest; this was removed on the next model.

The next version, the C.IV, was another of the major production versions like the C.I. This was one of the most successful of all the two-seat reconnaissance aircraft built by Rumpler. At altitudes exceeding 15,000ft very few Allied fighters were capable of even getting near it, let alone catching it. Almost identical to the C.I in appearance, the C.IV differed in that the wings had a slight sweep and stagger. The lower wing was considered to have an unusual profile inasmuch as it resembled the lower wing of the Liebelle form (*dragonfly*).

The fuselage spacers were of steel tube while the front section of the longerons from the cockpit on, were made of ash, which were spliced to the rear longeron section made of spruce. A trap-door was placed in the floor of the observer's cockpit for the photo-reconnaissance missions. The tail surfaces were constructed of steel tube and covered with doped fabric. The aircraft was powered by a six-cylinder, in-line, water-cooled 260hp Mercedes D.IVa engine which gave a top speed of 106mph, a climb rate of almost 1,000ft per minute and an operational ceiling of 21,000ft with a flight duration of between three and four hours depending on bomb load carried. It had a wingspan of 41ft 6½in, a fuselage length of 27ft 7in, and a height of 10ft 8in. The C.IV was armed with a single fixed forward-firing synchronised Spandau machine gun, a manually operated Parabellum machine gun and four bombs, totalling 220lb, carried in external racks.

The Rumpler C.V was no more than a C.III airframe fitted with the 260hp Mercedes six-cylinder, in-line, water-cooled D.IVa engine and constructed identically

Rumpler C.VII front three-quarter view

to the C.IV. The success of the C.IV prompted the manufacturers to produce an improved model and this they did at the end of 1917 in the shape of the C.VII. Almost identical in construction and design to the C.IV, the only difference was in overall dimension. The only visible difference was that the engine exhaust was shaped to exhaust sideways instead of upwards and over the top. Powered by a super-compressed, six-cylinder, in-line, water-cooled 240hp Maybach Mb.IV engine, which gave a top speed of 109mph, an operational ceiling of 23,944ft and a flight duration of four hours.

The British ace Major James B. McCudden VC gave an account of his encounter with a German reconnaissance aircraft which turned out to be a Rumpler C.VII. Flying an SE5, McCudden attacked the Rumpler at 18,200ft, but then the German aircraft started to climb until it reached 20,000ft. Struggling to keep up with it, McCudden realised that he was flying over enemy territory and the German aircraft was still climbing and flying away from him. Discretion being the better part of valour, McCudden turned away and headed back to his own lines. His report on the performance of this new German reconnaissance two-seater gave rise to concern and a wary eye was kept out for this type of aircraft. A large number were built.

A specialised version of the C.VII was built at the same time, the Rubild. This specially equipped photo-reconnaissance aircraft was fitted with highly specialised camera equipment and was capable of flying at heights in excess of 24,000ft.

The German Army's plans for a major offensive at the beginning of 1918 included the extensive use of reconnaissance aircraft. The continued success of the Rumpler C series prompted the Idflieg to request the company to produce a trainer with the emphasis on the training of observers. This meant it had to have the facilities for gunnery, photographic, radio and observation training. The aircraft had to be up to operational standard whilst still being economical. This was achieved by fitting a six-cylinder, in-line, water-cooled 180hp Argus As.III engine, which gave a speed of 87mph and an operational flight duration of four hours.

Rumpler produced C.VIII which was supplied to the Flieger Ersatz Abteilungen. Based on the C series design the construction was almost identical to that of C.IV and C.VII. The wing surfaces, however, reverted back to the C.I model both wings having angular raked tips. The C.VIII had a wingspan of 39ft 11½in, a fuselage length of 26ft 4in and a height of 10ft 6in. It was armed with one synchronised fixed forward-firing Spandau machine gun and one manually operated Parabellum machine gun. It had a flight duration of four hours which was ideal for training purposes.

At the end of 1917 an experimental model appeared, the Rumpler C.IX. Intended as a two-seater fighter, the C.IX presented a design with single I-type interplane struts and a smooth oval multi-stringered fuselage, and was powered by a 160hp Mercedes D.III engine. It was fitted with an 'all-moving' rudder which proved to be unsatisfactory. After a series of unsuccessful flight tests the aircraft was scrapped. A second version which had a totally revised rudder also proved to be unsatisfactory and that version too was scrapped.

The company went back to the existing C series design but with single-bay X interplane struts. The Rumpler C.X was powered by a 240hp Maybach Mb.IV engine which gave it a top speed of 121mph. The aircraft had a wingspan of 34ft 5½in, a fuselage length of 22ft 8in and a height of 10ft 3in. On returning from its first test flight it was in collision whilst on the ground and was damaged beyond repair. It was decided not to continue with this model.

Another model, the Rumpler Experimental C-Type, had a V-12 350hp Austro-Daimler engine was fitted into a C.IV airframe. Only one was built.

The design of the Rumpler C.IX surfaced again at the beginning of 1918 with the Rumpler 7D 1. This model was the first in a series of six experimental single-seater fighters which was to culminate in the production of the D.I some months later. The first, the Rumpler 7D 1, had the wrap-around streamlined fuselage which was plywood skinned and covered in a dope-painted fabric. It also incorporated the six-cylinder, in-line, water-cooled 160hp Mercedes D.III engine and radiator. One of the other features was wide chord I-section interplane struts between the wings.

The second of the six models, Rumpler 7D 2, had the fuselage plywood-skinned, only covering the fore and aft sections, whilst the middle section was just covered in doped fabric. The streamlined interplane I-section struts were replaced with the conventional twin struts. This too was powered by the 160hp Mercedes D.III engine. In an effort to reduce drag, the interplane struts of the next model, the 7D 4 (there was no 7D 3), were replaced with single struts of C-section and this too was powered by the 160hp Mercedes D.III engine. There was a 7D 5, but it appeared to be exactly the same as the 7D 4 and modifications were minor.

The next model to appear in the experimental series was 7D 6. This was a revolutionary quadruplane project, for which there is no information available.

The Rumpler 7D 7, which continued the series, was based on the design of the 7D 4, and had the bracing cables encased in streamlined casings. This was to be the last of the series and the one that was to be the prototype for the highly successful Rumpler D.I.

Two D.Is were entered into the 1918 mid-summer D-type competition and excelled themselves. Powered by a 180hp Mercedes D.IIIa engine, D.I had a top speed of 112mph and a climb rate of nearly 1,000ft per minute. It had a wingspan 27ft 7½in, a fuselage length of 18ft 10½in and a height of 8ft 5in. A number were produced, but the end of the war interrupted the production of any more aircraft. In the autumn of 1918 another version fitted with a 185hp BMW high-compression engine emerged, but it never reached the production stage.

Information obtained in 1970 from the papers in the A.R. Weyl collection indicated that the Rubild was in fact a Rumpler C.VI, but then as both the C.VI and C.VII were almost identical it really does not matter.

SPECIFICATIONS

Rumpler B.I

Wing Span	42ft 8in
Length	27ft 6¾in
Height	10ft 2⅛in
Weight Empty	1,650lb
Weight Loaded	2,134lb
Engine	One 100hp Mercedes D.I – six-cylinder, in-line, water-cooled
Maximum Speed	90mph
Service Ceiling	16,520ft
Duration	1½hrs
Armament	None

Rumpler C.I

Wing Span	39ft 10½in
Length	25ft 9in
Height	10ft ½in
Weight Empty	1,744lb
Weight Loaded	2,866lb
Engine (three tested)	One 160hp Mercedes D.III
	One 180hp Argus As.III
	One 150hp Benz Bz.III
	– all six-cylinder, in-line, water-cooled
Maximum Speed	95mph
Service Ceiling	16,660ft
Duration	4hrs
Armament	One fixed forward-firing Spandau machine gun
	One manually operated Parabellum machine gun mounted in the rear observer's cockpit

Rumpler C.IV

Wing Span	41ft 6½in
Length	27ft 7in
Height	10ft 8in
Weight Empty	2,376lb
Weight Loaded	3,366lb
Engine	One 260hp Mercedes D.IVa – six-cylinder, in-line, water-cooled
Maximum Speed	106mph
Service Ceiling	21,000ft
Duration	4hrs
Armament	One fixed forward-firing Spandau machine gun One manually operated Parabellum machine gun mounted in the rear observer's cockpit Four 55lb bombs

SABLATNIG FLUGZEUGBAU GMBH

Dr Josef Sablatnig was born in Klagenfurt, Austria, and was regarded as one of Germany's 'Old Eagles'. In 1903 he built his first aircraft, possibly a glider, although there is no record of it being flown. Deciding that there was more of a future for aviation in Germany, Josef Sablatnig moved to Berlin in 1910. That same year, he, and six other aviators, learned to fly on a Wright Biplane at Johannisthal, Berlin. He later entered a race in 1912 – the Austrian Circuit – and won.

In 1913 Josef Sablatnig became a director of the Union Flugzeug-Werke at Tetlow where he was responsible for developing the Bombhardt's Arrow Biplane into the Union Arrow Biplane and into an outstanding aircraft. During the next few years, Josef Sablatnig and another pilot by the name of Walter Höhndorf, who later became a German fighter pilot and holder of the Orden Pour le Mérite, flew the aircraft in a number of aerobatic competitions.

The exploits of these two early aviators did not escape the attention of the Kaiser's brother Prinz Heinrich who invited Josef Sablatnig to accept German nationality. The Union aircraft firm ran into trouble early in 1915 and went into liquidation. Josef Sablatnig, now a nationalised German living in Berlin-Koepenick, decided to found his own company – Sablatnig Flugzeugbau GmbH.

The first aircraft to come out of the new factory was SF.1. Powered by a 160hp Mercedes D.III engine, SF.1 was an unarmed, two-seat reconnaissance floatplane and was accepted by the navy. Only the one was built. The long sleek fuselage of the SF.1 was to become a characteristic of Sablatnig aircraft that were to follow.

The SF.1 was quickly replaced by the SF.2, again unarmed, but fitted with a radio transmitter. The first six were delivered to the navy between June and September 1916 and performance results were such that LFG and LVG began to produce the aircraft under licence. Seeing the potential of the seaplane, Josef Sablatnig started to explore the use of a heavy seaplane for escort duties. The result was SF.3. Powered by a 220hp Benz Bz.IV engine, the fuselage of the SF.3 deviated from the previous two models of having fabric-covered fuselages to one of plywood covering. In keeping with the CFT requirements it was fitted with a machine gun for the observer and a radio transmitter. It was sent to the Seeflugzeug-Versuchs-Kommando (SVK – *Seaplane Testing Centre*) at Warnemünde for testing and evaluation, but its fate is unknown. One school of thought thinks that it may have crashed during testing and no record of the event survived.

In the meantime Sablatnig continued with developing the SF model and on 17 February 1917 delivered Sablatnig SF.4 to the navy. Armed with a single synchronised fixed forward-firing Spandau machine gun, only one of these aircraft was built as it failed to make the grade when in competition with other seaplane manufacturers. The feedback from the tests laid the way open for the development of SF.5. This was an improved version of SF.2 and so successful was the aircraft, that 101 were built and delivered to the navy. This model carried no armament but was fitted with a radio transmitter.

What was rather strange was the fact that the Sablatnig factory in Berlin was in the Koepenickerstrasse which was almost in the centre of the city. Even more unusual was the fact that the company, in addition to its own production, took over sub-contract work for Friedrichshafen. Sablatnig did have a small dockyard at the Müggelsee for flotation tests. Efforts were made to acquire additional premises at Warnemünde, which were successful later in 1917.

The first of the landplanes made its appearance in 1917, the Sablatnig SF.6 (B.I). It was in reality an SF.2 with the floats replaced by an undercarriage and was intended for training duties only.

The company reverted back to making seaplanes with the SF.7 and dispensed with the bracing wires replacing then with I-type interplane struts. Three of these aircraft were built and accepted by the navy in September 1917.

A second land model was produced at the end of 1917, the SF.C.I. A conventional two-seater, the C.I was of wood and fabric construction and differed very little from the other two-seater aircraft manufactured by various companies. It was armed with one manually operated Parabellum machine gun mounted in the observer's cockpit and was capable of carrying six 50kg bombs. Only two were built as the aircraft did not come up to the requirements of the Idflieg.

A second C model, the C.II was built, incorporating the interplane I-struts that were a feature of the SF.7. It was powered by a 240hp Maybach Mb.IV engine which gave it a top speed of 94mph but only the prototype was built.

In January 1918 came Sablatnig SF.8. This was a dual-control seaplane designed and produced specifically as an instruction aircraft for flying schools. The SF.8 was sent to Warnemünde for intensive testing and passed, with the result that an additional forty were ordered. It is not known if all the aircraft were delivered, but at least twenty found their way on to the navy's inventory.

Sablatnig continued to try and develop a landplane without a great deal of success. The appearance of two Experimental C-Types in the spring of 1918, both variants of the C.II aircraft, gave some hope but only the single models were ever built. A C.III was developed and fitted with a large single wing, similar to that of the Fokker D.VII; again only one was built.

The need for bombers prompted Josef Sablatnig to produce a single-engine, two-seater night bomber, Sablatnig N.I. A small number were produced during the latter half of 1918, but the end of the war put an end to any more production of aircraft by Sablatnig.

During World War Two Josef Sablatnig was arrested and sent to Auschwitz concentration camp for assisting Jewish people to escape from Germany. He died in Auschwitz.

SPECIFICATIONS

Sablatnig C.I

Wing Span	52ft 6in
Length	28ft 6½in
Height	10ft 6in
Weight Empty	2,310lb
Weight Loaded	3,380lb
Engine	One 180hp Argus As.III – six-cylinder, in-line, water-cooled
Maximum Speed	75mph
Service Ceiling	21,000ft
Duration	2–3hrs
Armament	One manually operated Parabellum machine gun mounted in the observer's cockpit
	Six 50kg bombs

Sablatnig SF.5

Wing Span	56ft 9½in
Length	31ft 6in
Height	11ft 8in
Weight Empty	2,314lb
Weight Loaded	3,531lb
Engine	One 150hp Benz Bz.III – six-cylinder, in-line, water-cooled
Maximum Speed	92mph
Service Ceiling	21,000ft
Duration	2hrs
Armament	None

Sablatnig N.I

Wing Span	52ft 6in
Length	28ft 6½in

Height	10ft 6in
Weight Empty	2,618lb
Weight Loaded	4,092lb
Engine	One 220hp Benz Bz.IV – six-cylinder, in-line, water-cooled
Maximum Speed	78mph
Service Ceiling	21,000ft
Duration	3hrs
Armament	One manually operated Parabellum machine gun mounted in the observer's cockpit
	One synchronised fixed forward-firing Spandau machine gun

Siemens-Schuckert Werke GmbH

Although Siemens-Schuckert's first venture into the world of aviation was in 1907, the company actually started life back in 1847 when it manufactured telegraph equipment. It was known as Siemens-Halske OH then it merged with the Schuckert Werke and became the famous Siemens-Schuckert company.

In 1907 the German General Staff approached the company with a view to building a 'military' non-rigid airship. The Type-M, as it was called, was completed but was unsuccessful. This was followed by a much larger version which by all accounts was very successful, but for some unknown reason the project was dropped. After two years the company was approached again, this time to build three aircraft. Two years and three aircraft later, that could only be described as mediocre at best, the company went back to its original business of electrical manufacture.

In 1914, with the outbreak of war, the German government requested that all companies respond to the war effort. Siemens-Schuckert reactivated the aviation department under the control of Dr Walter Reichel, who was assisted by Dr Hugo Natalis and designer/pilots Franz and Bruno Steffen. The company's first effort was a single-engined monoplane that had been constructed for Prince Friedrich Sigismund of Prussia and was based on a design by Swedish aircraft builder Villehad Forssman. Two of the Siemens-Schuckert Bulldogs, as they were known, were built in 1915 and submitted to the Idflieg for testing. One of the aircraft was fitted with a 100hp Siemens-Halske Sh.I rotary engine, the other with a 100hp Mercedes S.I. Both the aircraft were rejected on the grounds of poor performance and even worse handling qualities.

Not put off by the rejection, Siemens-Schuckert produced the B model designed by Franz Steffen. Designed and constructed as an unarmed reconnaissance aircraft, the Siemens-Schuckert B was powered by a 100hp Siemens-Halske Sh.I rotary engine, which gave it a top speed of 95mph. It had a wingspan of 40ft 8in and a fuselage length of 20ft 4½in. The wing spars were constructed of tubular steel, a new innovation for the time. The one and only model built was delivered to the Brieftauben Abteilung at Ostend at the request of the commanding officer for testing purposes. During one of the test flights the aircraft crashed and what was left of the usable parts were returned to the factory.

One of the types of aircraft that had been requested by the government was a bomber. Siemens-Schuckert responded by submitting two R-plane designs. Two of the company's designers, Villehad Forssman and Bruno Steffen, based their designs on the Sikorsky-built, four-engined bomber 'IIIa Mourumetz'. Both men had been in Russia at the time the Russian heavy bomber had been built: Forssman building airships and Steffen as a pilot serving on the Russian Front.

The first design by Forssman, who can best be described as a man of vision and vivid imagination, copied the Sikorsky configuration line for line. The Forssman R, as it was called, had four uncowled 110hp Mercedes engines mounted on the lower wing driving two-bladed propellers. The top speed of the aircraft is said to have been 115mph, but there is a great deal of scepticism regarding this. The pilot's cabin was enclosed and fitted with ample transparent panels, giving him an excellent view all around. The observer/gunner was not so fortunate; his position in a pulpit fitted on the nose was completely exposed. The 78ft 9in wingspan initially had only single struts fitted, but it was soon realised that additional struts, including diagonal ones, were required.

There were a number of continuing problems; as one was solved more appeared. The aircraft was underpowered and had only been subjected to a couple of ground runs, when the first test pilot refused to fly the aircraft saying it was unstable. A second pilot, Leutnant Walter Höhndorf, was requested to fly the aircraft. On his first run the aircraft hopped into the air twice then went over on its nose. The aircraft was rebuilt and despite the glossy streamlined look of the aircraft it was riddled with structural weaknesses. After the accident no pilot could be found to fly the aircraft and it was placed in a hangar.

In an effort to save the reputation of the company, the Steffen brothers were approached to test fly the aircraft, which they did on the grounds that they were allowed to make certain modifications. This was agreed. Bruno Steffen was to fly the aircraft and five members of the Idflieg Acceptance Commission were invited to go along, not surprisingly all five refused. It was left to Bruno Steffen to fly the aircraft alone. The Idflieg acceptance specifications called for the aircraft to reach a height of 2,000m in thirty minutes whilst carrying a load of 1,000kg and enough fuel to sustain a four-hour flight.

The brothers installed a device that allowed all four throttle levers to be operated in unison. After examining the design drawings, Franz Steffen, warned his brother that the fuselage was weak behind the cockpit and to be careful on take-off and landings. The flight in October 1915 was relatively uneventful and the Idflieg accepted the aircraft, but only for training purposes. Shortly after acceptance the aircraft broke its back due to vibration when the engines were running up.

The second of the designs submitted was Siemens-Schuckert SSW R.I. It was designed by the Steffen brothers and given the designation SSW R.I 1/15 (the 15 referred to the year of manufacture) and was built at the SSW-Dynamowerk, Berlin. It was powered by three 150hp Benz Bz.III engines turning two twin-bladed propellers. Two of the engines were placed in the nose of the aircraft with their crankshafts facing aft; the third engine was mounted behind the gearbox on a lower

Siemens Shuckert D.III on its tail stand.

Siemens-Schuckert D.D5 seen at the factory. The aircraft in the background is a Siemens-Schuckert E.I.

Siemens-Schuckert R.I bomber.

level and facing forward. Each engine was connected to a common gearbox by means of a combination of leather-cone and centrifugal-key clutches. When the required number of revolutions was reached, the centrifugal-key clutch engaged automatically, whilst the leather-cone clutch was disengaged manually.

The SSW R.I had a wingspan of 91ft 10in and a fuselage length of 57ft 5in. It had a top speed of 68mph, an operational range of 320 miles and flight duration of four hours.

SSW R.II 2/15 was the next model to appear just three weeks after the first flight of R.I. It was the first of six aircraft contracted by the Idflieg at a cost of 170,000 marks without engines. The first model was powered by three 240hp Maybach HS engines, which were supplied by the government. There were problems right from the outset as the engines were no more than modified airship engines and totally unfit for operational use. Consequently the aircraft throughout the manufacture and operational time were plagued with problems. Eventually common sense ruled and the engines were replaced, initially by 220hp Benz Bz.IV types and later by the 260hp Mercedes D.IVa.

There followed a number of variations up to SSW R.VII 7/15 with different wingspans and engines. All these models gave sterling service to the German Army and carried out numerous raids.

The fighter aircraft side of the company switched back to the monoplane design and produced the Siemens-Schuckert E.I. Powered by a 100hp Siemens-Halske Sh.I rotary engine, E.I had a top speed of 93mph. It was of conventional construction, the box-type fuselage being covered in plywood with dope-painted fabric wings. With a wingspan of 32ft 10in, a fuselage length of 23ft 3½in, the aircraft had a flight duration of 1½hours. Armed with a single synchronised fixed forward-firing Spandau machine gun – twenty E.Is were ordered by the army and delivered at the beginning of October 1915.

A second model was built at the beginning of 1916, the E.II. It was powered by an in-line, water-cooled 120hp Argus As.II engine and was constructed using some

Siemens-Schuckert R.II under construction in the factory.

of the usable parts recovered from the crashed Siemens-Schuckert B. The only model built crashed during tests whilst being flown by Franz Steffen, brother of Bruno Steffen, one of the company's designers. This was followed by E.III which was an E.I fitted with a 100hp Oberursel rotary engine. Only six examples were built.

A return to the biplane design resulted in the appearance of the Siemens-Schuckert D.D5. Only one model single-seater fighter was built. Powered by a 110hp Siemens-Halske Sh.I rotary engine, the D.D5 bore more than a passing resemblance to the type B. Passed to the Idflieg for evaluation, D.D5 was rejected for its lack of handling and visibility from the cockpit. Using the information gained from the evaluation, Siemens-Schuckert set to work to produce another fighter. The Allies were having good success with their French Nieuport fighters and, whenever one was captured, the aircraft was handed over to the German manufacturing companies to see if they could use any of the refinements built into the aircraft. The Siemens-Schuckert company had recently received an enemy aircraft and set to work copying it; the result was the Siemens-Schuckert D.I. The first test flight of this aircraft was by Bruno Steffen, whose brother Franz Steffen died in the crash of the Siemens-Schuckert B.

The aircraft was then passed to the Idflieg for evaluation, resulting in an order being placed for 150. In November 1916 production started, but within weeks problems arose. It was nothing to do with the aircraft, but with the supply of the rotary engines, so it was decided to use the 110hp Siemens-Halske Sh.I engine that had recently been developed by another branch of the company. This was a revolutionary engine; the crankcase rotated in one direction at 900rpm and the crankshaft in the opposite direction at 900rpm. This gave an engine speed of 1,800rpm for a propeller speed of 900rpm, which resulted in greater efficiency.

Siemens-Schuckert E.I.

The engine was mounted within an open-fronted, horseshoe-shaped cowling with the lower half completely cutaway, thus allowing exhaust fumes to escape freely. The fuselage was of a box-girder construction with four main longerons of spruce with plywood formers. It was covered with slab-sided plywood and doped fabric, with the exception of the foremost section which had metal panels in which large ventilation slits had been cut. Tail surfaces and aileron were made of steel tubing and covered in doped fabric. The wings were staggered and the original French-designed planform retained, although the four centre-section struts were vertical in both side and front views.

The problems with delivery of the engines improved slowly, but by mid-1917 other fighters had improved markedly, leaving the Siemens-Schuckert D.I way behind; so much so that only ninety-five of the original order were completed before being cancelled by the army. The D.I ended up in training schools although a number did see action on the Western Front and gave a good account of themselves. There was a D.Ia model that had a slightly larger wing area and two D.Ibs with an improved Siemens-Halske Sh.I engine; none of which amounted to anything.

At the beginning of 1917 Siemens-Schuckert designers came up with a design for a triplane fighter, the D.Dr.I, which was powered by two 120hp Siemens-Halske Sh.I high-compression engines. The unusual fighter had a nacelle situated between the wings, with 'push-pull' engines mounted fore and aft with the pilot sitting in the middle. The tail assembly, with twin rudders, was mounted on tubular outrigger booms. It was fitted with twin synchronised forward-firing machine guns. Unfortunately, the Siemens-Schuckert D.Dr.I crashed on its maiden flight and no effort was made to rebuild it.

The natural successor to the D.I was the D.III. There were a number of D.II proto-types, but they only tested some of the ideas and theories that had appeared on the drawing board. The Idflieg, impressed with the D.II prototypes and with the relative success of the D.I, made a pre-production order for twenty D.IIIs in December 1916. This was followed by a further order for thirty more in January, but there was a proviso and that there was to be continued development of a D.IV model and three prototypes were ordered.

During the construction of D.III, two prototypes were built, the first being the Siemens-Schuckert D.III (short). Two prototypes, each having a tubby rounded fuselage, were built but with their own differences. The first model had a wingspan of 27ft 10½in and a fuselage length of 19ft 8in. The second, the D.III (long), had a wingspan of 29ft 7 in and a fuselage length of 19ft 8in. Both aircraft were fitted with the Siemens-Halske Sh.III engine.

Developed from these two prototypes, the Siemens-Schuckert D.III was one of the finest single-seat fighter aircraft in the German Army. It was powered by an eleven-cylinder 160hp Siemens-Halske Sh.III engine, which was one of the most powerful engines available at the time; the aircraft could reach a top speed of 112mph. There were teething problems with engine piston seizure. This manifested itself when the aircraft was supplied to Jasta 15 of JG.2. This was commanded by one of Germany's most experienced pilots Hauptmann Rudolf Berthold who, despite the problems he and his fellow pilots were having, continued to endorse the D.III. There were opponents of the aircraft, among them Oberleutnant Hermann Göring, whom one suspects was hand-in-glove with his friend Anthony Fokker in trying to get the Idflieg to purchase Fokker aircraft.

An improved engine was fitted to D.III. It was one of the aircraft, flown by Siemens test pilot Rodschinka, to be flown to an unprecedented 26,586ft in thirty-six minutes. The Siemens-Schuckert D.III was now looked upon differently and, because of its superb climbing ability, was used by Kest 4a, 4b, 5, 6 and 8 as inter-ceptors. It is recorded that on one sortie, Oberleutnant Fritz Beckhardt shot down two Breguet B.14s at a height of 23,000ft whilst they were on a reconnaissance mission.

The Siemens-Schuckert D.IV was produced in March 1918 with a redesigned upper wing, the lower half of the engine cowling cutaway and cooling louvres cut into the propeller spinner. The maximum speed was increased to 118mph and climb rate increased. A total of 280 D.IVs were ordered, but the war was over in November and not all aircraft would be delivered. Production of the aircraft was controlled by the rate of delivery of the engine and which was at times painfully slow.

The D.IV had a wingspan of 27ft 6⅜in, a fuselage length of 18ft 8¼in and a height of 9ft 2½in. It was armed with two synchronised fixed forward-firing Spandau machine guns.

The first deliveries of the Siemens-Schuckert D.IV went to the Marine Jagdgeschwader, which was under the command of Oberleutnant zur See Osterkamp, and Jasta 14. Later Jasta 22 and Kest 2 were to receive a small number of the aircraft, but a number of other Geschwaders, including the famed Richthofen Geschwader, did not.

In March 1918, the Siemens-Schuckert factory in Berlin produced SSW R.VIII the largest aircraft in the world at the time. The R.VIII had a wingspan of 157ft 6in, a fuselage length of 70ft 10in and a height of 24ft 3in. It was powered by six 300hp Bass & Selve BuS.IVa engines, which turned two tractor and two pusher propellers and gave the 35,000lb aircraft a top speed of 77mph, with a maximum operational ceiling of 13,124ft. The SSW R.VIII had a range of 559 miles.

The aircraft was given a new designation of R.23 in line with other R-planes. The cockpit, unlike the previous SSW models, was open, thus giving the two pilots an excellent all-round view. The aircraft commander/observer had a fully enclosed cabin situated behind the cockpit, which was fully equipped with a map table and navigation equipment. It also had a dorsal fin in which a ladder was fixed to enable the upper gunner get to his post. The aircraft was a revolution for the time, but the war ended before the aircraft was completed. The war's end also permanently halted the building of the R.24, which was running in tandem with R.23; it was only three-quarters completed.

One Siemens aircraft that spent a great deal of time as a prototype was the Siemens-Schuckert D.IIe. It had started life as D.II and built with dural-girder wing spars and unbraced wings. It was later fitted with I-type interplane struts with no bracing. On tests it was found that the wings flexed alarmingly and so was returned to the factory for bracing cables to be added. After more tests it was returned to the factory for refurbishment to D.IV standards and sent to Geschwader II for evaluation tests. It was returned to the factory for modifications and the fitting of a new engine, the Siemens-Halske Sh.III. It was returned to Geschwader II in July 1918, where it stayed until the end of the war and it is believed it never saw action.

Three prototypes of the Siemens-Schuckert D.V appeared in August 1918, all with different types of wing bracing. The last of the three competed in the D-type competition at Aldershof.

A deviation from the biplane heralded the arrival of the Siemens-Schuckert D.VI. Designed to replace the D.IV the D.V was a parasol fighter fitted with a jettisonable fuel tank beneath the fuselage. Powered by a Siemens-Halske Sh.IIIa engine, which drove a four-bladed propeller, D.V had a top speed of 137mph and a climb rate of 1200ft per minute. It had a wingspan of 30ft 9in and a fuselage length of 21ft 4in.

Only two of the aircraft were built, neither of which saw action as they were not ready for testing until after the Armistice.

The Siemens-Schuckert company was never the household name in aviation as Fokker, Dornier and Rumpler were, but they were without doubt one of the most innovative of all the aircraft manufacturers of World War One. A perfect example of this was that between 1915 and 1918 not only did they build some of the finest aircraft, but they also developed a number of glider bombs that were without doubt the forerunner of today's guided missile programme. In 1918 the company developed a 300kg and 1,000kg Torpedogleiter (*glider bomb*) and trials were carried out from the Zeppelin L.35. None of the bombs were launched in anger, but they did give the world an insight of what was to come.

SPECIFICATIONS

Siemens-Schuckert D.IV

Wing Span	29ft 6⅜in
Length	19ft 8¼in
Height	9ft 2½in
Weight Empty	1,190lb
Weight Loaded	1,620lb
Engine	One 160hp Siemens-Halske Sh.III Rotary
Maximum Speed	112mph
Service Ceiling	26,240ft
Duration	2hrs
Armament	Twin fixed forward-firing Spandau machine guns

Siemens-Schuckert E.I

Wing Span	32ft 9½in
Length	23ft 3½in
Height	8ft 11in
Weight Empty	1,041lb
Weight Loaded	1,481lb
Engine	One 100hp Siemens-Halske Sh.I Rotary
Maximum Speed	100mph
Service Ceiling	20,240ft
Duration	1½hrs
Armament	One fixed forward-firing Spandau machine gun

Siemens-Schuckert D.Dr.I (Dreidecker)

Wing Span	39ft 9¼in
Length	19ft 1in
Height	8ft 1in
Weight Empty	946lb
Weight Loaded	1,408lb
Engine	Two 120hp Siemens-Halske Sh.I Rotary
Maximum Speed	89mph
Service Ceiling	20,240ft
Duration	1½hrs
Armament	Two fixed forward-firing Spandau machine guns

ZEPPELIN WERKE STAAKEN GMBH

Companies like Siemens-Schuckert and LVG had made tremendous inroads into the development of long-range bombers during World War One, but the most successful company by far was Zeppelin Werke Staaken. Staaken R-planes bombed England during hostilities and were the only large bombers to carry out attacks on the Western Front.

The birth of Staaken R-planes can be traced back to the dream of one man – Hellmuth Hirth. In 1915 he planned to build an aircraft that would fly across the Atlantic and fly at the World's Fair in San Francisco. Financial backing was assured by Gustav Klein, Director of Robert Bosch Werke, but World War One put paid to his dream. However, the concept had not been forgotten, and the airship manufacturer Graf Zeppelin saw the potential for a terror weapon.

With the demise of Naval Zeppelin LZ., the German Naval High Command looked at Graf Zeppelin's design of the airship in whole and at Graf Zeppelin himself. Graf Zeppelin, whose relationship with German Admiral von Tirpitz had never been good and was now almost none-existent, turned his attention to the building of long-range bombers. Zeppelin approached the Robert Bosch Werke and persuaded then to allow Gustav Klein and thirty of their engineers, plus assorted other workmen, to join him in building bombers.

Large sheds were rented from Gothaer Waggonfabrik AG (Gotha) on Gotha airfield and work began on the giant bomber. A corporation was set up named Versuchsbau Gotha-Ost (VGO) which was financed by Bosch and Zeppelin. Among the engineers invited to join the company were Claude Dornier and Ernst Heinkel, but only Dornier accepted. Both were later to become famous aircraft manufacturers in their own right. Almost from day one it was decided to use two different types of material in the construction of these giant bombers: wood and metal. Claude Dornier was given a small hangar on Lake Constance, where he carried out experiments in building an all-metal aircraft with considerable success.

Work on VGO.I (RML.1 – Reichs Marine Landflugzeug) started in December 1914 but by the end of January 1915 had to be halted because engines were not ready. The 240hp Maybach HS engines which had been chosen were a modified version of the HSLu airship engine. The aircraft was powered by three engines: one mounted in the nose driving a tractor propeller, the remaining two mounted in nacelles, supported between the wings by inverted struts, driving pusher propellers. The wings were fitted with unbalanced ailerons.

The rectangular fuselage was of the conventional slab-sided structure and constructed with a mixture of spruce longerons and welded steel tubing. With the exception of the plywood-covered top decking, the fuselage was covered in doped fabric. The fuselage narrowed down to a horizontal knife-edge at the biplane tail, which consisted of four small fins with unbalanced rudders along the top. The control cables from the cockpit to the tail rudders passed along outside the fuselage to large quadrants situated in the cockpit.

The aircraft had a flight crew of six: two pilots, a commander/observer and three mechanics, one for each engine. The cockpit was large and open, with the observer in an enclosed section behind. Communications between the crew were limited and carried out by means of hand signals, blackboards and a series of bells. One wonders how during a flight in an open cockpit or standing by one of the engines, anyone could have possibly heard any bells!

By the beginning of April 1915, the aircraft was completed and on 11 April, piloted by Hellmuth Hirth, VGO.I took to the air on its maiden flight. The success of its initial flight prompted the manufacturers to make plans for a long-distance cross-country flight from Gotha to the Maybach Werke, Friedrichshafen. The reasons for the flight was firstly to see how the aircraft performed on long flights and secondly to obtain improved and more reliable engines from Maybach.

It took six months for reliable engines to be installed in the VGO.I, but on the return flight during a bad snowstorm disaster struck. Flying over the Thüringen Forest two of the three engines failed, leaving one in use. The aircraft could not stay airborne on one engine so – with tremendous skill – the two pilots, Hans Vollmöller and Flugmaat Willy Mann, put the giant aircraft down in a small clearing. The aircraft was severely damaged but the crew were uninjured.

Engineers collected the remains from the crash site and returned them to the factory at Gotha. There the aircraft was rebuilt; this time there were a number of modifications made. The VGO.I had cowled engines installed with gun positions for the now mechanic/gunner in the front of the nacelle. On the top of the centre-section cabane a large streamlined gravity tank was fitted. The rebuilt VGO.I flew again on 16 February 1916 and after tests was accepted by the navy and assigned to Navy Kommando LR.1, commanded by Leutnant zur See Ferdinand Rasch. On the side of the aircraft were painted letters RML.1. On the trip from Gotha to Alt-Auz, normally a three-day trip, problems arose from day one. The undercarriage collapsed, the engines overheated with the result that they had to be replaced, the end result was it took three months to complete the flight.

Over the next few months RML.1 was involved in a number of raids against Russian troop installations and air stations. In late 1916 it was involved in another crash. On 10 March 1917 the rebuilt VGO.I (RMK.1) took off on a test flight with Hans Vollmöller and Leutnant der Reserve Carl Kuring at the controls together with Gustav Klein acting as observer. Shortly after take-off there was an explosion in the port engine nacelle and the engine stopped. Circling the airfield and preparing to make an emergency landing, the rudder pedals jammed. Vollmöller cut the engines and prepared to land, but the jammed rudders forced the aircraft into a right-hand turn and the aircraft smashed into the doors of the airship shed. All three crew were killed instantly.

Claude Dornier, who had been working at Lake Constance, started constructing a giant flying boat at the beginning of 1915, the Zeppelin-Lindau Rs.I. Powered by three 240hp Maybach Mb.IV engines, the gigantic aircraft had a wingspan of 142ft 8in, a fuselage length of 95ft 2in, and a height of 23ft 7½in. The engines were mounted within the fuselage and drove three pusher propellers. The aircraft was wrecked before flight trials began, the exact circumstances are not known. A second machine was already in production and powered in exactly the same way. The main difference was the wingspan was considerably shorter at 108ft 11in and the fuselage

length 78ft 4in. With the flight test programme completed, the aircraft was dismantled and the parts used to construct the Zeppelin-Lindau Rs.III.

Whilst VGO.I was being rebuilt, work was continuing on VGO.II. The aircraft was
identical in construction and specifications as the VGO.I although there were a
number of modifications made in the tail area. The vertical tail surfaces were reduced
to two but the rudder areas were increased.

The aircraft was accepted by the Idflieg on 28 November 1915 and given the
designation R.9/15. Again VGO was dogged with problems, this time the aircraft
ran out of fuel on one flight after encountering very strong headwinds. The aircraft,
flown by Leutnant Lühr and Leutnant Freiherr von Buttlar, had to make an
emergency landing in which the undercarriage was ripped off. One experiment to
place a rear gunner in the tail failed miserably, when, after the test flight, the gunner
was removed from the aircraft barely alive. The oscillations experienced in the tail
were so violent that the gunner became violently ill soon after take-off and stayed
that way throughout the flight. Tests on a gun mounted internally were carried out,
but came to nothing as there were serious problems with its accuracy.

The third in the series of Staaken R-planes, the VGO.III, was well under construction in 1915. It had been decided to replace the three 240hp Maybach HS engines
with six 160hp Mercedes D.III engines. Although lower in individual output, the
total horsepower was jumped from 720hp to 960hp. Two engines were mounted
side-by-side in the nose driving a twin-blade tractor propeller; the remaining four
engines were mounted in pairs in outboard nacelles and drove twin-bladed pusher
propellers.

The aircraft was given designation R.10/15 by the Idflieg and assigned to RFA
500. Carrying a crew of seven, including a wireless operator, the aircraft completed
seven bombing missions, including the bombing of the railway station at Riga. On
24 January 1917, the aircraft was lost along with five of the crew, when it crashed on
landing and burst into flames.

A deviation from building bombers was made in November 1916, when the
Zeppelin-Lindau V.1 took to the air. This was an attempt at a single-seat fighter
constructed mainly of metal. It had an egg-shaped nacelle constructed of steel struts
that were covered in aluminium sheet and attached to open steel tail-booms and
struts. The tail and wings were covered in doped fabric. Wingspan was 34ft 5½in,
with a fuselage length of 20ft 7in. The aircraft was fitted with a 160hp Maybach
Mb.III pusher engine.

The Allied offensive began to pose the threat of an Allied air attack on the Staaken
factory. The German High Command decided that the factory should be moved to
a place of relative safety, so it was moved to Staaken, near Berlin. The first of the
Staaken-types came off the production line, the Staaken R.IV.

It was powered by two 160hp Mercedes D.III tractor engines that drove twin-
bladed propellers of 13ft 9in diameter, and four 220hp Benz Bz.IV pusher engines
that drove two four-bladed propellers of 14ft 1in diameter. The giant aircraft had a
wingspan of 138ft 5½in, a fuselage length of 76ft 1in, and a height of 22ft 3½in.
Machine gun positions were built into the upper wings directly above the engine
nacelles; these, together with one ventral, two forward and two dorsal machine gun

positions, made it one of the most heavily protected aircraft in the world. The aircraft was involved in a number of bombing missions on the Eastern Front and survived the war only to be broken up in 1919.

The Staaken R.V followed soon after the first test flight of the R.IV. The main difference between the two aircraft, was that the outboard engines were reversed with that the result that all the engines were tractor ones turning four-bladed propellers. The new positioning of the engines took some time to solve the technical problems that were thrown up, but eventually the aircraft was assigned to RFA 501 at Ghent and during its eight-month career flew sixteen combat missions. It crashed in October 1918.

The best known of all the German R-planes was the Staaken R.VI. This was the largest aircraft ever to go into production during World War One and nineteen models were built, including a seaplane version. The first six were built by Zeppelin Werke Staaken, the remainder built under licence by Luftschiffbau Schütte-Lanz (Zeeson), Ostdeutsche Alabatroswerke GmbH. (Schneidemühl), and Automobil & Aviatik AG (Leipzig-Heiterblick). The design was based on the earlier Staaken-types, the main difference being that the position of the engines were changed to four 260hp Mercedes D.IVa push-pull engines in tandem, installed in two nacelles in the wings. There were four radiators: two at the front and two at the rear, the rear radiators being mounted slightly higher than those in the front.

Eighteen of the aircraft were built: eleven were destroyed during the war, the remainder fought throughout the last part of the war. A couple of the aircraft were used commercially after the war.

The Staaken R.VII was similar to R.IV: unlike the R.VI, it had two of the engines powering a four-bladed tractor propeller were mounted in the nose, and the remaining four engines powered two four-bladed pusher propellers. The undercarriage was relatively short and consisted of two sets of four wheels on each side with a two-wheeled nose section.

After tests the aircraft was accepted by the Idflieg and assigned to RFA 500 on 14 August 1917. On its way to the Front, the aircraft stopped at the airfield of Flieger Ersatabteilung in Halberstadt for emergency repairs. With the repairs completed, the aircraft took off on 19 August 1917 and headed for the Front. As the aircraft rose in the air it became obvious that something was wrong. The aircraft was at 70m from the ground when the starboard wing dropped and the aircraft forced into a tight turn. As R.VII 14/15 reached a wooded hill at the end of the field, the starboard wing lurched suddenly downwards and hooked into a tree. The aircraft somersaulted into a rocky ravine on the other side of the hill. Only three of the nine crew members survived but were badly burned.

Claude Dornier's attention was drawn to the development of a two-seat reconnaissance aircraft, the Zeppelin-Lindau C.I. The fuselage was of an all-metal construction covered in a sheet-metal skin. The wings however, although constructed of aluminium, were covered in fabric. The Zeppelin-Lindau C.I was powered by a 160hp Mercedes D.III engine, which gave a top speed of 93mph, and had a wingspan of 34ft 5½in, a fuselage length of 24ft 4in and a height of 9ft (2.74m). It was armed with a forward-firing fixed Spandau machine gun and a manually operated Parabellum machine gun. Tested by the Idflieg, it failed to meet the requirements and was scrapped. C.II was almost identical and only differed in the type of radiator used. Only a small number were built.

Another two-seater was constructed by the Zeppelin Werke at the airship factory at Friedrichshafen. The models were designed by Paul Jarray and were entirely wooden machines covered in doped fabric. The Zeppelin C.I and C.II were almost identical, with the exception of the tail surfaces on the C.II being removed and the tail frame being made of metal.

Powered by 240hp Maybach Mb.IV engines which gave a top speed of 125mph, they had a wingspan of 39ft 4½in, a fuselage length of 26ft and a height of 11ft 9in. Six C.Is and twenty C.IIs were built, none of which saw action. At the end of the war they were sold to the Swiss Air Force who flew them until 1928.

Work was still continuing on the giant seaplanes and Rs.III, which arrived in October 1917, was a monoplane powered by four 245hp Maybach Mb.IVa engines that gave a top speed of 84mph. It had a wingspan of 121ft 8in, a fuselage length of 74ft 7½in and a height of 26ft 11in. The tail booms – so prominent on the Rs.II model – were removed and replaced by a fuselage made of steel longerons and alloy frames. The metal fuselage, with its biplane tail, was covered in fabric and mounted on top of the wing. The Rs.III had a short, wide hull which supported the two nacelles that contained the four tandem-mounted engines.

The first flight took place at Friedrichshafen on 21 October 1917 and was so successful that the aircraft was taken to Norderney, a flight of some seven hours. It underwent a series of tests but the Armistice intervened before it could be put into service. The last of the giant flying boats, the Zeppelin-Lindau Rs.IV, made its maiden flight in October 1918. The fuselage had a metal skin and a much simplified cruciform tail section. Like the previous model, it was powered by four 245hp Maybach Mb.IV engines, which gave a top speed of 90mph.

The Rs.IV had one test flight and was then dismantled. Claude Dornier, who had been spearheading the programme, was able to use a great deal of the information gained from the test flights of the giant aircraft, and incorporate them into the successful commercial flying boats he created after the war.

Zeppelin-Staaken R.VI 29/16 powered by four 245-hp Maybach Mb.IVa engines fitted with upper-wing gun positions. This aircraft was operational with RFA.501 and crashed on 10 May 1918 attempting to land in thick fog.

Zeppelin-Staaken R.VI being prepared for a mission. Note the ladders leaning against the fuselage as the ground crew carry out their servicing.

One of the most successful of the Staaken giant bombers was R.XIV. Three of the models were built – the R.XIV 43/17, 44/17 and 45/17. Four 12-cylinder 350hp Austro-Daimler engines initially powered R.XIV 43/17, but they proved to be unreliable. They were replaced by four 300hp Basse & Selve BuS. IVa engines which also proved to be unreliable, so were replaced by five 245hp Maybach high-compression Mb.IVa engines. The reason for the sudden switch from four to five engines was the increased weight of 2,000kg, which required additional power. All three aircraft were ready by the early part of 1918.

Each of the aircraft was armed with six-machine guns: two in the dorsal and ventral positions and one each in the engine nacelle positions. The cockpit was of the open type, whilst the bomb–aimer/observer/navigator's position was in an enclosed cabin situated in the nose.

At the beginning of December 1917, the German Navy ordered two Staaken seaplanes. They bore a strong resemblance to the Staaken R.XIV inasmuch as the cockpit area was completely enclosed for both pilot and navigator/observer. There were noticeable differences: the fuselage was raised 5ft above the lower wing which raised the tail as well to protect both the fuselage and tail from spray and rough seas whilst landing and taking off. The two models, numbered Types 8301 and 8303, carried a crew of five and were armed as the R.XIV with the addition of two 20mm Becker cannons in the rear position. Powered by for 260hp Mercedes D.IVa engines, the 8301 and 8303 had a maximum speed of 80mph, a wingspan of 138ft 5½in, a fuselage length of 68ft 10½in and a height of 22ft 3½in. Neither aircraft ever saw active service.

Zeppelin-Staaken VGO II R.9/15 just after it had crash landed. Both the gunners can still be seen in the nacelles.

Zeppelin-Staaken R.27/16 under construction.

An improved version of R.XIV, the R.XIVa, appeared in the middle of 1918 and was the last of the R-planes to be built by Staaken. Four of the aircraft were ordered by the Idflieg and given the designations R.69 to R.72. Only the first three were completed and were too late to see any active service. All three aircraft were used by the German Army to fly cargoes up to the end of the war, and afterwards by the Inter-Allied Control Commission.

In February 1918 there appeared another version of the Staaken R.VI, the Staaken L. Seaplane. The undercarriage was replaced with 39ft 4½in duraluminium floats and slightly larger ailerons. During the last of the test flights, carried out by Leutnant Haller, the engines failed whilst flying over land and the aircraft crashed killing all the crew. However, earlier results had convinced the navy that the aircraft had a great deal going for it, so placed an order for a further six Staaken R-seaplanes which were based on the design and construction of the Staaken L.

An experimental two-seater seaplane fighter was built in May 1918, the Zeppelin-Lindau CS.I. The aircraft was almost of all-metal construction with the exception of the wings and tail surfaces, which were covered by doped fabric. It was powered by a V-8 195hp Benz Bz.IIIb engine, which gave a top speed of 93mph. It had a wingspan of 43ft 3in and a fuselage length of 36ft, and was armed with one fixed forward-firing Spandau machine gun and a manually operated Parabellum machine gun. Only one was built.

The specifications of the Staaken giant bombers hardly differed, the only differences being in the variety of engines used and some minor modifications. Their contribution to the bomber aspect of World War One was modest to say the least, and although they had some impact it was not as great as the German Army had hoped for; nevertheless they opened a new page in the annals of aviation history.

SPECIFICATIONS

Zeppelin C.I

Wing Span	34ft 5½in
Length	24ft 4in
Height	9ft 1in
Weight Empty	1,712lb
Weight Loaded	2,350lb
Engine	One 240hp Maybach Mb.IV – six-cylinder, in-line, water-cooled
Maximum Speed	94mph
Service Ceiling	21,240ft
Duration	1½hrs
Armament	Two fixed forward-firing Spandau machine guns One manually operated Parabellum machine gun mounted in the rear observer's cockpit

Zeppelin-Staaken R.IV

Wing Span	138ft 5½in
Length	76ft 1½in
Height	22ft 3½in
Weight Empty	19,298lb
Weight Loaded	28,677lb
Engine	Four 220hp Benz Bz.IV – six-cylinder, in-line, water-cooled
Maximum Speed	78mph
Service Ceiling	29,240ft
Duration	6–7hrs
Armament	Six manually operated Parabellum machine gun mounted in the nose ventral and dorsal positions

Zeppelin-Staaken R.VI

Wing Span	138ft 5½in
Length	72ft 6¼in
Height	20ft 8in
Weight Empty	17,426lb
Weight Loaded	26,066lb
Engine	Four 245hp Maybach IV or four 260hp Mercedes D.IVa – six-cylinder, in-line, water-cooled
Maximum Speed	84mph
Service Ceiling	14,240ft
Duration	7–10hrs
Armament	Four manually operated Parabellum machine guns mounted in the nose, ventral and dorsal positions

The great majority of the German aircraft manufacturers after World War One disappeared, but some were absorbed into larger companies. The contribution these companies gave to aviation, however, will never be forgotten, nor will some of the men who flew their aircraft.

INDEX

Numbers in **bold** indicate illustrations.

Adam von, Hans Ritter, **38**, 39, 40, 144, 153, 179
Allgemeine Electrizitäts GmbH, 190, 192-98
Ago Flugzeug-Werke GmbH, 190
Albatros Werke GmbH, 199,-208, 269, 282
    Albatros C.II Gitterschwanz, 94, 201
    Albatros C.V, 90, 193, 201
    Albatros D.III, 29, 30, 39, 44, 59, 60, 67, 100, 204, 208, 269
    Albatros D.V/D.Va, 34, 39, 42, 48, 89, 90, 105, 120, 132, 153, 190, 204, 207, 287
Albert Rinne Flugzeug-Werke, 190
Allmenröder, Leutnant Karl, 32, 45, 46, 53, 63-66, **64**, 178
Alter-Ludwig-Werke, 190
Althaus, Oberleutnant Ernst Freiherr von, 34, 35, 36, **36**, 42, 53, 66-68, **67**, 72
Automobil und Aviatik AG, 188, 190, 193, 208-13
    Aviatik B.I, 188, 208
    Aviatik C.I, 25, 208-209, 213
    Aviatik C.III, 213
Avery, Lieutenant William USAS, 129

Baldamus, Leutnant Hartmuth, 30, 179
Banfield, Leutnant Gottfried, 259
Barker VC, Captain William, 118

Bassermann, Ernst, 186
Bäumer, Leutnant Paul, 53, **123**, 126, 177
Baur, Vizefeldwebel Johann, 68
Bayerische Flugzeug-Werke AG, 190
Bayerische Rumpler Werke GmbH, 190
Beaulieu-Marconnay, Leutnant Oliver Freiherr von, 53, **69**, 69-70
Beckhardt, Oberleutnant Fritz, 305
Bernert, Oberleutnant Fritz Otto, 30, 36, 39, 40, 53, 70-71, **71**, 178
Berr, Oberleutnant Hans, 53, **72**, 72-73, 126, 181
Berthold, Hauptmann Rudolf, 35, 36, 37, 53, 87, 88, 177, 305
Blume, Leutnant Walter, 53-55, **54**, 178
Boelcke, Hauptmann Oswald, 26, **27**, 28, 30, 53, 59, 60, 75-77, **75**, **76**, 79, 131, 134, 177, 203, 221, 223, 225-26
Boelcke, Hauptmann Wilhelm, 79
Boenigk, Oberleutnant Oskar Freiherr von, 36, 37, 53, 77-78, 178
Boes, Leutnant, 96
Böhme, Leutnant Erwin, 30, 50, 53, **59**, 77, **79**, 78-80, 132, 178, 203
Bomhard, Karl, 189
Bolle, Rittmeister Karl, 53, 80-81, **123**, 178

Bongartz, Leutnant Heinrich, 53, 81-83, **83**, **123**, 178
Booker, Flight Lieutenant C.D, 163
Brandenburg, Hauptmann Ernst, 53, 83-85, **84**, 119, 277
Brauneck, Leutnant Otto, 47
Brückmann, Oberleutnant, 194-95
Brunnhuber, Simon, 223
Buckler, Leutnant Julius, 53, 85-87, **86**, **123**, 177
Buddecke, Hauptmann Hans Joachim, 35, 36, 37, 51, 54, 87-88, 98, 180
Bülow-Bothkamp, Leutnant Walter von, 50, 54, 88-90, **89**, 132, 178
Burkhardt, Hauptmann, 272
Buttlar-Brandenfels, Kapitänleutnant Horst Treusch Freiherr von, 51, 53

Cadbury, Lieutenant Peter, RNAS, 156
Caspar Hamburg-Fuhlsbüttel, 258
Castiglioni, Camilo, 259
Childlaw-Roberts, Captain R.L, 133, 169
Christiansen, Oberleutnant zur See Friedrich, 51, 54, 115, 179, 260, 263
Clausen, Unteroffizier Fritz, 110-11

Daimler Motorengesellschaft Werke, 190
Degelow, Leutnant Carl, 54, 90-92, **91**, **123**, 178
Deilmann, Leutnant Karl, 140, 143
Deutsche Flugzeug-Werke GmbH (DFW), 190, 194, 210, 214-19
    DFW C.V, 215, **216**, 217, **218**
    DFW Floh, 214
    DFW R.I, 214, 219
Doerr, Leutnant Gustav, 56, 92-93, **93**, 178
Döring, Rittmeister Kurt-Bertram von, 34-35, 36, 37, 45, 144, 180
Dorme, Sous Lieutenant Rene Pierre, 153
Dorner, Hermann, 24, 186, 214, 254
Dornheim, Leutnant Ludwig, 65
Dornier, Claude, 145, 199, 306, 308-309, 311
Dossenbach, Leutnant Albert, 30, 42, 43, 54, 67, **94**, 94-95, 179
Dostler, Oberleutnant Eduard Ritter von, 34, 39, 40, 46, 50, 54, 95-97, **96**, 178

Eaton, Lieutenant E.C. RFC, 149
Eberhardt, Colonel von, 221
Ehmann, Vizefeldwebel Gottfried, 97, 180
Epstein, Ritter von, 103, 123
Eschwege, Leutnant Rudolf von, 97, 98, **99**, 179
Euler, August, 24, 186-87
Euler Werke, 190
Eversbusch, Alfred, 187, 188, 282, 283
Eversbusch, Ernst, 187, 282
Eversbusch, Walter, 187, 282, 283

Falkenhayn, General Erich von, 123
Festner, Vizefeldwebel Sebastian, 45, 47, 64, 65, 180
Fiedler, Max, 195
Fitzmaurice, Commander J., 119
Flugmaschine Fabrik Franz Schneider, 190

Flugmaschine Rex GmbH, 190
Flugmaschine Wright GmbH, 187, 188, 268
Flugzeugbau Friedrichshafen GmbH, 190, 230-40, 297
    FF.33 models, 232-33, 235, 237, 238
    FF.33e *Wölfchen*, 232-33, **233**, **234**, 237
    FF.49b/c, 235, **236**, **237**, 238
Flugzeugwerft Lübeck-Travemünde GmbH, 190
Foerster, Hauptmann, 223
Fokker, Anthony, 26, **26**, **28**, 85, 189, 219, **221**, 223, 225, 226, 267, 305
Fokker Flugzeug-Werke GmbH, 189, 190, 219-230, 265, 267
    Fokker E.V, **38**, 40, 140, 230, 274
    Fokker E.III, 87, 104, 112, 150
    Fokker D.VII, 34, 40, 42, 50, 70, 105, 121, 124, 139, 150, 164, 226-27, **228**, 229, 287, 288, 297
    Fokker Dr.I, 34, 36, 39, 42, 50, 92, 105, 165, 169, 175, 226-27, **228**, 229, 230, 286
Forssman , Villehad, 188, 299-300
Forstman, Oberleutnant zur See Walter, 231
Frankl, Leutnant Wilhelm, 30, 35-36, 37, 54, **67**, 99-100, 179
Fricke, Oberleutnant Hermann, 54, 100-101, **101**
Friedrichs, Leutnant der Reserve Fritz, 42, 43, 56, 179

Gabriel, Vizefeldwebel Willi, 47, **48**, 188
Garros, Roland, 26, 164, 222
Germania Flugzeug-Werke GmbH, 190
Goedecker Flugzeug-Werke, 191
Gontermann, Leutnant Heinrich, 30, 34, 50, 54, 126, 164, 177
Göring, Oberleutnant Hermann, 34, 35, 46, 47, 50, 54, 74, **102**, 103-105, 115, 122-23, 124, 145, 166, 178, 269, 305
Gothaer Waggonfabrik AG, 190, 191, 240-49, 308
    Gotha G.IV, **242**, **244**, 245, 246
    Gotha G.V, **243**, **244**, 245, 246, **247**, 248
    Gotha WD.11, 242-43, 245, 248
    Gotha WD.14, 245-46, 247, 249
Grade, Hans, 24, 186
Greim, Oberleutnant Robert Ritter von, 54, 105-106
Griebsch, Leutnant der Reserve Wilhelm, 54, 106-107
Grohmann, Konstrukteur, 199
Grone, Oberleutnant Jurgen von, 54m 107-108

Halberstädter Flugzeug-Werke GmbH, 191, 249-54
    Halberstadt CL.II, 97, 210, 250, **251**, 252-53
    Halberstadt D.III, 35, 41, 98, 254
Hannoversche Waggonfabrik AG, 188, 254-58
    Hannover CL.II, **255**, 255, 256
Hansa und Brandenburgische Flugzeug-Werke GmbH, 188, 254-58
    Brandenburg CC, 259
Hanseatische Flugzeug-Werke, 191, 258
Heinkel, Ernst, 258-60, 308
Heldmann, Leutnant Alois, 42, 43, 179
Hemer, Leutnant Franz, 39, 40, 179
Hengl, Leutnant George Ritter von, 68
Hillmann, Dipl.Ing, Wilhelm, 280
Hintsch, Leutnant der Reserve Hans, 47, 64
Hipleh, Alexander, 199

Hirth, Hellmuth, 308, 309
Hoenmanns, Oberleutnant Erich, 112
Hoeppner, General der Kavallerie Ernst von, 24,
    25, 27, 54, 84, 109-109
Höhndorf, Leutnant Walter, 37, 54, 180, 196, 296,
    300
Höhne, Leutnant Otto, 81
Homburg, Oberleutnant Erich, 54, 109-10
Horn, Oberleutnant Hans-Georg, 54, 110-11, **111**
Hoppe, Vizefeldwebel Paul, 73
Howe, Feldwebel Hans, 64
Hudson, Lieutenant Harold, 118
Huffzky, Vizefeldwebel, 97
Hünfeld, Baron von, 119

Ihde, Flieger Rudolf, 42
Immelmann, Oberleutnant Max, 21, 26, **27**, 28,
    54, 76, 77, 134, 135, 147, 176, 179

Jacobs, Leutnant der Reserve Josef Carl Peter, 54,
    112-15, **113**, **123**, 129, 177
Janzen, Leutnant Johann, 36, 37, 39, 40, 180
Jeannin Flugzeug-Werke GmbH, 191
Jahnke, Otto, 111
Junkers, Dr Hugo, 189, 264
Junkers Flugzeug-Werke AG, 107, 119, 189, 191,
    264-68
    Junkers J.1 (E.1) 'Tin Donkey', 189, 206, 264-
        65, 267
    Junkers J.1 (J.4), 265, 268
Junkers-Fokker Werke, 191
Justinus, Leutnant Bruno, 164

Kaiserlich Marinewerft Reichwerft, 191
Kalf, Leutnant, 118
Karjus, Leutnant Walther, 34, 45, 47
Keller, Hauptmann Alfred, 54, **55**, **123**
Kirchstein, Leutnant Hans, 34, 40, 54, 178
Klein, Gustav, 308, 309
Klein, Leutnant Hans, 34, 37, 42, 43, 54, **123**, 180
Kleine, Hauptmann Rudolf, 54, **115**, 115-16
Köhl, Hauptmann Hermann, 54, **117**, 117-19, **123**
Kohlhepp, Leutnant, 122
Kolbe, Oberleutnant, 220
Kondor Flugzeug-Werke GmbH, 191
Koner, Dr, 226
König, George, 189
Könnecke, Leutnant Otto, 50, 52, 54, 119-20,
    126, 178
Kreft, Leutnant Konstantin, 64, 59, 286
Kreutzer, Martin, 225
Küllmer, Vizefeldwebel Heinrich, 41, 144
Kuring, Leutnant der Reserve Carl, 309

Lackner, Oberleutnant Walter, 112
Lang, Oberleutnant Rudolf, 46, 64, 65
Langfield, Kapitänleutnant, 241
Laumann, Leutnant Arthur, 42, 43, 52, 54, 120-
    21, **121**, **123**, 178
Lawson, Captain G.E.B. RAF, 150
Lenz, Leutnant Alfred, 37, **67**
Leonhardy, Hauptmann Leo, 54, 121-22, **123**

Lewis, T.A. RAF, 59, 60, 152
LFG Bitterfeld, 188, 268
Leith-Thomsen, Oberleutnant Hermann von der,
    27, 54, 158-60, **159**
Linck, Oberleutnant Ludwig Karl Wilhelm, 41, 42,
    43
Linke-Hoffman Werke AG, 191, 269
Loerzer, Hauptmann Bruno, 50, 54, 74, 103-104,
    122-24, **123**, **124**, 177
Löwenhardt, Oberleutnant Erich, 34, 35, 42, 43,
    52, 54, 124-26, **125**, **144**, 177
Luftfahrzeugbau Schütte-Lanz, 191
Luftfahrzeug GmbH (LFG), 188, 191, 268-77
    LFG Roland C.II Walfisch, 269-71, **270**, 275
    LFG Roland D.II/IIa, **270**, 271, **272**, 275-76
    LFG Roland D.VII, 272-73, **274**
Luft Torpedo GmbH, 191
Luftverkehrs GmbH (LVG), 189, 191, 246, 277-
    82, 308

Mai, Leutnant Josef, 28, 56, 120, 126, **127**, 178
Mall, Herman, 231
Mallinckrodt, Leutnant Friedrich, 41, 43, 189, 265
Mann, Flumaat Willy, 309
Märkische Flugzeug-Werke GmbH, 191
McCudden, Captain James B, 169, 227, 293
Menckhoff, Oberleutnant Carl, 54, **128**, 128-29, 177
Mercur Flugzeugbau GmbH, 191
Meyer, Leutnant Georg, 56, 129-30, 178
Meyer, Hauptmann Willy, 286
Mix, Unteroffizer Erich, 130
Motorluftschiff Studiengesellschaft, 187, 188, 268
Müller, Leutnant Max Ritter von, 30, 50, 54, 77,
    81, 131-32, **132**, 178
Müller-Khale, Oberleutnant Albert, 54, **133**, 133-34
Mulzer, Leutnant Max Ritter von, 54, 134-35,
    135, 181

Naglo Boots-Werft, 191
Natalis, Dr, Hugo, 188, 299
Nathanael, Offizerstellvereter Edmund, **29**, 179
National Flugzeug-Werke GmbH, 191
Neckel, Leutnant Ulrich Ritter von, 39, 40, 41,
    54, **136**, 136-37, 139, 178
Nieber, Leutnantgeneral Stephan von, 186
Nielebock, Leutnant Landwehr Friedrich, 54, 137-
    38, **138**
Noltenius, Leutnant Friedrich Theodor, 37, 41,
    47, 56, 139-40, 179
Nordeutsche Flugzeug-Werke GmbH, 191

Oesterlein, Professor, 194
Oertz Werke GmbH, 191
Ostdeutsche Albatros Werke GmbH (OAW) 191,
    199, 311
Osten, Leutnant Hans Georg von, 36, 37, 47
Osterkamp, Oberleutnant zur See Theodor, 51,
    54, 114, **123**, 140-41, 178, 305
Otto Werke GmbH, 191, 277

Parschau, Leutnant Otto, 54, 222
Pätzold, Georg, 235

Pechmann, Hauptmann Paul Freiherr von, 54, 141, 280
Periere, Oberleutnant zur See Friedrich von Arnauld de la, 231
Pfalz Flugzeug-Werke GmbH, 188, 191, 271, 282-89
    Pfalz D.III/IIIa, 34, 42, **285**, **286**, 289
    Pfalz D.VIII, 60, 286, 287
    Pfalz Dr.I, 285-86, 289
Platz, Reinhold, 225
Pütter, Leutnant Fritz, 54, **142**, 142-43, 178
Pütz, Vizefeldwebel Johann, 106

Rasch, Leutnant zur See Ferdinand, 309
Redler, Lieutenant H.B, 163
Reichel, Dr, Walter, 188, 299
Reinhard, Hauptmann Wilhelm, 34, 35, 39, 40, 41, 47, 56, 143-45, **144**, 179
Rhys-Davids, 2nd Lieutenant Arthur, 169, 227
Richthofen, Oberleutnant Lothar Freiherr von, 32, 34, 43, 44, 46, 47, 52, 54, **61**, 65, **144**, 145-46, **146**, 177
Richthofen, Rittmeister Manfred Freiherr von, 30-32, 34-35, 39, 42, 44-46, 50, 55, 57-63, **58**, **59**, **60**, **62**, 64-65, 67, 77, 96, 143-45, **144**, 152, 168, 174, 177, 204, 207, 226-27, 286
Richthofen, Leutnant Wolfram Freiherr von, 34, 46, 47
Rieper, Leutnant der Reserve Peter, 55, 147
Rittberger, Baurat, 189
Robert Bosch Werke, 308
Robertson, Lieutenant, 260
Rodschinka (test pilot), 305
Roi, Hauptmann Wolfram de la, 23, 186
Röth, Oberleutnant Friedrich Ritter von, 55, 147-49, **148**
Ruff, Hauptmann, 220
Rüger, Unteroffizier Paul, 118
Rumey, Leutnant Fritz, 50, 55, 120, 126, **148**, 149-50, 177
Rummelsbacher, Oberleutnant Karl, 41-42
Rumpler Flugzeug-Werke GmbH, 187, 191, 208, 290-96
    Rumpler C.I/Ia, 195, 254, 290-92, **291**, **292**, 295
    Rumpler C.IV, 278, 284, 292-93, 296
    Rumpler C.VII (Rubild), 256, **293**, 293

Sablatnig, Dr Josef, 189, 296-98
Sablatnig Flugzeugbau GmbH, 191, 296-99
Sachsenberg, Oberleutnant zur See Gotthard, 51, 55, 114, **123**, 150, 178
Sander, Chief Engineer Ing, 194
Santa Elena, SMS, **233**, 235, **236**
Satchell, Lieutenant H.L. RFC, 152
Schäfer, Leutnant Karl Emil, 32, 45, 47, 50, 55, **61**, 65, 151-52, **151**, **152**, 178
Schelies, Richard, 186
Schilling, Leutnant Hans, 94, 95
Schlegel, Ernst, 286
Schleich, Hauptmann Eduard Ritter von, 55, 78, 152-54, 178, 207, 269, 288
Schmidt, Leutnant Julius, **30**, **31**, 41, 179
Schmidt, Oberleutnant Otto, 56, 179

Schneider, Franz, 190, 223, 277, 278
Schönfelder, Oberflugmeister Kurt, 114, 180
Schopper, Karl, 189
Schwade Flugzeug und Motorenbau, 191
Siemens-Schuckert Werke GmbH, 188, 193, 299-307
    Siemens-Schuckert D.III, **301**, 305
    Siemens-Schuckert D.D5, **301**, 303
Simon, Leutnant Georg, 48, 64
Soden, Captain F.O, 133
Sommermann, Hans, 235
Somerville, 2nd Lieutenant H.A, 133
SSW-Dynamowerk, Berlin, 300
Steffen, Bruno, 188, 299, 300, 303
Steffen, Franz, 188, 299, 300, 303
Strasser, Fregattenkapitän Peter, 51, 55, 154-56, **155**

Tantzen, Dipl.Ing, 269
Thelen, Robert, 202
Thom, Leutnant Karl, 55, 154, 156-58, **155**, 178
Thuy, Leutnant Emil, 55, **123**, 154, 160-61, **160**, **161**, 178
Trotha, Oberleutnant Freiherr von, 85
Tutschek, Hauptmann Adolf Ritter von, 21, 50, 55, **162**, 162-63, 178, **228**, 286

Udet, Oberleutnant Ernst, 34, 36, 37, 48, 50, 52, 55, 85, 92, 163-65, **165**, 177, **205**, 288
Union Flugzeug-Werke GmbH, 189, 191, 296
Ursinus, Oskar, 241

Veltjens, Leutnant Joseph, 37, 55, 69, 166, **167**, 173, 178
Versuchsbau Gotha-Ost GmbH (VGO), 308
Vollmöller, Hans, 309
Voss, Leutnant Werner, 30, 42, 44, 46, 50, 55, 68, 166-69, **168**, 177, 204, 226-27

Waggonfabrik Josef Rathgeber, 191
Walz, Hauptmann Franz, 55, **123**, 169-70
Warda, Flieger, 97
Weiss, Leutnant der Reserve Hans, 44, 46, 48, 56, 145, 179, 288
Wendelmuth, Leutnant Rudolf, **29**, 180
Wentsch, Leutnant, 278
Wenz, Leutnant Alfred, 42, 126
Wenzel, Leutnant Paul, 39, 40, 41, 181
Wenzel, Leutnant Richard, 41, 48, 180
Windisch, Leutnant Rudolf, 55, 120, 170-72, **170**, **171**, 178
Wintgens, Leutnant Kurt, **26**, 28, 55, 172-73, **173**, 179, 223
Wolf, SMS, 232
Wolff, Oberleutnant Kurt, 32, 34, 45-46, 48, 50, 55, **61**, 64, 65, 143-44, 173-75, **174**, 178
Wühlisch, Leutnant Heinz von, 76
Wulf, Leutnant Josef, 39, 40
Wüsthoff, Leutnant Kurt, 34, 36, 39, 55, **123**, **144**, **175**, 175-76, 178, 214

Zeppelin Werke Lindau GmbH, 191
Zeppelin Werke Staaken GmbH, 191, 308-316
Zorn, Dipl.Ing. Werner, 194-95